BALTIC SEA

KONIGSBERG

Insterburg Gumbinnen

I P

DANZIG

Rastenburg

XVII P

Lyck
Arys

XX P

ALLENSTEIN

Deutsch-
Eylau

Hammerstein

STETTIN

Gruppe Graudenz

II P

Bromberg Thorn

Gnesen

Warthe Lager

RUSSIA

Frankfort
a/Oder

POSEN

V P

Ostrowo

Glogau

Neuhammer Leignitz

BRESLAU

Bautzen

Schweidnitz Brieg

Lamsdorf VI P

RIA

Neisse Gleiwitz

Pless

Scales

0   50 Miles 100   150

0   50   100   150
Kilometres

MAP SHOWING
GERMAN ARMY CORPS DISTRICTS

NOTE: Berlin is the Head-Quarters of the Guard Corps as well as of the III Corps.
The Guard Corps is recruited from the whole of Prussia & from Alsace-Lorraine.

□ Army Corps District Headquarters ◉ Divisional District Headquarters
○ Brigade District Headquarters △ Training Ground (Truppen-Übungs-Platz)

P = Prussian W = Württemburg S = Saxon B = Bavarian

Reproduced from War Office Map of February, 1917, by permission.

ASSIZE OF ARMS

Au Général Morgan
mon souvenir fidèle.

F. Foch

ASSIZE OF ARMS

THE DISARMAMENT OF GERMANY
AND HER REARMAMENT (1919-1939)

J. H. MORGAN

WITH A PREFACE BY

LIEUT.-GENERAL SIR G. M. W. MACDONOGH

NEW YORK

OXFORD UNIVERSITY PRESS

1946

PREFACE

By LIEUT.-GENERAL SIR G. M. W. MACDONOGH,
G.B.E., K.C.B., K.C.M.G., late Adjutant-General

BRIGADIER-GENERAL MORGAN has given convincing proof, if any were needed, that the keen, well-trained legal mind assimilates very rapidly, and very thoroughly, every type of experience that it encounters. In the autumn of 1914, when I was in charge of the Intelligence Branch of the General Staff at G.H.Q., B.E.F., Mr. Morgan (as he then was) came out to France as the official representative of the Committee of Inquiry into Breaches of the Laws of War, and as Home Office Commissioner with the British Army, and I have had the pleasure of knowing him ever since, both when in the Army and as a colleague on the Executive Council of the International Law Association.

In order to give him facilities for carrying out his investigations, he was appointed a Staff Captain in the Adjutant-General's Branch at G.H.Q., and thus commenced a connection with the Army which lasted all through the Great War and during the first five years of the peace. His high professional knowledge of the law, coupled with the deep insight he acquired into the organization of the Army and the problems of recruiting and demobilization, made his services particularly valuable both to my predecessor, General Sir Nevil Macready, and to myself when Adjutant-General to the Forces. Thus in 1916 he attended, on behalf of the Army Council, the Court of Inquiry into irregularities on the Lines of Communication and, in the following year, he prepared for the Army Council the case for the Parliamentary Commission on Mesopotamia. In October 1918 he was appointed by the late Lord Birkenhead, with the approval of the War Office, Vice-Chairman of the British Government's Committee of Enquiry into 'War Crimes.' He was also British Military Representative at Versailles on the Prisoners of War Commission.

It was accordingly with full confidence in his knowledge and ability that I was able to nominate him as A.A.G. of the Military Section and as my 'personal representative' at the Paris Peace Conference in 1919 and subsequently as D.A.G., with the rank of Brigadier-General, on the Inter-Allied Military Commission of Control in Germany. In Paris he took the initiative in suggesting the necessity of a Convention to regulate the post-war occupation of the Rhineland and was accordingly instructed to proceed to Cologne and report on the conditions of the occupation under the Armistice. As a result he was instructed by the C.I.G.S., Sir Henry Wilson, and myself, to submit a draft Convention. After its acceptance by us, it was approved by Marshal Foch without alteration and was unanimously accepted by the Versailles Military Committee whose deliberations General Morgan attended when in charge of it. He also initiated, as A.A.G., the scheme for the organization of the Commission of Control for the execution of the Disarmament articles of the Treaty of Versailles. In Berlin he amply justified his appointment for, as Deputy President and senior British representative on the Effectives Sub-Commission of the Commission, his acute legal brain, aided by the sound knowledge of Germany and the German language he had acquired as a student at the University of Berlin, enabled him to disentangle the intricate provisions of the numerous German laws and Army Orders regarding conscription, mobilization, and military service in general, whilst his experience with the Adjutant-General's Department both at G.H.Q. France and at the War Office made him capable of understanding the full implication of those provisions and of the figures published in the German budgets.

When appointed to the Commission of Control, General Morgan quickly gained the full confidence of his French colleagues and particularly that of General Nollet, the Chief of the Commission. Consequently, when he resigned and left Berlin in September 1923, General Nollet issued a most appreciative 'Army Order' thanking him for the 'incomparable services' he had rendered to the Commission and expressing great regret at his departure.

I was, therefore, not surprised when in 1926 at a public luncheon in London, at which I had the honor of presiding, given to General Nollet, at that time Minister of War, and at which General Morgan was present, the French General, turning to his former colleague, said:

Mon Cher Morgan . . . vous nous avez ainsi montré qu'un homme, sans consacrer à l'étude des questions militaires l'intégralité de son temps et de sa carrière, peut cependant y exceller, s'il apporte à cette étude des brillantes facultés et une grande puissance de travail. Mieux que tout cela, vous avez été pour tous un ami.[1]

General Morgan's work on the Commission was equally appreciated by Marshal Foch, who brought his services specially to the notice of M. Briand, the French Prime Minister.

After these experiences and with these qualifications, it is safe to say that there are few persons, if any, who have the same claim to be listened to as General Morgan on the subject of German Disarmament. He published a most illuminating and prophetic article on this subject in the *Quarterly Review* in October 1924, and I can only hope that when the time comes to implement the clauses of the Atlantic Charter, the lessons which General Morgan has drawn in this book, *Assize of Arms*, will be given the attention due to them.

It is most earnestly to be desired that no false sentiment or longing for appeasement will cause history to repeat itself and thus enable Germany again to escape the destruction of her means of rapidly re-creating her armed forces and of supplying them with armaments. General Morgan has shown how she succeeded in doing so under the able guidance of General von Seeckt, as she had done under that of Scharnhorst after the Treaty of Tilsit.

Germany may well produce another such genius, and it will be for the draughtsmen of the new Armistice and Peace Treaty and for those charged with its execution to profit from the experiences of the past, of which General Morgan is so able an exponent, and to see that every loophole for evasion is securely closed.

G. M. W. MACDONOGH

[1] 'My Dear Morgan, You have thus taught us that a man, without devoting to the study of military problems the whole of his time and of his career, can, none the less, excel in them if he brings to such study brilliant faculties and a great power of work. Better still, you have been for all of us a friend.'

CONTENTS

ILLUSTRATIONS

xi

AUTHOR'S INTRODUCTION

THE AUTHOR of this book desires to express his obligations to many friends who, at one time or another, have read it, in whole or in part, and, in particular, to four distinguished soldiers, British and French, without whose encouragement it would never have been begun, much less resumed. Those obligations extend over a long period of time. The book was originally commenced in the year 1924 at the suggestion of Marshal Foch and others, and it was the Marshal's offer to write a 'Preface' to it which was decisive in determining the Author to undertake a task from which, in view of its magnitude, he might otherwise have flinched. Then, in 1925, came the fateful overtures by Herr Stresemann for a 'Pact of Security' known, and now notorious, as the Pact of Locarno. The price exacted by Stresemann for that Pact was not only the withdrawal of the Control Commission, but silence. He got it. It became 'bad form' for any one to question whether Germany was, or was not, in a state of grace in the matter of disarmament. To have proceeded, under such circumstances, with the publication of a history of the attempt to disarm her under the Treaty of Versailles would have involved such a revelation of the bad faith of Germany, in her all too successful obstruction to the work of the Control Commission, as to amount, in the language of diplomacy, to 'an unfriendly act,' particularly in view of her spectacular entry into the comity of the League of Nations. The only course open to the Author was therefore to abandon his unfinished task. With that decision Marshal Foch concurred, although he had no illusions whatsoever about 'Locarno,' regarding it, as he did, not as a sedative but as 'an opiate,' *une soporifique*, as he put it. The truth was too blunt, in his own words too *cru*, to be told to a 'pacifist' world in a state of ecstasy, bordering on hysteria, over the signature of the Pact. Nor would it have been believed if one had attempted to tell it. Such a book at such a time would only have been stigmatized as 'conduct calculated to provoke a breach of the peace.' But when, just ten years later, Germany threw off the mask, Foch's former Chief of Staff, General Weygand, reminded the Author of the Marshal's suggestion, and offered to write the Preface which Foch was no longer alive to write. About the same time, General, afterwards Field-Marshal, Sir John Dill, then Director of Military Intelligence at the War Office, who, like Foch, was not deceived and who foresaw the coming catastrophe, wrote to me to the same effect in a remarkable letter in the course of which he observed, *'The situation has never been squarely faced;* we, and the world, preferred to wait upon events and so, as you foretold, Germany's reconversion to the gospel of force is, I imagine, now complete.' Such encouragement, coming from soldiers so distinguished, was not to be lightly disregarded, but there were, by then, other and prior claims upon my time, involving, among other things, long visits to India as Counsel to the Chamber of Princes, and it was not till three years later that the work was sufficiently advanced to justify the redemption of General Weygand's promise. Thereupon he wrote the promised Preface. But the tragic fate which overtook him two years later, and the ambiguity attending his position after the collapse of France, appeared to impose upon me the painful necessity of dispensing with the publication of his Preface altogether. Thereupon General Macdonogh, of whom I took counsel, agreed to step into the breach and to write the Preface which now makes its appearance in this volume. He urged, however, after reading Weygand's contribution, that it was of 'such historic interest' that it would be a mistake to discard it altogether. It appears, therefore, as an Appendix to this volume. Three of these four great soldiers, Foch, Dill, and Macdonogh, have now passed away and the fate of the fourth is, at the moment of writing, still one of the dark secrets of the Nazi terror.

I have to thank General Sir Alexander Godley, Major-General Sir Ernest Swinton, Brigadier-General Harry Lewin, and Colonel Maxwell Earle for reading the present volume, and the greater part of the succeeding volume, in proof, with care and consideration. General Godley took over the command of the British Army of Occupation in the Rhineland in March 1922 and, when serving in Berlin, I had the advantage of his wise counsel and support on more than one critical occasion when I needed all the support I could get in the discharge of a none too easy duty. To the Right Hon. Sir

Malcolm Robertson, M.P., Chairman of the British Council, I am under many obligations as difficult to assess as they are impossible to repay. His knowledge of modern Germany is unique among Englishmen, for, in the course of his distinguished diplomatic career, he served as an *attaché* at the British Embassy in Berlin in the days of the First Reich and subsequently, in the days of the Weimar Republic, as Deputy High Commissioner for the Rhineland. More than twenty-one years ago, he, no less convinced than myself that Germany was already preparing for another war, urged me to undertake this task, and he has followed my faltering efforts to complete it with a solicitude which could not have been greater if the book had been his own. Indeed, but for him this book, at a critical moment in its progress in 1942, would, for reasons which it is unnecessary to particularize, have been abandoned altogether. I have also to thank Brigadier-General Sir Harold Hartley, F.R.S., the author of a masterly report, issued to me in 1919, on the German Chemical Industry, for reading the chapter in the second volume which deals with this vital but difficult and highly technical aspect of disarmament.

During the last year of my tenure of my appointment in Berlin, and for a considerable period after my resignation, I had the honor to be closely associated with two distinguished soldiers in the Directorate of Military Intelligence at the War Office, General Sir John Burnett Stuart, the Director, and Colonel, now General, R. G. Finlayson who was then head of M.I.3, and, as such, of the sub-department which was the channel of communication between the General Staff and the Control Commission. The nature of my obligations to them will be apparent in the book itself. Here it is sufficient to say that they and I were in complete agreement on the conclusions I reached, and duly reported, on the subject of German disarmament, and any difficulties I had had in convincing the War Office, before they 'took over,' completely disappeared with their appointment to the Directorate. 'We see eye to eye,' wrote General Finlayson to me at the time. 'We are aiming at the same thing: the destruction of German militarism,' wrote General Burnett Stuart a little later. It was this identity of view, thus at last attained, which made it possible for me to resign when I did. It would be almost unnecessary for me to say this but for certain somewhat sensational statements about myself which have appeared in a well-known book, *World in Trance*, by Leopold Schwarzschild. I have, indeed, to thank General Burnett Stuart and Colonel Finlayson, as he then was, for their approval of my acceptance of a request by General Nollet that I should continue, after my resignation, to advise the Commission in an honorary capacity for the subsequent three years down to the date of its withdrawal in February 1927. Such acceptance seemed incumbent on me, in view of Marshal Foch's having on his own initiative sought, and obtained, an assurance from the War Office that I should remain in Berlin till the end of the Commission, but without their approval acceptance would have been, to my mind, impossible. More than that, I have to thank them for having given me, in the most generous terms, official permission to disclose the substance of my official reports, and of many other confidential documents, in an article I thought it my duty to write in the *Quarterly Review*[1] soon after my resignation with the object of enlightening my fellow-countrymen as to the dangers to the peace of Europe implicit in the subtle plans of the Reichswehrministerium which, in those reports, I had attempted to unmask. It was, therefore, certainly not the fault of the War Office, nor indeed of the Foreign Office, that public opinion in England was so disastrously bemused, not to say 'doped,' in those fateful days as to the dangers lurking ahead of us. The responsibility for that tragic state of affairs lay elsewhere.

The two statements by Herr Schwarzschild, which occur at pages 224 and 172 of his book, have been so widely reproduced in newspaper reviews of that work, a valuable work, that I feel it incumbent on me to correct them. For they are curiously inaccurate. Mr. Lloyd George never sent me a 'telegram' of 'dismissal.' A British Prime Minister does not, and indeed cannot, send telegrams of dismissal to British officers. Nor can a British officer be dismissed from the Army at all except by sentence of court-martial. I did, indeed, receive in June 1922, a telegram of recall—not of dismissal—and it is true enough that the cause of it was a continuing difference of opinion between a certain higher authority and myself, he insisting

[1] As to the origin and occasion of this article, and its violent repercussion in Germany, see Appendix V, 'The State of German Disarmament in January 1925.'

that Germany was 'totally disarmed' and I insisting that she was not. So far as I am aware, Mr. Lloyd George had nothing to do with the telegram. It was cancelled by the C.I.G.S. within a few days of its dispatch but not, as Herr Schwarzschild says, on 'the intervention of Marshal Foch' but of General Nollet, whose letter on the subject will be found in Appendix VI of this volume. Foch's 'intervention' came later and was the request already mentioned, for an assurance by the C.I.G.S. that I should remain until the end of the Commission.

Mr. Schwarzschild's second statement is that '*in violation of military discipline*' I precipitately and, as he seems to think, heroically, disclosed in the correspondence columns of *The Times*, 'the sense' of a 'suppressed' Final Report of the Commission and thereby convicted two eminent statesmen, M. Briand and Sir Austen Chamberlain, of 'falsification' of the Report. This is altogether too imaginative. There was no 'violation' of military discipline whatsoever on my part, any more than there had been in the publication of my *Quarterly* article. Nor did I ever impute to these two statesmen, with both of whom I had been on terms of personal friendship, anything so dishonorable as 'falsification.' I did not even refer to them in my letter to *The Times*. What I did do was to disclose therein, after seven years of self-imposed silence on the subject of 'Locarno,' the fact that, down to the very day of the Commission's summary withdrawal as the price of the ill-fated Pact, Germany had 'done everything in her power to obstruct, deceive, and counter-control the Commission whose duty it was to disarm her'—a statement which has lately been endorsed in almost identical words by Mr. Anthony Eden in the course of a powerful speech in the House of Commons on 29 September 1944. The immediate occasion of my letter to *The Times* was an appeal to me by a distinguished officer serving in the Historical Section of the Committee of Imperial Defence, who had served on the Control Commission in Berlin. In a remarkable letter, dated 11 October 1933, he wrote to me expressing his deep anxiety about the credulity with which the English public was accepting the persistent statements of German propagandists that Germany had 'totally disarmed.' He asked me to deal with them in *The Times*, explaining that, as he was still in the service of the Crown, he could not so deal with them himself. With his personal letter to me, he enclosed a draft of what he had intended, or rather wished, to say himself in *The Times*, had he been free to do so. In the course of that draft letter he wrote:

No one who served in Germany on the Control Commission can fail to know that Germany never did fulfill the Disarmament provisions of the Treaty and that she never has been disarmed, materially or morally. The plain facts are that Germany has never acknowledged her responsibilities, has never accepted defeat, is determined to re-arm in any event, and is merely biding her time.

This draft, he added, he had shown to his superior officer, the greatest military historian of our time, who 'while agreeing' with all he had thus written, had expressed the view that, as he was still serving the Crown, it would be 'inadvisable' for him to publish it. 'You are the man,' my correspondent gracefully added, 'to make public these things, if you feel disposed to do so, and I very much hope that you will.' I had received many similar letters from other regular officers who had served on the Control Commission. In view of such appeals it seemed to me that the least I could do was to comply with their requests. The result was the letter in question which the Assistant Editor of *The Times*, my friend Mr. Murray Brumwell, of whom I took counsel, decided to publish on 4 November 1933, and to publish with considerable prominence. As for the public-spirited officer who wrote to me asking me to write as I did, there can, I think, be no harm in disclosing, at this distance of time, that he was Lieut.-Colonel Charles Hordern, R.E.

I have to thank the Directorate of Military Intelligence for granting me permission, on the initiative of Sir John Dill, to reproduce a map, showing the distribution of German Army Corps Districts, from a confidential War Office 'Hand-book' on the German Army of the 'first' Reich which was issued to me when serving on the Commission. I have also to thank the Admiralty for giving me details, refreshing my memory, as to certain German outrages at sea during the last war which will be found on pages 175-6 of this volume. To the Right Hon. Sir Donald Somervell, K.C., M.P., His Majesty's Attorney-General, and Sir William Malkin, G.C.M.G., K.C., Legal Adviser to the Foreign Office, I am indebted for certain assistance which, at Sir William Malkin's request, I do not particularize. That request and my compliance, as a matter of course, with

it do not, however, to my mind, discharge me from the pleasant
duty of expressing my acknowledgments to both my learned friends,
as I now do. I take this opportunity of expressing my appreciation
of facilities placed at my disposal for research in German books and
German military periodicals by the Librarian of the London Library,
Mr. C. J. Purnell, and the Assistant Librarian, Mr. F. J. Cox; by the
Deputy Librarian of the War Office, Mr. A. S. White; and by the
Librarian of Chatham House, Miss Eileen Stiff. Dr. W. M. Jordan,
who is the author of an admirable historical work [2] of patient and
discriminating scholarship published under the auspices of the Royal
Institute of International Affairs, kindly placed at my disposal his
transcript of passages dealing with the disarmament discussions in
Paris in the year 1919, which occur in a prodigious 'Diary,' in
twenty-two volumes, of the Peace Conference by an American
writer, Mr. D. H. Miller. Mr. Miller's book, however, although useful in refreshing one's memory, has told me nothing with which, as
a member of the British Military Delegation at Paris, I was not
already familiar. The proceedings of the Military Committee, appointed on 12 February 1919 to study under the presidency of
Marshal Foch the problem of how to disarm Germany, have in fact
never been published, either by Mr. Miller or any one else, and I am
fortunate in having had placed at my disposal by Marshal Foch,
shortly before his death, his unpublished papers on the subject.[3]

It may well be that some of the suggestions put forward in this
book for the effective disarmament of Germany have, owing to the
delay in its publication, lost something of the novelty they possessed
at the time they were originally written. I cannot regret this, for the
simple reason that they have now been adopted, and published to
the world, by those who alone are in a position to implement them,
in other words by the three great statesmen who are responsible for
the Report of the Crimea Conference. I have in mind, in particular,
the proposals in that Report for the total 'disarmament and disbandment of all German armed forces,' the total dissolution of the
German Officers' Corps, which is implicit in such disbandment, and

[2] *Great Britain, France and the German Problem, 1918-1939* (the Oxford University Press, 1943), by W. M. Jordan.
[3] Extracts from those papers will duly appear in a second volume, to be
published later.

the 'elimination of all German industry that could be used for
military production.' It is the only way. No one with any experience
of the Control Commission of 1919-27 can doubt that. But when, on
18 December 1942, I suggested these particular measures, in the
course of an address delivered, by request, to a 'Round Table Conference' in London, representative of the United Nations, there were
some newspapers which, in commenting, amiably enough, upon that
utterance, dissented from it. One thought it, as it may well have
been, premature, another considered it too drastic. Today, as the
result of the unanimous endorsement by the House of Commons
of the Crimea Conference's Report, and of Mr. Churchill's compelling speech on that historic occasion, these things are no longer
open to controversy. For that happy result much credit is, I think,
due to the 'Post-War Policy' Group of members of both Houses
of Parliament which, more than two years ago, commenced to
study, in secret session, the subject of the disarmament of Germany
with a view to the education of public opinion. On several occasions members of the Cabinet attended their sessions to hear their
views. In May 1943 and in August 1944 the Group issued two most
valuable Reports on the subject. These Reports recommended the
very measures of disarmament which are now the declared policy
of the Government. I had the honor of being invited by the Group,
on its formation, to attend its meetings regularly at Westminster
as its honorary adviser, and I take this opportunity of thanking
my friends Sir John Wardlaw-Milne, M.P., the Chairman, and Mr.
J. J. Craik Henderson, M.P., the Vice-Chairman, for the opportunity thus afforded me of laying my views before this most influential and distinguished body of public men.

There remains, however, and will for many years remain, the
problem of how these majestic plans of the Crimea Conference to
ensure that, in the words of its Report, Germany shall 'never again'
be able to disturb the peace of the world are to be enforced. Those
plans will require, to my mind, an armed occupation of the whole
of Germany for at least twenty-nine years, the financial burden of
which will inevitably fall upon the taxpayers of the three great
'United Nations.' Will those taxpayers 'stay the course'? Is there
no way of shortening, without grave risk, the term of that prolonged
occupation? I shall attempt to answer the second of these two ques-

tions, and to answer it, I hope, constructively, in the concluding chapter of a second volume of this book.

Exigencies of time and space make it impossible for the author to comment fully in this Introduction, as he originally undertook to do on page 166 of this volume, on the effect, if any, on the prerogatives of the German Officers' Corps of the sensational trials, resulting in conviction, by the Nazi 'People's Court' of a number of German Officers in July 1944. The subject will be dealt with in a second volume. Here it is sufficient to say that the convicted officers were, before they were put on trial, formally *expelled* from the Army by a military 'court of honor' (an *Ehrengericht*), consisting exclusively of their fellow-officers. They were therefore no longer, under German military law, officers at all. In *The Times* Report of 9 August 1944, it is significantly stated, on the authority of a German news agency, that at their trial they 'did not wear uniform.' In other words they were tried as civilians. The fact that, even on a charge of 'treason,' Hitler was unable, or unwilling, to put suspected officers on trial until he had secured their dismissal from the German Army by the Officers' Corps affords a striking confirmation of the persistence of the prerogatives of the military caste.—J. H. M.

PART ONE

PART ONE

I. THE ADVANCED GUARD

O N THE NIGHT OF 12 September 1919 a long 'special' train stood
waiting at one of the departure platforms of the Gare du Nord.
It was the first train to leave Paris for Berlin after five catastrophic
years. Even so, it had something of a belligerent look. It was uncommonly like a troop-train. The station, dark as a cavern under
the arched roof, was full of shadows, but high above us the great
arc lamps, suspended by invisible filaments, hung like so many
planets in the vault. Their hard, white light shone down upon a
little group of officers who stood upon the platform, by the doors
of the *wagon-lits*, talking in five languages. The searching radiance
of those lamps picked out with the intensity of a spot-light the
infinite variety of the uniforms of the three 'arms' of the Allied
Nations with a chromatic harmony of subdued colors—pale blue,
dark blue, dove-gray, and khaki in an infinitude of shades.

Beyond the barrier, jealously guarded by *gendarmes,* a curious
crowd of Parisians stared inquisitively at each officer as he passed
through. Two drivers stood on the footplate of the engine, engaged
in earnest talk with some Divisional Superintendent of the line. He
seemed to be coaching them in their duties—I heard the word
doucement oft repeated. No doubt it was necessary. For two frail
and precarious threads of steel were to bear our train during the
watches of the night across a desert. Behind the long chain of
wagon-lits, the saloons, and the carriages for 'other ranks,' twelve
great railway-trucks were coupled to the train. They were sur-
mounted by uncouth shapes and monstrous, lashed to the trucks
with stout ropes and hidden by black tarpaulins. Those shapes
might have been guns, but were not.

A group of French porters in belted blouses, having loosened their
straps and disengaged themselves of our kit, stood at ease within the
barrier and gazed at the tarpaulins. Now and again, one of them
pointed possessively at one tarpaulin or another with an air of grim
satisfaction, although none of them smiled. My own porter I de-

tained in casual conversation. His eyes had that neurasthenic look, the pupils dark and fatigued, which haunted the faces of men for many a long month after they had evacuated the fire-trenches. I asked him where his home was. 'I have none,' he replied simply, 'it is gone'—*C'est tout à fait disparu*. His home had been a village in one of the Eastern Departments. The village, he had been told, was so wasted by the enemy that not one stone was left upon another. As he talked of it, I recalled a dreadful drive through the devastated districts, soon after the 'Cease Fire' of the Armistice, and the sight of a heap of rubble with a stump of wood protruding from it like an amputated limb. On the stump some grim humorist had painted the words 'C'ÉTAIT CRÉPY.' It was the epitaph of a whole village, pounded into the soil. As I turned away, he drew my attention to an inscription, chalked in big scrawling letters upon each of the tarpaulins which shrouded our Army cars. The other porters, he explained, had done it. The inscription was 'À BERLIN.' Just five years earlier, the German troop-trains, carrying von Kluck's Army Corps towards the Belgian frontiers, had borne, chalked upon the windows by the exultant invaders, the inscription 'Nach PARIS.' Now came the repartee. We were not, indeed, a punitive expedition. But we were charged with the duty of destroying the terrible instrument which had ravaged the fair face of France and ruined millions of lives.

I noticed that, like his comrades, the village exile never smiled. None of them appeared vindictive nor were they even exultant. In those days, indeed, one very rarely encountered any exultation among the French. What one did encounter was a strange, pensive mood. It was not joy, neither was it sorrow. It was not even relief. It was suspense. On the night of the Fête de la Victoire in Paris, I saw a party of young British officers, who had dined a little too well at the Majestic and had swept with linked arms down the Champs Elysées singing 'Tipperary,' as they burst uproariously into the foyer of Claridge's where I and my staff-officer, Colonel Brinsmead, sat together. They invited the French guests to dance with them. No one responded. The French looked steadily and in silence at the joyous invaders, who thereupon stepped quietly out, puzzled and a little abashed. A few days later, I was home on leave in London, a guest at a dinner-party at the Berkeley to celebrate our own 'Day of Victory.' The restaurant rioted with merry laughter and the whole concourse of diners lassoed one another across the tables with streamers of multi-colored ribbons. Many of them danced ecstatically. And now, as I looked at that little group of porters with their calloused hands and tired eyes, so somber that they did not even raise a cheer as our train drew out of the Gare du Nord, I recalled the contrast between their people and mine in the triumphal hour. I remembered London on that night at the Berkeley, the brittle crackle of fireworks in the Park and the vociferous cheering of the crowds. And I remembered Paris on the night of the Fête de la Victoire, a pensive Paris, crowded but silent, and not less somber than silent, the Champs Elysées illuminated only by four great urns resting upon four great altars, each bearing the name of a martyred city, ARRAS, ST. QUENTIN, CAMBRAI, PERONNE, whence there emerged a smoky flame, as of a burnt offering, that was neither light nor dark but crepuscular against the night. Beside the mournful beauty of those flaming shrines, our London fireworks now seemed to me a meretricious thing. And like the voice of an ac- cuser, I seemed to hear the voice of France, 'Ye have piped but we have not danced; we have mourned but ye have not wept.' After all, her fairest provinces had been flayed by the invader twice within living memory and ours had not. With a strange, a mournful, clair- voyance, she seemed to divine that the end was not yet.

As one officer after another came through the barrier, we fell in- evitably into national groups. Our 'inter-allied' character reminded me of the Peace Conference, except that we did not talk so much. We were as yet, internationally, strangers to one another. But many a lasting friendship was to be forged between French and British offi- cers during the years of duress that lay ahead. In the little nucleus of British officers with me was Major F. C. T. Ewald of the South Staffords, an old friend of mine who had come all the way from Palestine to report to me in Paris on my nomination of him as D.A.A.G. on my staff. He was a typical company officer of the old B.E.F., one of the survivors of that first battle of Ypres—where he had won the D.S.O.—which is the epic of our race. Lean, sinewy, with a small bird-like head and twitching eyebrows, he walked like a man whose feet were more at home in the stirrups than upon the pedestrian pavement. He had ridden in the Grand National. When I first met him he was Inspector of Musketry to the Southern Command. In his way he was typically English. He had no use for foreign languages and not much for foreigners, whether French or German. When General Barthélemy appeared one day at our headquarters in Berlin in a black tail-coat, straw hat and brown boots, Ewald could hardly be persuaded that Barthélemy was a soldier. My assurances that Barthélemy had commanded a Division with heroic distinction at Verdun and had been head of the famous Deuxième Bureau at the Ministère de la Guerre in Paris left him still incredulous.

With us was Major Scott, to be known and endeared to us all as 'Scottie,' of the 4th Hussars. Scottie was diminutive, even for a cavalry officer, with a big head, a pale face, and round gray eyes set well apart, which looked at one with the ingenuousness of a newborn child first opening its eyes in wonder upon the world. Such was one's first impression, until you discovered that no greater artist in pulling one's leg ever entertained a mess. Small in stature, he did not know what fear was, and had been wounded by shrapnel so often that his body was said to be full of scrap-iron. On the platform I encountered, for the first time, Captain Tottenham, who was Senior Naval Officer of the advance party of the Naval Control Commission. He was a charming fellow with a subtle air of distinction, immaculate, debonair, witty, with large blue eyes that looked one straight in the face. His self-assurance was perfect. One of my friends in the Senior Service told me that Tottenham was in the habit of winding up his allocutions to 'subs' on deportment with the exhortation, 'Try to be like me—if you can.' Under a bland and courteous demeanor he concealed a will of iron, and when, as happened soon after our arrival, the German authorities began playing tricks on the Naval Commission, they discovered in no time that Tottenham was not a man to be trifled with.

As we four British officers stood and talked together, there was a stir at the barrier and all the French officers came smartly to the salute. A short, compact figure strode on to the platform. It was the President of the Military Commission of Control, General Nollet. I had only met him once and I looked at him with a quickening interest which now seems to me to have had in it some sort of unconscious clairvoyance. For little did I think, at that moment, that this great soldier of France and myself were, in course of time, to establish a close and enduring friendship. As he took off his gold-embroidered *kepi* for a moment on that September night, I noticed that he had an imposing brow, an intellectual face, a delicately chiseled nose, and sensitive nostrils. His hands were small, like Napoleon's, and finely shaped. He had a jaw of iron and his shoulders were broad and powerful. There was resolution in every line of him. Such was the man whose name during the years that lay ahead of us was to be a word of wrath and expostulation in the German Press. Week after week, particularly during the occupation of the Ruhr, the newspapers of 'the Right' assailed the German public with hints not to nail Nollet's ears to the pump, reminded them that he was to be seen daily lunching in the Adlon or walking, as indeed he did without escort, in the Unter den Linden, and enlarged suggestively on the scandal of his impunity. It all left him quite unmoved. When an excited mob beset our offices in the Hotel Bellevue one torrid summer day, he ordered the blinds of his room to be drawn up, saying to me, as the shouts grew ever more menacing, 'If they want to find me, they will know where I am.' Discoursing of such things, and worse, he once said to me, 'A man's strength is in his enemies.' The saying was characteristic.

The arrival of Nollet was the signal for our departure. 'En voiture, messieurs, s'il vous plaît,' cried the Divisional Superintendent. Doors slammed, farewell salutes were exchanged, the platform slowly receded. The train drew out of the station and gathered way. Soon the lights of Paris twinkled and disappeared. I sought my 'sleeper,' opened a German book—it was Goethe's *Dichtung und Wahrheit*—and fell once more under its wistful spell. I had left the door of my compartment open and from time to time I heard the laughter of the little group of British officers in the corridor, as 'Scottie' and Ewald capped one another's stories. Now and again my compartment was brilliantly illuminated by the lights of one station after another, as we flashed through and the noise of the train rose to a louder note with the vibration and then changed to a lower one as we gained the unconfined spaces of the open country.

Gradually everything seemed to change. As I glanced out into the night, I noticed that the telegraph poles and their filaments of wire had completely vanished. The time since we had passed a station or a signal-box now began to appear incredibly long. The landscape itself had changed. It had a curiously bleached look and not a tree was to be seen. Complete silence had fallen upon the merry group of officers in the corridor. Then I heard two French words uttered and no more. The words were 'Mon Dieu!' Then an Englishman spoke and I recognized Ewald's voice: 'Christ! It reminds me of the Dead Sea.' I rose and went out into the corridor. It was now nearly midnight and the moon was at the full. Everything was etched in black and silver. The air grew very cold.

A vast silence encompassed us, a silence so deep that not a sound could be heard except the panting of the engine which had now slowed down to a crawling pace. I looked out. Silhouetted in the cold moonlight there loomed up on either side of the line great gaunt shapes of a monstrous uniformity. There was something macabre about those shapes; it was as though we were passing through an interminable cemetery, a veritable *champ des morts*. They looked like gigantic tombstones. Then I saw that they were the gable-ends of ruined houses. Street after street of them, at right angles to the line, ran radiating past us and each street sparkled white in the moonlight with the splinters of shivered glass or gleamed gray with the pallor of crumbled masonry. The ruins were wrapped in a winding sheet of mortar, fine as dust, but where the wind had winnowed in the deserted streets the mortar lay in drifts against the walls as thick as sand heaps. The multitudes of those sepulchral shapes suggested that we were passing through what had been a great city. But its name none of us could tell. Like the buried cities of antiquity with their plaintive appeal to the historian, it seemed to await the archaeologist's spade, as though crying out for recognition. Nothing moved in that wilderness of stone and dust, nor did any living thing appear. Even the rats had deserted it. Now and again an open space told of a park or garden but the trees had lost all character. Not a leaf hung upon their stark limbs and I looked hard at their distorted shapes, shivered and blasted by gunfire, trying to decipher in them the filigree pattern of an oak or the fan-like outline of an elm. But those stricken shapes were as anonymous as the city itself. They reminded me of Delville 'Wood' in 1916. One poplar alone had escaped. Its tall, clean-limbed shape pointed to the sky like a note of exclamation.

The city vanished like a ghost into the night and we were once again out into the open country. Looking intently out of the windows of our train at the vast moonlit spaces, I understood now why the countryside seemed so bleached. Not a blade of grass was to be seen. Everything was withered into dust. Now and again the train slowed down, for our engine-drivers were wary of the shadows thrown in black patches by ruined houses across the track ahead. We crawled through another dead city, and then another and yet another. The journey seemed interminable. As the night grew colder and yet more cold, a deep depression seemed to settle on us all. Conversation in the corridor flickered and went out like a dying candle. Yet there we remained, fascinated by the weird horror of the scene. Weeks later, I read in the *Vorwärts* a description of it all by a German journalist who had passed that way and who gave thanks to God that the Fatherland had altogether escaped that awful disfigurement. Throughout the long night one little group of officers in sky-blue uniforms remained in the corridor and, after their first exclamation, never spoke. They were French.

'Le silence éternel de ces espaces infinis m'effraie.' I thought of Pascal's 'terror' as he contemplated the vast solitudes of inter-stellar space. At last, I could stand no more of it, and, leaving my companions in the corridor, I returned to my compartment, undressed, and fell into a troubled sleep. I dreamed that I was flying alone and through the Infinite until I landed with a terrific impact upon a dead planet, cold as ice. I woke suddenly to find my bedclothes on the floor and myself on top of them. The train was at a standstill. It had pulled up with a shock that had transmitted itself, like a current, from carriage to carriage—the buffers of the trucks behind us were still noisily nudging each other as I awoke. I heard afterwards that the drivers had sharply put on the brakes, shutting off steam, at the sight of a dark patch across the track ahead. One of them descended from the footplate with a hurricane lamp to investigate, only to find nothing there. It was the shadow of a ruined house projecting across the track. The shell-holes in the permanent-way had been hastily filled up only a few weeks before by a breakdown gang of platelayers, and the drivers never knew where there might not lurk a subsidence of the soil or of the layers of new ballast that covered it. There were many such halts during the long night.

I fell asleep again. When I awoke in the morning, the night journey seemed utterly remote and incredible. The sun was up and my eyes fell upon a green and living world. We were passing through the leafy vales of the Ardennes. A well-metaled road ran alongside us and an exhilarating sight caught my eye. A British battery in column of route was passing at a smart trot, the sun glinting on the brass-work of the guns and twinkling from the polished buttons of the drivers and the gunners on the limbers. They were doubtless *en route* for the Army of Occupation on the Rhine. Bailey, my batman, brought me a morning cup of tea and I joined the other British officers at breakfast. In due course, we arrived at Cologne and detrained. We found our way to the Dom Hotel, hard by the Hauptbahnhof. It was the Headquarters Mess of the Army of Occupation and was alive with British officers. Here I was joined by a gunner officer, Colonel T. R. Ubsdell, known throughout 'the royal regiment' as 'Tubby,' whose services I had secured as my A.A.G.

On an earlier visit to Cologne, when ordered by General Macdonogh to proceed there and report upon our occupation of the Rhineland with a view to drawing up the Rhineland Convention for the Peace Conference, I had strolled one day into one of those 'military courts' of ours which enforced 'peace, order, and good government' among the civil population by the exercise of summary jurisdiction. Between the occupied territory and the rest of Germany, we had erected a barbed-wire frontier which was also a Customs frontier, and a vast amount of smuggling went on by Germans coming to and fro by rail. This illicit traffic was lucrative and was highly organized by some German *Schieber* (profiteer), always in the background, who was ready to give the British soldiers ten marks for a packet of cigarettes purchasable in our canteens at a third of the price. A short, stoutish officer in the uniform of a lieutenant-colonel, sitting on the bench and presiding over the court, was dealing with a dozen such cases. I watched the procession of delinquents pass in and out of the dock. Their mendacity was inexhaustible and I observed that its exposure left them neither embarrassed nor ashamed. It is a German characteristic. One of them was a big man with a flat head and two rolls of fat at the back of his neck. With unblushing effrontery he told three different stories in succession, by way of defense, under the Colonel's cross-examination. Then he fainted—or appeared to faint. 'Pay one thousand marks,' said the Colonel laconically as he regarded the inanimate figure in the dock. 'Next case.' The big man made a surprisingly rapid recovery and took a thousand marks out of a well-filled wallet.

The 'next case' turned out to be an exceedingly small boy charged with smuggling cigarettes. He cried. 'Don't cry!' said the Colonel, whereat he cried the more. A military policeman gave evidence. It appeared that the boy had been employed by an undiscovered group of smugglers who, no doubt, traded on his innocent appearance as a useful tool. He had been caught red-handed with his schoolboy's satchel bulging with two thousand English cigarettes. 'Any witnesses for the defense?' asked the Colonel. There was only one. It was the boy's mother and she was a widow. She wept. She seemed to expect nothing less than a sentence of death. After all, it was a military court and the only militarism she knew was the jack-boot of Prussia. Her evidence, such as it was, was incoherent and agitated. 'Seien Sie nicht so aufgeregt,' [1] said the Colonel, interrupting her all too inadequate defense, 'How many children have you got?' 'Nur dieses!' [2] she said, indicating with a tragic gesture the little culprit in the dock. 'The case is dismissed,' said the Colonel, and, turning towards the mother, he added gently in German, 'Take care of him.' The Colonel was Ubsdell. From that moment I made up my mind that I had found the officer I wanted. To deal with our late enemy in Berlin I needed officers who could be hard when hardness was imperative, and gentle when it was not. I applied to the A.G. for Ubsdell's services in Berlin and he was gazetted A.A.G. in due course.

At mess at the Dom Hotel I met again many British officers whom I had encountered some months earlier when making my report to the A.G. on our Occupation. The 'Rhineland Convention,' regulating the post-armistice conditions of the occupation, was now on 'the Statute Book,' being duly engrossed on the parchment of the Treaty after I had succeeded in piloting my draft of it through its 'Committee stage,' at the meetings of the Supreme War Council at Versailles, with but little amendment.[3] But it was not to come into operation

---

[1] 'Don't be so excited!'
[2] 'Only this one!'
[3] It was subsequently amended, in spite of a strong protest by Marshal Foch, by a civilian committee appointed by the 'Council of Four' to reconsider it in consequence of criticisms by an American delegate, Mr. Noyes, obsessed with the strange idea of substituting what he called 'a civil occupation' for a military one. The result was the super-imposition of a 'Rhineland High Commission'

until the appointed day of the following January when the Treaty was to be ratified. In reply to my inquiries as to how things were going, an A.P.M. told me at lunch that, except in the matter of smuggling, the civil population were giving little trouble. If anything, they were rather too friendly—or the women were. An Army Order had warned our men against 'fraternizing' with the Germans, who, technically, were still an 'enemy' nation until the Armistice had expired. One of our soldiers was had up before his C.O. for being found under rather intimate circumstances with a German girl. 'I wasn't fraternizing, sir,' he pleaded in confession and avoidance. 'She said she'd be a *sister* to me and I said that wasn't good enough.' For sheer casuistry there is nothing like a British soldier at bay in the orderly-room.

With the civil population our relations, after a certain amount of friction at the outset, were, on the whole, good. Whether they would have been equally good had our troops been in occupation of other territories of Prussia, particularly East Prussia and Berlin, is extremely doubtful. The people of the Rhineland are of a very different breed from those of the Prussia to which they were forcibly annexed in 1815. They are, or rather they were, distinguished, as Heine observed, by 'a genuine love of liberty' (*eine echte Freiheitsliebe*) entirely alien to the Prussian tradition of autocracy and, for a considerable period of their history, they were attached, in more senses than one, to France and to French culture. Heine, writing from Berlin in 1822, remarked on the singular freedom of the Rhinelander from that 'hatred of the French' (*Franzosenhass*)[4] in which the youth of Old Prussia were even then, unhappily, being nurtured. It has been part of the curriculum of the Faculties of History in every Prussian University ever since.[5] A genial people, superficially at least, the Rhine-

upon the Commanders-in-Chief of the Armies of Occupation. This Commission proved, in practice, futile. In all other respects the Committee followed closely the original British draft of the Convention.

[4] Heine: *Briefe aus Berlin*, p. 216.

[5] A great historian, Fustel de Coulanges, summed it up, with no exaggeration, thus: 'La maison de Hohenzollern a travaillé à rendre belliqueuse l'opinion publique, elle en a fait une machine de guerre. L'opinion en Prusse a été disciplinée comme l'armée; elle a compris que, pour récolter plus surement la victoire, il faut commencer par semer la haine. Ses professeurs se sont attachés à travestir notre révolution française et à dénaturer toute notre histoire pour nous rendre haissables.'—*Revue des deux Mondes* (1871), vol. xci, pp. 21-2.

landers are distinguished, according to the opinion of German writers themselves, from other folk in other parts of the Reich by a 'happy temperament' (*ein glückliches Temperament*). Some things that occurred could, indeed, only be explained by the adulteration of the Prussian toxin. One of the few 'scraps' that arose between Briton and German was excited by an act of courtesy by a British soldier to a German woman, which occurred at just this time. One day, pursued my friend the A.P.M., a German civilian, accompanied by his wife, entered a tramcar in Cologne. It was full. A British soldier rose to offer the lady his seat. The husband promptly took it. Thereupon the soldier seized the marital despot and threw him out of the car. The story became the talk of Cologne, and some weeks later I read an article on our occupation in the Berlin *Vorwärts* by its Cologne correspondent, in which he reluctantly wrote, 'After all, we Germans have something to learn from the English.' Dr. Goebbels himself, although he would probably be the last to admit the source of his inspiration, was at one time determined that they should learn it, or rather ape it, on occasion.[6]

During the years that followed I was destined to see a good deal at first hand of the Allied occupation of the Rhineland when, on my journeys to and from London and Berlin, I diverged to spend a few days as the guest alternately of the British G.O.C., General Sir Alexander Godley, at Cologne, and of the French G.O.C., General Degoutte, at Wiesbaden. It became the fashion in England, largely as the result of the assiduous efforts of German propaganda materially assisted at a much later date, namely in 1923, by the French occupation of the Ruhr, to represent the British occupation as very soothing to the German civil population and the French occupation as proportionately irritating. To believe this was, of course, very pleasing to our national vanity. But neither proposition was true. The presence of the British in the Rhineland was about as welcome as the

---

[6] During the Olympic Games in Berlin, the Ministry of Propaganda, according to reports in *The Times* and the *Morning Post* from their Berlin correspondents, issued public instructions to the people of Germany to be polite to the influx of foreign visitors. One of these encyclicals ran: 'You are advised to give up your seats in tramcars, buses, and trains *during this period*, to any woman you see standing, even though she be a Jewess.'—*The Morning Post* (Berlin correspondent) 30 June 1936.

presence of a couple of bailiffs sitting in a house under a distress warrant. Soon after the arrival of our troops, a British officer, now a distinguished Member of Parliament, Captain Peter Macdonald, had occasion, in the discharge of his duties as billeting officer, to call at a commodious country-house near Duren. The door was opened by the householder, a large and corpulent German, who answered the British officer's polite explanation of the object of his visit by trying to shut the door in his face with the observation, 'We don't want any Englishmen here.' A Prussian officer, under similar circumstances, would unquestionably have drawn his revolver. Captain Macdonald, with his foot strategically placed inside the door, began to parley, but without result. He was alone. The householder became more and more unpleasant. Suddenly a weird, wailing shriek, as of a soul in torment, from the road startled the truculent German. A moment later, a battalion of Canadian Highlanders, marching in column of fours and headed by their pipe band, swung into view. The householder instantly capitulated. This sort of unpleasantness towards us soon disappeared. But later it recurred. Its recurrence coincided, curiously enough, with our reductions in the effectives of the Army of Occupation. The lighter we sought to make the yoke, the more unfriendly did the civil population become. Towards the end of the Occupation, when the British troops were quartered at Wiesbaden, there was more trouble, taking the form of a furtive slashing of the tires of British Army cars, until the British G.O.C., General Thwaites, who was not the sort of man to stand any nonsense, took drastic steps to stop it. They were effectual.

Sometimes it fell to 'the other ranks' of our Army of Occupation to teach the German civilians how to behave. Soon after our arrival a British sergeant in uniform, going home on leave, was making for the wicket of the booking-office at Cologne station when he was hustled by a stout German elbowing his way in order to get in front of him. The crowd at a booking-office in Germany invariably forms itself into a 'scrum,' never a queue, and it is always a case of *sauve qui peut*. It is the German idea of *Lebensraum*. The indignant soldier seized the thrusting German by the scruff of the neck and hurled him back with the laconic reminder, 'Half a mo! Who d'yer think won the bloody war?' 'Verzeihen!' said the German, probably apologizing for the first time in his life. As Erich Remarque has observed, 'A German never apologizes.' [7]

In the evening, we departed from Cologne and entrained for Berlin. As we left the Hauptbahnhof, a long train drew alongside of us, its carriage windows crowded with shaven heads of an unmistakable contour. Their owners were cheering lustily and waving their hands. They were the first batch of returning German prisoners of war. I reflected that perhaps my efforts, as the British Military Representative on the Prisoners of War Commission at the Peace Conference, to secure the early repatriation of the exiles, might have done something to soften the asperities of the war. But in this I was destined to be disillusioned. As we sped through the German stations beyond the Rhine, we noticed that they were garishly lighted and decorated with flags and evergreens. 'What's all this mean?' inquired Ewald, as we stood in a group in the corridor. 'It's to welcome us,' replied 'Scottie' with a face of the most convincing solemnity. Ewald believed this for quite a long time and began to revise his opinion of foreigners until I thought it time to explain that this flattering reception was not intended for us but for the returning prisoners of war.

We stopped towards midnight at a station whose name I forget. Here the Germans drew first blood. In fact, they scored heavily. It was in this wise—our party included two or three Japanese officers, among them Major Maurita of the General Staff, who was eventually attached to my staff in Berlin, and a diminutive 'Jap' interpreter. The interpreter was small, even for a Japanese, and, unlike Maurita, who came of an old Samurai family, he was quite exceptionally plain of feature. He was uncommonly like a small monkey, and he walked alone. He strolled to the end of the platform and stood there, a forlorn little figure. A group of German platelayers were at work on the permanent-way alongside and regarded him curiously and in silence. At that moment three or four French subalterns of our party, magnificent in new uniforms and, as is the way of youth, not unconscious of their splendor, strolled along, stretching their legs, booted and spurred, after the confinement of our journey. They looked, possibly they felt, as though they were treading the alien soil with the proud heel of the conqueror. The platelayers stared at them and

[7] Remarque: *Three Comrades*, p. 324.

they returned the stare with supercilious eyes. At last a huge German navvy, resting one hand on his long hammer, raised the other and pointed to the little Japanese, 'Das ist der schönster,' [8] he exclaimed.

The remainder of our journey was uneventful and in the early morning we arrived in Berlin. Our train was stopped short of the Friedrichstrasse terminus at a suburban station. The station master explained, with much unction, that the German Government had arranged for us to detrain there in order to spare us a 'hostile' (feindlich) demonstration. Some of us were ingenuous enough at the time to believe this. Later we grew suspicious of such solicitude, and with good reason. An imposing armed guard in steel helmets was posted outside the station. This was for our 'protection,' we were elaborately informed, although there was no crowd visible and none audible. We drove through the Tiergarten to the Hotel Esplanade where rooms had been requisitioned for us. Our uniforms excited something of a flutter in the lounge of that vast caravanserai. It was just sixteen years since I had last been in Berlin when, after coming down from Oxford, I had done a 'semester' at Berlin University. There seemed to be something unfamiliar, something missing in the streets and in the foyer of the hotel, and for a while I wondered what it could be. Then I recollected. It was the complete absence of the smart gray coats of those German officers who had lorded it everywhere over the civil population in the old days, sweeping civilians into the gutter. Not one such was now to be seen. The revolution had, for the time being, scattered them all like the leaves of the forest. They were to reappear one spring morning, a little later, in a dramatic resurgence.[9]

There were other changes. The great city had a blighted look. A 'prosaic' (prosaisch) town, as Goethe called it, and an 'insipid' (nüchtern) city, as Heine found it, it had never been beautiful with that classic beauty, that baroque elegance, which delights the eye in Dresden, in Stuttgart, and in Munich. A century earlier, Madame de Staël had been struck by the entire absence of stonemason's work in Berlin; even its palaces, she observed, were mere brick. So it remained till long after our departure when Hitler in fulfillment of his grandoise architectural dreams determined to go down to history as the ruler who found it brick and left it ferro-concrete. Our R.A.F. have now

---

[8] 'That's the best looking of the lot.'
[9] See below, Chapter IV, 'The Revolt of the Reichswehr.'

somewhat disturbed both the dream and the fulfillment. But, although never beautiful, Berlin had, in the days when I matriculated at its university, at least been smart, gay, and lustrous—a harlot among cities, if you like, but superb in its meretricious finery. Now it was incredibly shabby. It may have been the stress of war, the shortage of oils and gold-leaf, the mobilization of painters and decorators, or perhaps the indifference of the new Republic, but, whatever it was, the great city had a mean and disreputable appearance. The gilded dome of the Reichstag had lost its luster, the doors of the great mansions were dull with cracked and faded paint and the stained and crumbling plaster of the walls gave them a leprous look. The shop windows in the Friedrichstrasse and elsewhere were almost empty of merchandise of the commoner kind, a state of affairs which may or may not have been due to the Allied blockade, about the 'inhumanity' of which a great deal of spurious sentiment was being industriously excited at the very moment of our arrival.[10]

But there were many shops choked with things which had once been priceless. They were antique shops and they told their own melancholy tale. These shops were like a museum of French art without its loving curator. The masterpieces of all the great cabinet-makers of France, from the cunning marquetry of Boulle to the Imperial bronze and mahogany of Percier and Fontaine, the fine flower of the styles of Louis Quinze and the Empire, were piled, like so many trusses of hay, upon one another in doorways and passages. Engravings, brocades, tapestries, bronzes, Aubusson carpets, and Sèvres porcelain were strewn over the shop counters or hustled each other on the shelves. Each inanimate thing told its own tale of a ravished home. From the canvas of the painter in oils and the ivory of the miniaturist the faces of expatriated family portraits seemed to look out at one in their exile with the sad heart of Ruth 'amid the alien corn.' Whose were they? Whence and from what fair château had they come? Who was the illicit vendor who had deposited them at the shop for sale? If you asked the shopkeeper such questions, he became wary, and, like a receiver of stolen goods, affected not to know. We knew well enough who it was, collectively and individually, that had been guilty of this ruthless rapine. It was the German

[10] As to the Allied blockade during the war and for some time afterwards, see below, Chapter xi, 'Germany in Defeat.'

General Staff. At the very beginning of the war the plunder of private property had been organized like a campaign.[11] The trucks of
German supply trains, returning from the front, had been packed
with these things like the vans of a furniture remover. Many a German officer must have been either a principal or an accessory in these
heartless larcenies. Now, in defeat, he and his like had fallen on evil
times and were trying to realize their ill-gotten gains. What, I used
to wonder, were the thoughts of my French comrades on the Commission as they looked upon these things? It was one of those questions which one never asks.

This sort of rapine was, to be sure, nothing new. It had been practiced by the invading armies of Germany upon the French people in
three campaigns by three successive generations of German troops,
even as it has been practiced behind the veil of 'Vichy.' But never
before had it been practiced on such a colossal scale and certainly
never with such demoralizing effects on the practitioners. In 1870-71
the spectacle of it moved a great French historian, more in sorrow
than in anger, to mournful protest and a somber question—'These soldiers who fill their knapsacks with our silver and with the jewelry and
lace of our womenfolk, *will these men,*' he asked, '*return to their own
country the same men as they left it?* Will they not take back with
them sentiments such as they had never felt and lusts such as they
had never known before?' [12] Whatever the answer to that searching catechism was in 1871, there seemed to be no doubt about the
answer to it in 1919. For the Germany I had known, as a student at
Berlin University in the years before the war, was now morally disfigured almost beyond recognition. In those days, so near in time, so
incredibly remote in circumstance, Germany had affected to be the
home of the civic virtues and, among them, not the least conspicuous
was, or so it had seemed to me, a universal respect for life and prop-

[11] An acute neutral observer, the American Ambassador in London, Walter
Page, writing in the summer of 1916, expressed himself thus: 'As soon as the
Germans took a town in Belgium, they asked for all the money in the town,
all the movable property . . . If they got London, they'd be rich; they wouldn't
leave a shilling. If they got to Paris, there wouldn't be 30 cents worth of movable property there in a week.'—*The Life and Letters of Walter Page*, vol. ii,
pp. 252-3.

[12] Thus, Fustel de Coulanges in 'La politique d'envahissement' in the *Revue
des deux Mondes* (1871), vol. xci, p. 29.

erty. Now, on my return, the country seemed like a thieves' kitchen. The first notice that I encountered at my hotel, the proudest hotel in Germany and the chosen resort of her aristocracy, was a warning to guests not to leave their boots outside their doors at night. Those who disregarded it never saw them again. The next was a notice over the cloak-room that the management would accept no responsibility, beyond a nominal sum, for articles deposited therein. An identical notice was to be seen over the cloak-rooms of every hotel, theatre, restaurant, café, and public place in Berlin. *Quis custodiet custodes?* had become a problem of menacing proportions. Even the public services, once as efficient and as honest as any in the world, were corrupted by the universal lust for loot. The Reich postal service was infected from top to bottom. The police were hard put to stamp out the infection until their suspicion fell upon an *Ober Post-beamte*, himself the head of the Postal Detective Service. A search of his papers disclosed that he had accumulated a private banking account of two hundred million marks—at that time the equivalent of something like a million pounds.

A wave of larceny was spreading over the country like an epidemic. Day after day one read in the German Press of museums being looted of coins and medals, family vaults despoiled of rings, national monuments stripped of bronze. Nothing was too great or too small, too sacred or too profane, for the itching fingers of the spoiler. Soon after my arrival, I had occasion to proceed to Königsberg by train, taking my batman, Bailey, with me. We were both in mufti, and Bailey was wearing a new cap of excellent English tweed. During the night journey he fell asleep in his compartment. Perhaps his sleep was even as the sleep of Eutychus. When he awoke, he found his cap had been stolen from off his head. Poor Bailey could not have been more surprised, nor more indignant, if he had been despoiled of his trousers. I told him he was lucky to have been spared them, but he refused to be comforted.

One came across symptoms of this social malady in the most incredible places. On my first visit of inspection to Gross Lichterfelde, the 'Sandhurst' of the German Army, I noticed in the great hall a handsome glass case, a mural decoration with the glass broken and the case empty. It had contained their proudest trophy—the baton of

Napoleon, captured at Waterloo. 'But where is it?' I asked. 'Stolen,' was the laconic reply.

Nemesis, like coincidence, has a long arm. In the year 1920 it caught the great Blücher himself in a ghoulish clutch. It is a strange tale, and macabre, but I can vouch for the truth of it. Blücher, as all the world knows, it was who gave the Prussian Army a bad name for looting. His vast depredations on French soil in 1814-15 are a matter of history [13] and beyond dispute, although the classical story of his exclamation at his first glimpse of London—'What a city to sack!' —happens to be, like so many intriguing stories, untrue.[14] The universal acceptance of the story in England at the time was, however, the testimony of a shocked generation to its intrinsic probability. And now, a century later, came one of Time's most dramatic revenges. In the village of Wahlstatt, the family place of the Blüchers in Silesia, where the hero of Waterloo lay in the family vault, the Christmastide of 1920 was celebrated by some amateur theatricals in the village hall, with the historic triumphs of Blücher and the Prussian Army as their theme. The Field-Marshal was impersonated by an actor wearing a reproduction of his Waterloo uniform and of the decorations which, according to common repute, had been buried with him. Conspicuous among the actor's decorations was a counterfeit of a large gold medal. The next morning a horrified retainer, making his rounds of the estate, found the family tomb had been forced open during the night with a crowbar. And on the frozen grass beside it lay the skeleton of Blücher. He had been rudely evicted from his coffin by thieves as they rifled it for loot.

[13] See, for example, the sober pages of the *Cambridge History of British Foreign Policy*, vol. i, pp. 505, 506, 507-9, 510, and 513 on Blücher's pre-occupation, to the distress of Wellington, with 'spoliation and revenge,' with 'indiscriminate and destructive pillage' and a determination 'to bleed France white.'

[14] I am indebted to his great-grandson for the true version. Prince Blücher told me in Berlin that what his illustrious ancestor actually said was 'Was für Plunder!' which means 'What rubbish!' The old Field-Marshal thought London an ugly city, and said so.

II. RECONNAISSANCE

SUCH, AT FIRST SIGHT, was the country, and such its temper, in which we of the 'Advanced Guard,' a handful of Allied officers mustering some forty all told, found ourselves during the ambiguous days of the Armistice. Our impression in those early days that we had to deal with a nation afflicted with 'a mind diseased' grew ever stronger as time went on until we began to feel we were living in a madhouse. This dark hinterland of 'unoccupied' Germany, so incredibly remote from the orderly life of the Rhineland under the benevolent despotism of the British and French armies of occupation, was even as that 'savage forest,' that *selva selvaggia* of the lusts of the flesh, which haunted the somber imagination of the Florentine poet, 'the very thought of which renews the horror of it.' To attempt to describe it in all its savagery will require a chapter to itself.[1]

At the outset we found we had to 'disarm' a country in which, as we discovered almost immediately on our arrival as the result of a rapid reconnaissance, there were at least five hundred thousand men still with the colors, armament factories were continuing to turn out guns and munitions, while millions of rifles and tens of thousands of machine-guns were in the unlicensed hands of demobilized 'toughs' who were spoiling for a fight.[2] All over Germany irregular levies, known as Free Corps, were being raised in the name of hard-bitten officers turned *condottieri* who were ready for anything, except a quiet life. We ourselves were quite unarmed and the nearest Allied troops were hundreds of miles away. It was a long way to Cologne, almost as long as to Tipperary, for we had no 'lines of communication' and, indeed, no base. The Treaty, and with it our powers of 'control,' was not to come into operation until it was ratified, and

[1] See below, Chapter XI, 'Germany in Defeat.'
[2] After a year's effort, i.e. in August 1920, we succeeded with great difficulty in persuading the German Government to enact 'An Act for the disarmament of the civil population.' Its enforcement, which was only partial, resulted in the surrender of merely 1,300,000 rifles and 9,000 machine-guns. During the war Germany manufactured 10,000,000 rifles.

that date was four months ahead. The main force of the Commission would therefore not arrive until the following January. The reader may well ask what, under such circumstances, we were doing in Berlin. Our premature arrival was, in fact, due to an invitation from the German Government. In the preceding month of August they had addressed a Note to the Peace Conference inviting the heads of the Commission to Berlin to 'negotiate' the execution of the Disarmament articles of the Treaty. Foch, who then, as always, seemed to foresee everything, pounced upon the word 'negotiate' and would have none of it. Events were to justify his caution. Acting on his advice, the Allied Powers in accepting this enticing invitation informed the German Government that we were prepared 'to discuss' but not to negotiate.

Immediately on our arrival, General Nollet presented himself on 15 September to the Chancellor of the Reich, Dr. Müller, and to Herr Noske, the Minister of Defense. The two Ministers assured him that the German Government had every intention of 'loyally' executing the Treaty. Five days after this assurance a curious encounter took place. There were many things to be arranged with the German authorities, especially in the 'Q' department. The main body of the Commission was to consist of nearly four hundred officers, to say nothing of 'other ranks,' with headquarters in Berlin and district 'Committees' dispersed all over Germany at the H.Q. of the seven Army Commands or *Wehr-kreise*. Buildings had to be requisitioned for office accommodation and garages for our Army cars. Billets had to be found for officers and men. The German Government suggested a 'conference' with our A.Q.M.G. and his staff to discuss these and other such things. The suggestion was accepted and the hour fixed by the German authorities for 11.25 on the morning of 20 September. The rendezvous was also fixed by the German Government. It was one of the annexes of the Foreign Office in the Behrenstrasse. They further suggested to us that a limitation of the representatives to four on each side would be a sociable arrangement. Their choice of the hour and the place and the numbers seemed to be mere questions of detail and we accepted it as a matter of course. But nothing is too small for chicanery, as we were to find to our cost on many occasions in the years to come, when it comes to doing business with German diplomatists. And so now. When the four representatives of the Control Commission arrived at eleven o'clock at the Foreign Office, they were shown into a waiting-room. They asked a messenger if this was the Conference-room and learnt, to their surprise, that it was not. After being kept to cool their heels like suppliants in the ante-chamber, they were informed that 'the other gentlemen' were ready to 'receive' them in the Conference-room. Our A.Q.M.G., a shrewd Scot with an inquisitorial nose, began to smell a rat. After all, by the terms of the Treaty, we were 'to control' and not to be controlled. He therefore informed the messenger that the Allied officers would enter the Conference-room after 'the other gentlemen' had vacated it, and not before. Then he would do the receiving. The messenger disappeared and, after a long absence, returned to inform the Allied officers that the Conference-room was vacant.

It looked as if the Commission had won the first round. But, as the Allied officers entered the room by one door, the German delegation filed into it by a door opposite and took up a strategic position on the opposite side of the long table which ran down the center of the room. Our own delegation had been limited, in accordance with the suggestion of the German authorities, to 'four a side.' They now found themselves confronted with twelve Germans. Before they had time to protest against this breach of faith, Herr Geheimrat von Keller, the head of the German delegation, was on his feet, opening the proceedings as though he had been nominated to the chair. Our A.Q.M.G., recovering from his surprise, stopped Privy Councillor von Keller with the observation that it was for the Allied delegation to state their requirements. He was in turn interrupted by von Keller. 'This building in which we meet,' observed the Privy Councillor suavely, 'is part of the German Foreign Office and I am instructed to point out to you that no representatives of Foreign Powers can "receive" in the German Foreign Office; *it is for us to receive you.*' The cat was now out of the bag. The Allied delegation suddenly realized that, in accepting without demur the German choice of the rendezvous, they had walked into a carefully baited booby-trap. Our A.Q.M.G. immediately declared the proceedings closed. The members of the German delegation countered this move by declining to withdraw. They proceeded to open their cigar-cases simultaneously, as if at a word of command, and, turning their backs on the Allied officers, filled the room with an asphyxiating cloud of tobacco. Owing to the blockade, German cigars at this time were home-made and peculiarly rank. There was nothing left for the Allied officers to do but to withdraw with every appearance of dismissal. Herr von Keller and his colleagues remained in possession of the smoke-stricken field.

Flushed with this success, our 'opposite number,' in short the Opposition, proceeded to make things as difficult as possible for us. Their first thrust was at the Naval Delegation. Whether this was because it was predominantly British or because its numbers were even smaller than our own I do not know. But here they met their match. We officers of the Military Delegation were comfortably billeted at the Hotel Esplanade and had no reason to complain of our accommodation. But the naval officers were badly housed and could not even get a bath. Captain Tottenham, the Senior Naval Officer, protested five times in five successive days against what, in the light of subsequent events, was clearly intended to be his humiliation. At last, on getting no reply, he sent a Note to the Wilhelmstrasse informing the German authorities that he and the whole of the Naval Delegation would leave Berlin the following day unless they were provided with decent accommodation by the hour of 10 a.m. Within two hours of the dispatch of this ultimatum the naval officers were furnished with quarters in one of the best hotels in Berlin—the Hotel Bristol. It is true that Tottenham, on returning from a walk in the Tiergarten, found the drawer of the writing-desk in his new quarters, which he had locked before going out, prised open by an alien hand. But as Tottenham remarked to me with a smile in telling the story, the 'silent service' does not keep confidential papers in the writing-desks of hotel sitting-rooms.

The atmosphere was, in fact, very 'unhealthy.' The German military authorities were rapidly recovering their prestige after the debacle of the Revolution. The Republican Minister of Defense, Herr Noske, a large man with a furtive eye whom I was to meet later on, was little more than a tool in their hands. He discovered the fact only too late.[3] Discipline was rapidly being restored in the conscript army, and at least half a million men had not yet been demobilized. Those who had been passed into the Reserve were, as we were to discover later, being 'discharged' from the depots with passes re-

[3] See Chapter IV, 'The Revolt of the Reichswehr.'

minding them of their legal duty to rejoin the colors if and when called upon. The munition factories—and there were seven thousand of them—still had their vast plant intact, and in some of them, such as Krupp's, guns were still being turned out. Meanwhile, the Nationalist Press was being mobilized against us, and we got our first glimpse of that curious synchronization of official obstruction and newspaper vituperation against the Commission with which we were to be so familiar in the years to come. The one and the other were always perfectly timed. It was an equally curious fact, and indeed significant of much, that these attacks were almost invariably confined to the newspapers opposed to the Republic and its Ministers. And yet their departmental inspiration was unmistakable. The explanation is to be found in the fact that while the Republicans were in office, the Nationalists were in power. The old bureaucracy, headed by Baron von Maltzahn, retained possession of the Foreign Office like a garrison while the Ministry of Defense was held by the officer caste of the old Army like a fortress. In their joint opposition to Disarmament they found a natural ally in the Nationalist Press and it was only too clear that they were in close liaison with it. The Republican parties, on the other hand, which at this time held a majority of the seats in the Reichstag, were not so openly opposed to Disarmament. The Socialist workmen, who had polled fourteen million votes at the Reichstag election a few months earlier, were, however, as General Nollet wrote in 1931 in his little book of reminiscences, 'owing to their persistent deference towards the military, inflexibly opposed [*irréductiblement hostile*] to the very idea of reduction of armaments.'

On the morning of 25 September, just five days after the rupture of the Conference with Herr von Keller, I opened the pages of a German newspaper [4] and encountered the following in leaded type:

KILL THE LOT!

THE LAST GREAT JUDGMENT WILL HOLD YOU BLAMELESS

Every morning I walk through the 'Siegesallee' to gaze upon the monuments of our heroes, the monuments which commemorate the race which for 500 years slaved to make the lands of Brandenburg what they are to-

[4] The *Deutsche Zeitung*, 25 September 1919.

day; the race which, daring everything, struggled for the unity of their people and for the elevation of their race to that position of Power that was theirs before the war. Every morning, in the ALLEE, I see the triumphant soldiers of France and Britain, strolling carelessly, cigarette in mouth, and staring ironically at the statues of the Hohenzollerns. I went my way through the Brandenburg Gate and along the Budapesterstrasse to the Potsdamerplatz. On the way I met six English soldiers. The Germans stared at them sullenly, *they only laughed in return*. Workmen of Germany! It is time you realized the shame the Armistice and the quazi-Peace has brought upon you and your country. Do you not still carry in your hearts that pride of country, which you cast into the mud on the Ninth of November 1918? It will be difficult to abstain from rising under the influence of National Pride— The day will come when all your comrades will think 'We ought to thrash these fellows. KILL THEM! THE LAST GREAT JUDGMENT WILL HOLD YOU BLAMELESS.'

As I was reading these lethal lines in bed at the Esplanade, Bailey, my batman, brought in my morning tea. I seized the occasion to hold an informal Court of Inquiry.

'Been taking any exercise round the corner in the Budapesterstrasse lately, Bailey?' I inquired negligently. 'Or in the Siegesallee?'

Bailey's face immediately assumed a wooden expression. I knew that look. Bailey, who had been at Mons with the Cheshires, was a typical 'Old Contemptible.' Whenever his commanding officer asked him a question, his face immediately came 'on guard' as though anything he said might be taken down in a 'Summary of Evidence' and used against him.

'Yes, sir,' he replied, with a non-committal air.

'Any one else with you?"

'Yes, sir.'

'Who?'

'There was me, sir, and Sergeant Graham and Sergeant Pears, and there was Hodgkin and Smith and Scaplehorn.'

That made six. An incriminating number. 'Were you laughing?' I asked.

Bailey looked at me in astonishment. 'Sometimes, sir. But we weren't meaning no harm.'

'Of course, you weren't,' I said. Bailey was visibly relieved. 'Fetch me that book lying over there. You can go.'

I opened the book, a bedside companion of mine, at a certain page, for the homicidal outburst in the *Deutsche Zeitung* had struck a chord in my memory. And this is what I read:

A year before Waterloo I saw the Duke of Wellington's Highlanders in Brussels. They were indeed a fine set of fellows. The whole lot of them stout, robust, and smart as though fresh from the hand of God. They all carried their heads high, *looked so happy,* and stepped out with their muscular, bare legs so light of foot as though for them there was no such thing as Original Sin. It is a singular thing, whether it originates in their race or in their soil, or in their liberal constitution, or in their sound education, but the fact remains that the English, speaking generally, seem in some way to excel other peoples. We see it here in Weimar, although few of them come here, and not always the best of them, but what genuine, charming people they are! Young as they are, most of them, they don't feel in this German and foreign place of ours the slightest constraint or embarrassment. The explanation of it all is not birth, neither is it wealth. It is simply that they have the courage to be themselves, as God made them, nothing half-and-half or crooked in them. They are as they are— perfect men. Perfect fools too, I grant you. . . Their good fortune to know what personal liberty means, their consciousness of what the name of England stands for among other nations is such that their very children seem to have it. In their schools, and even their nurseries, they are treated with greater respect and much more freedom than any of us Germans ever enjoy among ourselves. I have only to look out of my window here in order to see how it is with us. When the snow lay on the ground the other day and my neighbor's children took their little sleds out into the street to give them a trial, a policeman immediately came on the scene and the poor little things fled like the wind.

Thus Goethe.[5]

This comparison set me thinking. Laughter in public, unless it be the licensed laughter of a theatre or music-hall or the mass-laughter of a political meeting, is discouraged in Germany. If a man smiles in the streets he is secretive; if he laughs, he is insulting; if he whistles, he is seditious. But why insulting? Why was the *Deutsche Zeitung* so enraged at the sight of six inoffensive British soldiers, all of them unarmed, laughing in public? Whether the answer be that the German suffers from a suspicious temper or the morbid sensitiveness of the egotist I do not know. It may be that the clue to it all is to be found in that short-tempered character in one of Congreve's plays who fell foul of a merry group of people with the words, 'I am sure

5 *Goethes Gespräche mit Eckermann* (Insel-Ausgabe), s.s. 391, 392.

they were talking of me, for they laughed consumedly.' Some of the British soldiers taken prisoner early in the war had laughed at first. They did not laugh long. The butt-end of a German rifle put an end to all that. But I suspect that the explanation lies deeper. The Englishman laughs, as a rule, because he is happy, the German because some one else is unhappy. The laughter of another, especially if he be a stranger, therefore moves him to a genuine feeling of uneasiness, provoking him to a disturbing introspection not unmixed with a sense of circumstantial inferiority. He laughs himself for the same reason as the primitive savage and can comprehend no other. My friend Herbert Ward, mighty hunter and great explorer, once told me that when he lay sick on the Congo with gastric fever, his face contorted with pain, his native bearers sat round him in a circle and howled with laughter. 'They meant no harm,' he charitably explained, 'they merely felt they were one up on me.' The Germans are a race of philosophers and there is one school of philosophy, or rather psychology, which has analyzed laughter and found it to be the expression of a sense of superiority. I sometimes think the theory must be of German origin. The shame or discomfiture of another always seems to excite the wildest laughter in Germany. Germans delight in derision. Perhaps this is the explanation of those political carnivals, so often reported in *The Times* of 1933 by its correspondents in Germany, in which Reichstag deputies, Socialist ex-Ministers of reputation, and Jews of high professional status were marched on foot, or driven in tumbrils, through the streets with degrading placards hung round their necks, on the *via dolorosa* that led to a 'concentration camp' amid the uproarious laughter of the crowd.[6] German humor is still medieval. Its spiritual home is the pillory.

But the *Deutsche Zeitung* article was not altogether a laughing matter. The lust to kill was there. Human life in Germany is very cheap, and there were any number of political murder societies

[6] This sort of derision reached a lamentable climax when a young German girl, who afterwards lost her reason, was led through the streets of Nuremberg in 1933 by Storm Troopers with her hair shorn and a placard round her neck bearing the superinscription, 'I loved a Jew.' No one lifted a finger to rescue her. The incident, which was one of many such, was fully reported, at the time, by English eyewitnesses in the columns of *The Times* and *Telegraph,* and is to be found in *My Years in Germany,* by Miss Dodd, the daughter of the American Ambassador, who also saw it with her own eyes.

abroad in the land. Hardly a day passed without some one being done to death by his political adversaries. The foul murder of Rathenau only attracted attention because of the eminence of the victim. The roll-call is to be found in a German book, *Four Years of Political Murder*.[7] How was it that the members of the Control Commission escaped? Some years after the Commission had been withdrawn, General Weygand remarked cheerfully to me, 'We never expected any of you to come back alive.' I think the explanation was a wholesome fear of Foch, a fear not unmixed with respect. A few weeks before our arrival, a French N.C.O., attached to the French Military Mission, had been murdered in Berlin. It was during the Peace Conference and Foch insisted that the 'Council of Four' should demand payment of a fine of one million gold marks by the City of Berlin. He got his way. There was, of course, the usual fatuous talk about 'the rapacity' of the French. But Foch was, as always, looking ahead. He knew that if an exemplary fine was not inflicted, the lives of the officers of the Control Commission, which was to follow hard on the heels of the Military Mission, would not be worth an hour's purchase. Even as it was, some of us had narrow escapes. Our men had been ordered to leave their rifles behind when they left Cologne. They neither liked nor understood the order, but they had to obey. Their rifles would have been of little use. We put more faith, on one critical occasion, in the hose-pipe at our headquarters at the Bellevue. We officers had our revolvers but we never carried them. I kept mine locked up in the drawer of my writing-desk at the Hotel Adlon, and always left it behind me when I went on an inspection. It was not pleasant to find oneself, as I did at Lyck in the uttermost parts of East Prussia, alone save for my staff officer, Major Bennett, and unarmed in the middle of an internment camp of Bolshevik soldiers incited by a Russo-German officer to do us in. But I feel pretty certain that Bennett and I owed our lives on that occasion to the fact that we so obviously carried no arms.

In the face of the Press campaign General Nollet preserved a complete equanimity. He was seldom indignant and never surprised. Nor did he allow himself to be disturbed by the guerrilla tactics of permanent officials like Herr von Keller. For the time being, he preferred,

[7] *Vier Jahre Politischer Mord* (Berlin, 1922), by E. J. Gumbel.

in dealing with the German Government, to assume that its Ministers meant to keep their word and to execute 'loyally' the Articles of the Treaty. With the unerring sense of political realities which always distinguished him, he knew that the 'balance of power' in the matter of disarmament was in the hands of the German generals rather than the Republican Ministers who indeed were, as we shall see, mortally afraid of them. He therefore determined to make a direct appeal to them for their amicable collaboration. He did not want, if he could possibly avoid it, to invoke the *force majeure* of an ultimatum from the Allied Governments and the Versailles Military Committee. On 5 November he attended at the Reichswehrministerium to meet the four German generals, von Cramon, Strempel, von Kessel, and Marschall von Bieberstein, who had been appointed by the German Government as heads of the Army Peace Commission (*Heeresfriedenskommission*) to 'co-operate' with us in the work of disarmament. It was not a pleasant task for them any more than it was for us, and Nollet, with characteristic chivalry, was quick to recognize the fact. Nothing could have been more tactful nor indeed more considerate than the graceful words with which he addressed them:

Gentlemen, we are entering together on a very delicate task. It is to your interest, as much as it is to ours, to make its duration as short as possible. We will do our best to adopt such a method of work as will conduce to the maximum of results in the minimum of time. Soldiers! we understand what you must be feeling today. None the less a nation honors itself in honoring its engagements, and a soldier grows in stature by loyally assisting his country to keep its word.

Noblesse oblige! Unhappily, these chivalrous words fell on deaf ears.

Nine days after this allocution the Council of the Commission, consisting of the Allied General Officers, met the four German generals of the 'Army Peace Commission' to discuss certain general principles put forward by the latter as to the scope and method of the control to be exercised by us. The discussion between them and us was not unfriendly, and, had we agreed with the utmost docility to their contentions, the subsequent unpleasantness [8] which put an end to all such oral discussions altogether might never have occurred. But such

[8] See the following chapter, 'Battle Joined.'

agreement on our part would have meant that we should never have been able to exercise any control at all. The German generals attempted to beguile us into accepting three interpretations of the Treaty which were totally inconsistent with the whole tenor of it, alike in the letter and the spirit. Their first contention was that the Treaty did not authorize the exercise of *local* control by the medium of the District Committees of Allied Officers which we proposed to establish at the headquarters of the seven territorial Commands representing the seven Infantry Divisions of the Treaty Army. For this contention we were not altogether unprepared. As early as 30 September, the Commission had received a letter from the German Foreign Office expressing 'grave perturbation' at the 'large number' of Allied officers who were due to arrive in the following January when the Commission got to work. With an air of strange ingenuousness the letter inquired what there could be for so many officers to do. The number of officers contemplated was, in fact, some four hundred or rather less. To secure the demobilization of five hundred thousand men still with the colors, to inspect the strength-returns of every battalion, troop, and battery of the new Army, to effect the disestablishment of the supply depots, ordnance depots, recruiting depots scattered all over Germany, their number running into thousands, which had ministered to the needs of an army of six million men, a Commission mustering only four hundred officers could hardly be regarded as excessive. To secure, in addition, the 'suppression,' as the Treaty put it, of seven thousand armament factories, the number of Control officers was even less excessive. In one alone of these factories, namely Krupp's, our ordnance officers discovered, when we got to work four months later, twenty thousand machines, every one of them an instrument of war, and, as such, calling for their attention. Thousands of guns, heavy, medium, and light, in gun-parks and fortresses all over Germany awaited our destruction if Germany was to be disarmed at all. Too often, indeed, in the years to come we felt ourselves as small and almost as indistinguishable in the execution of our tremendous task, as the needle in the haystack.

In its remonstrance on the score of our numbers the German 'Note' decidedly overdid it. It is, as we often found, a curious feature of the German way of stating a case that its exponents always seem to think that the greater the number of arguments advanced, the stronger the case. Sometimes an argument, weighty in itself, was reinforced by another argument so trivial as to suggest that the main argument was one in which its authors did not place any faith at all. On other occasions the arguments were multiplied so freely that they ended by being mutually contradictory, reminding one of nothing so much as the soldier who, when accused of stealing a watch, pleaded at one and the same time that he had never had it in his possession and, in the alternative, that he thought it was his own. The arguments of the German 'Note' on this occasion were equally multiple in character and not less inconsequent, if not quite so contradictory. A 'Commission' was, we were reminded, a word which, in the German language at any rate, meant a small number of persons, and the use of the word in the Treaty could therefore mean nothing else. Not feeling quite certain, apparently, that this grammarian-like line of approach would be quite conclusive in view of the sweeping definition of our functions in the Treaty, the Note proceeded to invoke the 'Wohnungsfrage' [9] and to suggest that to lodge four hundred officers would 'very gravely' complicate the difficulties of the German Government in finding housing accommodations for the working-classes. As we were to be billeted in luxurious hotels, all of them swarming with fat 'profiteers,' this argument was also, it appeared, not regarded by its exponents as conclusive, and yet a third was advanced. The German Government, proceeded the Note, could not be responsible for 'the grave incidents' which the presence of so many officers might excite among the civil population. With this argument was coupled a fourth, more in the nature of a demand. The Commission were requested to give an undertaking that, for our own 'self-protection,' the Allied officers should never appear in uniform. It was difficult to reconcile this solicitude for our safety with the fact that the Government took no proceedings whatsoever against the newspapers which were inciting the civil population to 'kill the lot' of us. As the substance of the Note, like nearly every official communication addressed to us, duly appeared in the German Nationalist Press, it is not uncharitable to suppose that the argument may have been designed to encourage the very 'incidents' which it professed to be so eager to avoid.

[9] 'The Housing Question.'

Be that as it may, the issue thus raised was one of vital importance. No one who knew anything of Germany could doubt that any officer of the Commission who attempted to conduct in mufti an inspection of a regimental unit in barracks would find himself exposed to the most stubborn obstruction, and indeed, to contempt if not worse. The authority conferred by uniform in Germany is a thing which has to be seen to be believed. The classical incident which convulsed the whole of Europe with laughter in the days before the last war, of the 'crook' who, donning the uniform of a captain of the German Army and calling himself Captain von Koepenick, so impressed the Bürgermeister of a German town with his air of authority that he delivered up to him the whole of the municipal cash, is characteristic. The difference between Germany and England in this respect is profound and significant. Before the Revolution of 1918 no German officer, even in peace-time, when off duty could appear in mufti without the consent of his superior; and that consent was rarely given. With us in England it is, of course, the other way about. The German rule was changed with the coming of the Republic at the instance of the astute von Seeckt, who realized that the more 'invisible' the Army the more plausible would be his contention that Germany was 'disarmed.' Accordingly, the German officers during 'the close season' from 1919 to 1935 conformed to the English rule and never appeared in uniform except when on duty.[10] But it was when they were on duty that we had to deal with them and, if we had been compelled to inspect their regimental units in mufti, even the N.C.O.s would have turned their backs on us. As for our safety, about which the German Government expressed much more concern than we ever did, it is quite certain that assaults on Control officers would have been far more common than they were if we had not performed our duties in uniform. It would always have been open to the assailants to pretend that they did not know who the objects of their assault and battery were. The demand of the Ger-

[10] Von Seeckt's astute policy was justified by results. An eminent American 'pacifist,' Dr. Nicholas Murray Butler, who visited Berlin during the years we were attempting to secure the disarmament of Germany, was so impressed by the absence of uniforms in public places that on his return to America he expressed his solemn conviction that the German Army had 'disappeared.' With the restoration of conscription in 1935, the old rule as to the wearing of uniform when off duty was, as a matter of course, itself restored.

man Government was at once refused by General Nollet, a refusal
confirmed by the Allied Governments, and it was significant that the
German Government, who as a rule would never take 'No' for an
answer, made no attempt whatsoever to repeat it. At the subsequent
conference with the German generals the matter was not even mentioned. Perhaps their 'Excellencies,' [11] meeting us, as they did, in
uniform, felt it was a demand which it would have been a little difficult for them openly to support with any degree of assurance.

The German generals stuck resolutely, however, to the contention, originally put forward some weeks earlier by the German
Foreign Office, that the Commission had no power to exercise local
control, in other words control outside Berlin, by the establishment
of District Committees. Their arguments were not very convincing.
The text of the Treaty had provided by one and the same Article
(Article 205) that the Commission might establish its organization
'at the seat' of the German Government, and that it should be entitled 'as often as it thinks desirable' to 'proceed' (se rendre in the
French text) to 'any point whatever in German territory' or 'to
send' (envoyer) Sub-Commissions to such points. With the verbal
ingenuity of a medieval schoolman, the German representatives fas-
tened on these words and contended that to 'send' a person to a
place was an entirely different thing from 'stationing' him there.
Nollet countered the argument by pointing out that a power to send
an officer to a point 'as often as' his superior, the Council of the
Commission, 'thought desirable' was indistinguishable from the
power to keep him there permanently unless the officer was to be
kept in a state of perpetual motion. In that case his labors would
have been even as the labors of Sisyphus and not less futile. Con-
trôler-c'est voir, 'to supervise is to see for oneself'—Nollet pointed
out with exemplary patience, unmoved by the plea of one of the
German representatives that all the information we wanted could
be supplied 'in documentary form' by the German Government.
With characteristic tenacity, the German military representatives
stuck to their point, one of them asking if we doubted 'the sincerity' of the Ministry of Defense and the veracity of the reports of the
progress of disarmament with which it proposed to supply us.

[11] A General Officer in Germany is accorded this ceremonial form of address.

The attitude of the German Government was now clear. It was for Germany to disarm herself and for us to sit in Berlin and accept her written assurances that the thing was done. This was not our idea of 'control' and it certainly was not the intention of the Allied Governments. Had we accepted it, we might as well have gone home at once. In the years that followed, almost every document put up to us by the Reichswehrministerium was found, after we had checked its statements by 'control' inspections, to be false. It was due entirely to the fact that Allied officers were permanently stationed in the District Commands and the great centers of the armament industry that we discovered, as we did in due course, that vast stocks of arms which never appeared in the official returns made to us by the German Government were being concealed all over Germany. Months after the Ministry of Defense had declared that all guns in excess of the establishment authorized by the Treaty had been surrendered, and had demanded from us a 'clean bill of health' for the armament factories, Colonel Beasley, one of the District Officers for Saxony, discovered hundreds of newly manufactured howitzers walled up in a single factory at Heidenau. There were scores of such discoveries of enormous *caches* of arms by Allied officers in the exercise of that 'local' control which the German military representatives at the conference in November 1919 sought to convince us was not only unjustified but a grave reflection on the good faith of the Ministry of Defense. It was the same with the vast 'gun park' of heavy artillery, exceeding the whole establishment of the German Army when it took the field in 1914, which, by our insistence on local control, we discovered a few months later secreted in the forts of Königsberg.

Having failed to carry their contention against local control, the German military representatives at the conference fell back on another, also aimed at contracting the sphere of control. With great ingenuity they sought to establish a distinction between the 'time clauses' of the Disarmament section of the Treaty and those to which no time-limit was attached. Certain clauses required certain prescriptions to be executed within a fixed period of time. Thus the German Army had to be demobilized 'not later than 31 March 1920' and the New Army to be constituted and organized in the prescribed formation by that date. Conscription was to be abolished

and the new Army, whose strength was to be limited to 100,000
effectives, was to be recruited by voluntary enlistment, the men being engaged on a long-term engagement for service with the colors
for twelve years, the formation of a reserve being prohibited. These
prescriptions as to the recruiting and enlistment of the new Army
were, of course, accompanied by no limit of time for their execution—the very fact that they were intended to be permanent negatived any such conception. It occurred to an astute mind in the
German Ministry of Defense to put forward the contention that as
the demobilization of the old Army had to be effected in a certain
period of time while the establishment of the new Army was for all
time, the Commission, although it could control the former, could
not control the latter at all. The acceptance of this distinction would
have meant that, the moment the old Army was demobilized and a
new Army nominally created, we should have been disabled from
making any attempt to discover whether the prescriptions of the
Treaty as to the recruiting and enlistment of the latter were com-
plied with or not. Not a single attestation-form or strength-return
would have been open to our inspection. The Ministry of Defense
would have been free to play the same trick on the Allied Powers as
Scharnhorst played on Napoleon in the execution of the disarmament
clauses of the Treaty of Tilsit. By engaging men on a short-term
enlistment of six months, instead of the long-term enlistment of
twelve years, and training them intensively to replace them by
others, they would have been able to build up a huge masked reserve.
That this was the intention of the German Military representatives,
in contesting our right to control the execution of those Articles of
the Treaty for which no time-limit was prescribed, subsequent de-
velopments gave ample proof. We did not know, at this stage, that
the German argument masked any such intention. We had still much
to learn. Needless to say, the German representatives did not so much
as hint at it. We rejected the argument on its merits, and the Allied
Governments upheld our rejection. To have admitted it would have
been to admit of a wedge being driven into the Disarmament section
of the Treaty, splitting it from top to bottom and leaving one half
of it unenforced and unenforceable.

Thus ended the conference with the German generals. It was the
last of its kind. An attempt to renew such conferences some two

months later came to a sudden and dramatic end.[12] The Council of the Commission now turned its attention to the drafting of 'interrogatories' (*Questionnaires*) for submission to the German Government, inviting the latter to disclose to us their military resources in men and material with a view to the demobilization of the one and the destruction of the other in accordance with the terms of the Treaty. In the matter of 'material' the stipulation of the Treaty was engagingly simple. A single sentence of a single Article was devoted to the subject in the following words:

Within two months from the coming into force of the present Treaty German arms, munitions, and war material, including anti-aircraft material, existing in Germany in excess of the quantities allowed, must be surrendered to the Governments of the Principal Allied and Associated Powers to be destroyed or rendered useless.[13]

Two months! It took us seven years and even then the 'surrender' was anything but complete. For this frustration the stubborn obstruction of the German Ministry of Defense was largely responsible. But not entirely. The moment we began to examine the problem of 'war material' we realized that it was almost insoluble. The thing defies definition. Is a field-kitchen war material? Or a field ambulance? Or a motor-lorry? All three are capable of civilian use. When are you to 'call a spade a spade,' and when should you call it an entrenching tool? How are you to distinguish between war explosives and 'commercial' explosives? The dynamite which serves to blast a quarry is as useful to the sapper in war as to the quarryman in peace. Where are you to draw the line, in seizing and destroying 'topographical material,' between the maps which serve for the construction of a railway in peace and those which serve a staff officer in a campaign or a gunner firing off the map? Is an ingot of gun-steel forged but not yet bored, turned, and rifled on the gun-lathe invested with a belligerent character or not? How were we to regard the vast stocks of nitric acid and the plant which manufactured it in the German chemical factories? Were we to stigmatize them as 'war material' and destroy them and all the plant which made them? If we had, we should have wiped out the German chemical

[12] See the following chapter, 'Battle Joined.'
[13] Article 169.

industry. I now think it unfortunate for a stricken world that we did not—Germany would then have been disarmed effectively enough. Nitrogen compounds are at once the most lethal and the most vital of chemical agents, a source of life and an instrument of death. Nitrates are equally indispensable as fertilizers and as explosives. Or chlorine?—the innocent and unsuspected agent of the dyeing and bleaching industries before the war until it revealed, in March 1915, on the fields of Ypres the dark secret of its potency for the most insidious of all forms of warfare.

All these things were still under the control of the Ministry of Defense, although many of them, such as motor transport, had, to be sure, been 'demobilized' to find, like the men themselves, employment in civil life. Like the men, they might at any moment be 'recalled to the colors' by the simple process of requisitioning. As we proceeded to draft our *Questionnaires* for the Ministry of Defense, the magnitude and complexity of the problem became more and more apparent. Our categories of war material grew and grew until they filled scores of pages of print. The species and sub-species extended to hundreds of articles. The list of 'optical' war material, from periscopes to range-finders, alone ran to fifty-two items. 'Signaling material' was almost equally multitudinous. In both cases many of the incriminated articles, such as field-glasses, telephones, and wireless apparatus, were unquestionably ambiguous in character, equally susceptible of use for war and for peace. We had, at the outset and before getting to work, to choose between the wholesale sabotage, which the words of the Treaty meant if they meant anything at all, of the vast stocks of such ambiguous material, representing millions of pounds in value, and, alternatively their dispersion by way of expropriation among private purchasers with every prospect of their being 'requisitioned' again from the purchasers by the Ministry of Defense the moment the Commission had been withdrawn. We chose the latter course. Our indulgence in thus tempering the execution of the Treaty may have been, and indeed was, misplaced, but we were not free agents. At that time the Allied Governments really believed that Germany was going to fulfill her obligations in the matter of 'reparations' and the German Government took full advantage of their credulity by pressing upon them the argument that the wholesale destruction of so many things capable of commercial use would seriously prejudice Germany's 'capacity to pay.' We were instructed accordingly. At this time more than one member of our own Government was also exhorting the British public to help to 'set Germany on her feet.' The result of our decision was that by far the greater part of Germany's 'war material' remained in German hands and the Article of the Treaty prescribing its total destruction was never enforced.

But, irrespective of such considerations as the effect of its enforcement on the payment of reparations, Article 169 of the Treaty was, in fact, largely unenforceable. Between war material and 'peace material' it is as impossible to draw a hard and fast line as it is to delimit 'contraband' and conditional contraband, or to distinguish an armament factory and its 'shadow' factory. Years later, after the Commission of Control had been withdrawn, the Disarmament Conference at Geneva never so much as faced the problem. It ignored it. In ignoring it, it abdicated. In other words disarmament is, and must for ever remain, largely an illusion. It can never be more than relative. You may beat your swords into plowshares and your spears into pruning-hooks but there is nothing to prevent the plowshare being re-forged into a sword and the pruning-hook into a spear. Wherever a country has reached a high degree of engineering, mechanical, and chemical development, there, however 'disarmed' she may appear to be, the race will be to the industrially swift and the battle to the industrially strong. If that country cherishes a tradition that war is its normal 'instrument of policy,' it has only to organize, in silhouette as it were, its industries in peace with a view to their conversion to war and it is already in an advanced stage of 'economic mobilization.' Such a country Germany was before the last war. With the advent of the 'totalitarian State' form of Government the process was complete. It would, of course, have been possible to spare the world the horrors of the present catastrophe if Germany had been deprived of her Army altogether, for then we could have made an end of the tradition which von Seeckt so ingeniously kept alive. Personally, I think that was what ought to have been done. But we should have had, at the same time, to 'neutralize' the Rhineland and garrison the Rhine bridgeheads for at least a generation, as Foch, quite rightly, insisted.

Exactly the same dilemma confronted us when we came to con-

sider another Article of the Treaty. By Article 168 'all establishments for the manufacture of arms, munitions or any war material'
other than those to be authorized for the limited requirements of the
new Army were to be 'closed down' (*supprimés*). Had we enforced
that Article of the Treaty in all its rigor, we should have reduced
industrial Germany to the condition of a 'devastated district.' Perhaps it was a pity we did not. Every factory in the engineering,
electrical, and chemical industries, and many others in Germany
had been converted during the war into such an 'establishment.'
Their number ran into thousands [14] and the number of machines
installed in them into tens of thousands. Many of these factories and
their machines had already been re-converted to their original 'peace'
production. Here again, as in the case of war material, the German
Government pressed on us, for all it was worth, the argument that
we should not impair Germany's 'capacity to pay.' After long and
anxious consideration, and as the result of instructions from our
masters, the Allied Governments, the Commission decided to spare
every factory and workshop which could establish, to our satisfaction, the fact of its re-conversion. The result was that Germany was
left with every lathe that ever turned a shell.[15] Even that great 'shop
of war,' Krupp's, was allowed to retain over 50 per cent of its twenty
thousand machines. Those great 'potential arsenals,' the chemical factories, which were now on our arrival ostentatiously turning over to
the production of drugs and dyes in place of the high explosives and
toxic gas they had manufactured during the war to the exclusion
of everything else, were left by us almost intact.

This momentous decision of ours was never made public and the
world was left to imagine that this vital article of the Disarmament
section of the Treaty had been enforced and that Germany had been
'totally disarmed.' Ministers told the House of Commons as much.
She never was. But the price exacted by her for her signature to the
ill-fated 'Pact' of Locarno was not only the withdrawal of the Control Commission and the evacuation of the Rhineland, whereby we

[14] Seven thousand, in fact, as we duly discovered after we had insisted on
'local control.' The German return to our Questionnaire on the subject was, as
always, false. It reported that there were only 'three thousand.'

[15] Not, of course, with shell-presses, which are machines exclusively special-
ized to the manufacture of shells, nor, as a rule, with gun-lathes.

surrendered the keys of the fortress. The moment we had made that surrender, she raised her price. She demanded silence. She got it. It became 'bad form' for any one to question her state of grace. During the years that followed the exchange of ratifications of that instrument not a single 'Allied' statesman, except on one occasion M. Briand, ever so much as hinted at the things which the Control Commission had been compelled to leave undone. The fable of Germany's 'total disarmament' became an article of faith with English pacifists and England was reproached by Mr. Lloyd George and others with not having laid down her own arms and taken Germany to her bosom. Hence the stupefaction with which the world awoke to the fact that, within three years of its accession to power, the Nazi Government and its predecessors had re-created the most powerful army of modern times. It was the forbearance of the French and British Governments, in dispensing with the execution of Articles 169 and 168 of the Treaty of Versailles, that was largely responsible for the swift and amazing renaissance of Germany's military power. The Control Commission was quite alive to the dangers of such a dispensation. But it must always be remembered that not only were we often overruled by a higher authority but also that we acted on the assumption that, after our withdrawal, the covenanted Committee of 'investigation,' responsible to the League of Nations, would, in accordance with the provision to that effect in Article 213 of the Treaty, be instituted to see that our indulgence would not be abused after we have been withdrawn. By her admission to the League, Germany appeared to give hostages for the application of this safeguard, but, as we shall see later, the cunning Stresemann succeeded in defeating its application altogether. It was only when, having completed her rearmament dispositions during 'the close season' created by Locarno and the sessions of the Geneva Disarmament Conference, which she so ostentatiously attended, she suddenly announced her withdrawal from the League that the world realized with a shock of dismay whither it had been drifting.

Thus did we of the Control Commission 'revise' the Treaty of Versailles almost as soon as we arrived in Berlin. A greater concession than this relaxation of Article 168 it would be impossible to conceive. Would Germany, if the position had been reversed, have

extended a similar indulgence to us or to France? The question
carries with it its own answer. As it was, we not only got no thanks
for it but for seven long years were held up to execration in the
Nationalist Press as the willful *saboteurs* of German industry. A
political cartoon in *Simplicissimus* represented General Nollet as a
tank crashing through a forest of factory chimneys falling like ninepins under his onset. Yet not a single factory which was devoted
to the commerce of peace was destroyed. On the withdrawal of
the Commission in January 1927, General von Cramon saluted our
departure with an inflammatory article in a Nationalist newspaper,
representing us as wreckers of German industry in terms which
would have been more appropriate to the studied destruction of
Belgian industry in 1914-18 by the German General Staff and its
camp-followers of the German 'heavy industry.' We, or at least
some of us, apprehended only too well that all this forbearance of
ours might be exploited, in no long time after we had been withdrawn, by the restoration of that very menace to the peace of Europe
which it had been our mission to destroy. Those apprehensions explain—and justify—the preoccupation of the French representatives
at the sessions of the Disarmament Conference at Geneva in 1932-4
with that problem of 'industrial mobilization' which the British representatives treated so lightly. For that lightness, if not levity, our
Foreign Office was certainly not responsible. The Foreign Office
had always been very wide awake, particularly Eyre Crowe and
Tyrrell, with whom I often discussed these matters when home on
leave. And, most notably of all, Lord Curzon. One day in 1921,
gravely disturbed as I was at the apparent indifference of our own
Government, i.e. of Mr. Lloyd George's Administration, one of
whose Ministers had astonished the Control Commission by informing the House of Commons that Germany was 'effectively disarmed' at the very time she was most obstructive to our efforts to
disarm her, I sat down and wrote a Memorandum on 'The Possibilities of a German Military Revival and the Means of Frustrating
It.' I sent it to Lord D'Abernon who received it with his usual
courtesy but without comment. It never got any farther. I was
not altogether surprised. Lord D'Abernon was the apostle of 'appeasement' and did not believe in the possibility, much less the
probability, of a German military revival. When the Parliamentary

Autographed: 'Au Général Morgan, après trois ans de la plus intime et la plus affectueuse collaboration

'29 Oct. 1922
G. Nollet'

GENERAL NOLLET
President of the Inter-Allied Military Commission of Control

GENERAL GOURAUD
(See page 252)
Autograph: 'Au Général Morgan, le Clairvoyant, amical souvenir
d'un compagnon de guerre—Gouraud, 11 Juin 1927'

Under-Secretary for Foreign Affairs, Cecil Harmsworth, an old friend of mine whom I met home on leave a few weeks later, heard from me of the existence of my Memorandum, he asked me to send the Foreign Office a copy of it. This I did. In no long time I received a letter dated 19 December 1921 from Harmsworth which I reproduce here not as a tribute to the writer of these pages but as a tribute to the Foreign Office:

I have shown your Memorandum to Lord Curzon. You may be interested to know the terms of the Minute he has written upon it. He has marked it 'A very significant, able and well-reasoned paper.'

Years afterwards I was told by Lord Salisbury that my Memorandum had been circulated to him as a Cabinet Paper, and that he had been 'much impressed' by it. I doubt if it made the slightest impression on any of his colleagues, except Lord Curzon.

But all these things were in the womb of the future. In those early autumn days of 1919 in Berlin we were still taking soundings in an uncharted sea and knew not what was in store for us. But some premonitions that our task was not going to be facilitated by those with whom we had to deal began to assail me. And one night, just fifteen days after our arrival, I sat down and wrote my first impressions to a friend. The letter was written *currente calamo* at the end of an arduous day and cast forth like bread upon the waters, to be immediately forgotten, in the stress of our strenuous task, by him who had written it. Sixteen years later, on the death of my friend, his nephew and executor, Lord Lansdowne, restored it to me along with many others. The letter now seems to me, in the light of all that happened after it was written, to have been not without an element of clairvoyance, though perhaps any man of average intelligence might have written it. Be that as it may, here it is:

Our difficulties are going to be very great. Already the Germans are forming a huge force of Security Police which will be a kind of masked reserve. The effectives of their police are, like their army, supposed to be limited by the Treaty but, even so, nothing is said as to how these police are to be armed and they have taken advantage of this to arm them with 'civil' aeroplanes, machine-guns, field-guns, and other engines of modern warfare, which is hardly what a Police Force requires. To escape the dissolution of their General Staff, they are transferring the topographical section of their Ministry of War to the Ministry of the Interior, their Intelligence section to the Ministry of Foreign Affairs, their Military Railway section to the Ministry of Transport, and a large number of staff officers are camouflaged as a Ministry of Pensions. We are going to encounter the same policy as baffled Napoleon after 'Jena' when he tried to reduce the Prussian Army to a Militia. Scharnhorst and Stein got the better of him. We have to see that von Cramon and the Reichswehrministerium do not get the better of us. Berlin is calm, but I think it is the sullen calm which precedes a storm. A Revolution in the near future is more than probable. We may then find ourselves isolated from the outer world but I hardly think we shall be the object of any direct attack.[16]

A few months later the revolution came like a thief in the night.

[16] To Lord Fitzmaurice, 25 September 1919.

III. BATTLE JOINED

O N THE 9 OF January 1920 the Commission of Control went over the top as the clocks of Berlin struck the hour of midnight— 'à l'heure de la mise en vigeur du Traité,' as the German Delegation in Paris had been forewarned, in a letter from the President of the Peace Conference, three days earlier. Its strength was three hundred and seventy-three officers [1] representing the five 'Allied' nations— Great Britain, France, Italy, Belgium, and Japan. For the Americans we waited and continued to wait. Their absence gave that pugnacious German publicist, Count Reventlow, an opportunity, in an attack on the Commission in a Berlin newspaper, for a somewhat elementary jibe at our expense. He called us a 'three-legged table,' regarding, apparently, the Italian and Japanese elements as negligible. In point of numbers they were. There were only twenty-one Italian officers and nine Japanese—among the latter my friend and staff officer, Major Maurita. The Japanese held, in fact, merely a watching brief. And very watchful they were. But they took no active part in our proceedings, except at the meetings of the Council.

The headquarters of the Commission and of its three Sub-Commissions—'Effectives,' 'Armaments,' and 'Fortifications'—were, necessarily, established in Berlin. The necessity was immediate and constant contact with the German Government and, more particularly, with the German War Office, now re-christened the Reichswehrministerium or 'Ministry of Defense.' The change of name sounded disarming, but was not. It deeply impressed some of our pacifists at home, as it was intended to do.[2] But a rose by any other name may still have thorns. It was, in fact, the first step in that union of all the armed forces of the country, Army, Navy and Air Force, which finally led to the development of the mightiest instrument of

[1] Subsequently, in July, raised to 383 officers and 737 men.
[2] Thus a Labour M.P., Mr. Day, naïvely demanded in the House of Commons that the War Office should follow suit and change its name to 'Ministry of Defence' as 'a contribution to World Disarmament.'

45

war the world has ever known. But the operations of control—the inspection of territorial commands and regimental units, the 'suppression' of thousands of munition factories, the dismantlement of fortresses, and much besides—were necessarily localized. The great majority of our officers had therefore to be posted all over Germany, in fact, wherever the old German Army had cast its shoe, in States and Provinces lying as far apart as Württemberg and East Prussia, Silesia and Westphalia, from the North Sea to the Bavarian Alps. We had made dispositions accordingly for the establishment of seven District Committees in duplicate [3] in the seven 'Wehrkreise' representing the territorial Commands of the seven Infantry Divisions allowed to Germany by the Treaty. Mainz and Cologne were our 'areas of concentration' for the assembly of the officers who were to proceed to their posts in the North and in the South respectively. Thither General Barthélemy and I repaired from Berlin to meet the officers under our command to instruct them in their duties.

The concentration at Mainz was in the French zone of occupation, that at Cologne in the British. The contrast in our reception at the two places was piquant, and characteristic of the difference in temperament between the two nations. At Mainz the Allied officers, to the number of about a hundred and fifty, were paraded with as much pomp and ceremony as for a trooping of the colors. Forming three sides of a hollow 'square,' each side representing one of the three Sub-Commissions, the Allied officers, who were in uniform and wearing their ribbons and decorations, stood in two ranks like so many companies on parade waiting to be numbered off from the right. Barthélemy and I took our places two paces in front of 'Effectives.' A bugle sounded a fanfare and we all came sharply to attention as a short, compact figure in blue-gray uniform and gold-embroidered kepi entered and took up a position in the middle of the 'square.' It was General Degoutte, the G.O.C. of the French Army of Occupation on the Rhine. He proceeded to address us. Ours, he reminded us, was an epoch-making task—'un devoir qui servira d'époque'—and unprecedented, the importance of which ex-

---

[3] i.e. seven Effectives and eleven Armaments District Committees, the Fortifications Sub-Commission being represented, in view of its topographically restricted character, by only three such committees. Effectives also had a Berlin Committee.

tended far beyond the confines of Germany. On its success or failure the future peace of the world would depend. His own country had sent the *élite* of its officers to discharge that duty and the other nations, he gracefully added, had doubtless done the same. 'Let us drink to the success of this momentous mission,' he concluded as a dozen orderlies arrived on the scene balancing trays of glasses which glowed like amber 'with beaded bubbles winking at the brim.' And a hundred and fifty glasses of champagne were raised to the toast. A day or two later, the second concentration of Allied officers for the northern area followed in the British zone at Cologne. Here there was no parade, no speech, no champagne. Our fellow-officers of the British Army of Occupation took no more notice of us than of our Allied comrades, beyond a casual 'Hello! What are you fellows doing in Germany?'

At Mainz and at Cologne Barthélemy held conferences of the officers of 'Effectives.' He spoke in French. My friend Colonel Lignard, a distinguished French infantry officer who prided himself on his mastery of the English tongue, volunteered to translate—with remarkable results. His translation was a kind of anglicized French, equally unintelligible to the French and to the English. He began with the words, 'I will now *traduce* what General Barthélemy has said,' and he traduced it vigorously. As he continued, the British officers looked at each other with a wild surmise. When he had made an end, he approached me and inquired, not without complacency, 'I hope you understood, *mon Général?*' I happen to know French very well and I could not resist replying—'My dear Lignard, I understood everything except the translation.' The gallant Lignard, not in the least offended, replied, 'Ah! but I make better next time.'

This done, we returned to Berlin. Little did we imagine the sea of troubles ahead of us in which the Commission was to be all but submerged. Our Headquarters Staff were, after much wrangling between our A.Q.M.G. and the German Government, at last accommodated in the Hotel Bellevue. This was a decidedly *déclassé* hotel, requisitioned for us by the German authorities, upon whom the obligation to accommodate us was imposed by the terms of the Treaty. It was an incredibly shabby place and, like the Pilgrim's parlor, full of dust. Ill-swept, ill-garnished, ill-kept, it was in the last stages of decay and incredibly dirty. German public buildings,

whether they be offices or hotels, are invariably as clean as the
kitchen of a German housewife, than which nothing could be more
clean. Wherefore I was sometimes moved to wonder whether the
choice of such a disreputable-looking place for the G.H.Q. of the
Commission might not have been carefully calculated and designed
to hold us up to public derision. 'The Germans,' as Lord Birkenhead
remarked on a memorable occasion, 'think of everything.' The Bellevue had, however, as things turned out, one advantage, if but a
minor one. Its site was the apex of a triangle formed by the approxi-
mation of two streets converging upon the great open space of the
Potsdamer Platz, into whose star-shaped formation three other streets
also converged in a common terminus. The Platz was thus like the
hub of a wheel, the five streets radiating from it like so many spokes.
An endless stream of life from each of these streets flowed into it
and, in troubled times, formed a kind of convulsive eddy, swirling
upon itself. At such times the Bellevue was not at all a bad observation post. From its windows we were destined to look down, within
a few weeks of our arrival, upon incredible things and terrible.

Of our billets we had no cause to complain. Those of us who
were general officers found suites of rooms reserved for us in that
sumptuous hotel whose teeming, feverish life during the hectic years
immediately after the war has been described with extraordinary
vividness by a gifted German novelist—Vicki Baum. The identity
of her 'Grand Hotel' is unmistakable. Some of its pages read like
an inventory of the Hotel Adlon. Nothing has escaped her observant
eye, from the silk upholstery, the mahogany doors, the damask walls,
down to the aquiline inkstands of bronze. Aquiline as became the
Hotel Adlon—the 'Eagle Hotel.' The predatory bird of German
heraldry was the prevailing note of design. Looking at the crowds
of profiteers, not more Jew than Gentile, who invaded the hotel,
I sometimes thought that a vulture would have been a more appropriate emblem for these days of its social decadence. Its lofty rooms,
with their marble overmantels, were richly appointed in the Empire
style and, amid so much opulence, it was sometimes hard to believe
that just outside its great swing doors, revolving continuously on
their axis with the ebb and flow of wealthy clients, there was to be
seen in the Unter den Linden, as everywhere else, men spectral with
hunger stalking the streets, men whose white hands could not dig

and who to beg were more than ashamed—the 'mark-fodder' of the middle classes. Life in this sumptuary oasis was, indeed, almost histrionic in its unreality. The Adlon seemed to offer everything that money could buy and nothing that the world outside it could afford. Dazzling jewels winked from the show-cases of privileged tradesmen and exotic blooms flamed in the window of the florist's stall. With German thoroughness the management saw to it that the wants of the 'Herrschaften' were supplied even before they were expressed. You had but to take out your cigarette-case, as you sat in the lounge, and a watchful little page in livery would dart towards you on winged feet and hold out a lighted match like a votive offering before you had time to extract a cigarette. If you gave a dinner party, the first violin of the orchestra, who was also its *Kapellmeister*, sent you his compliments and invited you to name your favorite air which, for a monetary consideration, he proceeded to play with consummate mastery. His playing of *Solveg's Lied* could bring tears to the fat cheeks of a war profiteer. But the *Geiger* was wholly mercenary and was prepared to play anything a guest chose to name, from *Deutschland über alles* to the *Sozialisten March*. He would, doubtless, have obliged with *Rule, Britannia!* or the *Marseillaise*, had any of us been so foolish as to ask him. This obsequiousness of his was to lead to serious trouble on a certain occasion, whereupon the *maître d'hôtel*, Herr Sizar, who no doubt envied him his unlicensed gains and was violently anti-Semitic, said it all came of employing Jews. Herr Sizar's sentiments towards Jews were both sinister and prophetic. 'No Jew,' he confided to me, 'ever fought in the war.' 'Wie so?' I asked in astonishment. 'They were all dead,' he replied with a grimace. 'Dead?' I retorted, looking round on the many evidences of resurrection. 'Yes, they used to bribe the Bezirkskommandos[4] to write *tot* [dead] against their names on the musterrolls.' It never seemed to occur to him that in calumniating the Jews he was incriminating the Gentiles. Such an imputation of wholesale corruption against the Army recruiting authorities carried with it its own refutation.

Built round the four sides of a stately courtyard in which a tall fountain played, day and night, a lullaby of falling waters, the front

[4] The recruiting depots.

of the vast building looked out upon the Unter den Linden and from the balcony of my rooms on the fourth floor I could see, right over the architrave of the Brandenberger Thor, the tops of the plane-trees in the Tiergarten. The balcony ran the whole length of the fourth floor, and late one night, as I sat in my room reading Heine's *Reisebilder*, I caught sight of three figures crawling stealthily along it outside my window, silhouetted against the moonlight like a moving frieze. They were policemen. There had been a burglary in the hotel. I got quite used to such excursions and alarms in the course of time. No doubt they were seeking Vicki Baum's Baron, for her von Gagern, highly individualized though he is in her dramatic pages, was a type and typical of the times. The Adlon, like every other hotel of fashion in Berlin, was haunted by gentlemen crooks, rendered desperate by their fallen estate. One of these picaresque characters paid my own rooms a visit later on. From this balcony I was destined, a few weeks after our arrival, to look down upon a tragic scene, lethal in its sudden fury.

Much that happened in the Adlon, and immediately outside it, was so interwoven with the existence of the Commission that, as will duly appear, it became almost as closely associated with our experience as the Bellevue itself. More closely indeed in the matter of social contacts, such as would have been quite impossible in the 'extra-territorial' atmosphere of the Bellevue. No French officer on the Commission ever sat at meat with a German—a gulf, deep beyond all sounding, seemed to separate the two peoples. But the British officers became the recipients of much hospitality, not perhaps altogether disinterested, and, of course, they returned it. In this respect, I was fortunate. In my rooms at the Adlon there foregathered in course of time men so representative of the old order as Blücher, von Donnersmarck, von Eckhardstein, Stresemann, Dr. Paul Meissner, Arnold Rechberg, and not a few officers *ausser Dienst* [5] of whom General Hoffmann was by far the most notable. This, however, was only when it became apparent that the Commission had come to stay. During the first three months we were as isolated socially as our French comrades themselves. Our presence seemed to be regarded as a joke, a bad joke, it is true, but none the less an occasion

[5] On the retired list.

for a jest, particularly in the cartoons of *Simplicissimus* and sometimes, in the Nationalist Press, for a threat.

The social life of the hotel reflected, as in a mirror, the social
upheaval of Germany at large, and, as such, was a phase of history.
This cherished creation of the ex-Kaiser, who had honored Herr
Adlon by approving its plans and was credited with having introduced into its design some characteristically flamboyant touches of
his own, had once been the social pride of Berlin and the chosen
haunt of the Prussian aristocracy. Now, immediately after the war,
it was the scene of a kind of drawn battle between the old order and
the new. In the catastrophic conditions of defeat it still maintained a
certain measure of exclusiveness, as though defying that article in
the Constitution of the Republic which declared all titles of honor
'abolished'—*abgeschafft*. In the Adlon guests were still greeted by
obsequious flunkeys in dove-gray liveries with the prefixes of 'Excellency' and 'Serenity' and 'High-well-born' when they were entitled to them and sometimes, if the tips were large enough, when
they were not. Tips—*Trinkgelder*—had, to be sure, also been abolished as unbecoming the dignity of the proletariat. They had been
commuted into a ten per cent *Zuschlag* for *Bedienung* which incontinently appeared, like a valediction, at the foot of the bill of the
departing guest. But they persisted. The new plutocracy, compre-
hensively known as the *Schieber*,[6] riotous in their living as only the
newly rich can be and eager to buy a deference which otherwise
they could not hope to receive, duly saw to that. Their presence in
the Adlon was in its way a portent. They were a new clientele dis-
placing the old like a barbarian invasion, to be endured but not to
be welcomed by those of the old order who still made the Adlon
their rendezvous. Looking round upon them, each with his bottle
of champagne reclining frigidly in its ice-bucket, Count Henckel von
Donnersmarck, as he sat at lunch with me one day in the dining-
room, made a wry mouth—'I would like to drop a bomb on this
place,' he growled, 'it is nothing but a home for these accursed
Schieber.' The smart uniforms which had colored the Adlon before
the war had wholly disappeared from the scene with the dissolution—
more apparent than real, for we had yet to dissolve it—of the German
Officers' Corps, and such officers as still frequented it were always

[6] Profiteers.

in mufti. But the bronze bust of the Kaiser still stood undisturbed upon the marble mantelpiece in the main corridor, as though confidently awaiting the return of the exile from Doorn. And, now and again, one or another of the Hohenzollern princes excited a flutter in the hotel by taking the place of honor at a small and select table of guests under the florid ceiling of the dining-room decorated with the luscious frescoes of a painter in an amorous mood. Men—the *Stahlhelm* [7] to a man—were still dreaming of the return of the monarchy and in the Adlon the visionaries found their spiritual home. But they were more than outnumbered by the real rulers of the new Germany—the great 'industrialists' who met at the Adlon to carry through big deals over their wine and cigars. Among these, the secretive figure of Stinnes, the despot of the 'heavy' industry, with his dark Assyrian profile, came and went, each sudden visit and equally sudden departure giving rise to feverish speculation on the Metal Exchange and wherever men bought and sold. He too, was a portent, attempting to achieve what another despot of a very different caliber, General Goering, later achieved—the control of the iron and steel industry. Stinnes, a ruthless gambler, had played the leading part in the organized spoliation of Belgian industry during the war on the assumption that Germany was bound to win it. He was destined to make his last throw of the dice at the coming Conference with the Allies at Spa. His sudden death was like the fall of a Colossus, bringing all his grandiose 'trusts' and 'cartels' down into the dust. The trade unions feared him, and the old aristocracy detested him—'a sinister figure,' was how Prince Blücher characterized him to me. 'He tried to blackmail me in his newspaper,' added Blücher, 'when I refused to sell him our family estate at Wahlstatt.' The defamation of the blackmailer and the dagger of the assassin had become in those disordered days the recognized means to unrecognized ends.

As day declined towards late afternoon, this crowd of *novi homines* gave place to a meretricious element which had something else to sell. The luxurious lounge, once the trysting-place of the 'best' people in Berlin, became a place of assignation for the worst. The smart crowd was flecked with young men with painted faces hovering and darting

[7] 'The Steel Helmets,' a union of ex-service men with pronounced Nationalist sympathies.

to and fro like dragon-flies. The artificial life on which they preyed was like a deadly iridescence on the face of the deep waters of proletarian life which ebbed and flowed, day by day, with a tidal rhythm in and out of the basements and kitchens of the Adlon, as crowds of wearied waiters, scullions, and chambermaids came and went in the small hours of the night from and to their impoverished homes in the outlying quarters of the city. Of them, and what they thought of those to whom they ministered, I should have known as little as the latter, had I been as indifferent. But it was a habit of mine during my long years in Germany to seek out, as is the way with most Englishmen serving in a foreign country, every chance of establishing contact with the people and discovering what they thought, how they lived, what they ate, and wherewithal they were clothed. Many a time after I had done an inspection of a regimental depot in Bavaria or elsewhere, I would get into mufti and, putting away my railway pass, with all its 'first-class' amenities, purchase a fourth-class ticket in order that I might talk with peasants and workmen as we sat huddled together in a community of discomfort on the wooden benches. In the Adlon that sort of fellowship was impossible and I should have been as ignorant, and perhaps as careless, of the toiling life of Berlin as all the other guests had it not been for my friend Herr Wilke.

Wilke was the head waiter on the fourth floor. For many years he ministered to my wants with unfailing solicitude. The first time he entered my rooms, he bowed deeply from the hips, addressing me as 'Excellenz,' and, as he retired with my order, retreated backwards as though in the presence of royalty. It was something of a problem to put him at his ease without losing caste, for during his service in the army these deep obeisances had clearly been exacted from him by the general officer whom he had served as batman, and he could conceive no other. When he saw that I treated my own batman like a human being, he recovered something of a man's poise. From that time forward we talked freely, and every morning he brought me an oral bulletin of what people were saying and thinking in the world without. Wilke was large, fat, and scant of breath, and his pallid face was sometimes suffused with a bluish tinge as though he suffered from an affection of the heart. He was a gentle soul. He had served during the war in the *Sanitätswesen* [8] and among such good Samaritans had

[8] The Medical Corps.

found his *métier* as a medical orderly—it was difficult to think of him as having been anything else. He was, of course, not of Prussian stock but a Saxon. The Prussians, as their great apologist, Treitschke, was proud to boast, have no use for gentleness.[9] Thinking of Wilke and his like, I once remarked to a Prussian officer of my acquaintance on the good nature of the Saxons. 'Good-natured!' he retorted, 'they're too afraid of hurting other people's feelings. Why, if I sat opposite a Saxon in a railway carriage and put my muddy boots in his lap, he'd leave them there for fear of offending me if he addressed me without being introduced.' He spoke as though he had tried the experiment.

Later I established a kind of contact with quite another type. It was Herr Kape. Kape was a masseur, recommended to me by a German friend, when, with little or no opportunities for exercise in Berlin, I found I was putting on too much weight. He was as unmistakably Prussian as Wilke was typically Saxon. He had a head like a flattened bullet, covered with a stubble of short, clipped hair, each hair standing up stiffly as though called sharply to attention. He was thick-set and enormously strong. If he was not an ex-N.C.O., he must certainly have been a *Kapitulant*,[10] for he always talked of the Army as though he still belonged to it—as perhaps he did. I learned more from him in his reminiscent moods about life in the ranks of the old Army than I could ever have learned from my friends among the officer class. A wide impassable gulf separated officers and men in the German Army. That personal solicitude for the comfort and well-being of his men which distinguishes the English company officer was quite unknown in Germany. But that was not quite all. I heard so much of the brutality of German N.C.O.s that I once asked General von Ofen not, indeed, whether it was true—that would hardly have been a tactful line of approach—but whether knocking the men about was in the German Army, as in the British, a military offense. Ofen's answer was curious. 'Well, you see,' he replied after a long pause, 'in my regiment, the Pomeranian Cuirassiers, there was quite a patriarchal tradition: not only did officers' sons join the same regiment from generation to generation but so with the men. So if a re-

[9] Thus, of the East Prussians: 'Much of their greatness lay in their total lack of that kind-heartedness (*Gutmütigkeit*) which is so wrongly exalted as a German virtue' (*Das deutsche Ordensland Preussen*, p. 6).

[10] A conscript who volunteers to serve a further term with the colors.

cruit shaped badly, the *Rittmeister* [11] would write to his father and the father would write back and *ask* that his son be given a good hiding.' This touching picture of a puzzled officer writing to the father of an unsatisfactory conscript, asking anxiously what he was to do with him, affected me deeply—indeed to the point of affectation. 'Wunderbar!' (Wonderful!) I replied. With which comment Ofen seemed deeply satisfied.

But my friend Lord Methuen, the Field-Marshal, who had been Military Attaché in Berlin, had told me rather a different story. 'It was always the custom in the German Army for the men to be knocked about, not only by N.C.O.s but by officers,' said Methuen. 'If you look at Hohenlohe's volumes on the Prussian Army, you will find a blunt admission of the fact—a statement that no Prussian recruit is ever any good until he's been knocked about.'

One day I thought I would tackle Kape on the subject.

'Did you have a good time as a recruit?' I asked.

He looked at me in astonishment, 'A good time?'

'I mean were the *Unter-Offiziere* [12] decent to you?' I explained.

He was still more astonished. 'Decent? Decent? Wie so?' he asked.

'What I mean is, how did they *treat* you?' I said with despairing emphasis.

'Ach, so!' replied Kape, his eyes widening as if he suddenly saw light. 'Well, they used to make me dance on the top of a hot oven with bare feet in my shirt while they whistled the tune of "Mariechen sass traumend im Garten." [13] The oven was so hot that I had to dance the whole time.'

'But, good heavens, man, why didn't you complain to an officer?' I asked.

'That wouldn't have been any good,' replied Kape with scarcely concealed impatience. 'I could only have complained to the *Feldwebel*.[14] And he would have said, "What! you pig-dog, you complain of an *Unter-Offizier!* Take that!" And he would have boxed my ears till I was deaf.'

---

[11] Captain (in a cavalry regiment).
[12] The N.C.O.s.
[13] 'Little Marie sat dreaming in the garden.'
[14] The Sergeant-Major.

'But why didn't you complain to the *Hauptmann?*' [15] I persisted.

'Ach! Das geht nicht,' [16] said Kape, as though his answer disposed of the subject. It certainly did. When I told him that I had known of a case—I had indeed had to 'vet' the court-martial proceedings—in which a choleric British officer, no less an officer than a brigadier-general, had been court-martialed for striking a man with his cane, when on parade, Kape was speechless with astonishment.

'Well,' I summed up reflectively, 'if we do nothing else, we shall at least make an end of that for you by abolishing conscription. There'll be no more of that in Germany with the new voluntary army.[17] If there is, men simply won't enlist.'

'We don't want conscription abolished,' was the astonishing answer.

'What! you want your young men to be treated like that?'

'Why not?' replied Kape cheerfully, 'I had to go through it. Why shouldn't they? *They'll have to.*'

The last four words were darkly prophetic. Kape never believed our Commission would succeed in abolishing conscription. Nor, as things turned out, did we—in the long run. He clearly thought we should never get anything done. He sometimes spoke as if he had secret information on that point. In other words, as if he had had a 'tip.' Later on I discovered what it was.

Such was the environment in which we lived and moved. For the first few weeks after our arrival our life was tranquil enough. We encountered little or no hostility, although we had good reason to know that we had nearly four hundred thousand officers and men [18] under arms to demobilize and equally good reason to suspect that they would not welcome the process. What we did encounter was

[15] Captain (in an infantry regiment).

[16] 'Ah! that's no use.'

[17] But there was! See below, Chapter VI and Chapter XI as to the persistence of brutality in the Reichswehr.

[18] The returns supplied to us as late as 17 February, after a delay of several months, by the German Government admitted the existence of 470,560 effectives still with the colors, i.e. 370,560 in excess of the Treaty establishment. These returns did not even profess to include a masked military formation known as the Security Police (see below) mustering at least 60,000, nor the thousands of soldiers of fortune organized into 'Free Corps.' Nor did they take account of a huge improvised militia known as the *Einwohnerwehren.*

an immense inertia and something more than inertia, in other words
a massive obstruction, in official quarters. Nearly every one of the
'Notes' and 'Questionnaires' which we had addressed to the German
Government several months earlier, when our 'Advanced Guard' had
come to Berlin by the Government's own invitation, remained un-
answered. We had asked at the outset for a copy of the current Army
Estimates. When the official copy reached us, we found that the
whole of the section dealing with the 'Supplementary [*überplan-
massige*] Estimates' had been blacked out. Our request for particulars
as to what had become of the Army Administrative Services which
had totally disappeared from their normal place in the Army Estimates—we subsequently discovered them in hiding in the Civil Departments—was ignored altogether. A questionnaire of ours on the
subject of military associations, the existence of which all over
Germany was daily reported to us by our District Committees, received short shrift with the laconic reply: 'Es gibt nicht.' [19] Yet
every hoarding in Germany was covered with placards inviting men
to join a force known as the *Einwohnerwehren* which the German Government affected to regard as nothing more than 'Special
Constables,' in spite of the publication in the Press of notices by local
authorities that service therein would 'count' (*gelten*) as 'active
service' (*Kriegsdienst*), and that the 'constables' would be subject to
the command of the local Reichswehr regiments. This 'huge militia' [20]
was, in fact, the germ of those tens of thousands of Storm Troops [21]
who, seven years later, almost immediately on the withdrawal of the
Commission, threw off the mask and proclaimed themselves to be
what they had always been. It is one of the ironies of history that this
very force which the Republican Government refused, in response
to our demands, to demobilize as an illicit organization, forbidden by
the Treaty, became the instrument with which, some twelve years
later, Hitler destroyed the Republic. The very notoriety of its existence, which the local authorities made no attempt to conceal, invested the denial of it by the Central authorities with all the character
of a direct defiance of the Commission.

[19] 'There are none.'
[20] This is a German writer's own description of this force, as it was in 1920,
in a book published long after the withdrawal of the Commission—*Hitler*, by
Konrad Heiden, p. 121.
[21] Heiden, p. 121.

The attitude of the German Government in regard to the *Sicherheitspolizei* (Security Police) was even more defiant. These 'police,' improvised during the Armistice, mustered in Berlin alone, where they were largely recruited from the demobilized battalions of the Prussian Guard, the flower of the German Army, no less than three brigades, or *gruppen*, of 9,000 men in all—and were equivalent in every respect to an infantry division. They were armed not only with machine-guns and trench-mortars but with field-guns and aeroplanes —a curious substitute for a policeman's baton. Their character as a reserve organization and, as such, violating the express provisions of the Treaty was so obvious, not to say flagrant, that their instant dissolution had been demanded by the Supreme Council in Paris as early as December 1919, in other words, several weeks before the Control Commission commenced its operations. Finding, on our arrival, that they were still going strong—indeed they were to be seen everywhere, with their side-arms, in their green uniforms and shakos, we addressed a note to the German Government asking that steps were being taken to comply with the demand of the Allied Governments. To this note we received no reply.

Such replies to our questionnaires as we did receive were not encouraging. In the very forefront of our huge task was the problem of demobilization. Before the provisions of the Treaty as to the authorized establishment of the new Army could be satisfied it was, of course, necessary to secure the demobilization of the old. The Demobilization—*Abwickelung* [22] as it was called—organization now adopted by the German War Office was based on the pre-war organization of the Army to be demobilized. The headquarters of the Home Commands, territorially represented by the Army Corps Districts, were accordingly transformed into Demobilization H.Q., each headquarters being known as an *Abwickelungsamt*, while each regimental depot within the Command did duty as a demobilization center, or *Abwickelungstelle.* Nothing could be more natural or more expeditious than this adoption of the military machine if it were really the intention of the German authorities to expedite demobilization. But was it? The more we looked at this organization, the more did it appear to be a huge reserve of officers. The official

[22] Literally translated, the word means 'winding up' or 'liquidation.'

returns we asked for disclosed that there were 3,579 officers serving in it, but these, we were disarmingly informed, were all *ausser Dienst*, in other words on the retired list, or else on half-pay. There were a few others, we were told, serving in it who were still on the active list but were awaiting retirement. A rapid inspection by Control officers disclosed that the 'few others' numbered at least 2,000. The number of N.C.O.s, ostensibly serving as clerks, in this demobilization organization we never knew, but they were legion. Among them was an obscure corporal named Adolf Hitler. I sometimes wonder to what extent our insistence on the eventual dissolution of this formidable organization was responsible for launching him on his meteoric career. Later on, as is related elsewhere,[23] we discovered that the demobilization organization was less concerned to demobilize the old army than to prepare for mobilizing it again when we had taken our departure. But what concerned us at the moment was that here was a huge organization, nominally 'demilitarized,' which secreted within it nearly 6,000 officers and a vast unascertainable number of N.C.O.s— all surplus to those on the establishment of the 'transitional' Army (*Übergangsheer*)[24] who were, heaven knew, numerous enough.[25] Our Commission was nominally due to leave within six months of our arrival, and was unquestionably expected by the German authorities to do so. We therefore naturally awaited with some impatience a reply to our 'note' inquiring as to when this formidable 'winding-up' organization of the old Army would itself be wound up and the demobilization of that Army completed. Eventually the reply came. It was laconic and consisted of two words—'Two years.'

On 29 January matters came to a head. For the first and last time the Allied general officers in a body and their antagonists of the German General staff saw each other not through a glass darkly but

[23] In a second volume to be published later.

[24] The Allied Governments had agreed to the temporary retention with the colors of 200,000 effectives, known as the *Übergangsheer*, but five weeks after the Treaty came into force this 'transitional' Army was still 470,560 strong.

[25] The German Government admitted the continued existence of 11,458 officers in the 'transitional army,' of 400 officers in the Army Corps H.Q.s and of 506 in the administrative services transferred to Civil Departments. Altogether there were at least 18,043 officers still serving in one capacity or another, exclusive of the 'Security Police,' a number nearly five times the establishment authorized by the Treaty of Versailles.

face to face. The German Government had addressed a note to General Nollet inviting us to a conference at the Foreign Office to discuss the operations of 'Control.' We accepted. The hour was fixed for eleven in the morning. We arrived with military punctuality, only to find ourselves kept waiting, like suppliants craving an audience, in an ante-room. We waited for a considerable time. At last a young German staff officer intimated, with a gesture towards the door of an adjoining room, that all was ready for us. As we filed into the conference-room by one door, a long procession of German officers entered by the other. The synchronization was perfect. We took up our positions on one side of a long table while the Germans executed a similar maneuver on the other. These movements took place in complete silence. Not a word, not a salute, was exchanged. There were seven of us and just fourteen of them. As the names of our delegation had, at their request, already been forwarded to the German authorities, this inequality in representation was presumably calculated. We were in service uniform, but the German officers were in full dress as though it were a levee, wearing their medals and decorations—I noticed that these still bore the Imperial crown. They stood with the immobility of statues, their faces as expressionless as masks but with watchful eyes. The head of the German delegation, General von Cramon and our own G.O.C., General Nollet, stood opposite each other. The two protagonists presented a striking contrast in racial types—Cramon a typical Prussian of huge physique, tall, thick, with cropped hair, a swollen face, prognathous jaw, and a bulbous nose, his hands like hams; Nollet shorter by a head but compact with resolution in every line of him, the full broad brow of a thinker, curiously reminiscent of Foch, a delicately chiseled nose, sensitive nostrils, and finely shaped hands. Nollet kept his eyes on von Cramon, but von Cramon never once looked at Nollet. He addressed all his remarks to a German civilian, who stood at his elbow interpreting, and addressed them as though not Nollet but the interpreter were his interlocutor. The atmosphere became charged with tension. Between the two men a duel, I felt, was bound to come.

It came with dramatic suddenness. Von Cramon had begun with some prolegomenous words about the necessity of mutual trust and confidence. He complained that the tone of Nollet's 'notes' had suggested mistrust—'Méfiance,' as the interpreter put it. Nollet replied slowly, articulating every syllable with immense nervous force so that every 'que' and 'si' sounded like a pistol shot. Nothing personal, he explained, had been intended, but 'control' implied supervision and supervision implied a measure of mistrust. 'I accept that,' said Cramon quietly and then, with sudden swiftness, 'I declare this sitting open.' Without even waiting for the interpreter to translate, he and all the German officers, as at a signal, suddenly relaxed and were about to sit down: 'Arrêtez-vous!' [26] rapped out Nollet, and the astonished Germans suddenly became rigid. The direct exchange of their two national tongues by the two men, thrusting aside the two interpreters as though they were 'seconds' who had got in the way, was like the clash of swords. There was a pause, a dead silence, as the two men seemed to measure each other. 'That won't do!' said Nollet, rapping out each syllable. 'There's an *attrape* there. It is for me to declare this sitting open. We are in control here.' Cramon replied, 'You are a foreign mission'—he skilfully avoided the word 'Commission'—'meeting the German Government on its own territory in time of peace. By all diplomatic precedents it is for me to preside.'

'There are no precedents,' replied Nollet sharply. 'The Treaty has made one. The Treaty placed us in control and control means supervision.' It was a polite way of saying that we were there to impose the will of the conqueror. I wondered whether, if the Germans had won the war and the positions had been reversed, the President of a German Commission of Control in Paris or London would have been equally polite.

'Very well,' said Cramon, after a pause, 'then that ends it. I must report to my Government.'

'And I to mine,' said Nollet.

We all marched out. As we left, Nollet said to me: 'C'était un piège.' [27] He was very pale but calm. After all, he had had to take a sudden decision and momentous, and we never quite knew, on such critical occasions, whether the 'Conference of Ambassadors' in Paris would support us. Already there were signs of dissension among the Allied Governments, and the Germans were quick to note them. What we did know was that, if we made the slightest *faux pas*, the

[26] 'Stop!'
[27] 'It was a trap.'

German Government would not only mobilize the Press against us with charges of insulting behavior but would address a complaint to Paris before we had time even to report what had happened. Wherefore Nollet assembled all the Allied generals in his room the moment we were back at the Bellevue, and asked us each in turn if we approved his action. He did not ask in vain. He presented an unforgettable picture. As he stood in the center of us in his long blue-gray coat, his hands thrust in his pockets, he said: 'I have beaten them four times in the field on the Western Front and von Cramon has never fought a battle.' There was always something Napoleonic about Nollet.

There could be no doubt whatsoever as to what all this meant. It was a trial of strength, deliberately prepared by von Cramon, to decide whether the German War Office should control the Commission or the Commission should control it. Nollet had divined this in a flash. The sequel to this historic encounter was immediate and significant—one might say sinister. The meeting at the Foreign Office had been a confidential one and was, in fact, never reported in the newspapers, but within a few hours the 'Nationalist Press' came out with a big headline: 'Verstärkter Schutz fur den Kontrol Kommission.' [28] The Berlin public were begged to keep calm, although they had never been less disturbed. Pickets of Security Police, added the newspapers, had been posted outside our hotels, to protect us from the just wrath of the German people. It was not the first time, nor the last, that the German public were ostentatiously exhorted not to nail our ears to the pump.

What did all this portend? We were not long left in doubt. Having declined to admit von Cramon's thesis that the German Government

[28] 'Increased protection for the Control Commission.' About the intimate relations of General von Cramon with the Press there could be little doubt, and in due course he came out into the open and proceeded to attack the Control Commission in the Press under his own name while still the accredited representative of the German Government with the Commission. A formal protest was eventually made by the Allied Governments on 2 November 1921, and four days later he was retired. But with unhappy pertinacity, not to say vindictiveness, he continued to write provocative articles in the Nationalist Press attacking General Nollet and the Commission itself in the columns of the *Lokalanzeiger*, in particular in its issue of 16 January 1926, while in the *Preussische Zeitung* of 3 July 1924, he pursued Nollet with extraordinary malevolence.

was to control us, we soon found ourselves submitted to a system of counter-control. In the course of time the system attained such proportions that the 'Army Peace Commission'—the *Heeresfriedenskommission* as it was called—became a kind of 'Shadow Commission.' A Shadow Commission it became in more senses than one, for some of its officers, in Pomerania in particular, 'shadowed' us everywhere, even when they—and we—were off duty. The Army Peace Commission had been instituted as early as the preceding November and at first we welcomed its institution. It was obviously necessary that there should be some responsible person with whom we could communicate direct in our requests for necessary documents, and the Treaty itself had prescribed that the German Government should appoint 'a qualified representative' for the purpose. The German Government had proceeded to appoint not one person but a whole Commission—the *Heeresfriedenskommission.* On the plea that a measure of decentralization would facilitate the operations of control, it then went a step farther and expanded this Commission until it was cast in our own image. Like the Control Commission, it was not only organized at the top into three Sub-Commissions, 'Effectives,' 'Armaments,' and 'Fortifications,' but projected itself all over Germany by the establishment of District Committees, corresponding to our own, in each of the seven *Wehrkreis* commands. This, it was pleaded, would expedite the local operations of control. Too late we discovered that it would do, and was meant to do, nothing of the kind. The German 'liaison' (*Verbindung*) officers in the districts, when confronted with any incidental question of control, always insisted that the matter, however trivial, must be referred to higher authority— and referred it was, in the best manner of the 'Circumlocution Office.' This Shadow Commission grew and grew until it became a kind of Secret Service mustering 140 'liaison officers.' The German liaison officers in the districts were always established in the same building as our own and invariably on the floor below, never on the floor above. The arrangement seemed very 'neighborly' but so, in a sense, is the removal of one's neighbor's landmark. In certain districts the German liaison officers intercepted the postman on his way up to us with an offer to relieve him of our letters. The offer may have been purely humane. After all, it saved the postman an extra flight of stairs. But at Stettin the postman, who was presumably a Communist with little love for the German Army, not only reported the offer to one of our Control officers on the floor above but, the next day, delivered the whole of the German liaison office's letters to the Control officer—with disconcerting results.

Of this powerful and pervasive instrument von Cramon was President, and with the rupture of relations between him and Nollet at the conference at the Foreign Office, he conceived the idea of using it to frustrate where he could not control. The German authorities, having failed at the outset in an attempt to dispute our right to any localized system of inspections at all, had then fallen back on their second line of entrenchments by insisting that no inspection should take place without the presence of a liaison officer. One of the reasons advanced for this contention was the necessity for our 'protection.' We had asked for none. As a matter of fact, it happened more than once in our inspections of the munitions factories (with our inspections of regimental units things were all the other way) that it was the German liaison officer who needed protection—and got it from our own officers. The sight of a German liaison officer in uniform in a certain factory in Saxony, which was being inspected by a British officer, Colonel Beasley, was greeted by the workmen with howls of derision and menacing shouts of 'Heraus! Heraus!' [29] Another reason, and a more acceptable one, advanced by the German Government was the necessity of a liaison officer to procure from the commanding officer of a unit the information we sought such as its strength returns (*Stärkenachweis*), pay-sheets (*Zahllisten*), nominal rolls (*Stammrollen*) and the like. To me, in particular, as G.O.C. the British section of the Effectives Sub-Commission and, as such, responsible for the demobilization of the old Army these documents were quite indispensable for my task. We accepted the condition accordingly. But as time went on we found that the liaison officers conceived it their duty, unquestionably with instructions to that effect, not to procure information but to prevent it being supplied. After nearly two years of this sort of thing, we had to insist on the right—and to exercise it— of making 'surprise' inspections without the presence of a liaison officer at all. When, owing to the attacks on our District Control officers, I decided to undertake some of these inspections of troops

[29] 'Out with him.'

in barracks myself, my car, the movements of which were always watched, was often chased by a liaison officer with the Jehu-like fury of a 'speed-cop.' Many and ingenious were the attempts made by Control officers, on the one hand, to make a surprise inspection and by the liaison officer, on the other, to frustrate it. In course of time the system of counter-control under the inspiration of General von Seeckt—and inspiring that distinguished soldier certainly was—developed into a fine art. But to von Cramon the credit of originating the system belongs. We were now to find it put into operation at our expense.

Within four days of the rupture of the conference with von Cramon,[30] the latter took the offensive. We received from him a 'note' informing our Fortifications Sub-Commission that a request for the plans of defense of the fortresses in the south and east of Germany could not be granted. This was a decided slap in the face. Stupendous demands had already been put up to us by the German Ministry of Defense for the armament of these 'fortresses,' many of which turned out, when at a much later date our sappers succeeded in gaining access to them, to be in fact museum pieces dating back to the Napoleonic wars and long dismantled. But on the pretext that they were part of an existing 'system of defense' [31] with the guns duly emplaced, the Ministry claimed to retain for their requirements an enormous establishment of heavy guns (two thousand in fact) such as would have endowed the new Army with more batteries of corps, i.e. heavy artillery, than the whole of the German Army possessed in 1913. As the Treaty expressly provided that the new Army should be armed only with field artillery, this claim was one which the Control Commission could not concede without first satisfying itself, by investigations conducted on the spot, that these 'fortresses,'

[30] General von Cramon appeared to have some misgivings that he had gone a little too far in his attempt at the conference to control the Control Commission. A few hours after it was broken off, a Foreign Office representative, Herr von Keller, waited on General Nollet to suggest a compromise by which Nollet and von Cramon should preside 'alternately' at such conferences. The suggestion was declined, and Nollet's refusal was upheld by Marshal Foch and the Versailles Military Committee.

[31] The Treaty expressly provided that the fortresses in the south and east, etc., should be allowed to retain their 'existing' system of defenses (see Articles 180, 195, 196).

a long list of which was submitted to us, really existed and were what they professed to be. The Control Commission therefore proposed to send a party of sappers to make a survey, or *recensement*, of them and their requirements. This proposal was, in turn, rejected by von Cramon's Commission on the ground that it was none of our business. The rejection was, indeed, expressed in more casuistical terms and supported by some elaborate arguments, based on a textual interpretation of the Treaty upon which the Reichswehrministerium now got to work with the misplaced ingenuity of a German professor editing the corrupt text of a classical author. We were quite in the dark at the time as to the daring scheme which lay behind these arguments. It was only later that we discovered that they masked an ingenious design to endow the new Treaty Army with the offensive arm of which the Treaty had been studious to deprive it. But one thing was already clear to us, and that was that our Fortifications Sub-Commission would, if we accepted this rebuff, be immobilized in Berlin and might just as well go home.

After this check, it was the turn of the Effectives Sub-Commission. Our right to inspect the strength-returns of the units in barracks was, indeed, not directly challenged, for we had carried the point some months earlier when an attempt had been made by von Cramon to question it. But the exercise of the right was frustrated. It was now that we began to realize our mistake in conceding the German claims that no inspection should take place without the co-operation of a German liaison officer. The liaison officers began to enjoy themselves by indulging in that particularly German form of humor, the playing of practical jokes, although, to be sure, there was a formidable earnestness behind it, the more formidable as they were unquestionably acting under instructions. Two of our Control officers presented themselves at the barracks at Potsdam accompanied by the inevitable liaison officer, only to be met by a tough-looking N.C.O. who informed them that the C.O. and all the officers of the unit were absent. Even the adjutant could not be found. The liaison officer professed, with an artless expression, complete ignorance of where they were. The inspection, of which due notice had been given by us in accordance with the agreement, had to be abandoned. At Duisburg the exact reverse happened. The C.O. of the unit to be inspected and its officers were all present, but the liaison officer was unaccountably absent and the C.O. professed to know nothing of his existence. No doubt in this case, as in the former, the comedy had all been carefully rehearsed on the telephone before the Control officers arrived. The result was the same in the one case as in the other—the inspection had to be abandoned. Occasionally the comedy was varied by the introduction of a new 'gag.' In one district the liaison officer professed, on his arrival at the barracks, to be new to his duties and suggested an adjournment of the inspection in order that he might obtain information from the liaison office (the *Verbindungstelle*) as to how to proceed. After compliance with his request, the Control officers came again on the appointed day, only to find a new liaison officer who requested another adjournment on the same ground as his predecessor.

This passive resistance soon hardened into something more active. As if at a given signal, the liaison officer accompanying the Control officers on an inspection would suddenly disappear. The next moment the soldiers of the unit to be inspected would pour out of the barrack-room, hoot the Control officers and assail them with clods of earth and a shower of stones. This happened, with a singular unanimity, at Prenzlau, at Bremen, at Doberitz and a score of other places. At Bremen two French officers were struck, thrown to the ground and threatened with bayonets. The troops were quite impartial in their unpleasant attentions—a British Army officer, Colonel Irvine, was their target at Prenzlau, while at Bremen—so we heard from the Naval Commission—a British naval officer was thrown into the water. It was difficult for any one who knew anything of the iron discipline of the German Army to believe that these assaults were not premeditated and approved. A 'row' in barracks is not a thing lightly tolerated in the German Army. The toe of the *Feldwebel's* [32] boot does not encourage spontaneous manifestations of feeling. The Control officers assaulted were in uniform. The fact aggravated the presumption of malice aforethought.

From all the District Commands reports came crowding in upon us at our G.H.Q. testifying to such tactical operations against us. In Berlin itself the air was thick with rumors of an impending *coup d'état*, but whether directed against us or against the Republic no one

[32] Sergeant-Major.

professed to know. Meanwhile one battalion after another of the
Reichswehr began marching up and down the Unter den Linden in
full field-kit, with their bands playing *Heil dir im Siegen-Kranz*. It
was their first appearance in the streets of Berlin since our arrival.
But Berlin, which is, according to Dr. Goebbels, 'the most excitable
city in Germany,' refused to be excited. The civil population, mostly
Republican in sympathy, was sullen and these parades excited no
enthusiasm, though, as things turned out, they were none the less
ominous on that account. My friend, Herr Wilke, confided to me
that never since the war had the Adlon been so full of officers. And
so it seemed. They were, it is true, not in uniform but the type was
unmistakable.

Then, one Sunday night, just six days before the blow fell, there
was a 'scene' in the Adlon which, in the light of later events, had all
the character of a premonition. A gunner would have called it 'a
premature.' The dining-room was crowded. Among the guests were
two French officers of the Control Commission. A group of German
officers in mufti were sitting at a table hard by in the company
of a cadet of the House of Hohenzollern, Prince Joachim, and the
Geiger, violin in hand, advanced towards the Prince with mincing
gait on his usual errand of solicitation. Prince Joachim whispered
something in his ear, the *Geiger* hesitated for a moment, then threw
up his violin under his chin and drew his bow across the strings. He
broke into the opening bars of *Deutschland über alles*. That trenchant
tune was now decidedly out of fashion under the Republic and, as
Prince Joachim and his party sprang to their feet, not more than half
the guests rose with them. The other half remained seated and, among
them, the French officers who might well be excused, under such
circumstances, for not knowing what to do. Ignoring the rest of the
recusants, Joachim, surrounded by his bodyguard of Prussian officers,
ordered the French officers to rise to their feet. They remained seated.
A sudden silence fell upon the room. 'You could have heard a napkin
drop,' as Wilke put it. The *Geiger*, by this time thoroughly frightened, stopped playing. The rest of the recusants now rose, not out of
deference but out of curiosity, not unadulterated, perhaps, by alarm,
to see what would happen. The waiters forsook their posts and clustered in an agitated group at the door. And alone, in the midst of this
alien crowd, the two French officers sat, and continued to sit, im-

mobile but with watchful eyes. The next moment there was a loud crash of crystal as Joachim threw his glass at one of them. His companions all followed suit with crash after crash, and one of the French officers, hit in the face, was unseated and fell to the ground. The other stood over him with shoulders squared, waiting the onset. Like all the rest of us, the two Control officers were quite unarmed. It was more than probable that the Prussian officers had the advantage of them in that respect, as well as in numbers. Ever since the Revolutionary troubles, when some of them had their epaulettes torn off, most German officers, whether in mufti or not, never went about without a revolver.

But the onset never came. One of the waiters must have given the alarm. Police suddenly appeared on the scene, the Republican element began to shout accusations at Prince Joachim while the *maître d'hôtel* threatened the chastened *Geiger*, now white and trembling, with his fists. The *chef de cuisine* suddenly appeared on the scene, all in white, like a ghostly apparition, from the depths of the vast kitchens, and told the *Geiger* that if he ever played that tune again he would 'do him in.' And, for the first time in the history of a proud dynasty, a cadet of the House of Hohenzollern found himself under arrest.

The next day, a little straw, light as thistledown, showed the direction of the wind, and an ill wind it was. With much solemnity, portentous in the more literal sense of the word, a German policeman called upon us at the Bellevue to complain that a British soldier had 'insulted' a German civilian. When asked the nature of the insult, the policeman reported with no less solemnity, 'er hat in ein Gelachter ausgebrochen.' [33]

Two days later the German Officers' Corps staged a scene of dramatic splendor. By the terms of the Treaty all 'military academies' were to be abolished within two months of the ratification of the Treaty. It was part of my duty to see that this was duly done by the appointed day, which fell to be 10 March. A few miles outside Berlin, in the suburb of Gross Lichterfelde, there was a great cadet school endeared to generations of German officers by the playful epithets of *Hat Keine Aussicht*, and *Homoeopathische Kur Anstalt*.[34] It was the

[33] 'He burst out laughing.'
[34] Which, freely translated, might be rendered: 'All hope abandon ye who enter here,' and, in the alternative, 'Homoeopathic Cure Institution.'

cradle of the German Officers' Corps, and its battle-honors were written large in the terrible casualty lists of the German Army. Here were nurtured von Moltke and all the paladins of the Great General Staff whose portraits adorned the walls of its great hall of ceremony with their mural bas-reliefs portraying the career of a cadet, from the day of his novitiate, his entrance, his drill, his musketry training, and his graduation. What Sandhurst and Woolwich are to the British Army, Gross Lichterfelde was to the German Army. This, and more than this, for Gross Lichterfelde was, in a country in which 'public schools' in the English sense did not exist, the one great public school. The officer's son—and an officer's son he almost invariably was—entered one of its 'preparatory' schools as a child of ten, and on his transfer to Gross Lichterfelde, was drafted into a company, instead of a 'house,' rose to be an N.C.O. instead of a prefect, and after passing his ensign's examinations proceeded by one route or another—by posting to a regiment, by passing into a 'Selekta' class, or by entering a 'War School'—to a commission, entering the German Officers' Corps, on the day he was gazetted, with two years' seniority over all other aspirants to that great caste. 'We were a caste within a caste,' said one of its sons, an officer of Cuirassiers, to me long afterwards when we sat at meat together and he talked wistfully of the past. 'Ludendorff is typical of us, narrow in outlook, if you like, terse in speech, with a touch of the drill-sergeant about him, but, then, at H.K.A. everything was "Kommando"; we even marched in to breakfast at the *Paradeschritt*.[35] You could always tell one of us in after-life, even if he lived to be ninety. *Ach*, yes, when I forget "H.K.A." may my right hand forget its cunning.'

Such was Gross Lichterfelde, such its pride of place and now, by an inexorable decree, its days were numbered. It was to close its doors on the eve of the 10th. The word went forth, and generations of officers who acclaimed it their *alma mater* attended the last parade, some decrepit with years, others disabled by wounds, some in mufti, others in uniform, and marched past the Commandant, with Ludendorff at the head of them, saluting the colors now brought forth for the last time. Of what happened at Gross Lichterfelde itself I only learned afterwards from two British officers whom I had sent there, in mufti,

[35] Parade-step.

to mix unobtrusively with the crowd. But sitting in my room at the Bellevue in the deepening twilight, I suddenly heard the stirring music of *Fredericus Rex*. I went to the window and below me I saw the cadets marching in column of fours across the Potsdamer Platz in their blue tunics with red facings and their gold-mounted Pickelhauben. A company of the Guards Schutzen Regiment followed them like a rearguard. At the head of the column marched the older generation of *alumni*, generals and colonels who had grown gray in the service, in a pageantry of uniforms representing the flower of the Army in dissolution and of the regiments doomed to disappear— Guards Cuirassiers, Foot-Guards, Death's Head Hussars, 'Fuss-Artillerie,' Uhlans, like a parade of ghosts. It seemed as though, like Heine's grenadier, they had risen from the grave:

> Dann steig' ich gewaffnet hervor aus dem Grab
> Den Kaiser, den Kaiser zu schützen.

In this roll-call of the years, youth and age marched together. The cadets marched at parade-step in perfect time with a precision of 'dressing' so faultless that they might have been a regiment of the Guards. As they kept their eyes fixed straight ahead on the colors of their Corps, their young faces seemed strangely expressionless and immobile as though they mastered some emotion too deep for tears. At a corner of the Platz, a German general, mounted on a gray horse, took their salute and, as their eyes turned towards him, it seemed to me as though a single cry went up from a thousand young hearts: 'Morituri te salutamus.'

The people on the pavement looked on incuriously. Not one of them cheered. Not one of them raised his hat as the colors were borne past. 'I wonder what all that silence means?' I remarked to Ubsdell who stood at my elbow, 'Emotion?' 'No,' replied Ubsdell tersely, 'indifference.' And so it was. The march through Berlin which had been staged by the German Officers' Corps without the knowledge of the Minister of Defense, Noske, was denounced by the Socialist papers the next day as both futile and provocative. As a political demonstration it fell flat. The only persons to feel its pathos were the British officers of the Control Commission. I felt as heretical as Cato. 'Victrix causa deis placuit,' I reflected, 'sed victa Catoni.' At the moment we all felt like that.

But any compunction I felt was rudely dissipated when I opened my German newspapers the next morning. Therein I found the allocutions of Ludendorff and Hoffmann at the last parade at Gross Lichterfelde. And, to my amazement, I read that they had hinted to the cadets that the suppression of their *alma mater* would prove to be only temporary. Clearly that march through Berlin was a carefully calculated act of defiance. 'What,' I thought as I reflected on all the assaults on our officers which had preceded it, 'does this mean?'

And then, just forty-eight hours later, the blow fell.

IV. THE REVOLT OF THE REICHSWEHR

'THERE'S BEEN a Revolution, sir.'

I opened my eyes. Bailey was standing by my bed with my morning tea. His homely features betrayed not a flicker of excitement. He spoke as though he were announcing a change in the weather. His face wore a somewhat self-satisfied expression as of one who felt that it is better to be the bearer of evil tidings than of no tidings at all. It was a habit of his, which I had encouraged, to divert my waking moments with barrack-room gossip, for which, however, he was careful never to accept any responsibility. I sometimes wondered whether Bailey had ever been 'crimed.' He seemed to know all about the inadmissibility of hearsay evidence. At any rate he always cast his statements in the form of *oratio obliqua*, prefacing them with the caveat, 'They say as how,' or 'I've heard tell.'

But on the morning of this fateful day Bailey confronted me with a direct statement in the form of *oratio recta*. He appeared to take complete responsibility for the truth of these catastrophic tidings. I was incredulous and proportionately annoyed.

'What the devil are you talking about?' I exclaimed with some heat.

Bailey's expression suddenly changed. He stood stiffly to attention. 'I've had nothing to do with it, sir,' he said.

'I don't suppose you had,' I retorted with ill-concealed amusement at this political disclaimer, at which Bailey was visibly relieved. 'But a Revolution! Where? When?'

'In the night, sir. Here in Berlin. Just outside. You can see what they've been up to,' he added with gloomy satisfaction. 'There's a lot of Jerrys about.'

I sprang out of bed and, throwing on a dressing-gown, I made for the balcony of my sitting-room and looked down. Below were four lethal-looking 'seventy-sevens,' commanding all approaches. A few yards to the right, where the Wilhelmstrasse debouched into the Unter den Linden, was a machine-gun post and barbed-wire entanglements. Field-kitchens were sending up wisps of smoke in the chill morning air. 'Jerrys' seemed to be everywhere—unmistakable Jerrys in tin hats and full service kit. Each man carried a pack, a rifle and a brace of bombs. On their tin hats was a new and mysterious emblem—the stigmata of a greater revolution yet to come. It was the first apparition of the 'Swastika.' Officers in long gray coats were giving orders.

I dressed hurriedly, got into uniform, and pressed the bell-button twice for the fourth-floor waiter. The large, moon-like face of Herr Wilke appeared. Always pale, his face now looked ashen gray with anxiety. His pendulous lip quivered.

'Die Revolution ist wiedergekommen, Euer Excellenz,' he said in quavering tones. 'Es ist schrecklich.' [1]

In reply to my questioning, he gave me such news as he had. Troops had marched into Berlin in the dead of the night from Doberitz and seized all the points of vantage, including the offices of the Government Departments in the Wilhelmstrasse. The Ministers had been warned just in time and had fled in their pajamas while Berlin slept. They were reported to have caught a train to Stuttgart.

'Well, a White Revolution is better than a Red one,' I remarked in an attempt to administer first aid to the unhappy Wilke.

But Wilke was not amused. He had, it appeared, rather painful recollections of an officer to whom he had acted as batman during the war.

'When I brought him his morning coffee,' Wilke told me with an air of acute depression, 'he used to shout, "Achtung Du! Dummkopf!" [2] and I had to come to attention immediately, with the coffee-tray in my hands. Often I dropped the tray and upset the coffee. Then he used to strike me with his fists and make me do it all over again with fresh coffee. Schrecklich! Schrecklich!'

I had always admired the peculiar dexterity with which Wilke, with bowed head and curved arms, extended like a suppliant, balanced the breakfast tray above him. He looked at such times like a caryatid. Now I knew where he had learned to do it.

At that moment of Herr Wilke's mournful reminiscences, a shout of 'Achtung!' in a rasping voice came through the open window from

[1] 'The Revolution has come back, your Excellency. It is terrible.'
[2] 'Attention! you blockhead.'

THE CLOSING-DOWN OF THE CADET SCHOOL AT GROSS LICHTERFELDE: THE LAST PARADE
(10 MARCH 1920)

The third figure from the left, in the background, is General Ludendorff

H.Q. EFFECTIVES SUB-COMMISSION (BRITISH), BERLIN, 1920

Front Row—Lieut.-Col. F. C. T. Ewald—Lieut.-Col. T. R. Ubsdell—Brig.-Gen. J. H. Morgan—

the troops below. Herr Wilke started. He did not drop my breakfast tray. Nothing so dramatic occurred. But something more poignant. His eyes blinked. He wept.

After a hurried breakfast, I descended to the first floor to take counsel with General Nollet. The hotel, which overnight had been full of guests and noisy, was strangely silent and had a subdued air. Many guests, I learned later, had already bolted for the railway stations to catch trains to the provinces before trains ceased to run. I found Nollet unperturbed, as always. His demeanor then, as at other and almost equally critical moments, brought back to me that ode of Horace in which he salutes the man who is at once just and tenacious of purpose:

> Si fractus illabatur orbis,
> Impavidum ferient ruinae.

The 'fractured world' was all around us. Anything might happen at any moment. Nollet, however, was as laconic as he was calm. It is a mistake to suppose that Frenchmen are always and everywhere excitable. I have often observed that the more critical a situation is, the calmer they become. Danger seems to act upon them as a sedative. With Nollet I found the not less imperturbable Walch, chewing his large drooping moustache with the meditative air of a cow chewing the cud. The other Allied generals, Barthélemy, Bingham, De Gouffroy and Calcagno, arrived a few moments later from their respective hotels. We were all in uniform. Together we held a 'council of war.' But what were we to do? None of us as yet knew what was happening. We had no instructions from our masters, the Conference of Ambassadors in Paris, as to how to deal with a Revolution. This was one of the things which, like much else, the Peace Conference had not foreseen. The *de jure* Government was in Stuttgart, the *de facto* Government was in Berlin. With which were we to treat, if we treated at all? To demand anything of the new Dictatorship would be diplomatically to 'recognize' it. There is a wise French proverb which says 'when in doubt, do nothing.' We followed it and decided to repair to our offices in the Bellevue as though nothing had happened and there await such instructions as might come from Paris. None ever came. The ultimate severance of all communications made them impossible in any case. We had no wireless.

Before we separated, Bingham, who was often a little premature, whispered to me in deep depression, 'This is the end. The Commission might as well go home.' And he urged upon Nollet that we should all get into mufti. To go about in uniform, he suggested, would be dangerous if not provocative. With the exception of the proposer, we were all opposed to this suggestion, but in matters like this we had, in view of our 'allied' character, to be unanimous. After some demur, Nollet agreed. Orders were issued accordingly. It was a mistake and might have cost many of us our lives. To thread your way, in pitch darkness in the dead of night, through barbed-wire entanglements and to be brought up sharply by a jumpy sentry fingering his stick-bomb while you fumbled in your pockets for your 'Ausweis' [3] was an unhealthy experience which we had to go through only too often during the days that were to follow. All German civilians had by that time been ordered by the troops to remain indoors after nightfall and, once we were in mufti, there was nothing to distinguish us from them. The sentries had a playful way of shooting first and inquiring afterwards, as many an innocent German civilian learned to his cost. I found it quicker to exclaim 'Englander,' than to fumble for my pass, and the disarming effect of that word was magical. It became my invariable pass-word.

As a matter of fact, the last thing the revolutionaries wanted to do was to quarrel with the Allied Governments, or with us as their representatives, from whom they were hoping to secure diplomatic recognition. Within the first twenty-four hours, General von Luttwitz, the leader of this *coup d'état*, sent a message to General Nollet requesting the honor of an interview. The request was politely declined. To have accepted it would have been fatal. None the less, we continued to be the recipients, individually, of uninvited assurances from German officers that the *coup d'état* was in no way directed against the Allied Governments. It was, we were assured, only a little domestic affair. To these blandishments we continued to turn a deaf ear. As usual, the German military mind gave us credit for no intelligence. We did not require the counsel of Ahithophel to divine that the establishment of a military Dictatorship in Germany meant our own extinction as a Commission, and, with it, the arrest of the process of disarmament at the very moment of its inception. The

[3] Pass.

streets were now swarming, under our very noses, with armed formations of the very men whose demobilization we had been continually
demanding and had failed to secure. These were the irregulars of
Ehrhardt's Marine Brigade, of von der Goltz's 'Iron Division' of
Baltic troops, and the Lutzow 'Free Corps.' They had been eating
their heads off in camp on the outskirts of Berlin, looking for
'trouble.' They had a particular bone to pick with us as, if we succeeded in demobilizing them, it would be a case of 'Othello's occupation's gone.' At their head was a typical soldier of fortune, Captain
Ehrhardt. These hard-bitten 'toughs' had been only too ready to
lend themselves to a military adventure when General von Luttwitz,
the G.O.C. of the First Gruppen Kommando, one of the four Home
Commands, and the prime mover [4] in this *coup d'état*, promised them
long life, re-engagement, and high pay. Germany at that time was
overrun with 'Free Corps' of this character, reminding one of nothing
so much as those marauding 'Free Companies' of the Middle Ages
which cut such a romantic figure in the glittering pages of Froissart.
Most of them were named after some popular general who had
'raised' them in the hectic days immediately succeeding the Armistice
and each of them had its own image and superscription. The skull
and crossbones [5] gave a macabre touch to one such unit in the streets
of Berlin. Many of these units, although nominally demobilized, had
been billeted on the farms of the great *latifundia* of the Junker landowners in Pomerania or were 'living on the country' in East Prussia
and in the sandy plains of Brandenburg. Others had been mustered
in Lower Silesia. Now, as at a signal, they suddenly emerged from
their rural seclusion, seized Königsberg, dominated Stettin and
swaggered in the streets of Breslau. But of all that was going on in
these outlying provinces and in the States we, at the time, knew
nothing. And of the fate of our officers posted in those distant storm-
centers we were equally ignorant.

These mercenaries were reinforced by hosts of officers, some of
them even serving in the ranks. The officers had flocked into Berlin
overnight and were now to be seen everywhere, like flies round a
honey-pot. As I drove to our headquarters in the Bellevue, I was

---

[4] The political leader was Herr Kapp.
[5] Later the insignia of Hitler's steel-helmeted bodyguard.

struck by the multitude of them in their smart gray coats, all of them
in cars which they acquired by the simple process of turning the
owner out at the point of a revolver. They called it 'requisitioning.'
I saw this happen several times. It might have happened to me but,
on each occasion when my car was stopped, I said 'Kontrol Kommission' and escaped all further molestation. My German chauffeur re-
sented it more than I did and was darkly prophetic. He was 'sick of
revolutions,' he told me, and hinted that the 'Arbeiterschaft' [6] would
have something to say to all this. The adhesion of all these officers
was not surprising for, as a class, they were ruined, desperate, and
sometimes starving. Only a few days earlier I had seen one such, clad
in the long gray overcoat of his caste, selling newspapers in the
streets of Dresden. Our 'Intelligence' had reported to us that scores
of them had placed their swords at the disposal of the Bolshevik
Government in Moscow, attracted by the offer of a thousand marks
a day. The age of the *condottieri* had returned.

On the first day the leaders of the revolt, anticipating no resistance,
were busy 'consolidating.' Their irregulars had taken their first objective with the occupation of the Government quarter in the Wilhelmstrasse, and their military success appeared to be complete. The
defection of the 6th Reichswehr regiment turned the scale in their
favor. The police had already been 'squared.' But it remained to
square the public. And it was here that Herr Kapp failed. His experiment in the technique of revolution and its failure must, I often
think, have been the secret of Herr Hitler's astonishing success just
thirteen years later. For Herr Kapp made one fatal mistake which
Hitler was careful not to repeat. He forgot 'die Gewerkschaften.' [7]
Had he arrested all the trade union leaders, sequestrated their funds,
shot a few 'pour encourager les autres,' beaten up the others, and
interned them in a concentration camp, he might have succeeded. Instead of doing anything so drastic, Herr Kapp began with a decree
prohibiting the publication of all the newspapers of the 'Left,' whereupon the Compositors' Union, who were Socialists to a man, struck
work and the newspapers of his own faction of the 'Right' failed to
appear. The bewildered public were therefore, at the outset, left

[6] The working-classes.
[7] The Trade Unions.

completely in the dark as to what kind of New Jerusalem Kapp and Luttwitz proposed to rear upon the ruins of the monarchy. A negative assurance that it would contain no Jews left the people of Berlin completely cold. Another assurance, equally negative, but not equally sincere, that they were not aiming at the restoration of the Prussian monarchy annoyed the Nationalists without convincing the Republicans.

Kapp and Luttwitz duly produced, however, a political program of a kind, intelligent enough in everything except the means by which they sought to put it into execution. Papen, Goering, and Hitler himself, all in turn, appropriated certain pieces in Kapp's repertoire some twelve years later, of course without acknowledgment. No politician ever acknowledges any source of inspiration but his own. According to Goering, the Führer has always been his own oracle, with some assistance from the Almighty,[8] and his ideas have owed nothing to any one. But the master-stroke initiated by von Papen in 1932, and consummated by Hitler a few months later, of destroying the autonomy of Prussia by merging the office of Prime Minister of the State in that of the Chancellor of the Reich, was, in fact, one of the unhappy Kapp's 'four points.' And a very astute point it was. The hegemony of Prussia, with its overwhelming resources alike of wealth and population, was almost as marked a feature of the constitutional structure of the new Reich as of the old, and, under the new republican franchise, Prussia was a Socialist State with a Socialist Cabinet destined to endure right down to 1932. As such, it presented a formidable obstacle to the recapture of the Reich by the political reactionaries. To capture Prussia was to capture the key of the citadel. When, in 1932, von Papen, as Chancellor, sent a Reichswehr lieutenant and a file of soldiers to the office of the Socialist 'Home Secretary'[9] of Prussia, Herr Severing, and told the astonished Minister to 'clear out,' he merely accomplished what Herr Kapp had hoped to accomplish twelve years earlier by more constitutional methods. But then Papen had the President of the Reich, whose nominee he was, behind him.

But the days of Hindenburg as President were yet to come, and

[8] See Goering's *Germany Reborn*, p. 79.
[9] 'Minister des Innern,' an office which closely corresponds to that of the Home Secretary in England as carrying with it the control of the police.

Herr Kapp had to deal with a Socialist President of the Reich, Herr
Ebert, who, ignoring his overtures, refused to recognize his existence.
From their refuge in Stuttgart, Herr Ebert and the Socialist Chancel-
lor, Herr Bauer, proscribed Herr Kapp as a traitor to the Republic.
Thereupon, Kapp, failing to secure the Presidential nomination as
Chancellor, proceeded to nominate himself. This was an unfortunate
move for one who, like Kapp, was vociferous in his assurances to the
public that he had come not to destroy but to fulfill. The Weimar
Constitution itself, he contended, prescribed that the President of the
Republic should be elected by the people and no such President had
ever been elected. This was true enough. Therefore let the people be
summoned to a plebiscite to elect the man of their choice. This was
Kapp's second 'point' and it was a good one. It would have been a
better one if he had not compromised his constitutional propriety by
nominating himself to be Chancellor. Four years later the plebiscite
took place and the man of destiny whom Kapp and Luttwitz probably had in mind, namely Hindenburg, was duly elected, to nominate,
in due course, Herr Hitler to the office which Kapp, in the absence
of a Hindenburg, had felt constrained to confer upon himself.

Kapp was not, in fact, the fool which, once he had failed, every
one, friend and enemy alike—for such is human nature—agreed, while
agreeing in nothing else, in stigmatizing him. He had clearly grasped
the fundamental trick underlying all successful revolutions of the
post-war period. And that is, as a profound student of the technique
of such movements has recently observed,[10] that, if you want to bring
a revolution to a successful issue, you should conduct it *under
cover* of the very laws which, once you have succeeded, you intend
to subvert. You should use the constitution in order to destroy it.
Demand a dissolution of the legislature to ascertain 'the will of the
people' and, if the result is not to your liking, demand another. In the
meantime get busy with all the arts of propaganda, loud-speakers,
wireless, cinemas, spot-lights, in proclaiming that you are 'out' not
to make a revolution but to save the State from one, from one which
does not, in fact, exist. Proclaim the sanctity of freedom of speech
and prevent your opponents from exercising it by breaking up their
meetings with the assertion that they are bent on denying it to you.

[10] *British Rule and Rebellion*, by H. J. Simson.

When, by these black arts, you have got the legislature you want, put an end to it. It was given to Dr. Kapp to see all these things as it was given to Moses to see the Promised Land, but he was in too much of a hurry, lost his nerve and tried to do all things at once. He demanded an immediate dissolution of the legislature—it was his third point—contending that it had exhausted its mandate, and here also he was adopting an attitude of constitutional correctitude which was nothing if not plausible. Finding Herr Ebert unwilling to treat with him on this point, as on the others, he was betrayed into making yet another unconstitutional step. He issued a decree dissolving the Reichstag himself and conjured up a 'Red Peril' which did not exist. Having failed to beguile the Socialist Government into going shares in a new Administration, he suddenly affected to discover that the Socialists were Communists, which they never were, and attempted to brand their Government accordingly. But his writ did not run and no elections took place. Kapp was, in fact, trying to do in a few days what it took that blessed pair of sirens, Goebbels and Hitler, with all their arts of oratory and their elaborated organization, ten years to accomplish. The science of physics had not yet placed at his disposal, as it was to place at theirs, the microphone and the wireless as instruments of propaganda, and, even if it had, Nature had not endowed Kapp with those gifts of demagogic oratory which enabled his successors to use them. He had to fall back on pamphlets, distributed, like tracts by an evangelist, among the wayfarers in Berlin at the point of the bayonet with a soldier, armed to the teeth, as the evangelist. He had no time to mobilize the *Einwohnerwehren* to do duty as an armed 'democracy' of Storm Troopers. That civilian touch was lacking, with the result that his movement was too obviously a military one to be popular. 'You can do everything with bayonets except sit on them.' Here too Kapp's successors learned a good deal from him, if only negatively. They learned from him that they could not make a Revolution with the Reichswehr and equally that they could not make one without it.

The 'Kappists' began, however, by purely peaceful persuasion. About ten o'clock in the morning, the first of a whole series of armored cars appeared in the Potsdamer Platz, to be followed a little later by motor lorries mounted with machine-guns. In the car, or upon the lorry, three or four soldiers shed pamphlets which fluttered down like a flock of pigeons among the crowd. They were eagerly snatched up by the populace, in default of newspapers, read, passed from one hand to another and then discussed in small conventicles which formed and re-formed in the Platz. While these pamphlets were being distributed by the four soldiers, a fifth lay prostrate upon the bonnet of the lorry with a machine-gun ready in case the crowd did not like their literary style. I sent out an orderly to secure one of these fly-sheets. It promised all things to all men with a profusion hardly exceeded by the author of *Mein Kampf*. The most seductive effort in this direction was a Proclamation to the students of the University of Berlin, which appeared in the course of the afternoon, announcing that there should be no more examinations. From that moment the students were with the Revolutionists to a man. They flocked to join the *Zeitfreiwillige*.[11] In all this the Revolution did but conform to type: 'There shall be seven halfpenny loaves sold for a penny, the three-hooped pot shall have ten hoops and I will make it a felony to drink small beer.' Luttwitz and Kapp were not more original than Jack Cade.

All day long, bodies of troops marched and counter-marched in column of fours across the square in front of my window at the Bellevue, playing every tune in their repertoire from *Alte Kameraden* to *Deutschland über alles*. Despite these demonstrations, the public appeared listless and unmoved. Even the stirring chords of *Fredericus Rex* failed to move them. I noticed that the officers, riding at the head of the columns, were almost solicitous in the care with which they saluted every time a civilian raised his hat—which was not often. The day passed without further incident. There had been no bloodshed. On the third day, which was a Sunday, a cloud appeared on the horizon. The 'Kappists' arrested the Minister of Transport who had remained behind in Berlin. Thereupon the railwaymen threatened to strike and the Kappists hurriedly released him. It was their first check.

At seven o'clock on the Sunday evening I returned from the Bellevue to my quarters at the Adlon. I went into the bathroom to wash my hands and turned on the tap. There was a gurgling sound, suggestive of some internal complaint in the pipes, but no water

---

[11] The *Zeitfreiwillige* were a Reichswehr Volunteer Reserve.

appeared. Clearly a matter for the hotel plumber, I reflected. The next moment the electric light went out. 'Fused!' I said to myself and, having found the wall in the darkness, I pressed the electric button twice for the fourth-floor waiter. No one appeared. This seemed strange, as Wilke was invariably very prompt in answering my signals. The room was now, of course, in darkness. But there are shades of darkness even as there are gradations of light and, as I waited with growing impatience for Wilke's appearance I was vaguely conscious of something peculiar about my room. Normally a faint light, like early dawn, suffused it even in the watches of the night. Its two big windows, leading on to the balcony, looked out on to the Unter den Linden, and the great arc lamps of that thoroughfare, and the 'sky signs' opposite, diffused so much light that my windows were, always, even in the dead of night, faintly visible in silhouette from within. Even the furniture could be just located in this crepuscular setting. But the room was now shrouded in an impenetrable darkness. Failing to find a match, I took an imaginary bearing in the direction of the windows, passed my hand over the wall like a blind man and suddenly felt the coldness of glass. I found the catch and throwing the window open, got out on to the balcony and looked down. I could see nothing.

A wall of blackness seemed to shut in the hotel like a fog. For a moment I was stricken with a horrid apprehension that I had lost my sight. To this fear succeeded another, as I gripped the iron railing of the balcony. Had I become stone-deaf? I could not hear a sound. The vast city lay at my feet but of its multitudinous hum not a sound reached me. The voice of the great cities in which we live and move is like the air we breathe—we are only conscious of it when it is withdrawn. The effect was like a sudden asphyxiation. The next moment I heard clearly enough the butt of a rifle, grounding on the pavement below, and the voice of a soldier so distinct in the stillness that he might have been standing at my elbow on the balcony. Then I saw the faint light of a match far down beneath me. I stepped back into my room, and, feeling my way to the door leading into my suite, threw it open and found myself on the great landing of the fourth floor. It was as dark as my room and not less silent. The lift had ceased to run. I groped my way along the interminable corridors until I came to the main staircase. There I saw the faint light of a pocket-

torch like a glow-worm, and encountered the holder of it. His face I
could not see but his torch must have made my own visible to him.
'Schrecklich, Euer Excellenz! und noch mehr Schrecklich!' exclaimed
a familiar voice. It was Herr Wilke. The faithful soul was on his way
to my rooms to inform me that he could no longer attend to my
wants. My bell he had never heard. It had never rung. But he had
been ordered to 'down tools' and had been given five minutes' grace
to tell me as much. The whole staff was being evacuated like the
withdrawal of a garrison. He had pleaded hard, he explained, to be
allowed to stay at his post, but 'Die Gerwerkschaften' were inexorable. 'Die Gewerkschaften!' I recalled the confident prophecy of my
chauffeur that the 'Arbeiterschaft' would have something to say to
the Kappists. The trade unions had now struck and struck heavily.
They had proclaimed a General Strike with the gloves off. No 'essential services' had been exempted. Water, light, power, communications, the very arteries of life, were completely cut off.

There ensued a period of existence which even now, at this distance of time, seems to me like a nightmare. The few remaining
guests in the Adlon fled as though the place were stricken with the
plague. Only myself and one or two other Allied officers were left.
For four days I never had a bath and had to shave myself with soda-
water. Life became more and more disgusting, and had the strike
lasted long there must have been an epidemic. Our existence threatened daily to become ever more like Hobbes's State of Nature—
'nasty, poor, brutish, and short.' We were without light, without
heat, without water, and without food. It was well for us that we
had a small Inter-Allied Officers' Club, supplied by stores from our
canteen, and here we managed to subsist on such tinned goods as the
canteen could, for the time being, provide. But we could not sleep
there, and to get to and from our respective hotels at night was a
ticklish business. The last thing our A.Q.M.G. did, before our telegraphic communications with the outer world broke down, was to
wire to the British forces at Danzig for ten thousand rations to be
sent to Stettin by a destroyer with a view to their dispatch thence to
Berlin by motor-lorry. They never reached us. After a hurried con-
sultation we decided to send all the British officers' wives in Berlin
to a safe refuge at Cologne. There were many wifely protests but
they were packed off that night. It was the last train to run.

the square, playing *Deutschland über alles*. The troops, having done
their bloody business, fell into step behind them. 'The bloodhounds!'
exclaimed a German civilian sheltering in our doorway. 'First they
shoot us down and then they play music.'

This was the prologue to a lethal drama to which the whole city
served for many days as both stage and auditorium. Sometimes one
heard the actors without seeing them, as when a burst of musketry
or the explosion of a bomb echoed from some distant street or quarter of the city. Looking out from the windows of the Bellevue,
forming, as it did, the apex of two converging streets and confronted,
as it was, by the approaches of three others, one never knew whether
the actors would appear from behind us, or in front of us, or to the
right or left of us. It reminded me of nothing so much as the setting
of *Danton* in Reinhardt's production at the Grosses Schauspielhaus
whereat the actors were not only upon the stage but scattered behind
one among the audience, and assisting the spectacle with their
frenetic cries. At times I saw from my window the first scene, missed
the second, and saw the third, as when an armored car, its coming
always heralded by a sinister whistle, crossed my field of vision and
disappeared. The sound of firing would follow and, a few minutes
later, four red cars, the cars of the Police Ambulance, would cross
the square with a loud clang of bells and disappear in the same direction. The drama lost nothing of its horror in that, as in a Greek
tragedy, the murders were committed off the stage.

The entire absence of any sort of resistance to the troops invested
this studied co-operation of the soldiers and ambulance men with a
sinister significance. Clearly the latter had been told to expect a 'kill'
and the battue of the helpless civilians was carefully premeditated.
Where, I reflected, had I encountered this sort of thing before? And
then I suddenly remembered that amazing 'White Book' of 1915,
in which the German Government attempted, with a bold plea of
confession and avoidance, to divert the execration of the world at
the massacre of nearly seven hundred men, women, and children by
the German invaders at Dinant, and other such infamies. 'Success had
to be striven for in every way,' explained the apologists of the
German White Book, but after the one-sided 'strife' was over and
the wounded had been raked out from the dead, 'We gave them

coffee.'[14] The presence of the ambulance men in Berlin suggested the same sinister solicitude. Clearly the temper of German militarism had not changed. There was a strange, a mournful Nemesis in all this. As it was with the invasion of Belgium in 1914, so it was with the occupation of Berlin now. So long as the Revolution had proceeded 'according to plan,' the conduct of the troops had been exemplary. The moment they had encountered a check with the declaration of the General Strike, their commanding officers, unable to defeat the strikers by a frontal attack, 'took it out' of the people at large. Opposition, which cools the blood of the Englishman, always seems to enrage the German. It accounts for the internecine fury of German politics. And as in peace, so in war. Surely it must have been of the German way of looking at things that La Fontaine was thinking in grave irony when he wrote of the 'evil' character of the animal which dares to defend itself when it is attacked. Belgium, having defended itself in the field, was defamed as an evil-minded nation of *franc-tireurs* and the innocent civilians suffered, at the hands of the German firing-parties, a vicarious atonement for the gallantry of the Belgian soldiers whose spirit the German armies had failed to subdue. And so now. The people of Berlin were expiating the opposition of the trade unions. But was it merely the savagery of thwarted troops? Was it not rather an example of that scientific ruthlessness with which the manual of the German General Staff indoctrinates its officers when it urges[15] the necessity of breaking the *Geist*, the spirit, of the civil population by every possible means. The cold collusion of the firing-parties and the ambulance men suggested the scientific co-operation of a surgeon and his 'dressers,' except that there was no anaesthetist.

Clearly the Kappists were getting desperate. There was the specter of the Allied Armies on the Rhine and wild rumors were spreading among the public that this resurgence of German militarism might encounter some hammer-stroke from Marshal Foch. Hence a procla-

[14] The German White Book, Document C (Summary Report–Dinant). See below, Chapter VII, at page 149.

[15] See the Introduction to *Kriegsbrauch im Landkriege*, and Chapter VII, below, at pages 147-8. It is the traditional German doctrine–cf. Clausewitz in his *Vom Kriege*, I, Kap. 1 (2) and V, Kap. 14 (3), where he argues that 'ill-treatment' of the civil population, in order to break 'the spirit' of the enemy, should be 'without limit.'

mation by Herr Kapp that the Revolution had no designs on the
Treaty of Versailles which was to be fulfilled so far as was com-
patible with 'the honor'—*die Ehre*—of the German nation, a significant qualification anticipating in so many words the blandishments
of Herr Hitler just thirteen years later. This ingenuous disavowal
had failed to elicit any response from the Control Commission. We
sat tight and waited. And so it was with the other Proclamation,
designed for domestic consumption, in which Kapp, like General
Monk at the Restoration, had declared for 'a free Parliament' and
announced that the National Assembly was dissolved. The Republic
countered with a summons to the deputies to join the Ministers in
their refuge at Stuttgart, and some two hundred rallied round them.
A 'general election' conducted under the supervision of bayonets
at the polling-booths had no charms for the trade unions on strike.
And when Herr Kapp sought to present the German people with
a rival Cabinet, and began to look round for colleagues, they all
with one consent began to make excuses. All the likely men upon
whom he had counted for success were waiting to see if he would
succeed. Portfolios went a-begging. The Foreign Office was offered
to four men of repute, one after the other, and none of them would
look at it. The Foreign Office staff took leave of absence and the
whole of the bureaucracy in the Wilhelmstrasse refused to take
orders from the new Government. Herr Kapp was taken unawares
and suffered from the improvised character of his *coup d'état*. He
had no concentration camps ready for refractory officials such as
General Goering so thoughtfully prepared for the reception of
'thousands of officials' [16] twelve years later. Then came another
check. The Imperial Bank declined to give Kapp's Administration
credit. Thereupon General Luttwitz ordered one of the *condottieri*
to take ten millions from the Reichsbank by force with the aid of
three armored cars. His shocked subordinate asked to be excused.
He drew the line at such sacrilege, as though he had been asked to
rob a church. It did not occur to Luttwitz to suborn a bank clerk.
Like the priests who volunteered to assassinate Lorenzo de' Medici
at his devotions in church when the professional assassins declined

[16] Goering, *Germany Reborn*, p. 128.

the commission in horror, a bank clerk with political views might
have felt no such compunction.

A kind of creeping paralysis began to overtake the unhappy Kapp.
He was not a man of blood, much less of iron, and the excesses of
the troops no doubt distressed him.[17] The officers could not understand such compunction [18] and came very soon to the conclusion that
this was a cock which would not fight. How many of the Reichswehr generals were principals, and how many accessories, in his conspiracy, whether before or after the fact, no one ever knew. That
stormy petrel Ludendorff was said to be implicated and he certainly
left his card on Herr Kapp.[19] He was presumably doing a little political reconnoitering, for he was careful to pay his call in mufti, with
the disconcerting result that the 'victor of Tannenberg' was challenged by a young sentry, who failed to recognize him, and ordered
him to produce his 'pass.' 'It's Ludendorff! you fool!' whispered an
agitated young lieutenant. But the damage was done. Ludendorff
had no further use for Kapp. As for the generals still on the active
list and holding Reichswehr commands, all of those in Berlin, when
implored by the Minister of Defense, Herr Noske, a few hours before the blow fell to take action against the rebellion, of which Noske
had been warned, declined on the ground that the rebellion was
'bound to be successful.' [20] In the territorial Commands the General
Officers commanding the Reichswehr Divisions declared themselves
neither for the rebellion nor against it, and as a rule, the troops were
confined to barracks. All the generals were in sympathy with Luttwitz's last demand to Noske, before the latter fled to Stuttgart, that
there should be no such reduction in the Army to the Treaty
strength as we were there to enforce. Noske subsequently disclosed
as much. But Luttwitz had undoubtedly offended the other generals

[17] He had, according to one of Ehrhardt's lieutenants, forbidden all resort to
shooting of the civil population—Rudolf Mann's *Mit Ehrhardt durch Deutschland*, p. 189.

[18] When Kapp's *coup d'état* had failed, Ehrhardt's lieutenant, searching for
the causes of its failure, wistfully concluded that if only they had shot a few
more people all would have been well. 'Und doch wäre mit Schiessen zur
rechten Zeit vieles besser geworden'—Rudolf Mann, at p. 189.

[19] Thus Rudolf Mann (p. 164) who was an eyewitness of what followed.

[20] 'Da der Erfolg der Rebellen sicher sei'—Noske in his reminiscences, *Von
Kiel bis Kapp*, at p. 209.

by acting so precipitately and without consulting them, and by the time he sought to concert with them a common plan of action the strike of the trade unions had paralyzed all his communications. It was too late.

On the fourth day an aeroplane appeared over Berlin and dropped counter-revolutionary fly-sheets reminding the people that the Republican Government was still reigning if, like the God of the Deists, not governing. The Kappists replied with a last fly-sheet declaring with most plaintive emphasis that there was only one government—'Es gibt nur eine Regierung'—and exhorting a listless public to beware of imitations. Of these there promised to be many, for Communism was beginning to rear its unlovely head in the industrial suburbs of Berlin. Like Herr Hitler, thirteen years later, Herr Kapp 'reacted' promptly to these manifestations by stigmatizing all the opposition to him, including the Republican Government itself now that it turned a deaf ear to his overtures, as inspired from Moscow. But this 'cut no ice.' It was hitting below the belt and a manifest lie. He found it convenient to ignore, even as Herr Hitler was to ignore, the fact that it was the leaders of the Republican Government, and its backbone the Socialist party, who had saved Germany from Communism in the October Revolution. But that revolution was still too near, and the popular memory of it too fresh in 1920 for Herr Kapp to 'get away' with this defamation of his opponents as Herr Hitler got away with it in 1933. The German public refused to hail him as the saviour of his country from the specter of Bolshevism.

On the fifth day it was clear that the revolution was petering out. The apparition of a civilian motor-car in the Unter den Linden—the first motor-car I had seen for five days without a machine-gun—distributing pale green fly-sheets, was like the return of the dove to the ark. Clearly the waters were subsiding. For the first time in five days I heard the sound of cheering, as the bystanders clutched at the news-sheets as though they were manna in the wilderness. I sent Bailey out to get one. It announced the 'Zusammenbruch der Militärdiktatur.' [21] Soon afterwards the old Imperial flags hoisted by the revolutionaries—a big black cross with an eagle in its center and

[21] 'Collapse of the Military Dictatorship.'

quartered with the iron cross—disappeared from the public buildings
in the Wilhelmstrasse.

But the crowd was to pay dearly a few hours later for its cheering.
As I passed down the Wilhelmstrasse after lunch I saw guns limber-
ing up and teams hooked in. The 'Baltic' troops, after their brief and
inglorious adventure, were preparing to evacuate the city over which
they had lorded it for five days. Their faces were surly and I looked
for trouble. It came. They formed up in the Unter den Linden,
guns in column of route, troops in column of fours. A dense crowd
watched them in silence. A boy laughed. Two soldiers broke out of
the ranks, clubbed him with the butts of their rifles and kicked his
inanimate body as he lay prostrate upon the ground. No one dared
interfere, but the crowd hissed. At that, an officer shouted some
words of command of which only the word 'rücksichtlos' [22] reached
me. The troops opened fire. The crowd was an easy target. The
street suddenly resounded with the 'rat-tat' of machine-guns, the
whistling of bullets, the crack of splintered glass, and the cries and
groans of the wounded. The people ran. The rest lay where they
had fallen. The stricken bodies had a strangely shrunken look. They
seemed like heaps of old clothes. Then came another command—to
cease fire—followed by 'Quick March!' The troops marched out
under the arch of the Brandenburger Thor in the direction of Charlottenburg, some of them occasionally breaking out of the ranks to
run on to the pavement and beat an unoffending civilian, whose
face they did not like, over the head with the tail-end of their
stick-bombs.

Life in the Adlon now resumed its normal course. All the frightened birds came back to roost. Every little dovecote of a room was
once again occupied. The lounge was once more crowded with the
wealth and fashion of Berlin, even more hectic in its gaiety than
before, as if a little hysterical after the strain on its nerves. Once
again the bells rang on the upper floors and the little signal discs
above the bedroom doors importunately flashed their ruby light.
The bookstall, its shutters now reopened, was gay with political
'squibs' wet from the printing-press, deriding Herr Kapp and his
'Kappists' and comparing him to that figure of farce, 'Herr Hauptmann von Koepenick.' The revolution was now stigmatized by the

[22] 'Ruthless,' i.e. 'No quarter.'

mocking Berliners, recovering from their mortal fright, not as a revolution which had nearly succeeded, but as a *putsch* which had ignominiously failed. A *putsch* in German means a political movement which, aiming at a revolution, succeeds in achieving nothing more than a riot. It is a derisive term. Only one man in Germany has ever lived down a *putsch* and survived to accomplish a revolution. It was Herr Hitler, and it took him over nine years. Herr Kapp, the puppet of General von Luttwitz and of the Reichswehr, who, as the black-coated civil servant he was, had served to invest the military *coup d'état* with a spuriously civilian character found himself proscribed. None of the Reichswehr officers intervened to protect him. Perhaps they felt that, like the discomfited conspirators in Machiavelli's immortal story of another *putsch*, the conspiracy against Caesar Borgia, he 'already gave out the odor of a corpse.' In any case, he was only a civilian. He fled incontinently amid the catastrophic laughter of a city which had trembled at his nod.

It was now the turn of the Communists. They had no more use for the Republic than the Kappists except that they were more sincere about it. Kapp and Luttwitz had been aiming at a military dictatorship decently veiled under constitutional forms. But the Communists now openly proclaimed the end of parliaments and constitutions, and called for Soviets, demanding the head of Herr Noske, the Minister of Defense, on a charger. They had never forgiven that stout Social Democrat for his resolute part in their suppression at the time of the October Revolution. The General Strike, which the Republican Government had invoked against the Kappists, now proved to be a Frankenstein whose monstrous features grew larger and uglier every hour. The workmen out in the suburbs of Spandau and Koepenick plundered the arms depots and lay in wait for all who might come against them. I drove out on a tour of inspection to the Alexander Platz, the nerve-center of Eastern Berlin and a point of strategical importance controlling the lines of communication from east to west. But I found it impossible to proceed farther. All the arteries converging on the Platz, except the road along which I had advanced, were blocked with barbed wire as with a pair of forceps. The barbarities of the troops had infuriated the workmen, and any officer or soldier who fell into their hands received short shrift. It went hard with any patrols who found themselves cut off.

The Army Chiefs, General Maercker and General Ofen, had persuaded Luttwitz to 'call off' the revolution and resign his command in the Reichswehr, but the military were still masters of the situation. The Republican Government could do nothing without them, for the General Strike continued. The moderate element among the workmen wanted an industrial charter, the immoderate a 'dictatorship of the proletariat.' The latter element, to wit the Communists, were decidedly a mere minority in comparison with the former, the Socialists, but like all minorities, they were much more vociferous even as they were more honest. They appealed to the workers with a slogan faintly reminiscent of Rousseau: 'You have lost everything but your chains.'

The restored Government collapsed almost as soon as it returned. The Chancellor, Herr Bauer, finding himself unequal to the situation, resigned, and his successor, Herr Müller, was hard put to it to form a Ministry. Then, as later in the history of the Weimar Republic, no man of repute was inclined to accept responsibility. No Minister knew when he might not find the poniard of the assassin in his back, as Scheidemann, Erzberger, and Rathenau were to learn in due course. When his opponents desisted from taking his life, they did their best to take away his character. Not only calculated defamation but savage violence became one of the fine arts of politics. And with that curious habit which Germans have of rationalizing everything, even brutality,[23] it became a cult.[24] As in war, so in peace—opposition seems to provoke the Germans to lethal fury. Not of them can it be said what Carlyle said of himself and a friend: 'We spent a pleasant evening, *except in opinion not disagreeing*.' You must agree to differ before you can differ without being disagreeable. It is just what the Germans, in politics at least, seem quite unable to do. As it was in the days of Tacitus, so it is now. The deliberative assemblies of the early German tribes are gravely recorded by the Latin

[23] See, for example, the manual of the German General Staff (Introduction) where it is argued that 'ruthless severity' in war is 'true humanity.'

[24] See, for example, Dr. Goebbels' Reminiscences wherein, after recording an attack, by the Nazi deputies, in the Prussian Parliament on 28 March 1932, on their opponents (one of whom had made an 'insufferable speech') resulting in eight of the latter being 'seriously wounded,' he concludes blithely and ethically, 'What a lot of *good* a row like that can do!'—*My Part in Germany's Fight*, p. 71.

historian to have settled their debates with a loud shout—'si displicuit sententia, fremitu aspernantur.' What happened to the minority Tacitus has not told us, but presumably they were knocked on the head. The infrequent meetings of Herr Hitler's 'Reichstag,' at which no one spoke except the Führer and the proceedings were summarily concluded, under the watchful eye of General Goering in the chair, with a stentorian cry of 'Heil Hitler,' would appear to be a true reversion to 'Nordic' type.

Weak and uncertain as it was, Herr Müller's Ministry appeared to have given the Reichswehr, assisted by the police, who had mostly maintained an attitude of benevolent neutrality during the Kapp Revolution, a free hand. They took it. Once again we were the eyewitnesses of 'A short way with the civil population' and the German doctrine of 'Frightfulness.' Five days after the collapse of the Kapp Revolution, I saw a cyclist patrol of twelve 'Security Police' enter the Potsdamer Platz, where a handful of civilians were moving about. The Platz had never been, at any time during the troubles, and was not now, a center of disaffection. It was far removed from the quarters which were the strongholds of the Communists. Trafalgar Square was not more respectable—and pacific. The people were at the moment strolling to and fro upon their lawful occasions, regarding the advent of the police patrol with the same indifference as Londoners regard the relief of one policeman on point duty by another. Perhaps their very indifference was their offense. Suddenly the police dismounted, fired an automatic pistol at one of them and brought him down. They then mounted their cycles and forgot to pick up the victim. He lay under a lamp-post with his toes turned up.

A little later in the afternoon the Reichswehr indulged in like pleasantries in front of our headquarters in the Potsdamer Platz. Once again I saw, as I had seen a week earlier, a scurrying of people like frightened rabbits across the Platz. I heard the staccato notes of a machine-gun and the next moment the cause of their frenzied agitation appeared. A motor-lorry emerged in the direction of the Leipzigerstrasse. It was packed with soldiers, all standing up, and I noticed a machine-gun mounted above the cab. The lorry stopped. There was a dead silence. The soldiers lifted down machine-guns and placed them so as to command the Potsdamerstrasse. Bennett, my D.A.A.G. and I, from the angle of our window, watched them curiously. Two of them crouched behind a machine-gun, as though sighting it. Bailey and some of my soldier clerks were leaning out of their windows, in the room next but one to ours in the Budapester-strasse, to get a better view. Their curiosity seemed to annoy one of the German soldiers. He raised a miniatory hand and shouted in a stentorian voice, 'Fenster Zu!' [25]

The effect of those two words on Bennett was electric.

'Damn them!' he vociferated. 'Don't I know those words! The last time I heard them was in Clausthal.'

'Clausthal!' I echoed. 'What do you mean?'

'The Gefangenenlager,' [26] he replied. 'I had three years of it. One day I leaned out of a window to hang out my socks to dry. A sentry promptly fired at me. I got three days' solitary confinement for it. I suppose my punishment was intended to console the sentry for having missed me.'

I did not want our 'other ranks' to be included in the bag of the day's sport. I therefore sent an order to our men to shut their windows. We waited to see what would happen next. But by this time there was not a civilian in the field of fire. They were all flattened in doorways or hiding behind kiosks and lamp-posts. After deliberating for some time, the soldiers took their machine-guns off the tripods, clambered into the lorry and drove off. Sport was apparently poor and the birds were too strong on the wing.

After some four days of this sort of thing, the General Strike came to an end with the Government's acceptance of the 'Nine Points' of the Trade Unions, and the Communist elements among the workmen were left to stew in their own juice. They were ruthlessly suppressed. The Communists were then, as always, no match for the disciplined forces of the Reichswehr and Security Police. Of these forces there were 31,700 quartered in Berlin and its immediate neighborhood, all of them involved in the Kappist plot, either as principals or as accessories, and its frustration had left them in anything but an amiable mood. They were now out for blood. They instituted a house-to-house search for arms in the industrial quarters

[25] 'Shut that window!'
[26] 'Prisoners of War Camp.'

of the city. If they found any, the householder was taken off to the barracks and shot without trial. How many such executions took place no one ever knew. The Communists had aggravated their offensiveness by demanding the punishment of the Reichswehr officers directly implicated in the Kappist revolt. Of such officers there were some seven hundred and fifty, and to demand their punishment was an affront not to be overlooked. The Republican Government could not have granted the demand even if it would. Not a single officer was ever so much as put on trial for treason against the Republic. But the Communists were shot without mercy as a matter of course.

The defeat of the Kapp Putsch was, in fact, the victory of the Reichswehr and its auxiliaries.[27] Henceforth the Weimar Republic was a prisoner in the custody of the Reichswehr, a prisoner let out on parole, it is true, but only on the conditions imposed by the captor. Not without reason did one of Ehrhardt's lieutenants, writing on the morrow of the event, declare, 'We felt ourselves the victors even if, as victors, we evacuated the field of battle.' [28] Ehrhardt's Brigade returned to its camp at Doberitz from its massacre of the people in the Pariser Platz, there to receive a mild reproof from the Commander-in-Chief of the Reichswehr for having allowed themselves to be 'misled' (*missleitet*) by 'political influences,' although the Commander-in-Chief 'recognized' (*anerkannt*), as he was quick to add, that they had been animated by the most 'patriotic' (*vaterländischen*) motives. The Army Order, addressed to them, in which this gentle scolding was conveyed, proceeded:

I recognize the excellent discipline (*die ausgezeichnete Disziplin*) of the Marine Brigade and the troops which accompanied them, and I thank them for having put themselves under me.

[27] An English writer, Mr. R. T. Clark, who has written a judicious and well-informed book on *The Fall of the German Republic,* has gone sadly astray in his estimate of the significance of the Kapp 'Putsch' which he treats as though it were a mere incident, not as an event. He describes it as a movement confined to a single Free Corps from which 'the new Army stood aloof.' As a matter of fact, no less than three Free Corps and all the Reichswehr units in the Berlin District took part in it. He misses entirely its significance in establishing the ascendancy of the Reichswehr. The Kapp 'Putsch' was, in fact, as a distinguished German writer has described it, 'one of the most important episodes in the history of the German Republic'—Konrad Heiden in *Hitler, a Biography* (1936), p. 108.

[28] Rudolf Mann, at p. 201.

This astonishing tribute to the troops whose hands were red with the blood of innocent civilians was signed, 'von Seeckt.'

But the Reichswehr were not content with establishing this prerogative of complete immunity from the course of justice. They wanted exemption from all control by the Civil Power. They got it. Herr Noske, the Minister of Defense, had to go. In a remarkable Memorandum, published a few weeks after the Kapp Putsch,[29] he told a lamentable story of his failure to secure, for the Reichswehr, officers who would faithfully serve the Republic. He could not, he wrote plaintively, find any. Worse than that, those on whom he relied betrayed him. Having heard rumors of the impending *putsch,* he instructed an officer of high rank, von Trotha, to visit the camp of Ehrhardt's Brigade at Doberitz, on the very eve of it, to discover if 'anything unusual' was happening there. The officer returned to report that he had found 'all quiet' (*ganz ruhig*) in the camp and that there was nothing to worry about. Within a few hours the Brigade was marching on Berlin. After it was all over, the unhappy Minister of Defense discovered that von Trotha had played the same trick on him as von Cramon's liaison officers were in the habit of playing on us. Trotha had telephoned to the camp to warn Ehrhardt that Noske was sending some one to inspect them. Even so, Noske was suspicious of Trotha's report from the outset, and the night before the march on Berlin he convened a meeting of the Reichswehr generals at the Ministry of Defense to concert action in order to defend the Republic against the threatened insurrection. All of them with one exception, General Reinhardt, refused on the ground that 'Reichswehr will never shoot at Reichswehr.' [30] It was a momentous utterance, and the course of the Kapp insurrection established the formidable truth of it beyond refutation. Henceforth the Reichswehr was an *imperium in imperio,* a State within a State. Whatever this Praetorian Guard demanded from the Republic it got. We were destined to learn this to our cost and to find that, the more we 'reduced' the Army, the higher the Army Estimates became until the reduction lost all meaning. Whether Noske would or could have exercised any control over the Army in this direction, had he re-

[29] 'Die Kappisten' and 'Der Putsch' published in his Memoirs, *Von Kiel bis Kapp,* pp. 194-211.

[30] 'Reichswehr werde nicht auf Reichswehr schiessen.'—Noske, p. 209.

mained in office, is a matter of speculation. But having dared on more than one occasion to refuse to allow Reichswehr generals to dictate to him, he had to go. His place was taken by a man of straw, Dr. Gessler, a 'Democrat' in place of a Socialist, whose purely ornamental character was to be sufficiently indicated, in due course, by his continuing to hold his sinecure, through every mutation of Governments, for eight years. Ministries rose and fell, parties came and went, coalitions formed and dissolved, but Herr Gessler continued to sit in the Ministry of Defense—*sedet et aeternum sedebit*. After all, he had nothing to do except say 'Yes' to the new Man of Destiny, who now became Commander-in-Chief of the armed forces of Germany. In him we were to meet our match. He will go down to history with another great German soldier, that Scharnhorst who outwitted Napoleon by 'torpedoing' the disarmament clauses imposed on Prussia by the Treaty of Tilsit. And so with the new Commander-in-Chief and the Treaty of Versailles. The name of this new antagonist with whom we were now confronted was General von Seeckt. In the German Army he was known as 'the Sphinx with the eye-glass.' The Sphinx had many secrets in store for us.

Behind him, as the instrument of his policy, von Seeckt had, like a solid phalanx, the indestructible confederacy of the German Officers' Corps. Wherefore, in the next four chapters, we must first deal with that corps and all that it stood for, beginning with a curious encounter of mine with one of them who, although he was, unlike von Seeckt, on the retired list, was typical of all the rest of them.

PART TWO

PART TWO

V. 'AUSSER DIENST'[1]

HIS EXCELLENCY was a homely looking man and elderly, with a rosy, wrinkled face which reminded me of nothing so much as a puckered apple. It was not quite a refined face. The lips were thick, the nose broad and flat, the brow somewhat insignificant. His teeth were strong, almost equine, and he had a jaw of iron. His hands were swollen and shiny with rheumatism. He wore a rough woolen waistcoat. But for a somewhat incongruous frock-coat, his appearance was almost bucolic and suggestive of a Prussian 'Bauer' from the Ostmark. I noticed that the frock-coat was rather shabby, and I felt rather drawn to him at the sight of it. For I too, in the days of my youth, had known the *res angusta domi*. And I knew well enough that many of the paladins of the old Army were having a hard fight for existence on pensions which, with the ever declining value of the mark, were shrinking to almost negligible proportions. Or was that shabby frock-coat merely indicative of the indifference of old age, to which nothing matters very much? But such indifference also has its pathos.

As our host introduced us to each other, his Excellency advanced towards me with outstretched hand. 'Herr General, pray allow me to say what I have long wanted to say to the first British officer I might have the honor to meet. The British Expeditionary Force was the finest Army of its kind that ever took the field in Europe.

I bowed deeply. 'What a *beau geste!*' I reflected. Could anything be more chivalrous? I did not know at the time that this was a formula which his Excellency invariably used whenever he encountered a British officer. And of such encounters there were many. It always acted like a charm. And so with me.

We sat down to lunch. The room was distinguished by a certain massive opulence, a ceiling of panelled oak, panelled walls and a stupendous Swabian sideboard in the baroque style. The table was

[1] *'Ausser Dienst'* is the German equivalent of 'on the retired list.'

sumptuously furnished with Bohemian cut-glass and old silver. We were a party of four—our host, Arnold Rechberg, his Excellency, my staff-officer Francis Norris, and myself. As the meal progressed, his Excellency unbuttoned his waistcoat a little and ate lustily.

'Your Excellency,' I said tentatively, 'do you care to talk about Mons and Le Cateau? I have read your book *Der Marsch auf Paris* with the greatest possible interest, and I should like, if I may, to put one or two questions to you.'

His Excellency beamed upon me. 'Of course (*natürlich*),' he replied.

'Why did you not pursue us after Le Cateau?' I asked, wondering whether the interrogatory was not a little too blunt.

'My cavalry was not equal to it,' he replied. 'Your cavalry were incomparable (*unvergleichlich*). *Unvergleichlich!*' he repeated.

I felt yet more charmed. But his Excellency seemed suddenly to reflect that I might think he acknowledged defeat at the hands of the British and that possibility clearly set a limit to compliments. 'You see,' he proceeded to explain, 'I thought originally that the British were coming from Ostend or Dunkirk, and I extended my right in order to have freedom of movement (*Bewegungsfreiheit*) to deal with them.'

'Then what,' I reflected, 'was your Intelligence Service doing to make a *gaffe* like that?' I did not say this, but he seemed to divine my thoughts.

'You see, Herr General,' he proceeded, 'it was all the fault of von Moltke. He made one mistake after another. Three mistakes, in fact. He tried to direct the campaign from too great a distance. He ought to have made Rheims his headquarters instead of Luxemburg.'

'And the second mistake?'

'He was too slow, too timid, too talkative. No Army Commander is of any use who harangues his staff. I never kept my Corps Commanders more than fifteen minutes. The great thing is to get your orders out to units as soon as possible and always before midnight.'

'And the third?'

'Ah, that was his worst mistake of all. He ruined von Schlieffen's plan. If I had had six more Divisions, I should have won. And I *was* to have had them. Instead of that, he reinforced his left under Prince

Rupprecht and dispersed his strength. His nerves got the better of him.'

'And the battle of the Marne?' I asked. 'It was touch and go with Manoury's army, was it not? You had nearly enveloped his left?' I did not think he had, but I was casting a fly.

His Excellency 'rose' to my cast like a famished trout. 'Yes, certainly. Most certainly. Why! when Hentsch burst in from G.H.Q. with the order for retirement, we simply couldn't understand it. My troops said, "Why have we got to retreat? We've got them!" I had Manoury at my mercy.'

He paused. His face became contorted and the little blue and red stigmata of the veins on his face were suddenly swollen with excitement. 'Ah, if that damned (*verdammter*) Hentsch's motor-car had only broken down and he had arrived six hours later, the war would have been won.'

'Six hours!' I reflected. I remembered an aphorism of Nollet's— 'Many a battle has been won or lost by half an hour.' But instead of saying anything so disturbing, I thought it prudent to change the subject. The charming old gentleman was getting rather explosive and I did not want to see him succumb to a stroke. Although, to be sure, he seemed as hard as iron.

'I hope your Excellency will bring out a second edition of your most admirable book,' I said by way of a sedative. 'You could then make all that clear. You see, so much has been written about the Marne campaign since your book appeared.' And that much, I reflected, showed that the German Army had had a terrible licking by the Allied Armies, not to be explained away by the Jehu-like driving of Colonel Hentsch's chauffeur.

His Excellency eyed me—a little suspiciously, I thought. 'I have not paid any attention to any books about it except those published immediately after the war,' he replied. 'What I have written, I have written. I wanted to show the state of my mind at the time the battle was actually fought. Any arm-chair critic can be wise after the event. When you come out of the Ratshaus [2] it's easy enough to think differently.' And he began to shout again, as Germans always do the moment they become argumentative.

[2] The Council-chamber.

Perhaps our host thought the conversation was getting a little too controversial and his Excellency a little too *schroff*, in other words gruff. He had been watching me as though anxious to see that the right impression was produced. For Rechberg was a born propagandist and very fond of arranging these little Anglo-German *ententes* by way of hospitality. He beckoned imperiously to the butler who now produced coffee, liqueurs, and cigars.

'Mahlzeit!' [3] said Herr Rechberg as he held up his gilded liqueur glass, bowing slightly to me.

'Mahlzeit!' echoed his Excellency, Norris, and I in a chorus.

Our host struck a match, and having lit his cigar, handed the match to me. I lit up and was about to extinguish the match when I observed that his Excellency was holding out his hand to me for it.

I extinguished it none the less and, striking another match, held out its virginal flame to him. 'With us, your Excellency,' I explained, 'it is considered unlucky for more than two persons to light their cigars with one and the same match.

'Ach, so!' exclaimed his Excellency. 'That's curious. Now I remember—let me see, when was it? After Le Cateau, I think—when I and five officers of my staff succeeded in lighting our cigars from one and the same match. One of us had made a bet about it.'

'And after that, you lost the battle of the Marne,' I said to myself. It seemed as good an explanation as the 'damnable' behavior of Colonel Hentsch.

By this time we were all mellow and *gemütlich* [4] under the influence of our host's most admirable cognac. His Excellency became sentimental.

'I was really very popular with the civilian population in Belgium and France,' he said, addressing himself directly to me after a luxurious expiration of aromatic smoke. 'Very popular.'

I don't know whether I have a 'poker-face,' but I must have been very successful in disguising the consternation I felt. After all, I knew a good deal at first hand about the 'popularity' of the German invading armies in France. It had been my mournful duty to follow

---

[3] 'Mahlzeit!' is a kind of grace after meat, a North German form of greeting signifying 'A blessing on your meal!' or less sacramentally, 'Good eating to you!' by way of a digestive.

[4] Genial.

GENERAL HANS VON SEECKT

Reichswehr Von Seeckt is the figure on the right, and is seen, on the occasion of the celebration of his seventieth birthday in 1936, conversing with Field-Marshal von Blomberg

GENERAL VON KLUCK

up their trail through the stricken country and to investigate certain things which I had ever since tried hard to forget. Those things haunted me like a nightmare.

'Yes, very popular,' his Excellency continued, as though encouraged by my silence. 'In the French villages I was called *unser General*.[5] I hadn't bread to give them but I always had my pocket full of sweets—for the children, Herr General. I remember offering a little French girl some chocolate. She took it eagerly, whereupon I said, "Are you willing to take chocolate from a Boche?" And do you know what her father said?'

'What, your Excellency?'

'He said, "Your Excellency, I am thoroughly ashamed of my fellow-countrymen for using such a name as *Boche* about your gallant and kind-hearted troops. Your soldiers are so kind, so kind."'

I suddenly lost all consciousness of my surroundings. 'No,' I thought. 'I can't forget. I can't. Would that I could! They knew no pity and now they know no contrition. If they get the chance, they'll do it again.' For my mind was traveling back, far back, across the vale of years. The luncheon-table appeared to be receding into a mist, his Excellency's honeyed voice seemed fainter and yet more faint, his face farther and farther away. My cigar smoldered in my plate.

I was back in the first winter of the war, driving in a French Army car with a French officer from Crépy-en-Valois to Senlis. As we left Crépy, we entered the forest of Compiègne, a majestic forest of noble beeches which rose tall and straight and gray like the piers of Beauvais Cathedral, their arms meeting overhead in an intricate vaulting through which we saw the winter sun in a sapphire sky. We turned southwest and, keeping to the left bank of the river, skirted the forest. Death, although so near, seemed far away. The countryside was already quick with the promise of life. Faint premonitions of spring appeared; catkins drooped upon the hazels, primroses made patches of sulphur in the woods and one looked for the blackthorn in blossom. Silver birches gleamed against the purple haze of the woodlands. The road ran straight as an arrow. As we neared Senlis, I was struck by the complete absence of all traffic on the roads. No market-carts came and went, neither did any wayfarer appear. Not a wisp of smoke arose from the chimneys above the screen of trees. We passed up a double avenue of elms—just such an avenue as that along which Monsieur Bergeret discussed metaphysics and theology with the Abbé Lantaigne—yet not a soul was to be seen upon the *trottoir*. A brooding silence

[5] Our General.

hung over the little town, a silence so deep as to be almost menacing. As we entered the main street, I encountered a spectacle which froze my heart. As far as the eye could see, along the diminishing perspective of the road, were burned-out homes, houses which once were gay with clematis and wistaria, gardens which had blossomed with the rose. And now all that remained were trampled flower-beds, tangled creepers, blackened walls, calcined rafters, twisted ironwork and fallen masonry. And this was Senlis! Senlis which had been to the Department of the Oise as the apple of its eye, a little town of quality, beautiful as porcelain, fragrant as a rose, and as a rose as sweet. As I looked upon these desecrated homes it seemed to me that the very stones cried out.

In all this desolation we looked in vain for any signs of life. It was not until we sought out the house of a captain of dragoons, a friend of my companion the Comte, that we found a human being in these solitudes. The house was, indeed, a melancholy ruin, but by the gate was a lodge, and in the lodge a concierge. He was a small man and middle-aged, and as he spoke he trembled with a continual agitation of body as though he suffered from some shock. He led us into his little house, the walls of which were blackened as with fire and defaced in many places with the impact of bullets.

And this was his tale: One afternoon early in September 1914—it was the second day of the month, he remembered it because there had been an untimely frost overnight—he heard the crackle of musketry on the outskirts of the town, and a column of German troops in field-gray uniforms appeared in the street. An officer blew a whistle, and, as some of them broke through the gates of the mansion, the concierge fled across the lawn with bullets buzzing about his ears. Shouts of laughter pursued him as he ran. In and out among the elms he doubled like a frightened hare, the bullets zip-zipping against the tree-trunks, till he crawled into a disused culvert and lay their panting and exhausted. From his hiding-place he heard the crash of furniture, more shots, and the loud, ribald laughter of the soldiers. And then the crackle of flame and a smell of smoke. And after that, silence. At dusk he crawled forth from his culvert, trembling, his hands and face all mottled with stinging-nettles and scratched with thistles. He found his master's house a smoldering ruin, and a thick pall of smoke lay over the town of Senlis like a fog. Somewhere a woman shrieked and then was still. About the hour of nine in the evening, the concierge heard voices in disputation outside the lodge-gates, and, as he hid himself among the shrubberies, more men entered, and, being dissatisfied with their work, threw hand-grenades into the mansion and applied a lighted torch to the concierge's humble dwelling. They were very merry and sang lustily. The concierge thought they had been drinking. They sang thus, 'comme ça!' said the concierge as he mournfully hummed a tune, a tune he had never heard before, but which he would remember all his life. I recognized it. It was Luther's hymn: 'Eine feste Burg ist unser Gott.'

Thus had passed the day. Meanwhile the Mayor, Monsieur Odent, 'a good man and greatly beloved,' said the concierge sadly, had been arrested at the Hôtel de Ville. His secretary proposed to call his deputies. 'No, no,' replied the Mayor tranquilly, 'one victim is enough.' He was dragged along the streets to the suburb of Chammont, the headquarters of General von Kluck. Others were dragged with him. His guards buffeted him and spat upon him as he went. They stopped in a field and told him he was to be shot. He asked 'Why?' and was told *'By the order of General von Kluck.'* There had been no fighting at Senlis and the terrified inhabitants, by the orders of Monsieur Odent, had behaved with fearful correctitude, remaining indoors. But the Mayor knew it was useless to argue with his executioners. He paused a moment, and then took his companions in captivity one by one by the hand, embraced them 'with great dignity,' *tres dignement* the concierge told me, handed them his papers, and bade them adieu. Two minutes later he was shot. His body was thrown into a shallow trench with a sprinkling of earth. The concierge had seen it the next day. The feet were protruding.

'Excuse me, sir.' It was Norris, whispering as he nudged my elbow. He had been keeping the conversation going with Rechberg and his Excellency while I had been sunk in the stupor of that tragic reverie, and my long silence had apparently passed unnoticed. I came to with a start.

'What's the matter?' I exclaimed.

'Sorry, sir,' Norris explained in a low voice, 'but you seem to have forgotten the time,' as indeed I had. 'You know you've got an appointment with General Nollet at three o'clock. We ought to be leaving soon.'

I turned to our host and apologized for having been so *distrait.* 'It's your generous hospitality,' I explained. 'I don't usually eat and drink so much in the middle of the day, and it makes me sleepy. What was it you were saying?'

'We were talking about the *Gewerkschaften,*' [6] Rechberg explained. 'They are giving us no end of trouble. Always going on strike since we had this accursed Republic.' Our host was a great industrial magnate and seemed to feel strongly on the subject. But his Excellency appeared to feel even more strongly. Perhaps he had taken too much cognac.

'Well, what are you going to do about it?' I asked languidly. 'After all, your working classes are going through a rather hard time. Many

[6] The Trade Unions.

of them,' I added as I looked at the sumptuous table, 'are none too well-off, now the mark is playing fast and loose with their wages. After all, a strike is their only weapon.'

'*Do about it?*' echoed his Excellency with unaffected surprise at my remark. 'Do about it?' All the soft persuasiveness with which he had cooed like a dove as he spoke of his endearing ways with the French civilians suddenly vanished. He seemed transmuted into another man. It was as though, in encountering an argument, he had encountered an insult. His face became almost livid. He brought his swollen fist down on the table with a bang which set the glasses ringing. 'There's only one way to deal with such fellows,' he shouted. 'Only one way! *Gewalt! Gewalt! Gewalt!*' [7]

And I found myself looking into the blazing eyes of his Excellency General von Kluck.

[7] 'Force! Force! Force!'

VI. THE GERMAN OFFICERS' CORPS

IKE HIS Excellency General von Kluck, thousands of German
officers had now fallen on lean times. But, unlike him, most of
them found themselves retired, or rather threatened with retirement,
in the prime of life. The Treaty of Versailles limited the establishment of the new Army to four thousand officers. The 'peace-strength'
of the old Army which we were called upon to demobilize had mustered at least thirty thousand of them, and another fifteen thousand
were commissioned during the war.[1] Wherefore we were now confronted with some thirty-four thousand [2] resolute hard-bitten men
with a professional grievance. They were to be 'axed.' But they had
not the slightest intention of laying their heads upon the executioner's
block if they could help it. They were determined to defeat our enforcement of the Disarmament clauses of the Treaty if they could. In
this they largely succeeded. From first to last they were our most
formidable antagonists. Thirty-four thousand men among a population of some sixty millions governed by a Republic which had not
only accepted the Treaty of Versailles, however reluctantly, but had
repudiated the Emperor to whom these officers had, each and every
one of them, on the day they were first gazetted sworn an oath of
'unconditional' obedience, would appear to an untutored mind to
constitute a negligible fraction of the nation with whom we now had

---

[1] These numbers refer to regular officers, *aktiv* officers as they were called.
They do not take account of the 'Reserve' officers of the *Beurlaubtenstand* who
were called up on mobilization or commissioned during the war. The number of
regular officers in the year immediately preceding the war was, according to a
German official publication 30,450—*Die deutsche Armee, 1871-1914*, by L. R. von
Collenberg (*Reichsarchiv* publications, No. 4, Berlin, 1922), at p. 108. The number of 'Reserve' officers during the war was no less than 226,130 according to the
figures given by Lieut.-General von Altrock in *Vom Sterben des deutschen Offi-
zierkorps* (Berlin, 1921), at p. 52.

[2] The number of regular officers at the date of the Armistice cannot have been
less than 34,000 as the official figures given by General von Altrock, *op. cit.*, at
p. 60, state that out of 45,923 such officers, 'participants in the war' (*Kriegsteil-
nehmer*), 11,357 'or 24 per cent' were killed in action or died on active service
during the four years 1914-18.

to deal. But they were, even after the catastrophic defeat of the
troops they had commanded, very far from being negligible. They
were, in fact, and continued to be during the whole time the Control
Commission was stationed in Germany, the most potent element in
the community. Indeed, it would be no exaggeration to say that, even
in retirement, they were the only element of any potency in the body
politic. This sounds like a paradox. But the truth of it the present
chapter will establish. The Weimar 'Republic' was itself, as we shall
see in a later chapter [3] a gigantic paradox.

One day, on entering the lounge of the Adlon on my return from
our headquarters in the late afternoon, I noticed an athletically built
man, in the prime of life, sitting before one of the little marble-topped
tables around which, in close proximity as though huddling together
for social warmth, the society of Berlin clustered like a swarm of bees
at that hour of the day. And like hiving bees they seemed to cling to
each other, in a buzz of conversation, for mutual support as they
swarmed in that vast *foyer*, the last refuge of a society in dissolution.
The man wore a monocle, and amid all that gregarious crowd he sat
alone. His seat confronted the revolving doors like a *poste d'observation*, and he scrutinized with a supercilious eye every new-comer
who passed through them, as though waiting for somebody who
never came. There was something about him which at once suggested
to my mind that he was a German officer. It was not merely the
monocle, although I have never known any German except an officer
to wear one. In the Army a monocle was very fashionable, which no
doubt explains why no civilian was ever so presumptuous as to adopt
one. Nor was it the smart cut of his lounge suit, although few Germans except the officer caste seem to know how to dress. It was rather
a certain aloofness amid the civilian crowd as of one who soliloquized,
'What have I to do with all these untouchables?' He sat there like a
dethroned monarch, a *roi en exil*. Thereafter I observed him, always
in the same strategic position at the same hour every afternoon. And
always alone. *Sedet et aeternum sedebit*, I reflected, and not more
happy than Theseus himself. His face wore a perpetual scowl.

One day, a few weeks later, Norris said to me, 'I've got to know a

---

[3] See below, Chapter IX, 'The Scent of Muscovy,' also Chapter XI, 'Germany
in Defeat.'

German flying officer. *Ausser Dienst*, of course. An interesting chap. He was an "ace" in the war. One of Richthofen's squadron, in fact. He's very anxious to be introduced to you. Do you object?'

'Not a bit,' I replied, 'so long as you remain after you've introduced me.' For I always made it a rule never to meet a German officer alone. For this rule, I had, as will duly appear, very good reasons.

That afternoon I returned at my usual hour to the Adlon, accompanied by Norris who, like myself, was billeted in the 'Grand Hotel.' As we entered the lounge, I saw the man with the monocle, alone, as always, and in his accustomed seat. At the sight of Norris he rose with alacrity, his scowl disappeared as though he had wiped it off his face with a sponge, and he was all smiles.

'Good afternoon, Herr Oberst,' he said to Norris. Norris presented him to me. 'Delighted to have the honor to meet you, Herr General,' he exclaimed. Von Kluck himself could not have been more flattering. 'Let's get away from all these lousy civilians,' he exclaimed as he swept the thronged lounge with a devastating eye, the eye of the *Ober-Kommando*, and we adjourned to the smoking-room.

My new acquaintance was Major Hans Steffen. His visiting card, which he presented to me with great solemnity as though it were a votive offering, was inscribed with the words 'Major a.d. der Fliegertruppe.' And we began to talk. I was destined to see a good deal more of Major Steffen during the years that followed and to learn a good deal from him. And still more about him, far more, in fact, than he ever knew that I knew. Every German officer *ausser Dienst* whom we met was watching us and duly reporting everything we said, in these social encounters, to the Reichswehrministerium by way of the freemasonry of the German Officers' Corps and of his regimental mess—for, as I discovered in due course, every regimental mess still met in secret, like the disembodied ghosts of the regiments we demobilized. What these 'retired' officers, who were so forthcoming and so endearing to us, did not know was that, while they were watching us, we were watching them. The French Secret Service, which had an uncanny way of getting to know everything and was always at my disposal, told me all I wanted to know about Major Steffen. He was doing a thriving business in *Schleichhandel*, which is the German name for smuggling. And rather impudent smuggling at that, I thought when I considered his anxiety to be on friendly terms with me. For he was engaged in smuggling arms out of Germany, a noxious form of trade expressly forbidden by those disarmament clauses of the Treaty which we were there to execute. No doubt Steffen had come to the conclusion that it would be useful to him in persuading German armament manufacturers to do a deal with him in this illicit disposal of their stocks if he could claim acquaintance with as many British officers as possible. I have never known a German do anything without a motive—no, not even so much as offering you a drink. It is rarely an altruistic motive. Of course I had to give him my own visiting card in return for his. That is a rule of etiquette on the Continent. And I have no doubt he made use of it in his business.

Now from Steffen, as from every German officer who sought my acquaintance, I learned, and made it my business to learn, everything I could about the caste to which they belonged, and continued, in spite of the dissolution of the old Army, to belong, the German Officers' Corps. That was why I never refused these contacts, although I never sought them. Except in the case of the liaison officers, nearly all the German officers I met, from Ludendorff, Hoffmann and von Kluck down to Major Steffen, were on the retired list. There was a kind of unwritten rule that we British officers should not consort with German serving officers, in other words the officers of the new Reichswehr. It would only have compromised our work of 'control' if we had, and the French officers on the Commission, who never under any circumstances consorted with any German officer at all, retired or not, would, quite rightly, have objected. In the case of the German liaison officers the rule was relaxed. They were, it is true, serving officers but they were officers 'zur Disposition,' supernumerary to the Reichswehr, and either due for retirement or called up from retirement for the special duty of liaison. Whenever I undertook an inspection of a Reichswehr unit in place of our local Control officers, or rather in company with them, which I did when, as frequently happened, they had trouble with the Commanding Officer of the unit or, as also happened but less frequently, they had been mobbed by the men themselves, I was inevitably thrown into close contact with a German liaison officer. He and I traveled in the same car, lunched in the same restaurant, and, if it was a long overnight journey, stayed in the same hotel—sometimes a wayside inn in the

uttermost parts of East Prussia or Suabia—and I always made a point
of inviting him to sit at my table. Under such convivial circumstances, these German officers talked freely, and not always discreetly, especially in the evening when they were in their cups. It
was thus that I learned from Major Wolff, of the 25th Württemberg
Dragoons, of the persistence of the regimental messes of all the regiments of the old Army and, what was even more remarkable, of the
Ehrengerichte, those 'courts of honor' the long arm of whose jurisdiction extended, on occasion, even to the tens of thousands of officers
of the Reserve. And many other things that the Reichswehrministerium never intended me to know. In the performance of this duty my
itinerary covered scores of thousands of miles—across the great inhospitable plains of East Prussia, through the deep limestone defiles
of the Black Forest, over the wooded uplands of Thuringia, the sandy
wastes of Brandenburg, the great *latifundia* of Pomerania, last strong-
hold except East Prussia of the Junkers, the suave undulating country
of Saxony, the hills and plains of Silesia, the miniature States of the
Mecklenbergs, the highlands and lowlands of Bavaria, wherever indeed, a garrison, a depot or one of the recruiting stations of a *Bezirks-
kommando* might happen to be. For the old German Army cast its
shoe very wide. In the course of these long journeys the German
liaison officer and I often beguiled our leisure by discoursing of military manners and customs in our respective countries and I learned
more than I could have discovered from all the German military text-
books that were ever written of what the German Army really was,
its *Geist* [4] as a German would say.

And so with Major 'a.d' Hans Steffen. A little encounter of his with
the 'Security Police' in the streets of Berlin, the story of which he
related to me at our first meeting that afternoon in the smoking-room
of the Hotel Adlon, revealed to me like a flash of light the *Geist* of
the German Officers' Corps, a *Geist* which nothing we could do, and
nothing the new Republic could do, would ever exorcise. I should
explain that the Berlin 'Security Police,' known from the color of
their uniform as the 'Green Police,' was supposed to be a peculiarly
Republican institution. And so it was if the appointment of a Socialist to be its Chief Commissioner, its *Polizei-President*, could make it

---

[4] i.e. the indwelling spirit of an institution.

one. All over Germany the new Republic had been busy in replacing the police presidents, who before its advent had invariably been either retired officers or officers of the 'Reserve,' with civilian Republicans. But the men themselves in the Green Police in Berlin were ex-guardsmen to a man, even as the 'Blue' Police all over Germany were, and always had been, *Kapitulanten*, in other words ex-service men. The German Army set an ineffaceable mark upon such men before it parted with them. Hence the explanation of Major Steffen's strange story, a story which to an Englishman who did not know Germany would appear quite incredible. And this was his tale:

'Yesterday I was walking along the Unter den Linden with my dog, a *Schäferhund*.[5] I had slipped his lead to give him some exercise. Suddenly a policeman stopped me. And do you know what the stupid fellow, *der dummer Kerl*, said to me? He said: "What are you doing with an unmuzzled dog without a lead? Don't you know it is against the Police Regulations?" He said *that* to me, Herr General! I asked him what he meant by stopping a Prussian officer in the street. I was in mufti, of course, but that's no fault of mine. I was naturally extremely angry [*sehr böse*],' added Major Steffen who obviously expected from me a sympathy I did not feel. But I was not so tactless as to say so.

'Quite so, Herr Major,' I said encouragingly.

'Well, when I asked him what he meant by stopping a Prussian officer, he took to his heels. He bolted. I chased him. It was rather a long chase, as I am not as fit as I was. But at last I cornered him in a cul-de-sac. By this time a large crowd had gathered. I was glad of that as I thought it would do those lousy civilians a lot of good to hear what I had to say. I told the policeman what I thought of him. I told him I had a good mind to give him a box on the ear [*eine Ohrfeige*].'

'And did you?' I asked.

'No,' said Steffen reflectively with an air of great magnanimity tempered by some regret. 'No. I let him off. He apologized. The crowd heard him apologize. After all, that was the main thing.'

Steffen's eyes, as he told me his tale, gleamed fiercely, especially

[5] Literally a 'sheep-dog,' but a dog of the breed known in England as an Alsatian.

the right one in which his monocle was fixed. He was obviously moved as, like the Ancient Mariner, he held me 'with his glittering eye.' And like the Ancient Mariner, his 'ghastly tale' had given him 'strange power of speech,' for he was not usually so eloquent. The incident had clearly made a deep impression upon him. Indeed, he told me the tale again on subsequent occasions. No doubt he told it to every one he met, and had already told it to all the comrades of his old flying squadron who, one may be sure, had sworn a solemn collective oath that such a state of things must not be allowed to last. In a way, a very different way, it made a profound impression upon myself, and I told the story in full in my next letter to my friend Thomas Hardy. Hardy was moved in his reply to a historical reminiscence of considerable significance.[6] Steffen's story made a profound impression upon me for the simple reason that I saw at once what we were up against. If a policeman, with all the power of the law behind him, could be thus intimidated, not to say hypnotized, when he was simply doing his duty, by an officer and a retired officer at that, no longer in uniform, what sort of support were we likely to get from the Government, who were the policemen's masters, in enforcing disarmament in the very teeth of the German Officers' Corps? The Ministers of the Republic had been conscripts themselves and the Army had set its mark upon them, as the German Army invariably does upon every man who is 'put through' it. Listening to Steffen's twice-told tale, I suddenly thought of what another German officer, Captain von Schmerling, had told me about Noske. Noske, the Socialist Minister of Defense, a big man with a furtive eye whom we shall meet again, was, or had been, one of the idols of the new Republic. He was a working-man and a trade unionist. During the

[6] Mr. Hardy wrote to me from Max Gate on 12 October as follows: 'I have quite recently been reading a yellow old letter, written from Berlin in June 1815 by a Dorset man whose daughter is a friend of ours, and who lately sent it to me. The writer says what is oddly in keeping with your remarks on the annoyance of Prussian officers. "Buonaparte has rendered Germany completely military; at the inns and post-houses a private Gentleman exacts not half the respect exacted by a soldier. This contempt for those who wear no swords displays itself in no very pleasant shape to travellers. About 3 weeks ago I might have died of damp sheets if my German servant had not taken upon him to assure a brute of a Post-master that I was an English General travelling for my health. . . . I have since girded on a sabre, got a military cap, and let my moustache grow: soldiers now present arms as we pass." '

Revolutionary days, just after the Socialist Provisional Government, with the assistance of the Army, had put down the Communist movement for the establishment of a 'Soviet,' Noske was commissioned by his Cabinet colleagues to wait upon General Maercker and the Army Delegation at Weimar to invite their acceptance of the new Republican Constitution. Von Schmerling, who had been present with the other officers, told me, with evident enjoyment, of an illuminating incident on that fateful occasion when I asked him what sort of speech Noske made. 'Speech?' replied Schmerling, 'Oh, he was eloquent enough, *to begin with*. All these Social Democrats are. It's their trade. Very eloquent and very confident, he was. But the moment the General asked him a question, *he came sharply to attention*. You see, Noske had been a N.C.O.'

It would have required at least a generation to exorcize the demon of Prussian militarism in the body politic. From the top to the bottom the civil service itself had been, and still was, militarized, if not militarist. By a most ingenious system, known as *Zivilversorgung*, the 'Reich' of the Kaisers had enacted, by a whole series of laws, that, in order to induce conscripts, after the expiry of their two years' compulsory service with the colors, to volunteer for a further term of service, any man who served for twelve years should be entitled, as a matter of right, to an appointment in the lower civil service, at the end of that term.[7] Such men were known as *Kapitulanten*. Most of them, before the expiry of their term, became N.C.O.s, and the object of it all was to build up a huge *cadre* of N.C.O.s available for the expansion of the Army, on mobilization, from peace-strength to war-strength. As a result, the whole of the lower civil service in Germany, with the exception of purely clerical or technical posts, was staffed by ex-servicemen, and hard-bitten men at that, men hammered by years of discipline into the Prussian pattern. Hence the obsequiousness with which every German officer, whether still serving or on the retired list, was treated wherever he went. The postman who delivered his letters, the inspector who clipped his railway ticket, the customs official who examined his luggage, the policeman whom *he* accosted, all came sharply to attention whenever they encountered him. If he

---

[7] At the end of his service he received a certificate, entitling him to such employment, known as the *Zivilversorgungschein* which, literally translated, means 'a certificate for civil provision,' i.e. a civil appointment.

was in uniform, no policeman would dare accost him, for reasons which will presently appear. And, as was explained in an earlier chapter,[8] so long as he was on the active list he was never out of uniform—except when he went to bed. It was not only 'bad form,' it was a serious breach of discipline, and punished accordingly, for an 'active' officer to appear anywhere in public except in uniform.[9] Not, indeed, that he ever wanted to do anything of the kind. For what the rods and axes of the lictors were to the Roman magistrate, *submovere turbam*, such was his uniform to the German officer. Every one had to make way for him. If he entered a restaurant, the waiters rushed to serve him first. No wonder Major Steffen found the lounge of the Hotel Adlon in the days of his enforced retirement a 'lousy' place. Doubtless he could never forget the times when he had sat there in uniform, the cynosure of every eye, waited on hand and foot. So, too, if an officer walked along the pavement, every one moved aside. Never, under any circumstances, did he 'queue up' before the box-office of a theatre or the wicket of a booking-office. It was unnecessary. The civilians always made room for him. Indeed, it was extremely dangerous for them to do anything else, for he always carried his sword and, if he was hustled, used it. If he was called as a witness in a civil court—and no court could subpoena him without the leave of his commanding officer—he gave evidence in uniform as a matter of course. If he was a party in the case, the scales of justice were more than likely to be tilted in his favor, for, as often as not, the civil judge was an officer in the Reserve and was nothing if not obsequious. In the higher civil service, including the judiciary, you had, indeed, not much chance of getting very far or climbing very high if you had not done a year as an *Einjährig-Freiwilliger* [10] in some crack regiment and been duly gazetted to a commission in the Reserve. However high his civil appointment, such a one would give

---

[8] See above, Chapter II, 'Reconnaissance,' at p. 33.

[9] Hohenlohe, the Field-Marshal, in his autobiography (*Aus meinem Leben*) says that officers who were hard up and could not afford a seat in the stalls of a theatre sometimes ventured to get into mufti, *im verbotenen burgerlichen Kleide*, in order to get a cheap seat in the pit, but only at the risk of being punished by their C.O. if they were recognized—*Die Königliche Preussische Kriegsakademie*, by Professor von Scharfenort, at p. 188.

[10] A 'one-year volunteer,' a term the significance of which is explained in the next chapter.

pride of place on his visiting card not to his High Court Judgeship, or whatever his appointment might happen to be, but to the superscription 'Leutnant der Reserve' as setting him above the 'swinish herd of civilians' (*Zivilschweine*) a habit which, as an anonymous writer observes, persisted even under the Weimar Republic.[11]

The immunities enjoyed by the German officer invested him with the divinity that doth hedge a king. They were, indeed, nothing less than prerogatives. It is no mere figure of speech to say that, so far as the civil courts were concerned, a German officer on the active list could, like the King, 'do no wrong.' It was, in fact, a rule of German law. To an Englishman accustomed to the legal maxim that a soldier, at any rate in time of peace, 'is only a civilian armed in a particular manner' and, as such, as much subject to the jurisdiction of the civil courts as the civilian himself, such a prostration of a whole people before a military caste as I describe in this chapter may well appear incredible. But in Germany the soldier, whether he were an officer, a N.C.O., or a private, was never subject, even in peace-time, so long as he was serving with the colors, to the civil courts, no matter what offense he might commit. If he committed murder, robbery, rape, or any other felony he was triable only by a military court, in other words by a court-martial. If the accused was an officer, the offense charged murder, and the victim a civilian, it might, and indeed sometimes did happen, that the officer would be 'honorably acquitted' in circumstances where, if the homicidal act had been committed in England, by an English officer, the accused would have been sentenced to death and hung. The German officer had only to plead in such a case that his civilian victim had 'insulted' him and the chances were that he would 'get away with it.' [12] For an officer to insult a

[11] 'Sie betrachteten die Eigenschaft eines Leutnants der Reserve als lebenserfullenden Beruf der sie weit über *Zivilschweine* erhob. Auch in der deutschen Republik von heute ist das noch üblich'—*Die Tragödie Deutschlands*, von einem Deutschen (Stuttgart, 1921), at p. 60.

[12] A terrible illustration of the traditional attitude of German officers towards unarmed and inoffensive civilians was published by the British Foreign Office, and duly reported in *The Times*, early in the last war. A few hours before the outbreak of the war, namely, on 3 August 1914, an English gentleman, old and infirm, Mr. Hadley, who had been residing in Germany, was traveling with his housekeeper, Mrs. Pratley, in one of the last trains to leave Germany for Paris. A German officer, Lieutenant Nicolay, on hearing of his presence on the train, entered his compartment and, in the presence of Mrs. Pratley, shot Mr. Hadley dead with a revolver as he sat helpless in his seat.

civilian was no offense, for, even if the insult was, in the language of English law, 'calculated to provoke a breach of the peace,' the civil courts could neither fine him nor bind him over—he was immune from their jurisdiction. But for a civilian to insult an officer was, according to the German military code, an offense to his uniform which it was the duty of the officer himself to punish by drawing his sword without a moment's hesitation. Wherefore an officer who cut down an unarmed civilian in the street because of an affront, whether real or imaginary, whether provoked by the civilian or by the officer himself, always 'got away with it.' He could neither be arrested by the police nor tried by 'the Civil Power.' He could, of course, be placed under arrest by his commanding officer, who might, or might not, report the matter to the G.O.C. and the latter, in his turn, might then, or might not, convene a court-martial to try him. The consequences of such a trial, for the officer, were never serious. I once discussed this matter with an eminent German lawyer, Dr. Paul Meissner, of whom I saw a good deal in Berlin. Meissner, whom we shall meet again, has achieved the remarkable feat of commencing his public career as confidential secretary to the Socialist President of the Weimar Republic, Herr Ebert, and finishing it off by eventually serving the destroyer of the Republic, to wit Herr Hitler, in the same capacity. Wherefore he is now known among German lawyers as 'Noah,' having survived the Deluge of 1934. His observations about German officers were illuminating. He told me of two cases, typical and within his knowledge, of officers who had cut down unarmed civilians with their swords. They were duly tried by court-martial. The court sentenced each of them to one year's 'fortress detention' (*Festungshaft*) which is a kind of honorable confinement, leaving no blot on the officer's escutcheon. Indeed, the consequences for an officer who *omitted* to cut down a civilian in the case of a scuffle with him were much more serious. If he were in uniform, as he always was, and a drunken civilian bumped into him with impunity, the officer might be tried by a military 'Court of Honor,' an *Ehrengericht*, for not avenging the slight to his uniform by drawing his sword. If the Court found him guilty, it was all up with him. The sentence in such a case was just the reverse of the medieval sentence of outlawry, of *civiliter mortuus*, but it was outlawry none the less, not because he was not returned to civil life but just because he was. Stripped of his commis-

sion, despoiled of all his prerogatives as an officer, deprived of his
right to wear uniform, he was an outcast. The places that had known
him knew him no more. As a soldier he was dead or worse than dead,
for in Germany it is not better to be a living dog than a dead lion.
The only course open to him, if he wished to avoid a lifelong disgrace, was to shoot himself. He usually did.

The new Republican Constitution did, indeed, purport to make
an end of all these prerogatives. The Weimar Constitution not only
abolished the privileged jurisdiction of courts-martial in the case of
offenses at common law committed by serving soldiers, but abolished
courts-martial altogether 'except in time of war' (*Kriegszeit*). In this,
as in so many other directions, the Weimar Constitution, like the Republic which it consecrated, was little better than so much 'hot air.'
These revolutionary changes were more apparent than real. The
Reichswehr officers, to a man, were officers of the old Army, steeped
in its traditions, and they had not the slightest intention of accepting
this attempt at 'demilitarizing' their jurisdiction over the men in the
ranks. When I interrogated them in the course of my inspections of
regimental units, they made no secret of their contempt for the law
purporting to abolish military jurisdiction [13] altogether. So far as the
orderly-room jurisdiction of an officer over his men was concerned,
the Minister of Defense, a civilian, Dr. Gessler, acutely conscious of
his lack of caste, made no attempt to interfere with its exercise. That
exercise frequently, as we shall see,[14] took the form of the officer giving the soldier who was 'crimed' a knock-out blow. It was 'law' all
right from the German officers' point of view, that sort of law for
which the Germans, characteristically, have a word of their own—
'the law of the fist,' *Faustrecht*. A cavalry officer, a *Rittmeister* acting
as liaison officer to our Commission, when discussing with one of my
Control officers the *morale* of the new Reichswehr, made the significant observation: 'When an officer comes on parade, *every man on
the barrack-square should tremble in his shoes.*' Tremble they always
had done in the old Army and tremble no doubt they did in the new.
Frederick the Great had laid down that Prussian soldiers should be
so handled that they should be 'far more terrified of their own officers

[13] Known as the *Gesetz betreffend Aufhebung der Militärgerichtsbarkeit*.
[14] See below, Chapter xi, 'Germany in Defeat.'

than of the enemy.' [15] So they had been ever since and so were they now.[16]

Tradition was, in fact, too strong for the infant Republic. Every one of the seven hundred serving officers who were implicated in the Revolt of the Reichswehr, colloquially known as the Kapp Putsch, had committed treason. Treason is, of course, in German law, as everywhere else, a capital offense, unless the charge is reduced to one of 'treason-felony.' With the abolition of the immunity of officers on the active list from the jurisdiction of the civil courts, these seven hundred officers ought, of course, to have been brought to trial. None of them ever were. But what was even more remarkable was the way officers *on the retired list* 'got away with it' under the Weimar Republic. By a strange paradox they were even more privileged, in fact though not in law, under the Weimar Republic than they were in the days of the Kaiser. Under the Kaiser an officer, when placed on the retired list, ceased as a rule, but not always, to be immune from the jurisdiction of the civil courts. And a retired officer who had conspired against the Kaiser's régime or against one of the Ruling Princes would certainly have got short shrift from the civil courts. But, in case after case of such conspiracies by retired officers against the new Republic, the offenders were either never brought to trial at all or, if they were, got off with a nominal penalty. Judges of the civil courts seemed to be afraid of them, reflecting, perhaps, that, but for the Treaty of Versailles, they, or most of them, would still be on the active list and might be again after we were gone. The climax of this paralysis of the Civil Power before the specter of the mailed fist was reached in the trial which followed on the collapse of Hitler's 'Putsch' in Munich in 1923. Seven retired officers appeared in the dock in company with Adolf Hitler who must have felt that he was now at last moving openly in high society. He had, it is true, been

[15] *Was danken Wir unserem Offizier Korps?* (Berlin, 1919), by General von Freytag-Loringhoven, at p. 12.

[16] As to the brutal treatment of the men in the old Army, see below, Chapter XI, 'Germany in Defeat.' As regards the new post-war Army, the following figures, which I extract from the Berlin periodical, the *Finanzpolitische Korrespondenz* of 25 May 1925, tell their own tale: the number of suicides among the *civilian* population of Germany for the year 1923 was 21 per 100,000, while in the Reichswehr it was more than five times as high, i.e. it was 111, and rose in 1924 to 160.

living for some time, like a lady of easy virtue, under the 'protection' of Ludendorff, but, as is usual in the case of such *liaisons*, not openly. It was certainly the first time that an ex-corporal had found himself sitting on the same bench in a court of law with a regular officer. Among the accused was no less a person than Ludendorff himself. The spectacle was altogether too much for the Public Prosecutor, who completely lost his nerve. The trial became an uproarious farce in which, as an eyewitness observed, 'the accused took the initiative and became the accusers.' Hitler, taking his cue from Ludendorff, shouted everybody down until the court became a bear-garden. The judges seemed paralyzed. It is possible that if Hitler had been tried separately, nothing could have saved him. But with such illustrious company in the dock the result was a foregone conclusion. Ludendorff was acquitted and the ex-corporal, who in the Kaiser's time would have got a long term of penal servitude or more probably a capital sentence, shared with a lieutenant-colonel and other officers the honorable distinction of being sentenced to *Festungshaft. Festungshaft*, as I have previously explained in this chapter, means detention in a fortress. It was, and is, a punishment involving, as German legal writers are at pains to point out, no reflection whatsoever on the delinquent's character. As such, it was generally, though not exclusively, reserved for officers who had committed such a venial offense as killing their man in a duel. I doubt if any corporal, or any ex-corporal, had ever in the whole of German history been so distinguished by the award of such a sentence. The guard-room and the detention-barracks were the place for him, if he was still serving with the colors; if he was not, then the convict's cell. After his sentence to *Festungshaft* in such distinguished company, Hitler's social position was almost, if not quite, assured, however dubious his political future might appear to be. Such a sentence was, as a German writer observed at the time, 'as good as an acquittal.' Perhaps better. Under the Weimar Republic there was only one greater distinction, in the eye of the military caste, than to be acquitted of treason against the Republic. It was to be convicted of it.

In the Reich of the Kaiser, that 'first Reich' as it is sometimes called to distinguish it from the Reich of the Weimar Republic which succeeded it, the German Officers' Corps was like the Praetorian Guard of the later Roman Emperors, in one respect if in no other. It was, in the last resort, the sovereign power. In times of civil disturbance, of which more in a moment, the Kaiser could, by a mere stroke of the pen, invest it with the whole of the Civil authority both judicial and executive, throughout the Reich.[17] A mere Proclamation of what was called *Belagerungs-zustand*, a conception so alien to English ideas of liberty that we have not even a word for it, was sufficient. No court dared question it. Any judge who ventured anything of the kind would have found himself under arrest in no time and his court closed. A subaltern and a file of Grenadiers would have seen to that. What happened, if and when such an intimidating Proclamation was issued, we shall see later on. But even in normal times the German Officers' Corps was the one authority about whose 'imperial,' and indeed imperative, character there could be no doubt. To explain this in detail would involve an excursion into German constitutional law, which God forbid!—in this chapter at any rate. For there never was any form of government so complex and so full of contradictions as the constitution of the First Reich. German jurists wrangled interminably as to its exact juristic character. Was it a Federation or a Confederation? Was it a Union-State (a *Bundesstaat*) or was it merely a union of States (a *Staatenbund*)? Was it one 'legal person' or many? Was it a union of peoples (a *Völkerbund*) or merely a union of Ruling Princes (a *Fürsten-bund*)? And if it *was* a union of peoples, was the resulting union 'a people'? Was there really a German *Volk*, a German people, at all? Or were there only German peoples, the peoples (the *Völker*) of Prussia, Bavaria, Saxony, Württemberg and all the rest of the constituent States? Eminent German jurists reveled in these contradictions with the passion, characteristically German, of a metaphysician involved in the mysteries of the Hegelian dialectic, and nearly came to blows about it. One of them saw in the Reich a mysterious ghostly entity which he called a *Staat an sich*, smacking strongly of that wraith of German metaphysics known as the *Ding an sich*, a term almost as untranslatable into our common-sense English speech as unintelligible to an Englishman. German philosophy is a tortuous, one might even say a tricky, thing. In that respect it is a true reflection of the German mind. But one plain fact emerged from all this riot of speculation about the body politic and

[17] Except Bavaria, which was exempt under the Constitution.

that was the glaring dispersion of political authority. It was, as it were, at once everywhere and nowhere. In their scrambling search, resembling nothing so much as a 'treasure-hunt,' to discover the hiding-place of 'sovereignty' in the Reich, one of these jurists, and by far the most distinguished of them, got as near the mark as any of them when he came to the conclusion that each of the twenty-five German States, 'looked at from below, is a sovereign, while, looked at from above, it is a subject.' [18] Hitler, characteristically, called all this dispersion of authority, alike under the first federal Reich and under the second, 'damned nonsense' (*Unsinn*) and merely an instrument of politicians for their own 'dirty' (*schmutzig*) ends.[19] From the point of view of an aspirant to Dictatorship it was certainly disturbing—unless he happened to be Commander-in-Chief of the Reich, in which case, as we shall see, he could make short shrift of it.

Now the point of this brief excursion into the jungle of German jurisprudence is this: in all this dispersion of civil authority under the federal confederation of the first Reich of the Kaiser, the one great instrument about whose authority there could be no dispute was the Army and its principals the German Officers' Corps. It was an authority at once overwhelming and penetrating, throwing its vast shadow over the whole Reich and intruding into every one of the constituent States from the North Sea to the Bavarian Alps. The German Officers' Corps was the spear-point of Prussian hegemony throughout the Reich. Three of the States, the kingdoms of Bavaria, Saxony, and Württemberg had, indeed, armies of their own and, with them, their own Officers' Corps. The 'contingents' of the remaining twenty-one States were incorporated in the Prussian Army, by a number of conventions entered into by their rulers, and were in consequence identical with it and not only identical but an integral part of it. But by special covenants, or by 'Imperial' legislation, the Military Code of Prussia had been extended to the three kingdoms, in common with every other German State, and their Armies and Army Corps were in their formations, as in their discipline, identical with hers. An officer, on being gazetted to a commission in Saxony,

---

[18] 'Der Gliedstaat ist, nach unten, Herr; nach oben, Untertan,' Laband in *Deutsches Reichsstaatsrecht* (7th edition), vol. i, p. 21.

[19] *Mein Kampf* (135th German edition), at pp. 642-3.

Württemberg, or Bavaria, did indeed bind himself by his military oath, his *Fahneneid*, to be faithful (*getreulich*) to the kingly ruler of his State. But by the same oath he also bound himself to render 'unconditional (*unbedingt*) obedience' to the King of Prussia as 'Kaiser' of the Reich, and there can be no doubt as to which of the two obligations he regarded as superior. It was, as German lawyers were ready to remind him, his duty to the Kaiser. The Imperial Constitution itself reminded him of the fact in so many words.[20] The same oath of unconditional obedience was exacted from all German officers by Hitler in his capacity of *Führer*. Indeed, as if to put the matter beyond doubt, the King of Prussia in his capacity as Kaiser could transfer any officer, 'even against the officer's will' as Laband pointedly puts it, from the armies of the three other kingdoms to his own. Nor could any officer in any one of those three kingdoms be promoted to the rank of general except with the Kaiser's consent. There was therefore no substantial distinction between the Officers' Corps of Prussia and the Officers' Corps of the three kingdoms. Like Aaron's rod, the rod of Prussia swallowed up all conceivable rivals. Moreover, in spite of the strictly territorial distribution of the twenty-five Army Corps and the restriction of regimental recruiting, except in the case of the Prussian Guard, within the territorial limits of each Army Corps Command, the promotion of German officers came to depend more and more on the arm of the service to which the officer belonged and less and less on the regiment to which he had been originally gazetted. As a result, a regiment recruited in Württemberg might be, and sometimes was, commanded by a colonel from Prussia. And so in other German States, with the single exception of Bavaria which had certain coveted privileges peculiar to itself, generically known as *Sonderrechte*. The Germany Army was in the days of the Kaiser, as it was under Hitler, to the body politic as a shirt of steel, flexible indeed but encompassing it like chain-mail.

At any moment the Kaiser might invest this Praetorian Guard with absolute power, a power of life and death, over every human being in Germany. If he once elected to do this, every civil authority, high or low, was bound, at their peril, to render to his officers the same

[20] Cf. Article 64 of the Reich Constitution: 'All German troops are bound to render unconditional obedience to the commands of the Kaiser. This obligation is to be included in the military oath.'

'unconditional obedience' as those officers were already pledged by their military oath to render to him. Germany might be in a state of profound peace with all her neighbors, with never a cloud upon the frontier. But that had nothing to do with it. If the Kaiser chose to think that 'the public security' (*die oeffentliche Sicherheit*) was 'threatened' (*bedroht*) in any part of Germany, even if the 'threat' were nothing more than a street brawl, he could, by Proclamation, declare the whole of the Reich, or any such part of it, to be in 'a state of war' (*Kriegszustand*) or, to be more precise, in 'a state of siege' (*Belagerungszustand*).[21] The question of whether the threat to public security was real or imaginary was, as the learned Laband observes, entirely for the Kaiser 'alone'[22] to decide. The hand that signed the Proclamation was, indeed, the mailed fist. No counter-signature by a Minister was necessary nor indeed would any such intrusion of the Civil Power have been conceivable. It would have been no more conceivable than the counter-signature by a Minister of a Brigade Order to troops in the face of the enemy. The only formality prescribed by the law—it was the law of Prussia—was eloquent of its whole character: the reading of the Proclamation 'must' be accompanied by 'beat of drum or blast of trumpet' (*Trommel-schlag oder Trompetenschall*). From that moment all power passed to the military. Every law, whether a law of the Reich or of one of the constituent States, relating to the liberty of the subject, might be 'suspended' by military decree. The Corps Commanders of the Army Corps Districts were invested, subject always, of course, to the orders of the Kaiser, with absolute power. Any civilian could be tried by court-martial without even the formalities as to court-martial procedure prescribed, in the case of a soldier's trial, by German military law itself. He might be tried, if trial it could be called, by a drumhead court-martial and shot immediately. The scope of the death-penalty was, in some sense, defined by the Prussian law in question, the *Belagerungszustandgesetz*. But, as it rested entirely with the

---

[21] The term used in the Reich Constitution was *Kriegszustand*, but in Prussia, which was 'the spiritual home' of this despotic conception and the law of which was expressly adopted for the purpose by the Reich Constitution, it was called *Belagerungszustand*, a more precise term in that it serves to distinguish such a condition of affairs from 'war' in the international sense. *Belagerungszustand*, literally translated, means 'a state of siege.'

[22] Laband, *op. cit.*, vol. iv, at p. 46.

Army officers to interpret the definition and as no civil court could under any circumstance, either at the time of the 'disturbance' or after it was all over, entertain any proceedings whatsoever to question what the officers had done, they could do exactly what they liked and hang or shoot any man out of hand.

The effect of all this was, as the sober Dr. Laband observes,[23] 'the introduction in all essentials,' whenever the Kaiser might think fit, 'of a military dictatorship.' In other words, there has always been in the background of German law the haunting specter of dictatorship as a legitimate exercise of power. The fact accounts for the readiness with which the German people accepted the dictatorship of Hitler when it came. The whole community had been schooled, or rather drilled, in this conception of supreme authority and knew no other. The fact that during the forty-seven years of the First Reich none of the three Kaisers ever exercised this particular power is immaterial. The material fact is that the power was there and that every one knew it. Indeed, the last of the Kaisers, William the Second, lost no opportunity of reminding them of it. One day in March—it was 28 March —in the year 1901, at the regimental dinner of the 'crack' regiment of the Prussian Guard, the 'Kaiser Alexander Grenadiers,' the Kaiser, in proposing the toast of the regiment, made a speech, reported the next day in every newspaper in Germany, in which he reminded the officers that, if the people of Berlin showed any symptoms of 'impudence' (*Frechheit*), it was the duty of the Guards to deal with them 'at the point of the bayonet.' Indeed, it was not necessary to issue any Proclamation of a 'state of siege' at all if it was merely a question of using the bayonet against civilians. Any officer, down even to a junior subaltern in command of a platoon, could do that if he thought the occasion demanded it, and no civil court could ever call him to account. Reading quite lately the biography, recently published, of a certain German officer with whom I had a good deal to do when I was serving in Berlin, I came across a remarkable passage on this aspect of the matter, and all the more remarkable as the author of the book was himself a highly placed German general, Lieut.-General von Rabenau, the *Chef der Reichsarchiv*, an appointment corresponding,

---

[23] Laband, *op. cit.*, at p. 44. It should be observed that the Weimar Constitution itself, by Article 48, endowed the President of the Republic with similar and even more despotic powers.

more or less, to the Head of the Historical Section of our Committee
of Imperial Defense. Therein General von Rabenau, whose enthusiasm for the subject of his biography falls little short of hero-worship,
tells with much relish a story of his hero when serving as a young
lieutenant in the Alexander Regiment of the Guards. The occasion
was the public lying-in-state of the aged Emperor William I in the
Cathedral of Berlin in the year 1888. Enormous crowds gathered, full
of 'love and loyalty' (*Liebe und Anhänglichkeit*) as the biographer
tells us, to pay their last tribute of respect to their dead Emperor. But
the queue was badly controlled, the barriers gave way and the queue
became a seething mass of people. In London, in such a case, the
police would, of course, have dealt with the crowd and dealt with it
with all that persuasiveness and good temper which invariably char-
acterizes such little encounters in that country. But the scene was
Berlin and a company of the Guards, inevitably, lying in wait near by.
The Company Commander was temporarily absent and the young
lieutenant, taking command, pounced upon the crowd. The sorrow-
ing people, von Rabenau naïvely tells us, meant 'no ill' (*nichts Böses*),
but his hero 'saw immediately that nothing was to be done by kindness' (*mit Güte*). He therefore, without a moment's hesitation, ordered the soldiers to 'fix bayonets' and marched them against the
crowd, who fled panic-stricken in all directions. 'A true soldier!'
soliloquizes von Rabenau by way of comment, adding that never in
the distinguished career which lay ahead of him did that young
Guardsman hesitate to use arms against his own fellow-countrymen
if he thought it the best way. The god of von Rabenau's idolatry, the
young Guardsman who is the hero of his story, was our great antagonist in Berlin, the future General von Seeckt.[24]

The reader will now understand the significance of the military
oath of 'unconditional obedience' in the German Army. In our own
Army there is no such oath nor indeed, for reasons which will presently appear, could there be. An English officer takes no oath at all
on being gazetted to his commission, while the only oath a private
takes on attestation is the ordinary oath of allegiance. In England an
officer's duty of obedience, and equally a soldier's, towards his military superior can never be 'unconditional'—at any rate in peace-time

[24] *Hans von Seeckt*, by Generalleutnant F. von Rabenau (Leipzig, 1938), at
pp. 29-30.

—for the simple reason that it is conditioned by his duty, as a citizen, to obey the law, in other words the common law of the land. If an order is manifestly unlawful at common law, it is not only his right, it is his duty, to disobey it. Hence the maxim of English law already quoted in this chapter—it is a *dictum* of Lord Justice Bowen—that 'a soldier is,' in peace-time, 'only a civilian armed in a particular manner.' In case of a civil disturbance in England a soldier is at common law in exactly the same position as a civilian. 'Red coats or white coats, it makes no difference.' [25] It is the duty of civilians to assist the police when called upon to do so—it is, indeed, a misdemeanor to refuse. But the police themselves can only use such a degree of force as is strictly relative to the degree of force with which they are met. An ordinary riot [26] cannot be suppressed with firearms or indeed any such lethal weapon as a bayonet. If a magistrate calls in the assistance of the military to deal with a disturbance, the officer in charge of the troops is not absolved from the duty of using no more force than is necessary, and if he orders his men to fire on a crowd which is not guilty of felonious violence, he is liable to be indicted for murder before a civil court. Neither the order of his military superior nor the summons of the magistrate will exculpate him. And so even with the men under his command. He and they are, of course, subject to military law, and if they disobey his command or he, in turn, disobeys the command of his military superior he, or they, may be court-martialed for disobedience. Hence the English soldier's dilemma. That dilemma has been put in its sharpest form by an English jurist in the epigram that, in such a case, a soldier is liable 'to be hanged if he obeys an order and to be shot if he does not.' Like most epigrams, it is a little too clever to be true. A soldier is never, under English law, liable to be shot for disobeying a command unless he is 'on active service.' Active service means, as our Army Act is careful to point out, service in 'operations against the enemy.' In England English civilians are not, and never can be, treated as 'enemies' by the military. England is not Prussia. None the less, the position of a British officer, to say nothing of his men, when called out by the Civil Power to assist in

[25] The case of the *King* v. *Gilliam*, reported in the Appendix to Clode's *Military Forces of the Crown*.

[26] i.e. a riot not accompanied by the commission of any felony or not coming within the terms of the Riot Act.

suppressing a disturbance, is a difficult one and there is no duty that a British officer dislikes more. The King's Regulations remind him, in almost so many words, that in such an event, a very rare event in our country, he had better 'mind his step.' If he does not, he may find himself in the dock on an indictment for murder or, more probably, for manslaughter.

In the German Army the officers were never troubled by any such dilemma. The 'unconditional obedience' they swore to their military superior had 'no legal limits.' [27] They were thus, in the most literal sense of the phrase, a law unto themselves and they behaved accordingly. Their men, who had had to take a similar oath on being conscripted, knew it and they, in their turn, behaved accordingly. 'Take a Prussian,' said a distinguished German scholar to my friend, the late Sir Frederick Pollock to whom I owe the story, 'and put him into a blue coat with red facings and tell him to shoot his grandmother, and he will shoot his grandmother.' No German soldier ever dreamed of disobeying the order of an officer to fire upon a crowd, be the crowd never so peaceful. He knew quite well that he would get five years' penal servitude in a military prison if he did not. But by the time he was court-martialed for his act of disobedience he would, in all probability, have become quite indifferent to what happened to him. He would have been so knocked about by his N.C.O., while under arrest and awaiting trial, that he would probably have preferred death to penal servitude. Arrest itself, even as a minor punishment for something much less serious than disobeying the command of his superior, could be a very intimidating thing, calculated to break the nerve of any German recruit who was sentenced to it. Such was 'close arrest,' *strenger Arrest*, as it is called, a punishment reserved for refractory recruits—it can never be inflicted on a N.C.O. The man who was sentenced to it was confined in a cell in impenetrable darkness, *complètement privée de lumière* as the writers of a French military text-book on the German Army put it, and his diet was bread and water. This punishment might last for four weeks. It was apt to have, as the French text-book dryly remarks, 'a very debilitating effect' on the nerves of the unhappy man subjected to it. Which, no doubt, is why the Gestapo applied it to the

[27] *Keine rechtliche Grenzen*—thus Laband, *op. cit.*, vol. iv, at p. 157.

most distinguished of Norway's citizens.[28] But brutal though such punishments, licensed by the Army Penal Code itself, were, they were as nothing to the unlicensed brutalities of the N.C.O.s who had an absolutely free hand in ill-treating the men, as has already been remarked in an earlier chapter of this book. At all costs the Army must be taught, as a German military periodical of recent date insisted, that war demands 'the highest brutality.' [29] Wherefore the German military hierarchy decided that if you want your men to be brutes in war, you must brutalize them in time of peace. The policy was successful. In this savage treatment of the men the officers were content, as a rule, to leave it to the N.C.O.s—except in the orderly-room. There the commanding officer would himself, as a German liaison officer, Major Wolff, naïvely explained to me, give a delinquent a knock-out blow with the utmost correctitude.[30] But a soldier never knew when an officer might not lay his hands on him. If the officer was in a temper, anything might happen to him at any moment. When serving in France in the first year of the last war, I was lunching one day, together with a French officer, at the inn at La Ferté sous Jouarre, a pleasant little town on the banks of the Marne which had been in the occupation of the German troops before the great battle which was the turning-point of the war. The landlord's wife, who waited on us, had many stories to tell of the German occupation, but one incident, of which she was an eyewitness, had left an ineffaceable impression on her mind. It was the treatment meted out by a German cavalry officer, a certain von Bülow, who was quartered at the inn, to one of his own men. The soldier had been ordered to hang up a lantern outside the officer's quarters, and had been either slow or forgetful. Bülow knocked him down, and then, as he lay prostrate, jumped upon him, kicked him, and finally beat him about the head and face, alternately, with saber

[28] The punishment is to be found in the Army Penal Code, the *Militärstrafgesetzbuch* (sections 24 and 25) itself. In *The Times* of 21 January 1942 will be found a report from Stockholm describing its infliction, in a concentration camp in Norway, on the venerable Rector of Oslo University and the fears expressed by the Swedish Press that the Rector's mind 'will break down in consequence.' In this brutality, as in every other, the Gestapo and the German Army are indistinguishable from one another.

[29] Thus the *Deutsche Wehr* of August 1936.

[30] See Wolff's remarks below in Chapter XI, 'Germany in Defeat.'

and riding-whip. 'The soldier lay quite still,' Madame told us, 'and never uttered a word—*pas un mot!*' She shuddered at the recollection —'*c'était épouvantable, Messieurs.*'

Such was the character, such the temper, of the German Officers' Corps. Ludendorff in no way exaggerated when, in his *Reminiscences* he described the Corps as constituting 'in the last resort the pillars of authority' in Germany. I have said, and in due course I will show, that it was the Officers' Corps who were responsible for the defeat of our attempts to enforce the Disarmament Clauses of the Treaty. For a year or two after the Revolt of the Reichswehr in March 1920, they were more or less unobtrusive, though by no means inactive, in their opposition to our 'Control.' They relied, not without reason, on the prospect of General von Seeckt, in collusion with Herr Gessler, the Minister of Defense, wearing us down by a policy of continuous evasion of our demands until British Ministers and a certain British Ambassador would turn a deaf ear to all our reports, convinced that either Germany was disarmed or, if she was not, never could be. Neither proposition was true. But with the growing tension between the British and French Governments, divided and, as regards the issue of German disarmament, distracted, as they were, by differences of policy on a multitude of other issues elsewhere such as Syria, Russia, the Near East, to say nothing of Reparations, the German Officers' Corps became more and more confident, not to say audacious. Their opposition ceased to be unobtrusive. One day, in March 1924, they boldly threw off the mask and came out into the open. They issued a manifesto, the audacity of which, or, if the reader prefers it, the impudence may be measured by the fact that the Treaty expressly forbade them to do anything of the kind.[31] On 12 March 1924 the following appeared under the heading 'Against the Control Insult' (*Gegen die Kontrollschmach*) in *Der Tag* and all the Nationalist newspapers in Germany.

The National Union of German Officers, the German Officers' League, the Naval Officers' Union take the strongest exception to the latest Note of the Ambassadors' Conference in Paris. Our Associations demand of the Government of the German Reich that the Note be decisively rejected.

[31] Societies of discharged soldiers and, generally speaking, associations of every description, whatever be the age of their members, must not occupy themselves with any military matters'—Article 177 of the Treaty of Versailles.

The unanimous shout of the German people must ring in the ears of the foreigner: 'Out with all these Control Commissions! Clear them out of Germany!'

Well might General von Seeckt, when, nine years later on the eve of Germany's repudiation of the Treaty, he himself threw off the mask and avowed that his consistent policy had been 'to neutralize the poison' (*das Gift*) [32] contained in its Articles of Disarmament, declare that, in fashioning the Reichswehr into the instrument of Germany's military revival, he owed everything to the German Officers' Corps.[33] The explanation of his success, he tells us with engaging frankness, was that the Officers' Corps 'survived' (*überdauert*) the war and all that followed it. And so, as will presently appear, we were destined to find to our cost.

[32] *Die Reichswehr*, by Generaloberst a.d. Hans von Seeckt (Leipzig, 1933), at p. 30.
[33] *Ibid.*, at p. 16.

VII. THE GERMAN OFFICERS' CORPS
(*continued*)

THE SEMI-FEUDAL PREROGATIVES with which the Officers' Corps was thus endowed were not more remarkable and, in this modern age of ours, more unique than its constitution. It was, it is, the most exclusive corporation in the world, and resembles in its exclusiveness or *Abgeschlossenheit*, as German military writers proudly call it, nothing so much as a medieval Order of Knighthood without its chivalry. Clausewitz described it as 'a kind of guild' (*eine Art von Innung*) with 'its own laws, ordinances, and customs,' and no description could be more apt. For, like the guilds of the Middle Ages, one of its most cherished privileges was the inexorable right to reject any candidate for admission to it, whatever his qualifications, of whom it did not approve. No Jew, no young man of 'Liberal' views, still less of 'Socialist' convictions, could ever hope to obtain a commission. Least of all could a conscript who had served in the ranks. In the German Army a 'ranker' was quite unknown, even in wartime. A 'Labour' member of the Opposition in our House of Lords, in a now notorious article attacking the officers of the British Army in the columns of an American magazine a few years ago, and accusing them of being a snobbish caste, invited his readers to admire the superiority of the German Army as 'a People's Army' in which such 'caste prejudice' was quite unknown. 'If Rommel,' he declared, 'had been born in England, he would still be a sergeant-major, indeed he would probably now be a retired sergeant, perhaps keeping a country inn.' A more fatuous, a more ignorant, statement has never been made to the world, even by an unemployed politician. Rommel never was a sergeant-major. If he had been, he would never have been commissioned. The Field-Marshal of World War II could never have hoped to be gazetted at all, even as a second-lieutenant. Compared with the German Army, the British Army is the most democratic, certainly the most liberal-minded, in the world,[1] even as it is the most humane. In Germany no youth could aspire to a commission unless he was either the son of an officer or the nominee of one, and even when he had gone through all the stages of his novitate as a cadet, including admission to a Cadet School or a 'War School' (*Kriegschule*), or both, and had passed his Officers' Examination with or without distinction, he still had to run the gauntlet of 'election' by the German Officers' Corps when his name was submitted, as it had to be, to the officers of his prospective regiment. If, after all his years of military education, those officers, assembled in the Mess in secret conclave like the committee of a very exclusive London club, decided to 'black-ball' him, he had to choose another and a civil vocation. The Supreme War Lord himself, the Kaiser, could not, or dared not, put his signature to the document, the *Patent* as it was called, granting a cadet or a *Fahnenjunker* [2] his commission unless the Officers' Corps had first decided to admit him. As we shall see later, the same rule persisted in the Reichswehr, and in all probability will persist. The officers took good care never to elect any youth of whom they were not quite certain that he was thoroughly 'broken in,' *dressiert*, as General Freytag-Loringhoven puts it,[3] to their own caste prejudices, their *Kastengeist*, as the German military writers, not without pride, call it. The officers had already, as we shall see in a moment, had abundant opportunities of keeping the youth under observation with a view to making sure of that.

There were only two ways of entering the German Army as a prospective officer. One was admission to a Cadet School. The other was nomination by the Commanding Officer of a regiment as a 'volunteer,' as distinct from a conscript, who served for a few weeks in

---

[1] In the British Army a Chief of the Imperial General Staff, the late Field-Marshal Sir William Robertson, a Deputy Chief, General Nye, a famous Divisional G.O.C., the late Hector Macdonald, were all promoted from the ranks after having served for years as an ordinary trooper or private. Of the German Army one of its officers has written: 'The well-known saying: "Every private carries a Marshal's baton in his knapsack"—never held good of our army in the Great War'—*Das alte Heer*, at p. 49. So also Franz Endres in *Reichswehr und Demokratie* (Leipzig, 1919), where the writer says (pp. 36 and 39) the German Army 'never was a People's Army (*Volksheer*),' adding that no man who was a Social Democrat could hope to be an officer.

[2] The meaning of this term, *Fahnenjunker*, is explained below.

[3] *Was danken wir unserem Offizier-Korps?* (Berlin, 1919), at p. 49.

the ranks but in a category peculiar to him and his kind, for he was soon given his own quarters and from the first sat at meat in the Officers' Mess. Such a one was known not as a 'cadet' but as a *Fahnenjunker* or *Avantageur* or, more colloquially, as an 'Aspirant,' aspiring to be, in the fullness of time and by the grace of God and the Officers' Corps, an officer. Socially, the cadets and the *Fahnenjunkers* belonged to the same class, except that a cadet was, more often than not, the son of an officer. As such, his education cost, and was meant to cost, his parents next to nothing, for the fees at Gross Lichterfelde, the Central Cadet School or *Haupt-Kadetten-Anstalt* as it was called, were only £37 a year, and even that payment was sometimes dispensed with. The cadet, unlike the *Fahnenjunker*, whose age of nomination was usually seventeen or eighteen, was 'caught young.' He entered a Cadet Preparatory School at the age of ten, was immediately put into military uniform, enrolled in a 'company' instead of a class, his 'house-master' was a Major and his teachers were officers holding the rank of Captain. He was drilled from his rising up to his lying down, he paraded for meals, he fell on his knees in the morning at the order 'Attention! Pray!' and closed his eyes at night at the order, shouted by the officer on duty, 'Attention! Go to sleep!' The first thing the infant cadet was taught, on his day of entry, was that all civilians were 'swine,' or, to be more precise, 'pig-dogs' (*Schweine-hunde*).[4] It is not surprising that the officers who had entered the Army by way of these Cadet Schools were notoriously even more arrogant than the rest of their kind. At the age of fifteen, the cadet was transferred from his preparatory Cadet School to the Central Cadet School, the curriculum of which corresponded to that of a civilian semi-classical school (a *Real Gymnasium*). After reaching the Upper Fifth Form in the Central Cadet School, he was, as a rule, posted to a regiment as a 'brevet ensign,' or *Fahnrich characktisiert*,[5] in other words, as an N.C.O. of a special

---

[4] Thus *Das alte Heer, von einem Stabsoffizier* (Charlottenburg, 1920), at p. 2. As to the German officers' attitude towards civilians, see further, Chapter XI, below.

[5] The term 'ensign' which is sometimes used in English about the German Army, is really a very misleading translation of the German word *Fahnrich*. An 'ensign' in the British Army was a second lieutenant; a *Fahnrich* is an N.C.O., ranking immediately after a *Vize-Feldwebel* (a Vice-Sergeant-Major), but, as explained above, a privileged N.C.O. in a social class by himself.

KRUPP'S—COMMENCEMENT OF DESTRUCTION OF SHELL-PRESSING PLANT BY THE
CONTROL COMMISSION

THE LATE FIELD-MARSHAL SIR JOHN DILL

category, dining in the Officers' Mess and occupying quarters of his own instead of sharing a barrack-room dormitory with the men. After six months with the regiment, he proceeded to a 'War School,' sat for his 'officers' examination,' and, on passing it, returned to the regiment as a full-fledged *Fahnrich*, to await election by the Officers' Corps before being commissioned.

The *Fahnenjunker*, as distinct from the cadet, was a 'public schoolboy' who, having either reached the Sixth Form or passed a special examination conducted by the military authorities, presented himself, at the age of seventeen or eighteen, to the Commanding Officer of a regiment with a view to acceptance as an 'aspirant officer.' If, and only if, the Colonel was satisfied that his birth, antecedents, and social position were such as to make him desirable as an officer and that his parents could make him a satisfactory 'allowance,' the Colonel might, or might not, accept him. Without the Colonel's nomination he had no chance. If he was lucky enough to secure it, he joined 'the other ranks' for a few months, not, like the favored cadets, as a privileged N.C.O. of the *Fahnrich* category, but as a private, in the first instance, drilling on the barrack-square, doing a musketry course, and all the rest of it. But he soon got his stripe as a corporal and his own quarters, while from the day of his joining up he was admitted to the Officers' Mess. In due course he proceeded to a War School, sat for his officers' examination, and returned to the regiment for a short period to await the ordeal of election. In the mess his 'table manners' were closely watched. The principal test was a capacity to get as drunk as was humanly, or bestially, possible, and 'Woe to the *Fahnrich!*' (*Wehe dem Fahnrich!*) as a German officer puts it,[6] or to the *Fahnenjunker*, if he failed to pass it. A German cadet or *Fahnenjunker* of ascetic habits who, like our own General Montgomery, forswore alcohol would

[6] *Das alte Heer*, at p. 125. The testimony of German writers, themselves officers, is almost unanimous on this point, e.g. the author of *Das alte Heer*, also Halkett in *Dear Monster*, at p. 78, where he says that initiation into the Mess required of the candidate 'the utmost limit of drunkenness'; also General Gleich in *Die alte Armee*, at p. 58, where he deplores what he calls 'the wholesale alcoholism' of the Officers' Messes and its debasing effects. Freytag-Loringhoven's attitude to the subject is curious; after arguing that drunkenness in the Mess was only 'occasional' (*gelegentlich*), he proceeds to say that 'Lemonade Lieutenants' could never have achieved the mighty deeds done by German officers in the War (*op. cit.*), p. 72.

most certainly have been 'blackballed' by the Officers' Corps when he came up for election. The governing idea of this sottish drinking seems to have been to 'harden' the aspirant for a commission. The most essential quality in an officer, von Seeckt once wrote, is 'to be hard' (*hart zu sein*), and to the German military mind 'hardness' is impossible without brutality. This, presumably, is also the explanation of what, according to the author of *Das alte Heer*, happened 'under the eyes' (*unter den Augen*) of the Officer-Instructors at Gross Lichterfelde. There, we are told by a German officer who had been through it, the senior cadets practised 'orgies' (*Orgien*) of torture on the junior boys, 'sticking them with knives and needles,' sewing their trouser-buttons into their flesh, tying the victim up for hours in a kind of improvised pillory with his limbs extended until he 'collapsed' (*zusammenbrach*),[7] and numerous other malpractices equally ingenious in their cruelty. Even when he had joined his regiment, on probation as a *Fahnrich* or a *Fahnenjunker*, the aspirant to a commission, although by that time at least seventeen or eighteen years of age, might be exposed to physical violence from the officers until he was actually commissioned, after which he was, of course, as immune as one of the Lord's anointed. Major Wolff, of the 25th Württemberg Dragoons, told me that the Captain (the *Rittmeister*) in his regiment had a playful habit of whipping the *Fahnrichs* all round the riding-school with a long riding-whip. 'I was covered with bruises for weeks afterwards,' he added. He spoke of it without a trace of resentment. No doubt he thought it a necessary part of a cadet's military education, and had practised this form of tuition himself when his turn came.

The Officers' Corps had a long arm. It not only controlled admission to its own order, but even admission to the Reserve, in other words, the choice of Reserve officers. The 'Reserve' of the German Army, so far as its officers were concerned, resembled, in some respects, our Territorial Force, but the analogy only holds good up to a certain point. Its officers, like our own Territorial officers, were not actually officers by profession, they were only called up on mobilization, and, for most purposes, they were in the

---

[7] *Das alte Heer*, at p. 3, where the writer describes in detail these and other sadistic practices.

eye of the law civilians, without the peculiar prerogatives attaching to the regular or *aktiv* officer. The rank and file of the Reserve were always ex-conscripts who, after their two-year term with the colors, passed into the Reserve and then, after five years therein, into the *Landwehr*, a force which at one time in German history stood in much the same relation to the standing army as the old Militia occupied in our own country. The officers of the Reserve had also served in the Army, but not as conscripts. If a German youth wished to be a Reserve officer he volunteered to serve as a 'one-year volunteer' (*Einjährig-Freiwilliger*). Such service was neither a right nor an obligation. It was a privilege. Instead of being conscripted at the age of twenty to serve for two years, the volunteer served for only one and joined up at the age of seventeen or eighteen. A certificate that the aspirant had reached the Upper Fifth Form in a public school, or its equivalent, was indispensable. But before he could be accepted, he had to present himself to the Commanding Officer of a regiment, who was of course invariably a regular officer, and satisfy him that he was socially desirable and, in particular, that his parents were in a position to pay for his board, lodging, uniform, and equipment during his year with the colors. For the one-year volunteer, although a 'private,' lived out of barracks in lodgings and at his own expense. The whole object of the institution of these volunteers was to provide officers for the Reserve and, like the cadets and the *Fahnenjunkers*, these young men were therefore admitted, from the day they joined up, to membership of the Officers' Mess, and for the same reason, namely, in order that they might be under the observation of the Officers' Corps. If, at the end of their year with the colors, the C.O. reported on them favorably and they passed a qualifying examination, they returned home as N.C.O.s and 'aspirant officers' until, at the end of two years, their names came up for a commission as a Second Lieutenant in the Reserve. Then, as in the case of an aspirant to a 'regular' commission, they had to run the gauntlet of election—election not, indeed, by regular officers but by the Corps of Reserve Officers of all arms residing in the same recruiting district, the *Landwehr Bezirk*, as themselves. But the scrutiny to which their claims were subjected was as strict, as jealous, and as intolerant of any civilian heresy in the candidate, as the scrutiny which the regular Officers' Corps brought

to bear on those who sought admission to its freemasonry. This because the Commandant of the *Bezirk* was always a regular officer,
and so were the senior officers 'detached' from the Standing Army
to hold commands in the Reserve (a Reserve officer in peace-time
rarely got beyond the rank of Lieutenant), and their influence in
such elections was immense if not decisive. Moreover, the Reserve
officers were, in their way, more snobbish, even as they were more
self-conscious, than the regular officers themselves. They had little
hope of being given a 'regular' commission, for such transfers were
not encouraged. Wherefore their only ambition was so to ape a
regular officer, the god of their idolatry, as to be mistaken for one.
Their 'naïve reverence' for the regular officers made them in this
respect, a German officer tells us, 'more Catholic than the Pope.' [8]
The 34,000 regular officers who constituted the German Officers'
Corps in 1919 thus acted and reacted on the spirit of all the Reserve
officers in Germany, who at that date numbered over 200,000, in-
fecting them with their own *Kastengeist*, their caste-spirit. The Officers' Corps was even as that 'little leaven' of the Scriptures which
'leaveneth the whole lump.'

The war of 1914-18, so far from enlarging the outlook of the
German Officers' Corps, actually narrowed it. The intrepid behavior
of the men in the ranks in that great ordeal of fire raised, as was
to be expected, the question of the promotion to officer's rank of
men who had distinguished themselves in the face of the enemy. It
was raised only to be negatived. The Officers' Corps would not
hear of it. A concession, more apparent than real, to popular sentiment was made by an Army Order that a sergeant-major (a *Feldwebel*) who had exceptionally distinguished himself under fire, might
be 'promoted' to the rank of 'Sergeant-Major-Lieutenant' or, in the
alternative, to that of a 'Deputy Officer' (*Offizier-Stellvertreter*),
titles which tell their own tale. It was, in fact, as General Schwarte
bluntly admits, 'no promotion.' [9] They were only 'acting' officers,
and at the end of the war reverted, in every case, to their original

---

[8] *Das alte Heer*, at p. 43. Hence the exclusion of Jews extended even to commissions as Reserve officers. With the suspension of 'elections' during the War,
Jews could no longer be excluded, and quite a number were commissioned, but
never as regular officers.

[9] 'Kleine Beförderung'—General Wrisberg in *Der Grosse Krieg*, Vol. 1 (*Die
Organisationen der Kriegführung*), at p. 34.

rank of N.C.O. or private. Even so, the number 'promoted' was very small, and the conditions which had to be satisfied before the 'promotion' was granted were so exacting as to be satirically described in German Socialist newspapers as 'nothing less than the capture of a live enemy General in single combat.' [10] 'After all,' said the Emperor's Military Cabinet, 'what on earth should we do with these fellows in peace-time if we really made officers of them?' [11] From the point of view of the German Officers' Corps a 'ranker' would have been 'untouchable' and, even as a leper, unclean.

The reader will now, I think, have no difficulty in understanding what I mean when I say that the German Officers' Corps has blighted like a pest every green shoot of modern thought and progress that might otherwise have taken root in Germany. It is like that exclusive oligarchy, the Venetian Senate of the seventeenth century, of which Harrington wrote that 'always changing, it is for ever the same.' Officers came and went, were placed on half-pay, or on the retired list, or went the way of all flesh, but the Corps itself invariably remained exactly what it had always been. Its ethical character never changed, its rules of conduct were never altered. The great humanitarian movements of the nineteenth century, in particular the humanization of the laws of war, the growth of international law, the development of a 'social conscience' and all that is meant by the word civilization, left the moral standards of the Officers' Corps as primitive and as ruthless as they were in the days of Frederick the Great and indeed of Attila. From all liberal and progressive movements, such as they were, within Germany itself it was equally estranged, and to them it was equally hostile. Examples of its 'successful' resistance to 'the inner development of our people' (*die innere Entwicklung unseres Volkes*), writes one of its apologists, General von Rabenau, in a remarkable panegyric, 'are innumerable,' [12] adding, not without pride, that 'throughout the nineteenth century, and in particular in the last quarter of that century, it shut itself off [*sich abschloss*] more and more from the outer world [*die Aussenwelt*].' [13] The somber significance of this admission will be more apparent

[10] Quoted by General Wrisberg in *Heer und Heimat* (Leipzig, 1921), at p. 200.

[11] *Das alte Heer*, at p. 47.

[12] Rabenau in *Hans von Seeckt*, at p. 62.

[13] *Ibid.*, at p. 28.

when we come to consider the sinister attitude of the Corps to the laws of war formulated by the 'outer world' in The Hague Conventions. 'Of course,' adds von Rabenau cheerfully, the Officers' Corps was 'an absolutist survival in a State changing over from Constitutionalism to Parliamentarism.' As such the Corps might well be called 'an anachronism' (*ein Anachronismus*), he concludes, 'and a good thing too both for the Army and the People.' [14] He instances among the many admirable achievements of the 'anachronism' its success in maintaining the immunity of the Army from Parliamentary control. Successful in this direction it certainly was, not only before the Revolution of 1918, *but after it*. The Chief of the General Staff, from the time of the elder von Moltke onwards, had always been completely independent of the Prussian Minister of War who, indeed, was himself, right down to 1918, responsible much less to the Prussian Parliament (the *Landtag*) than to the Kaiser as King of Prussia. The Weimar Constitution, while appearing, by the institution of a 'Reich' Minister of Defense, to introduce Ministerial responsibility for the Army and, with it, Parliamentary control, in reality did nothing of the kind. By an Ordinance (*Verordnung*) of 11 August 1920, transferring the functions of command to the 'Chief of Army Direction' (*Chef der Heeresleitung*), General von Seeckt was made virtually independent of the Minister of Defense, Herr Gessler, who was reduced to the menial direction of mere administration. This departure was followed by a series of changes which concentrated all military powers in the hands of von Seeckt—Recruiting, Inspections, Training, Promotion, Mobilization, Operations, Intelligence, with the result that the General found himself invested with all the powers of the pre-war Military Cabinet and the pre-war Chief of the General Staff. There had been no such concentration of military authority in the hands of one man at any period in German history. The Minister of Defense became a mere puppet. In this respect, as in so many others, the 'republican' constitution of Weimar can only be described as little better than a 'scrap of paper.' For six years von Seeckt ruled with a rod of iron in all Army matters.[15]

[14] *Ibid.*, at p. 6.
[15] Von Seeckt's resignation, in October 1926, was not, as was commonly supposed at the time in England, due to the Minister, Herr Gessler, who had

In no direction was the success of the Officers' Corps in its resistance to 'the development,' the moral development, of the German people more complete, nor indeed more terrible, than in its opposition to all attempts of the civilized world to humanize the laws and usages of war. Hence the melancholy spectacle of its behavior in every campaign it has undertaken during the last hundred years and more. Always and invariably it reverts to type, like a *recidiviste*. In 1848, in 1870-71, in 1914-18, and now again, it has periodically shocked the conscience of the civilized world by outrages which are no sooner forgotten than they are repeated. The story of its treatment of the Poles in 1848 will be found later in this volume,[16] where the reader will find a contemporary description by an English eyewitness which, in all its horror, might have been written of the behavior of the German Army in Poland in 1939. Its treatment of the French village of Bazeilles in 1871 reads like the undying shame of the treatment by its jackals, the Gestapo, of Lidice a few years ago. Of the massacre of Bazeilles, where every man, woman, and child was shot, bayoneted, or burned to death by German troops acting under the orders of their superiors, it is sufficient to cite the words of an English writer of repute whose impartiality is beyond suspicion: 'It is not too much to say that the incident sent a thrill of horror throughout Europe.' [17] Barely another generation had elapsed when, in 1914, the German High Command, represented by General von Kluck, ordered the massacre, in one Belgian town after another,[18] of inoffensive civilians, men, women, and children, on a

nothing to do with it. Still less did it establish the principle of Ministerial responsibility for the Army. In fact, it had just the opposite effect. Gessler was forced to go by a clique of Generals a few months later and with him disappeared the last remnant of civilian control over the Army. He was succeeded as 'Minister' by a General, Groener, who in due course was succeeded by another General, Schleicher. The Officers' Corps thus scored all along the line.

[16] See below, Chapter XI.

[17] Mr. Walter Spaight, in his *War Rights on Land*, at p. 39. After the massacre a German Proclamation was issued by the High Command accepting full responsibility for it as 'a sentence executed against the village in virtue of the laws of war.' Of this official massacre, the *Daily News* correspondent, quoted by Mr. Spaight, wrote, 'I saw the charred corpses of the women and the tender little ones—a sight I dream of to this day and wake in a cold sweat of horror.'

[18] i.e. at Dinant, Aerschot, Louvain, Andenne, Jamoigne, Titigny, and many other places. The facts are to be found in the famous Report of Lord Bryce's Committee published in 1915, after the most careful investigation, by the British

scale far exceeding anything that had happened at Bazeilles. The number of victims ran into thousands. When the tidings of these things first reached England in those somber days they were received with incredulity as the wild inventions of a stricken people suffering from war hysteria. That incredulity, as I happen to know, was at first shared by the Committee appointed by the British Government to inquire into them, whose representative I was in France with the B.E.F. It was only when the dreadful evidence put before us established the facts beyond the possibility of doubt that we ceased to disbelieve. But we did not cease to wonder. Had not the German Government, we asked ourselves in troubled consternation, put its signature, only seven years earlier, to the international conventions, negotiated and signed at the second Hague Conference, which outlawed for all time the very possibility of such things? And then suddenly, by a mere accident, I discovered a copy in German of a certain military manual recently issued by the General Staff for the use of German officers, the very existence of which was quite unknown in England and in America and indeed almost everywhere else. That manual explained, with a truly lethal logic, the terrible things done by the German troops in Belgium in 1914, even as it explains the terrible things which they did in Russia [19] and elsewhere during World War II.

On the publication of this manual in an English translation, for which I was responsible,[20] in January 1915, public opinion alike in England and in America was, it may be said without the slightest exaggeration, both astounded and horrified. *The Times*, in a remarkable leading article devoted to the English translation of the book, described it, only too truly, as 'a code of savagery.' *The New York Times* summed up the doctrines of the book as 'most astounding.'

Government. The number of victims at Dinant alone was no less than 674 men —mostly old men—women, and children, forty of whom were under fifteen years of age. They were put up against a wall and shot.

[19] A certain weekly journal, which I have seen described as the spiritual home and last refuge of 'pro-Germanism' in England today, has persistently sought to exculpate the German Army from responsibility for the atrocities committed in the war, by pleading that they are all due to the Gestapo. It is to be hoped that after the publication of German Army Orders by the Russian Government on 6 April 1943, we shall hear no more of this sort of thing.

[20] It was published by Sir John Murray under the title, *The German War Book*.

And so with every other newspaper of importance in both countries. The explanation of the shock thus caused by this disclosure of the book and of its existence is to be found in what had happened, only a few years earlier, at the Hague Conferences of 1899 and 1907. During the third quarter of the nineteenth century there had been a growing consensus of European opinion in the direction of humanizing the laws and usages of war. A great jurist of European reputation, Bluntschli, a Swiss by birth, gave eloquent expression to the principle that the civil population of every country ought to be immune from violence at the hands of an enemy belligerent. This principle, formulated by the Declaration of Brussels in 1874, duly found the fullest expression in the Hague Conventions and Regulations, which another jurist, a Russian by birth, De Martens, succinctly described as 'a mutual insurance by the nations for the protection of their civil populations against the abuse of force in time of war.' They were saluted by an English jurist of repute, Professor Pearce Higgins, as 'one of the greatest triumphs of civilization in having brought about the distinction between the treatment of combatants and non-combatants' by securing the latter from violence. The German plenipotentiary at the Conference of 1907, Baron Marschall von Bieberstein, was particularly eloquent on the subject. He almost suggested that the Conventions did not go far enough.[21] All the contracting parties, Germany included, agreed to issue to their armed forces instructions in conformity with these Conventions.

The British War Office duly and faithfully incorporated in full the text of all the Conventions and Regulations in its Manual of Military Law, colloquially known to British officers as 'the Red Book,' and devoted a chapter of the manual to enforcing on all our officers the principles they embodied for strict observance in the field. The German General Staff did exactly the opposite. It issued to all its officers a manual, the *Kriegsbrauch im Landkriege*, in which not only were the texts of all the Regulations and Conventions

[21] 'Military acts,' declared von Bieberstein, 'are not governed solely by principles of international law; there are other factors: conscience, good sense, and the sentiment of duty imposed by principles of humanity.' (*Actes et Documents* (1907), Vol. I, pp. 282 and 286.) But whenever it came to the point, the German representatives at the Conference always seemed to prefer ambiguity, in drafting the terms of the Conventions, to explicitness; the British attitude was just the opposite.

totally omitted but the German officer was warned, in so many words, to be 'on his guard' against 'the humanitarian notions' embodied in them.[22] They were derided as the outcome of 'sentimentality and flabby emotion' (*Sentimentalität und weicheler Gefühlsschwärmerei*). 'The only true humanity,' the German officer was instructed, 'very often' lies in being as ruthless as possible. He must, the manual insisted, never forget 'the frequent necessity of terrorism' (*Terrorismus*). Each and every provision of the Hague Regulations, although the Regulations themselves were hardly ever mentioned, much less published, in the book and never respectfully, was studiously repudiated. For example, the German manual posed the question: Can an officer compel the peaceful inhabitants of an invaded country to give information about the strength and disposition of their country's forces? 'Yes,' was the answer of the manual; it is doubtless regrettable, but it is often 'necessary.' Should they be deliberately exposed to the fire of their own troops? 'Yes,' such a measure may be indefensible, but its 'main justification' is that it is often 'successful.' Should the forced labor of the inhabitants be limited to works which are not designed to injure their own country? 'No,' this is an absurd distinction and impossible. Should prisoners of war be put to death? It is always 'ugly' but it is sometimes 'expedient.' May one hire an assassin, corrupt a citizen, or suborn an incendiary? 'Certainly'; it may not be reputable (*anständig*), but the 'law' of war is less 'touchy' (*empfindlich*). Murder, lying, treachery, bribery, and 'fifth column' methods were expressly recommended by the German manual and were justified by the amazing argument that, as international law did not explicitly forbid them, it must be taken to have implicitly sanctioned them.

Thus did this sinister book 'give,' in the words of *The Times* leading article, 'the highest official sanction, the sanction of the German General Staff, to principles and practices which are in flat contradiction to those of all civilized peoples.' With the invasion of Belgium its 'principles' were put into practice with the utmost fidelity. Just a century earlier, Clausewitz, on his appointment as Director of the Staff College, the *Kriegsakademie*, in Berlin, had indoctrinated the Prussian Officers' Corps with exactly the same principles. 'A

---

[22] See the English translation, *The German War Book* (1915), at pp. 54, etc.

man of rare tenderness of heart,' as the official historian of the *Kriegsakademie* describes him with unconscious irony,[23] he warned his pupils against attempting to disarm an enemy without *the maximum* of 'bloodshed,' begged them to avoid a 'benevolent' spirit towards a stricken foe, dismissed all humanitarian restrictions on the conduct of war as 'hardly worth mentioning,' and denounced 'moderation' in an officer as 'an absurdity.' [24] His great ambition, the historian tells us, was to leave behind him a book, embodying this teaching, such as German officers would never forget. 'He achieved it' (*er hat sein Ziel erreicht*). The same authority tells us with admirable candor, 'all the victorious Army Commanders in the famous campaigns of our Fatherland have taken his book and its teaching as their model; innumerable officers (*unzählige Offiziere*) have adopted it.' [25] When, in due course, the German General Staff, in 1915, found themselves compelled, by the horrified comments in neutral countries on the facts disclosed by the Bryce Committee's report, to attempt some answer to that report, they fully admitted what they had done in one of the strangest pleas of confession and avoidance ever published,[26] justifying, or rather excusing, their massacres of the Belgian civilians in words which might have been taken straight out of Clausewitz's ruthless text-book—'speedily to overcome opposition had to be striven for *in every way.*' And with characteristic cynicism they accused their Belgian victims, without a shred of evidence to support the charge, of having violated those laws of war which, in their own manual, the *Kriegsbrauch im Landkriege*, they had so contemptuously repudiated.

Such was the German Officers' Corps at the time we came to grips with it in the year 1920. *And such it remained to the end.* This

[23] *Die Königliche Preussische Kriegsakademie*, by Professor von Scharfenort (Berlin, 1910), where, at p. 53, the author, in a glowing tribute to Clausewitz, describes him as a man '*von seltener Weichheit*,' and of the most exquisite delicacy of feeling.
[24] Thus Clausewitz in his book on the art of war, *Vom Kriege*, 1 Kap. 1 (2).
[25] Von Scharfenort, *op. cit.*, at p. 54.
[26] I refer to the 'White Book' published by the German Government in 1915 under the title of *Die Völker-rechtswidrige Führung des belgischen Volkskrieges*. This truly amazing document was never published in England, but our own Foreign Office had it translated for official use and placed a copy of it at my disposal. Some account of it will be found below in Chapter XI.

persistence of the character, the temper, the constitution, and the omnipotence of this armored despotism is, as I hope to show in due course,[27] one of the great problems, in my opinion the chief problem, which we shall have to solve when the time comes to disarm Germany effectively and once and for all. The thousand and one devices by which it defeated our 'control' it will be the task of this volume and its successor to disclose and explain. At this stage I will confine myself to saying that von Seeckt succeeded in converting the Treaty Army of 100,000 effectives into nothing less than a vast Officers' Training Corps. There never was a more fatal delusion than that which prevailed, alike on the Continent and in England, right down to September 1939, a delusion finding sensational expression in a fantastic book published on the very eve of World War II, namely, the delusion that Germany 'couldn't win' in a European war because, as a result of the Treaty of Versailles, she was suffering from 'a serious shortage of officers,' commissioned and non-commissioned.[28] Never, at any time since the Treaty of Versailles was signed and ratified, had she suffered 'seriously' from anything of the kind. The campaigns of 1939-40 in which she overran with her giant armies, admirably officered and led, nearly the whole of Europe, to say nothing of her later initial successes against Russia, gave the *coup de grâce* to that comfortable delusion.

Another delusion, equally ill-founded but in this case still widely entertained, was, and is, a belief that the German Officers' Corps, under the Nazi régime, lost its exclusive character and, with it, its independence. The truth is exactly the opposite. Under the Weimar Republic the officers of the new Reichswehr, all of them, at the outset, officers of the old Army, jealously maintained the traditional prerogative of the Corps to reject any candidate for a

27 See below, Chapter xi.

28 Thus, at pp. 43, etc., of a book by a Hungarian writer, Dr. Ivan Lajos, translated into English, and published in London in August 1939, under the title, *Germany's War Chances*, with the sub-title (on the wrapper) 'Germany Can't Win.' The imaginative author of this book put the number of N.C.O.s of the Reichswehr, before the restoration of conscription, at '8,000.' There were in fact, as we discovered, no less than 40,000 as early as 1921. And so on. From beginning to end this sensational book was vitiated by two fundamental fallacies, (1) its naïve assumption that Germany was disarmed under the Treaty of Versailles, (2) its uncritical acceptance of German statements in German publications from 1935 onwards as to German armaments and effectives.

commission, and there is every reason to believe that it was still maintained in the *Wehrmacht*.[29] During the Second World War the election of candidates for a commission by the regimental Corps was no
doubt suspended, as it was during the last for obvious reasons,[30] but
at that time, all its suspension meant was that the veto on the 'aspirant's' appointment to a commission was placed in the hands of the
Commanding Officer of his battalion as representing the Corps. I
discovered the persistence of this cherished prerogative under the
Weimar Republic as the result of an inspection of the new Infantry
School at Munich, which I made in November 1921, in the company
of our local 'Control' officer, my friend Colonel J. L. Likeman. We
had, under the terms of a certain article of the Treaty,[31] closed down
the Cadet School at Gross Lichterfelde, but by the same article,
decreeing its suppression, Germany was authorized to establish 'one
school per arm' for the 'recruitment' of officers. In effect, this meant
one *Kriegschule* per arm. I was curious to discover how officers, i.e.
officers other than the original establishment of 4,000 authorized by
the Treaty, all of whom, as I have already observed, were officers
of the old Army, were going to be 'recruited' by von Seeckt. Were
they being nominated as in the old days by the Commanding Officer
of the regiment, admitted to the Officers' Mess from the day they
joined the 'other ranks,' promoted almost immediately to be N.C.O.s
of a category peculiar to themselves, and, most important question
of all, subject, in due course, to 'election' by the officers of the
regiment? If so, the German Officers' Corps would, obviously, be
perpetuating itself and its character exactly as before. In other words,
I was searching for traces in the new Army of *Fahnenjunkers*, who
after all had been even more important, quantitatively though not
qualitatively, in the 'recruitment' of officers for the old Army than
the 'cadets.'[32] The enormous number of surplus N.C.O.s which we

[29] I use the term *Wehrmacht* to describe the German Army since the transformation of the Reichswehr by the restoration of conscription in 1935.

[30] By an Order of the Military Cabinet in 1915, see Wrisberg's *Heer und
Heimat*, at p. 201.

[31] Article 176.

[32] Only one-third of the regular officers of the old Army were cadets in the
technical sense of the word; the remaining two-thirds entered the Army direct
as *Fahnenjunkers*, instead of through the portals of the Cadet School at Gross
Lichterfelde.

discovered in the Reichswehr—over 40,000 in an Army limited by the Treaty to 96,000 effectives,[33] suggested to my mind a line of inquiry, the inquiry which took me to Munich. Either these N.C.O.s, I concluded, were nothing less than a vast cadre of instructors training an untold number of men enlisted for a few months, instead of the twelve years' term prescribed by the Treaty, and thereby building up a masked reserve. Or else they, or rather a considerable proportion of them, were a cadre of 'aspirant' officers equally out of all proportion to the legitimate requirements of the Reichswehr. As we shall see in due course, both these surmises turned out to be correct. They were, indeed, not mutually exclusive, for, if a masked reserve was being nursed, it would obviously require a proportionately larger number of officers, in excess of the Treaty establishment, to take over the command of it on mobilization. But at the time of my visit to the Infantry School, I was concerned only with the 'recruitment' of officers, not of instructors.

On my arrival at Munich, I was received by the famous General von Lossow, at that time Commandant of the new Infantry School. I took Likeman with me. He was an extremely able regular officer, and absolutely fearless, who had distinguished himself at Stettin by standing up to many a 'rough house' when inspecting the Security Police and Reichswehr in barracks, which was one of the reasons why I had transferred him to Munich, a transfer which amounted to promotion. He had served in France with great distinction all through the war as an officer of the Suffolks, ending up by serving at Murmansk under General Ironside, who told me, years afterwards, that Likeman was 'one of the bravest officers in the British Army.' A perfect stranger to me in 1919, he had come to see me at the War Office, when I was home on leave from Berlin, to ask if I could find room for him on the Control Commission. I had already chosen, after personal interviews in Cologne and in London, the full complement of British officers for the Effectives Sub-Commission, but I was so impressed by Likeman that I determined to find room for him and, with General Macdonogh's support, I succeeded. It was a lucky day for

[33] The Treaty of Versailles limited the new Army to 100,000 of which *not more* than 4,000 were to be officers. Unfortunately it imposed no limitation on the number of N.C.O.s, an oversight of which von Seeckt was quick to take advantage.

me when I met him—he was one of my most loyal supporters on the Commission at a time when I needed support in face of much obstruction, not to say detraction, in a certain quarter. But I knew that Likeman, if he made the inspection of the Infantry School by himself, would get 'no change' out of von Lossow, who, indeed, would probably, as a general officer, have refused to see him at all on the ground that he would not submit to interrogation by a Lieutenant-Colonel. He could not refuse to see me, which was why I decided, as I often did in such cases, to undertake the inspection myself. Von Lossow received me quite genially, a fact which at once put me on my guard, for I knew by experience that Germans are only genial to Englishmen when they hope to make a fool of them. Geniality is not natural to a German, as Treitschke himself once admitted. It is a fact which the many Englishmen who visited Germany during the years of 'appeasement,' when she was preparing her second 'tiger-spring' at the throat of Europe, and were highly gratified to find themselves received with open arms, quite failed to grasp. Many of them came home quite bewitched by the warmth of their reception and were promptly ensnared by Ribbentrop into joining his pet booby-trap, the 'Anglo-German Fellowship.' Today they are wiser and sadder men. Certainly von Lossow did his best to fool me. He began by assuring me that the status of *Fahnenjunker* or *Avantageur* no longer existed. A prospective officer, he explained, must enlist for twelve years 'in exactly the same way as the ordinary private,' without any expectation or guarantee that he would eventually be nominated for a commission. Before being admitted to the Infantry School, he would, he added, have, of course, to sit for an entrance examination, but 'any man' in the ranks might sit for it. This answer at once aroused my suspicion because I knew from our inspections of units in barracks that not a single private had been enlisted for twelve years. They were all enlisted for six, or, at most, twelve [34] months. The only enlistments for the twelve years' term were the N.C.O.s or —a cunning trick of camouflage—men who, although appearing in the nominal rolls as 'privates,' were found, on our examination of the

[34] The cases of a twelve-month enlistment were significant. They suggested the reintroduction of the 'one-year volunteers' (*Einjährig-Freiwilliger*), described above, in order to provide a nucleus of Reserve Officers.

pay-rolls, to be receiving pay as N.C.O.s. I therefore tried a 'ranging shot' with von Lossow. The full strength of his school, of which he was obviously proud, was, he told me, 250 'aspirants' for a commission. 'Are they all *gentlemen?*' I asked. This was, as things turned out, a lucky shot of mine. 'Of course,' was the complacent reply. 'But how, then,' I proceeded, 'do so many "gentlemen" come to have enlisted in the Reichswehr as ordinary privates for twelve years without any expectation or guarantee of a commission?' 'Well, naturally,' replied von Lossow, who obviously did not see where I was leading him, 'a prospective officer before enlisting always has an interview with the Colonel, and so, as a rule, do his parents.' The idea of a German officer of the rank of Colonel deputizing as a sergeant-major and condescending to interview every man who turned up with his family at the barracks, wishing to attest as an ordinary recruit, was almost too funny for words, but I took good care not to smile. 'Well, and what happens to him after he has been nominated by his C.O. and passed through your school?' I pursued. 'Oh, he goes back to his regiment,' replied von Lossow, 'to wait for *a report of all the officers* upon him before he is gazetted.' 'And how long does he have to wait for that?' I continued. 'Oh, not very long,' was the answer. 'You see, they have had him *under their personal observation from the day he enlisted.*' 'Thank you,' I concluded with that agreeable forensic feeling which counsel has when he has the rare good fortune to encounter a 'hostile' witness who unwittingly tells him all he wishes to know and a great deal more than he had ever hoped to be able to find out. That decisive 'report' of *all* the officers of the regiment or battalion was clearly nothing less than the old system of election by the Officers' Corps. And their 'personal observation' could be nothing other than observation of the young aspirant in the Officers' Mess. The Corps of officers in a unit could not possibly observe collectively the habits of every ordinary private in the ranks. Subsequent investigations fully confirmed my interpretation of the ingenuous—or disingenuous—replies of his Excellency General-Leutnant von Lossow.

Did this prerogative of the German Officers' Corps to exclude elements of which they did not approve undergo any derogation with Hitler's accession to power? Certainly not. The idea that the professional Nazis, whether Police or ordinary Storm-troopers, had 'gatecrashed' into the Officers' Corps is a complete illusion, although not an uncommon one. Such evidence as has been produced in support of it proves exactly the opposite. In saying this, I have in mind the incorporation of the 'Police' in the Reichswehr on the morrow of the day on which Hitler restored conscription. That incorporation has been cited in some English newspapers as evidence that the German Officers' Corps had, by the admission of Police officers, lost its old homogeneity of character. But the 'Police' so incorporated were the *Sicherheitspolizei*, i.e. the 'Security Police,' who were the creation neither of Goering nor of Himmler, but of Noske and von Seeckt. They came into existence long before the Gestapo and the Storm-troopers were ever heard of, in other words, in 1919. They were, to a man, officered entirely by regular officers of the old Army, and in the year 1922 I was able, after much travail, to convince M.I.3 War Office once and for all that they were identical with the Reichswehr, in other words, were second-line troops. Much travail, because until 23 December 1922 the War Office had long hesitated to accept my reports to that effect owing to the dissenting opinion of my British colleague, General Bingham, on the Council of the Commission who, although in a minority of one, insisted that the German police were completely 'demilitarized'—for no better reason than that the German Government said they were.[35]

As for the Gestapo and the Storm-troopers, I doubt very much if any of them ever, as such, secured admission to the Officers' Corps at all. Any ambition they may have cherished of dominating, or even permeating, the Army perished with Hitler's sacrifice, as a burnt-offering on the altar of the Officers' Corps, of that unhappy Nazi organizer, von Roehm, who dared to cherish just that particular ambition. Hitler's massacre of Roehm and his adherents on 30 June 1934 was a victory for the Officers' Corps over the Storm-troopers, and a decisive one. The incidental murder of General Schleicher on that bloody occasion, although no doubt inspired by Hitler, who had an old political grudge against the General, was not only an isolated

[35] The instantaneous incorporation of the whole of the Security Police in the Reichswehr on the very day when Germany threw off the mask and restored conscription, i.e. in 1935, showed, dramatically enough, how utterly false the German Government's assurances, that they were demilitarized, were and always had been.

incident,[36] but the immediate occasion of Hitler's greatest humiliation. The German Officers' Corps made him 'eat dirt' by calling a meeting of the Corps and passing a resolution, and, what is more, publishing it, in which they condemned the murder of Schleicher as the felonious act it was. Hitler never dared to repeat any such lethal action against a German officer, and the reader can dismiss altogether the sensational stories, occurring and recurring in the Press during the last war, about German generals, who had incurred Hitler's displeasure, being 'bumped off' by the Gestapo. The German Officers' Corps would have made short work of any Nazi agent who ventured to attempt anything of the kind. Hitler did, of course, retire Generals from their commands, but that was a legitimate exercise of his prerogatives as Supreme Head of the State, and, as was the Kaiser, *Bundesfeldherr*. The Kaiser did the same—he retired the younger von Moltke, Falkenhayn, and Ludendorff himself. Yet the Kaiser's authority was more apparent than real, and it is quite possible that Hitler's action in this respect was, as was the Kaiser's, dictated to him and not by him, in other words, inspired by the senior members of the German Officers' Corps itself in which there have always been, so far as the general officers are concerned, fierce personal rivalries, due to a 'jealousy' which one of them, von der Goltz, has deplored as a fundamental characteristic of all his tribe.[37]

---

[36] It is strange to find such an accomplished American journalist as Mr. E. A. Mowrer, who served as a newspaper correspondent in Berlin, describing the murder at the same time, of von Kahr, the retired Minister-President of Bavaria, as that of a 'General,' which von Kahr never was. He was not an officer by profession at all but a civil servant. And stranger still to find Mr. Douglas Reed, in an interesting article in the *Daily Mail* of 20 April 1943, on 'The Missing Years in Hitler's Life,' falling into the same error. I say 'strange' because Mr. Reed's knowledge of 'Hitlerite' Germany is beyond challenge, and England owes him a debt of gratitude, which has never been paid, for the intrepid and prophetic book, *Insanity Fair*, a classic of its kind, with which he strove, early in 1938, to awaken his fellow-countrymen to the danger ahead of them.

[37] 'Jealousy (*Eifersucht*) is an inborn characteristic of the German, and I had to contend with it all through the war,' wrote General von der Goltz in referring to commanding officers (see his *Meine Sendung in Finnland*, Leipzig, 1920, at p. 10). The author of *Das alte Heer*, himself a staff officer, describes (at p. 16) the General Staff as 'dominated' at all times by 'a bitter and reckless (*unbekümmert*) struggle' among its officers for the higher Commands, particularly the command of an Army Corps. The German Officers' Corps, although united as one man against German civilians, was not exactly 'a band of brothers.' The various arms of the service in the Officers' Corps were equally jealous, and

It was a council of Army Corps Commanders which, on at least one occasion, dictated to the Kaiser during the First World War what he should do or not do. Hitler could indeed confer the honorary rank of 'General' on any one he pleased, and I understand that he had done so more than once in the case of his Nazi advisers, but that is a very different thing and has its precedents. The Kaiser conferred the rank of 'Colonel-General-Field-Marshal' on Bismarck, on his enforced retirement, although Bismarck was not, and never had been, a regular officer. It was nothing more, if nothing less, than a decoration, and conferred on him no military authority whatsoever.[38]

In the late summer of 1936, when on a visit to Germany, I was the witness of a remarkable, not to say dramatic, incident which has left an ineffaceable impression on my mind, an incident which revealed with the velocity of light and all its illumination—it was like a flash of lightning and all over in a moment—the overlordship of the Army and the prostration, in more senses than one, of the Nazis before it. Never have I seen such a public humiliation inflicted on men who aspire to rule. That incident, of which more in a moment, was the more remarkable because, until that moment, everything I had seen on my visit seemed to conspire to impress the visitor with the authority and prestige of the Nazis themselves. Certainly they had done their best thus to impress me. On hearing of my presence at a great country-house in the very heart of the lovely pine-woods of the Taunus, where I was the guest of an American friend of German parentage, Mrs. Greenough of New York—the Bürgermeister of Wiesbaden waited on me to convey an invitation from the Gauleiter of Hesse. It was an offer to show me some of the mighty works of 'Wieder-

sometimes contemptuous, of one another—see the anonymous author of *Kritik des Weltkrieges, von einem Generalstabler* (Leipzig, 1921), at p. 30, where he hints at this sort of thing, while the author of *Das alte Heer* bluntly says (at p. 28, etc.) that a cavalry officer always looked down on an infantry officer, both looked down upon a gunner as 'middle-class' (*bürgerlich*), while a sapper was regarded by all three as being 'not quite the thing' because his was not a 'fighting arm.'

[38] In what I have written above, I have not been unmindful of the existence of Himmler's *Waffen S.S.* But to describe it, as I have seen it described, as 'a fourth arm,' on an equality of footing with the Army, and a serious challenge to the Army's supremacy, seems to me a wild exaggeration. See Introduction to this book.

aufbau,' to wit 'social reconstruction,' wrought by the Nazi régime.
I accepted and, as a result, I was for several days in succession conducted on long tours through the Rhineland, escorted by two gigantic Storm-troopers in a large and powerful 'Nazi' car. I noticed that,
wherever we went, everyone humbled himself before us or rather
before the two Storm-troopers. At every hotel at which we stopped
for a meal, an obsequious landlord ordered the waiters to serve us
before any one else. The driver of every car on the road, on hearing
the long blast of our screeching siren which, presumably, sounded a
familiar Nazi note of its own, or on seeing the large swastika flag on
the bonnet of our car, frantically made way for us as though the siren
was that of a fire-engine. Some of them, indeed, in their trepidation,
steered their cars right into the ditch. Those two Storm-troopers
appeared to be invested with all the prerogatives of the German
Officers' Corps.

But the most spectacular, not to say histrionic, item in the program
arranged for my entertainment and instruction came last and, ironically enough, on the very eve, 4 October, of that public humiliation,
as I have called it, which was to be its anti-climax. The item was an
invitation to attend a great meeting at the Ratshaus to which the
good people of Wiesbaden had been invited in their thousands, a
meeting to do honor to what might be called the fellowship, whether
goodly or not, of the apostles of the Nazi creed, in other words, the
Blut-Orden.[39] The *Blut-Orden* was an 'Order' founded by Hitler
to commemorate the day, 9 November 1923, on which, with a
few hundred followers, he attempted that unsuccessful *coup d'état*
known to history as the Munich 'Putsch.' The survivors of that encounter with the carbines of the Munich Security Police, in other
words, those who escaped the fate of the sixteen of their comrades,
left dead on the stricken field of the *Odeonplatz*, by either throwing
themselves on their stomachs or, like Hitler, running away, were, on
his accession to power, enrolled in the new fellowship as the original
disciples of the Nazi gospel, while the sixteen dead were canonized
as the noble army of martyrs on whose graves Hitler, with much

[39] The word *Orden* in German means either a knightly or monastic 'Order,'
or a decoration. In the case of the *Blut-Orden*, literally the 'Blood Order,' it
does duty for both. One of my hosts at the *Bierabend* showed me, not without
pride, this decoration—a kind of metal of red enamel, bearing, if I recollect
rightly, the superscription 'Munich, 9 November 1923.'

solemnity, laid a wreath once a year on the anniversary of the day he deserted them. Since the foundation of the Order, its members, the survivors, lived like fighting cocks as the pensioners of the Third Reich and the self-invited guests of any municipality they decided to honor with a visit, no man daring to refuse them anything. I accepted the invitation to the Ratshaus, although had I known the sort of reception which was in store for me I should probably have refused. But if I had, I should have missed an experience which, as far as I know, has fallen to the lot of no other Englishman, namely, a private *Bierabend* [40] with the *Blut-Orden* which, following on the conclusion of the meeting in the Ratshaus, lasted until three o'clock in the morning and gave me such an insight into the Nazi mentality as I would not have missed for words, which is why I dwell upon it.

When I arrived at the Ratshaus, accompanied by a young relative of mine, an officer in the Swiss Army, and entered the vestibule, I could see through the doors of the assembly-hall a vast audience, excited and expectant. I had hoped to slip in unobserved, as I had a card of admission on which the Bürgermeister had inscribed my name. But the two Storm-troopers who had escorted me on my Rhineland tour were there in the vestibule, and one of them promptly came forward to greet me, while the other whispered something to a third Storm-trooper who was wearing a decoration of red enamel. At the same moment my eye fell on forty men, all wearing a similar decoration. They were drawn up in two ranks in the vestibule, one to the right, one to the left, with a space between the two ranks in the center of which the third Storm-trooper stood importantly. Those forty men were the paladins of the *Blut-Orden*. Never have I seen such a choice collection of 'toughs.' And, to my amazement, I found they were waiting for me. That third Storm-trooper was their 'Führer,' a generic term not confined to Hitler, as we shall see. Before I go any further, let me assure the reader that I did not feel at all flattered by what followed; any more than I had felt any complacency about the attention showered on me during my conducted tour of the Rhineland. Other former officers of the Control Commission besides myself, notably my friends Colonel J. H. M. Beasley and Colonel P. B. O'Connor, who had revisited Germany under the Nazi

---

[40] Literally a 'Beer Evening,' i.e. a drinking party.

régime had been the subject of similar attentions at the hands of the Nazi authorities, if not on quite the same scale. When they were not being entertained, they were, as one of them discovered, being 'shadowed.' [41] So, no doubt, was I. But they, like myself, had been thoroughly inoculated, by years of experience when we were serving in Germany, against the toxic effects of German 'geniality' in ministering to one's vanity, by the anti-toxin of German mendacity of which we had had so many unpleasant proofs in our work of 'control.' I had little doubt that all this calculated hospitality was, in the case of those of us who had served on the Control Commission, designed not only to secure recruits for the 'Anglo-German Fellowship,' but to exhibit us as ostentatiously as possible to the German public as proselytes who had seen the error of their ways and who, having been guilty of what Ludendorff once stigmatized to me as the 'scandalous' attempt (*die Schande*) to disarm a stricken Germany, now, by our acceptance of official hospitality, did obeisance to the restoration of her armed might by the Führer. It is the only explanation I can offer—and I think it is the true one—of my extraordinary reception at the Ratshaus.

The moment Storm-trooper Number Two had whispered my

[41] If any of us former 'Control' officers had visited Germany two or three years later, i.e. in the summer of 1939, our reception would, no doubt, have been very difficult. Indeed, I doubt if we should have returned alive. In saying this, I have in mind a ghastly story which has never been made public but which was told me by the late Lord Lloyd who, as Chairman of the British Council, had all the facts communicated to him. A certain British officer went to Germany for a short holiday in the summer of 1939. He was not engaged on 'secret service,' but he knew Germany well, perhaps too well to please the Nazis. His people never saw him again. They received a communication from the German Government, through the usual official channels, informing them that he had committed suicide and offering, if so desired, to transmit his ashes, with the intimation that it had been found 'impracticable' to arrange for the preservation and transport of his body. He had left England in the best of health and spirits, and one of his friends informs me that he was 'the last man in the world' to commit suicide. A few hours before the German authorities had his body cremated they notified our local consular authority of the 'suicide,' and invited the consul to view the body. He went. The body was lying on a bed and bore no signs of wounds, although the face was strangely contorted. Just as he was about to leave, the consul took a closer look. Under the chin there was a faint impression of a pair of huge hands like those of a gorilla. It was impossible to prove anything, but the consul had no doubt about what had happened. He had been strangled.

name to Number Three, the latter shouted a word of command to his forty fellows, and they all saluted me with a stentorian shout of 'Heil Hitler!' and the usual sacramental gesture. Of course I had to return it in the same fashion—it would have been discourteous to do otherwise, although I had an uncomfortable feeling that I was doing public obeisance. But there was no escape. I was politely requested to proceed into the hall up a broad gangway leading from the huge entrance doors to the platform and dividing the hall into two sections with the audience packed on either side. Storm-trooper Number Two fell in behind me and the whole cohort of the *Blut-Orden* followed in double file until we reached the front row of seats, which were all vacant. An arm-chair in the center had been reserved for me; twenty of the *Blut-Orden* took the seats on my left, the other twenty on my right. The leader, Herr Bart, mounted the platform to deliver the oration of the evening, and I soon forgot my uncomfortable feeling of self-consciousness in listening to him. He was extremely eloquent, at times torrentially so. Afterwards, in the convivial privacy of the *Bierabend* at the Hotel Vier Jahreszeiten, in a large room specially reserved for the *Blut-Orden* and guarded by Storm-troopers like a fortress, Herr Bart asked me if I 'understood' his speech. 'Yes,' I replied. 'But did you understand *with your heart* as well as with your brain?' he persisted. 'Do you mean—was I in sympathy with it?' I answered with some embarrassment. 'No,' he explained, 'what I mean is—did it appeal *to your emotions?* Or was it too like a lecture?' 'Not at all,' I replied somewhat equivocally, 'I found it most emotional'—as indeed it was. Herr Bart had almost reduced his audience to tears by comparing the young Hitler to Jesus Christ, and himself and his handful of comrades to the fishermen of Galilee who had left all and followed him. They had been ridiculed by their fellow-countrymen (which was true enough in 1923), dismissed from their jobs, and despised and rejected of men. And so on. As I listened to Herr Bart, I felt more and more, although I had never heard him, much less met him, before, a curious sense of recognition. The gestures, the rasping voice, the straining of the vocal cords, the sudden changes from *pianissimo* to *fortissimo*, the *crescendo* at the end of long, involved sentences, where had I seen and heard it all before? Then, as I closed my eyes for a moment in a concentrated effort to remember, I had it. Adolf Hitler! Herr Bart's oration might have been delivered by Hitler himself. And, curiously enough, like Hitler, he was short, 'stocky,' dark, square-headed—'not the Nordic' type at all, but that 'Alpine' type, as anthropologists call it, so frequently found in Bavaria and the Tyrol. When I told him, as we sat drinking together tankard after tankard of *helles* or *dunkles* at the *Vierjahreszeiten*, how strongly he reminded me of the Führer, his eyes lit up with unaffected pleasure. And then he told me something. 'There are thousands of just such speakers as I in Germany today,' he confided. 'You see, we are *taught* how to do it.' There was, in fact, a 'Führer-schule,' [42] indeed many a one, in Germany. Wherefore it may be that Hitler 'being dead, yet speaketh' on the microphone. I do not think so myself. But the German Officers' Corps, whose foundling he himself was, had at any rate any number of understudies from whom to select another, so far as broadcasting was concerned.

That festive evening at the hotel taught me many things, but it would take me too long and too far afield to relate them here, important though they were, and are, if one is to take the proper measure of the generations of the young and middle-aged in Germany today. I will only mention one or two. At the *Bierabend*, every one of the forty comrades came in turn to the table where Herr Bart and I sat together. And whatever was discussed—and we ranged over every question of current world-politics—each and every one of them used exactly the same arguments in the same language. Even their replies to my questions were identical. When you had talked to one of them, you had talked to them all. There were none of those individual points of view which are so characteristic of Englishmen. They had been drilled to think as recruits are drilled to form fours (or threes) on the barrack-square. It was mass-thinking, if thought it can be called at all. They seemed to have no reasoning power whatsoever. They had a sense of humor, but it was a rather sinister sense. A famous German comedian had been hired, or commandeered, to entertain them as a kind of licensed jester—he even made jokes, in the privacy of our conventicle, about the Nazi leaders, with the single exception of the Führer, such as he would never have dared to make in public, and always with a wary eye on the forty who constituted

[42] A Führer-school.

his sole audience. A characteristic jest of his, funny enough but cruel in view of its topical significance, took the form of a series of questions to which, after a pause, he gave the answers. 'What sort of a woman does a German like to possess most?' he asked. 'A blonde? No! A brunette? No! A slender woman? No! A buxom one? No!' Then came, amid roars of laughter, his answer to the riddle. 'An Aryan grandmother!' I did not laugh. For I was thinking of my friend Professor Gerhard Lassar, who had held, when I first met him, the Chair of Constitutional Law in the University of Hamburg. Tall and fair, he looked typically 'Nordic.' A great scholar,[43] a charming man, with a gallant record as a Reserve officer in the last war, he told me one day, when on a visit to London, that he had been deprived of his Chair. When I asked him why, he replied sadly, 'Well, you see, they—the Nazis—wanted my Chair for one of their Storm-troopers, and they discovered that one of my grandparents was a Jewess.' Poor, wounded name! A few months afterwards he committed suicide.

Just as I was leaving, *somno vinoque defessus*, in the small hours of the morning, in spite of the hospitable entreaties of Herr Bart, who insisted that the night was still young, he made a supreme effort to convince me of the pacifist sentiments of the Nazis. And a very remarkable effort it was, reminding me of nothing so much as my encounter with his Excellency General von Kluck. They did not want war, he explained, with any 'civilized' country. They had only re-armed to defend Europe against the dark forces of Russia. 'What about France?' I said, thinking of a notorious passage in the 135th German edition of *Mein Kampf* which I had bought the day before at Wiesbaden—in the authorized English translation it had been thoughtfully omitted. 'Ah, you English people don't understand,' replied Herr Bart. 'The Führer *loves* the French. We all do!' '*Wirklich?*'[44] I replied, trying hard to look as if I believed this astonishing statement, and apparently succeeding. 'Yes,' he said dreamily, 'I served in France during the Great War. We were very popular with the French people behind the lines. Very popular. You see, we used to share our last crust with them.' '*Wunderbar!*'[45] I exclaimed, and

[43] At my request, as Legal Editor of the *Encyclopaedia Britannica*, he wrote the article on German Law for the 14th edition.

[44] 'Really?'

[45] 'Marvelous!'

Herr Bart evidently thought I was impressed, as indeed I was, though not quite in the way he thought. 'When the Armistice came,' he continued, 'the French people threw their arms round our necks and wept.' 'For joy?' I asked. 'No! *for sorrow*. We were leaving them, you see.'

The next day, which was 5 October, came the anti-climax, as I have called it, to all this impressive display of Nazi authority and prestige. The 38th Infantry Regiment of the old Army, now numbered the 80th, was to re-take possession of the barracks which it had been compelled to evacuate by the 'demilitarization' of the Rhineland and the Neutral Zone—in which Wiesbaden was situated—under the terms imposed on Germany by the Treaty of Versailles. A day of triumph, you would think, for the Nazis and their claim to have brought about the restoration of Germany's military power. Enormous crowds, massed on the pavements behind the police who lined the route, assembled to witness the march of the troops into Wiesbaden. The lamp-posts and houses were profusely decorated with huge swastika banners. The thousands of window-boxes without which no window in Germany is complete blazed with ivy-leaved geraniums and petunias in a riot of red and purple color. The sun shone with the splendor of midsummer and not a little of its heat. I had been given a post of vantage just behind the 'base' from which a General was to take the salute, with the result that I was a witness at very close quarters of the dramatic anti-climax, for it was just at this point that it all happened. The saluting-base was a raised, circular platform half-way down the broad avenue of the Wilhelmstrasse at a point, known as the Theater-Platz, where, on the opposite side of the avenue, the long line of tall houses is broken by an open square known as the Kursaal-Platz. These details are, as the reader will duly see, important in order to understand exactly what happened. Right across the Kursaal-Platz was posted a mass of Storm-troopers drawn up in close formation, in ranks about ten deep, like a solid phalanx. And very imposing they looked. Their position suggested a guard of honor, and as such no doubt they and their 'Führer' regarded themselves. They were in their yellowish uniforms with white armlets bearing a big swastika in black. In due course the triumphant music of a military band playing, appropriately enough, 'Die Wacht am Rhein,' reached our ears and the head of the column of troops appeared. They marched with the precision of a machine, doing the goose-step, and had been so marching in the blazing heat for at least four miles. I noticed that the rigid faces of the men were glistening with sweat. The officers, of course, were mounted, and magnificently mounted. The General's hand came smartly to the salute, as the long column with 'Eyes right' saluted him. The cheering of the crowds became deafening as company after company, separated by a few paces with the Company Commander riding at the head of each, passed the saluting base and continued straight on up the avenue. Two companies, forming the tail of the column, followed, and then suddenly, as they reached the saluting base, made a sharp turn to the left and headed straight for the Kursaal-Platz, occupied by the Storm-troopers who were only some twenty yards away. The movement took the Storm-troopers completely by surprise, and before they had time to do anything the soldiers of those two companies of the Reichswehr were upon them. Their impact upon the Storm-troopers was like that of a living wall —perhaps a tidal wave would be a more appropriate metaphor. The Nazis were knocked down like ninepins and fell in all directions. The Reichswehr marched over their prostrate bodies without even changing step. The soldiers neither pushed nor shoved, but continued to march onwards with perfect 'dressing,' their rifles still at 'the slope' at the exact angle, their legs continuing to do the goose-step as their heavy iron-shod feet came down on the bodies of the Storm-troopers. The latter, I noticed, never moved, but lay like so many corpses, reminding me of nothing so much as the story I have told above [46] of the man who lay silent and immobile under the blows of a German officer's riding-whip. A dead silence fell on the cheering crowds. As the rear rank of the last company of the Reichswehr disappeared in the direction of the Kursaal, the fallen Storm-troopers picked themselves up, many of them no doubt badly bruised and with dislocated joints, for I noticed that they rose with difficulty, and limped painfully away. Their Troop-Führer, quite dazed, made no attempt to get them to re-form. The next moment the line of police, guarding the route along the avenue, withdrew, the crowds broke up in surging masses, and all was over. But not quite. The General, who, standing like a statue on his platform, had watched the humiliation of the

[46] At page 133.

Storm-troopers with an impassive face, now descended from his pedestal which was surrounded by the crowds who were pushing and shoving one another in all directions as though struggling for *Lebens-raum*. How, I wondered, for I was close to him and was myself unable to move in the crowd, would he get away? I need not have wondered if I had recalled the pride of place of the Officers' Corps as I had seen it in the streets of Berlin in the days of my youth. For, the moment he descended the bottom step of the saluting base and advanced, a striking figure in the long gray coat of his caste, booted and spurred, his head crowned with a spiked silver helmet, his left hand resting on the pommel of his sword, the crowd precipitately fell back in silence on both sides of him, as though in mortal fear of touching the hem of his garment. He strode right through them as though they were not there, looking neither to his right nor to his left. Then I knew that the German Officers' Corps had come into its own again.

Postscript: The sensational trials of certain German officers, some by court-martial, others by the civil 'People's Court,' in July 1944, for 'treason,' and their subsequent execution, which have occurred since this chapter was written and in type, may appear to qualify what I have said as to the ascendancy and the prerogatives of the German Officers' Corps. In my opinion they do not. I have dealt with this episode in the Introduction to this book.–The AUTHOR.

VIII. THE OFFICERS' CORPS TAKES THE FIELD

THE 'REVOLUTION' OF 1918, in other words the establishment of a Republican Government in Berlin, enabled the German Officers' Corps to shift on to the shoulders of the Majority Socialists the odious office of signing the Armistice and, in due course, the Treaty of Versailles. Indeed, as will be explained in the following chapter, the Republican Government could not have come into existence at all without the collusion of the German General Staff. But the new form of government did not outlive its usefulness to the Officers' Corps with the signature of the Treaty. If it had, they would not have tolerated it long. The wiser heads among the German General Staff, such as General von Seeckt and General Groener who had held aloof from von Luttwitz's ill-fated attempt against the Republic [1] in March 1920, realized that a Republican Government could still be immensely useful to them by serving to secure from the Allied Governments, particularly the British Government, concessions, amounting to so many revisions of the Treaty, in their favor, which they could never have hoped to secure if the Prussian monarchy had been restored or an avowedly Nationalist Government installed in Berlin. A 're-public' in the custody of the Reichswehr, as I have described it in an earlier chapter, could ask for concessions, particularly in the matter of disarmament, which the Reichswehr could not ask for itself. And the custody of the Reichswehr meant the custody of the Nationalist parties who, like the bureaucracy, were both militarists and monarchists to a man. Republican Ministers, particularly if they were Socialists, had only to represent to the Allied Governments, or rather to the British Government, that if the Treaty were enforced in all its rigor, they could not guarantee the continued existence of the Republic and of Parliamentary institutions—they had only to represent this to secure the most anxious attention in Downing Street. And something more than attention, namely support, in our Liberal Press, with the result that 'pacifist' elements in England, growing stronger

[1] See above, Chapter IV, 'The Revolt of the Reichswehr.'

167

every day, fell headlong into many a trap thus baited for them by the German militarists. The supreme example of this extraordinary and indeed paradoxical development was the fate of those Articles of the Treaty [2] which dealt with 'Penalties,' or, to use the expressive word employed by Mr. Churchill a little while ago, 'Retribution.' It was on this issue that, as early as February 1920 within barely four weeks of our arrival in Berlin, the German Officers' Corps took the field against the Treaty of Versailles and, as always, behind the screen of a 'Republican' Minister of Defense, in this case Herr Noske.

'Penalties' meant the trial and punishment by military tribunals, convened by the Allied Governments, of German officers, particularly the High Command, responsible for the outrages committed in the conduct of the war. This was a matter with which I had been intimately concerned from the day on which Lord Birkenhead appointed me Vice-Chairman of the British Government Committee, constituted on the eve of the Armistice, to inquire into breaches of the laws of war by the armed forces of Germany. Thousands of depositions which were, unfortunately as we shall see, never published, depositions taken down by our sub-committees and a staff of junior barristers employed for the purpose, established, as similar inquiries by the French and Belgian Governments had established, beyond the possibility of refutation the commission of 'grave offenses against international justice and against humanity' as the Allied Governments put it in their reply to the protest of the German Government against the draft conditions of peace.[3] In the covering 'Letter' accompanying their reply, the Allied Governments drove home this charge in language not a word too strong.[4] Indeed, it is a significant fact that, in their immensely long and detailed note of protest against the harsh-

---

[2] Articles 227, 228, 229, 230.

[3] *Réponse des Puissances alliées et associées*, at p. 27.

[4] *Lettre d'envoi au Président de la Délégation allemande*, at p. 3 where, to quote the English text, the following words were used: 'Germany is responsible *for the savage and inhuman manner in which the war was conducted*,' for 'a series of promiscuous shootings and burnings with the sole object of terrifying the inhabitants of Belgium into submission by the very frightfulness of their action,' for 'a piratical submarine campaign and the destruction of great numbers of innocent passengers and sailors by ruthless submarine crews.' The 'Letter' went on to recite a whole catalogue of other such crimes, committed during the years 1914-18, in language which, word for word, would apply equally to the conduct of the German Armed Forces in World War II.

ness of the terms of the Treaty, a Note which occupied no less than four columns of very small print in *The Times*, the German Government, while denying much else, made no attempt whatsoever to deny this trenchant accusation. By the Articles of the Penalties Section of the Treaty, Germany undertook to 'hand over' to the Allied and Associated Powers all persons accused of having committed such outrages whose names should be specified. It was a great mistake not to have insisted, as a term of the renewal of the Armistice, in February 1919, on the *immediate* surrender of the accused instead of making it a term of the Treaty. But this, as I will show in the 'Postscript' to the present chapter, was not the fault of the British Government. A List specifying these offenders was in due course submitted to the German Government. This 'Black List,' as it was called, contained originally no less than three thousand names. It was subsequently reduced to nine hundred in order to confine it to something like manageable proportions, and also to cases which left no room whatsoever for doubt as to the guilt of the accused. This was a vital matter, vital if, as the Allied Governments' Note had put it, that 'reign of Law among nations' was to be established 'which it was the agreed object of the Peace to set up.' Vital and, added the Allied Governments, 'necessary as a deterrent to others who, *at some later date*, might be tempted to follow the example of these crimes and inhuman acts.'

Immediately on the publication of this 'Black List,' there took place the first great trial of strength as to whether the Treaty of Versailles was to be enforced or not. As such, its issue was momentous. It ended in a victory for the German Officers' Corps and a capitulation on the part of the Allied Governments which can only be described as ignominious. When the List, the *Auslieferungsnote*, or Extradition Note, as it was called, was handed to the German Government's representative in Paris, Freiherr von Lersner, on 4 February 1920 he, with singular effrontery, refused to receive it, and it had to be sent to the German Foreign Office in Berlin by courier. The moment it arrived, the Nationalist Press were in full cry. 'The extradition,' trumpeted the *National Zeitung*, 'is out of the question.' [5] 'If the German Government'—it was a Socialist Government—'attempt to execute this surrender,' threatened the *Deutsche Allgemeine Zeit-*

---

[5] *'Die Auslieferung ist unmöglich'*—the *National Zeitung* (Acht Uhr Abendblatt), 6 February 1920.

ung, 'they will encounter the strongest opposition,' hinting very plainly that none of the police would 'dare' to carry out their orders. 'Do the Government really think,' demanded the *National Zeitung*, 'that the Reichswehr officers are prepared to see their former comrades handed over to these foreign Governments for trial?' The Socialist Press seemed frightened by all this outcry. A still small voice, that of the Independent Socialists (the *Unabhängigen*), who were a tiny minority [6] and not represented in the Socialist Government, did, indeed, venture to point out that 'After all, we have signed the Treaty, *and it must be fulfilled*' (*Er muss erfüllt werden*). 'Fore God and men' (*Vor Gott und den Menschen*), retorted the *National Zeitung* with pious indignation, 'this is a disgraceful utterance.' The organ of the party nominally in power, the Socialist *Vorwärts*, was sorely perplexed and did not quite know what to say. It made no attempt whatsoever to exculpate the offenders on the Black List, at the head of which appeared, with every justification, the name of Ludendorff, for he, even more than von Kluck whose butchery of 674 old men, women and children at Dinant stank to heaven, was notoriously responsible for the greatest of the crimes, for the miseries of the Belgian deportations, the horrors of 'unrestricted' submarine warfare and for much else besides. The leading article in the *Vorwärts* was, indeed, a curiously damning plea of confession and avoidance:

We cannot too decisively reject the standpoint of those who would make heroes and martyrs of the accused. Granting that they have committed the acts with which they are charged, acts of which the German people ought to be ashamed, it is by these acts that they have brought upon us the fearful situation in which the German people now finds itself. Sympathy for the accused therefore simply cannot enter into any consideration of what should be the attitude of our Government and the mass of our people on this question.[7]

'But,' was the lame and impotent conclusion of the writer, 'even those of us who view the accused with the strongest repugnance, cannot but feel that the reckoning (*die Auseinandersetzung*) with them is a domestic matter for Germany herself to deal with and not for a foreign tribunal.'

The next day a curious, not to say sinister, Proclamation to the

---

[6] They had only 22 out of 469 seats in the Reichstag.
[7] The *Vorwärts*, 4 February 1920.

German people was issued by the Socialist Minister of Defense, Herr Noske, who was strongly suspected by many of his party, and not without reason, to be hand in glove with the German Officers' Corps. It was signed by the *Oberbefehlshaber* [8] and countersigned by Noske as Minister. And this was what it said:

KEEP YOUR DIGNITY!

Great though the excitement in the people is on account of the Entente Governments' Extradition demand, expression must be given to our expectation that a dignified demeanor be observed to the extent that every molestation of members of the foreign Military Commission must come to an end, so that I am not compelled to take far-reaching measures for their protection.[9]

'Don't nail his ears to the pump.' There was not the faintest sign of 'excitement' in Germany, except in the Nationalist Press, and least of all in Berlin. No one had made the slightest attempt to 'molest' any of us, least of all myself who, for obvious reasons, was the person most likely to be molested. 'If the Germans have been compiling during the war a Black List of their own of British officers,' said General Macdonogh, with grim pleasantry, to me, discussing these things when he and the C.I.G.S., Sir Henry Wilson, invited me to proceed to Berlin, 'you may be sure your name is at the head of it.' It was not unlikely. My appointment as Vice-Chairman of the 'War Crimes' Inquiry Committee towards the end of the war had been announced in *The Times* and the German Government, who think of everything, had, no doubt, duly noted the fact.

Noske's Proclamation was exploited, as no doubt its authors meant it to be, for all it was worth by the Nationalist Press. Within a few hours they all came out with big headlines, 'PROTECTION FOR THE KONTROL-KOMMISSIONEN STRENGTHENED.' An 'inconspicuous' (*unauffällig*) police patrol was, they declared, taking special care of us. I never knew until that moment that we were being 'protected' by the police at all, and I doubt if we ever were. Their protection was only too conspicuous by its absence on really critical occasions as, for example, when we were doing an inspection of units in barracks and were the objects, as we were at times, of hostile demonstrations

[8] Commander-in-Chief.
[9] Published in the *Deutsche Allgemeine Zeitung*, 5 February 1920.

by the troops. Unfortunately, my British colleague on the Council of the Control Commission, General Bingham, took all these things at their face value, which was a way he had. He was now asked by our own Government for a report on the situation and discussed it with me accordingly. 'We might as well all go home at once,' he said to me gloomily, 'if the British and French Governments persist in this demand.' To this I strongly demurred. 'We might just as well go home if they do not,' I retorted bluntly, 'for if our Governments throw up the sponge on a major issue of the Treaty like this, we shall be kept here for years instead of months,[10] and will never succeed in disarming the country at all; it is all a try-on and, what is much more serious, a trial of strength.' My arguments had no effect on him, and he dispatched an alarming report to London.

On the day after von Lersner's impudent refusal in Paris to accept delivery of the 'Black List' the *Daily News* came out with a leading article in which the following strange passage occurred:

> One cannot understand how reasonable and honorably minded people can view with other than anxiety the demand of the Allied Governments for the Extradition in the form in which it has been published. There are very strong indications that the threatening behavior of the Entente in this matter has produced more unrest in Germany than all the other measures which the Peace Treaty carries in its train.

Great was the joy in the Nationalist Press of Germany over this first sign of repentance in England for what an ex-Editor of the *Daily News*, going one better, was to call, a little later, '*the criminal Treaty of Versailles*,' an epithet which was joyfully circulated all over the world in hundreds of thousands of copies of a propagandist pamphlet put forth by the *Fichte Verein* of Hamburg. The *Deutsche Allgemeine Zeitung*, in particular, reproduced the *Daily News* article in 'leaded' type.[11] Nor was this all. 'Why not,' the *Daily News* obligingly suggested, 'drop the idea of trying *only German* offenders and of trying them before *Allied Tribunals?*' The innuendo that we ourselves, or our Allies, might have committed such outrages was meat and drink to the German Press. The suggestion that 'neutrals,' of

---

[10] The terms of the Treaty provided that the Disarmament of Germany was to be carried out in six months. As the result of obstruction, we were kept there seven years.

[11] The *Deutsche Allgemeine Zeitung*, 5 February 1920.

which there were none to be found except very small Powers like
Switzerland, Holland, and the Scandinavian countries, all neighbors,
and fearful neighbors at that, of the still mighty power of Germany,
should constitute the tribunal, was even more acceptable in Berlin.

What followed was no less ludicrous than lamentable. The ardor
expressed in Mr. Lloyd George's famous Newcastle speech on the
eve of his 'Khaki Election,' colloquially known as the 'Hang the
Kaiser speech,' had been cooling long before matters now came to a
head. Even at the Peace Conference, Mr. Lloyd George seemed to
take but a languid interest in the matter. A story, for the truth of
which I cannot vouch, went the round of the British Delegation that
Clemenceau, getting impatient at the British Prime Minister's delay
in producing the Black List to be compiled by the British Government, said to him one day at the council-table: 'Mr. Prime Minister,
I can understand your growing indifference to this matter: *you have
a General Election behind you*, but we have one in front of us and
the French people feel very strongly about this question.' Be that as
it may, Mr. Lloyd George appears to have been only too ready to
give ear to a compromise which the German Government, in due
course, put before the Allied Governments. It was that a kind of
'token trial' of some of the offenders should be conducted by a German Court, sitting in Germany. The proposal was accepted by the
Allied Governments on 13 February 1920. I have called this a capitulation and an ignominious one. For, barely eight months earlier, the
Allied Governments, in their reply of 16 June 1919, to a German protest that Germans accused of 'war crimes' could only be tried, if at
all, by German courts, had retorted by saying 'it is *impossible* to en-
trust in any way the trial of those directly responsible for offenses
against humanity and international right *to their accomplices in their
crimes.*' The result of the compromise was an equally ignominious
farce. To call it 'window-dressing' would be to pay it too high a
compliment unless the metaphor be taken to mean that nothing but
'dummy goods' were exhibited. The trial took place at Leipzig before
the 'Criminal Senate' of the Supreme Court of the Reich. I attended
it. A handful of cases, twelve out of the three thousand, were selected.
Only three of the accused were Generals, the rest, with the exception
of a Major, were junior officers or N.C.O.s, and one private. When
I told General Barthélemy this, he exclaimed, not without irony,

'Generals! Then of course they will be acquitted.' They were. The case against one of them, General Karl Stenger, accused of ordering a massacre of French prisoners and wounded, was pretty black, but he was not even put on trial. The Public Prosecutor asked the Court to dismiss the charge against him, and they did. And so with the other two Generals. The Major, who was a sort of scapegoat, got two years' imprisonment—two years for murder.

Three of the accused, Neumann, a private, Heynen, an N.C.O., and Muller, a 'Reserve' officer, were charged with ill-treating British prisoners of war in camps in which thousands of our men had died like flies as the direct result of such ill-treatment.[12] Neumann kicked our men in the stomach and systematically knocked them about with the butt of his rifle. The Leipzig Court found the charges against him proved. But a German General, von Fransecky, was present in court, holding a 'watching brief' for the German Officers' Corps. The Court treated him with almost servile deference. After hearing the evidence, General Fransecky, without disputing a word of it, gave it as his 'expert' opinion that Neumann had only done 'his duty' and was 'a model of a dutiful German soldier.' The Court, suitably impressed— or intimidated—let Neumann off with two months' imprisonment. Heynen had struck a sick man in the face, kicked men too weak to stand up, as they lay on the ground, and tortured a man mentally deranged till he 'cried every night in his sleep.' The Court again held the charges proved and General Fransecky again came forward to justify these brutalities on the ground that 'obedience in camps' must be secured 'at all costs.' Heynen got off with ten months. The Re-serve officer, Captain Muller, was almost too hard a nut even for General Fransecky, although he did his best for him. Muller, a huge man who continually interrupted the proceedings in Court, habitually thrashed sick men with his stick, kicked them as they lay on the ground, rode them down when he was on horseback, and amused himself by taking snapshots of them with his camera as they were using an exposed latrine. These charges were also proved to the satis-

[12] A British Committee of Inquiry had overwhelming evidence of this. A sub-committee reported, after investigating seventy thousand cases, that they dis-closed 'a system of shocking barbarity such as would be unbelievable, were it not established beyond the possibility of doubt.' A certain report which has never been published is given in an Appendix to this book.

faction of the Leipzig Court which, after insisting that Muller took the photographs 'with no ill feeling' but merely 'to commemorate his service as Commandant,' sentenced him to a nominal six months' imprisonment—nominal because they thoughtfully deducted from his sentence all the time he had been in detention awaiting trial.

But what happened in the case of two German naval officers, Lieutenants Dittmar and Boldt, accused of one of the most atrocious outrages of the war,[13] was even more significant. On 27 June 1918 a British hospital ship, the *Llandovery Castle*, returning from Canada, was torpedoed without warning by a German submarine on which Dittmar and Boldt were serving. The human freight of the *Llandovery Castle* consisted entirely of non-combatants: a crew of 164 and 80 officers and men of the R.A.M.C., together with 14 nurses. Three boats were hurriedly launched. Only one was ever seen again. As she rowed away out of sight, her crew heard the sound of continuous firing from the submarine. A number of witnesses from the crew of the submarine and two captured British merchant service officers, who were on board of her, gave evidence that the U-boat turned her gun on the remaining two ship's boats, one of them containing the fourteen nurses, and continued firing until they were sent to the bottom with all their living freight. The accused officers, Boldt and Dittmar, who had the most villainous faces I have ever seen, refused to give evidence. But their defending counsel had the audacity to call a number of German 'witnesses' in an attempt to prove that the British Navy frequently committed such atrocities at sea. Their 'evidence' was all 'hearsay,' and bad hearsay at that. After this had gone on for some time, the British Delegation, headed by the Solicitor-General, Sir Ernest Pollock, who was present and held a kind of 'watching

[13] I know of only two worse cases. They came before the British Government Committee of which I was Vice-Chairman and I am indebted to the Admiralty for having recently given me details of them which have refreshed my memory. They were the cases of two British merchant ships, the S.S. *Belgian Prince* and the S.S. *Torrington*. The former was torpedoed on 31 July 1917. The Master was taken prisoner by the submarine and sent below. The crew were ordered to line up on the submarine's deck. Their life-belts were taken away from them and the submarine then submerged, leaving them to drown. Three only, who had managed to hide their belts under their coats, survived to bear witness to the atrocity committed. They were picked up the next morning by our patrol boats. The crew of the *Torrington* were treated in exactly the same way.

brief,' protested. Thereupon the President of the Court suddenly affected to discover, what he had known all along, that this impudent diversion was irrelevant and such 'evidence' inadmissible. The Court eventually held the charge against Boldt and Dittmar proved. For this murder of some thirty or forty [14] defenseless men and women in open boats, these two scoundrels received a sentence of four years' imprisonment. They never served it. Within a few weeks I read in the German Press the news that they had 'escaped' from prison. They were never rearrested. They were quite young and were soon probably once again engaged in the conduct of 'unrestricted' submarine warfare on the high seas.

Thus ended the Leipzig Trials. They were never resumed. Nearly three thousand inculpated German officers, Ludendorff and von Kluck among them, were never so much as brought to trial at all. Only one regular Army officer, the Major, was convicted. The Allied Governments acquiesced and threw up the sponge. A shout of triumphant laughter went up all over Germany.[15] The German Officers' Corps had 'got away with it.'

[14] In addition to the two score or so—their exact numbers were never known —thus massacred as they attempted to row away from the sinking ship, nearly 200 souls on board, who were unable to lower boats, were drowned. Only twenty-four persons, namely those in the one boat which managed to escape the submarine's murderous fire, were saved.

[15] A German comic weekly with an immense circulation, *Kladderadatsch*, in its issue of 5 June 1921, came out with a parody of the evidence against Neumann, Heynen, and Muller in which the British prisoners of war were represented as complaining that they were not served with eggs and bacon for breakfast. The Nationalist Press, in particular the *Deutsche Zeitung* and the *Lokalanzeiger*, saluted the trials as a complete vindication of the German Army. Even a Radical paper, the *Vossische Zeitung*, defended the brutalities of Heynen and denounced the almost nominal sentence he received as 'unjust.' The result of the acquiescence of the British Government, particularly as none of the Reports of its Committee of Inquiry into breaches of the Laws of War by the German Armed Forces were ever published, was to give countenance to German propaganda which now got busy with the accusation that all German atrocities were entirely the invention of our own Ministry of Propaganda during the war. Even in England this German propaganda was not without its effect among the post-war generation. At the beginning of the Second World War a letter by a Cambridge undergraduate appeared in the *Spectator* expressing the pious hope that there would be no such talk in England of German 'atrocities' such as had 'disfigured' our conduct of the last war.

POSTSCRIPT

I have said in the foregoing chapter that it was 'a great mistake' on the part of the Allied Governments not to have insisted, as a term of the renewal of the Armistice in February 1919, on the immediate surrender of the German officers accused of 'war crimes' instead of making the surrender a term of the Treaty. In saying this, which is pretty obvious to every one today, I, at least, am not being 'wise after the event.' There can be no harm, at this distance of time, in disclosing what actually happened in Paris in February 1919. On 21 January of that year Lord Birkenhead, who had just been appointed Lord Chancellor, visited Paris in company with his successor as Attorney-General, Sir Gordon Hewart, and, after a long talk with me on the subject of 'War Crimes,' asked me to prepare the British Case for the use of the Law Officers of the Crown as the British representatives on the Inter-Allied Commission of the Peace Conference which had just been empaneled to deal with its subject. Accordingly, I wrote on 24 January a long 'Opinion' which was accepted without amendment by Birkenhead and Gordon Hewart, the latter of whom, when he was unable to attend the sittings of the Commission in Paris, was represented by Sir Ernest Pollock, the Solicitor-General, with the Prime Minister of New Zealand, Mr. Massey, attending as the 'Dominion' representative. I was requested to attend the sittings of the Commission as a kind of 'junior devil' to the Law Officers, but I also held a 'watching brief,' as A.A.G. in the Military Section, for the Adjutant-General who was closely concerned in view of a proposal of my own, strongly supported by General Macdonogh and eventually adopted, that any trials should be held by British, French, or Belgian *military courts*, in other words by courts-martial. In the course of the Opinion I wrote as follows:

The exercise of a *post-bellum* jurisdiction can only be secured by special covenants to that effect in a Treaty of Peace, but the surrender of offenders and the delivery of documents is a proper subject for the imposition of conditions in an Armistice, and I recommend that these two objects be secured by this means *at the earliest possible moment*. Offenders may escape to neutral countries and documents be destroyed if this is not done at once, and indeed there is reason to apprehend that such evasive operations are already being practised. The Allies are at present practically in the position of being able to send what may be called their process-servers into any part of Germany, they can extend the area of occupation *manu militari* and they can dispatch missions into any part of Germany as part of the terms of the Armistice. The state of war gives the Armistice a recurrent sanction but *once Peace is signed this instrument of compulsion will be gone*. It would, therefore, be fatal to defer the formulation and presentation of these demands until the Treaty of Peace is presented to the German Government. If, under the Treaty, the German Government agreed to such demands and subsequently after its ratification and the consequent termination of the Armistice failed or refused to comply with them, it might be almost impossible to enforce them. Moreover, it is in every way desirable that the courts, or divisional tribunals, for the trial of offenders should begin to sit *at once*, exercising an uncovenanted military jurisdiction such as they undoubtedly posses so long as the Armistice lasts, *but no longer*, under the laws and customs of war. Not only may the offenders otherwise escape or conceal themselves under assumed names but, with the rapid acceleration of Demobilization among the Allies, many of the witnesses may return to civil life and be lost beyond recall.

This proposal, after its adoption by the British Government, was strongly urged upon the Inter-Allied Commission at their second sitting in Paris on 7 February, at which I was present, and received almost unanimous support. But, to everybody's consternation, the American representative, Mr. Lansing, President Wilson's Secretary of State, vehemently opposed it, declaring that, if it was carried, he would decline to present it to the 'Supreme Council.' None the less, it was carried. But, no doubt on Mr. Lansing's representations, President Wilson secured its rejection by the Council. In the hope of averting a similar fiasco at the end of the second war, I drew the attention of the present Lord Chancellor, Lord Simon, soon after his accession to the Woolsack, to all that had happened in 1919-20, sending him a copy of the Opinion in question and, if I may judge by his public utterances since then, he, like his predecessor Lord Birkenhead, agrees, in language identical with that of my Opinion, with all that I ventured to urge, only too vainly, in January 1919. But I find it difficult to understand what Lord Simon means when he speaks, as he did in the House of Lords on 7 October 1942, of the *next* 'Armistice.' At this point he has paid me the compliment of following the language of my Opinion a little too closely. An Armistice is a cessation of hostilities, nothing more if nothing less, and it was the declared policy of the 'United Nations' not to grant an Armistice at all but to insist on an 'unconditional surrender,' which is not an Armistice but a capitulation, although, of course, it admits, like an Armistice, of the resumption of hostilities if necessary.

. . . .
. . . .
. . . .

PART THREE

IX. THE SCENT OF MUSCOVY

I

A 'Red Army' in the Ruhr—'All is not quiet on the Western Front'—
The Neutral Zone and its significance—The Reichswehr takes the field—
Commandant Graff and his mission—The Reichswehr's butcheries—The
truth about 'the Red Terror'—The French occupation of Frankfurt—The
legend of 'The Black Shame'—Sir Malcolm Robertson's observations—
General Demesse and his Moroccan troops—The advent of the *agents
provocateurs*—The truth about the French occupation of the Ruhr—Von
Kahr and his tragic fate.

II

The Bolshevist specter and German Propaganda—English half-heartedness about the Disarmament of Germany, and its explanation—The English character and the German—The English delusion about Germany 'going Red'—The German Revolution and its Russian affinities—Its repudiation of them—Rejection of the Russian ideology—'The Revolution is
ended'—The fate of the Workers' and Soldiers' Councils in Germany—A
Revolution 'made with rose-water'—The persistence of the Monarchist
tradition—The exploitation of the Revolution by the German General
Staff—The myth of the 'Stab in the Back' and Hitler's appropriation of it
—Hitler on the Jews as the real assassins—The Russian Revolution in the
light of history—'Reversion to type' in Germany and in Russia—German
incapacity for self-government, and its cause.

FOR FIVE WEEKS after the revolt of the Reichswehr had petered out
in Berlin, the Reichswehrministerium were singularly coy in their
communications with us. They were desperately busy, they subsequently explained, dealing with a 'counter-revolution,' a revolution
which threatened the peace not only of Germany but of the whole of
Western Europe. A 'Red Army' had suddenly risen out of the ground
overnight in the great industrial district, the *Industriegebiet*, of the
Ruhr immediately east of the Rhine, three Reichswehr battalions
policing the Neutral Zone [1] had been compelled to take refuge in
Cologne, the hidden hand of 'Moscow' was strongly suspected, and
the Reichswehrministerium had been reluctantly compelled, in view

---

[1] For an explanation of what was meant by this term, see below, p. 185.

of the urgency of the situation, to dispatch without first asking our permission heavy reinforcements, including no less than twenty-eight batteries of field artillery, in excess of the local garrisons authorized by us, in order that they might deal with this grave menace. Such was the tenor of a laconic communication we received from the Ministry on 27 March. It was very polite, not to say propitiatory. We had, however, already dispatched two of our officers, Commandant Graff and Captain Wauchope, to the scene of hostilities, and we immediately instructed them to investigate the truth of these representations and report to us. This they did in due course. And a very illuminating report it was. After which interlude, the Reichswehrministerium found time, on 24 April 1920, to give their attention once more to us, although, as they were careful to explain, one must not assume that all was quiet on the Western Front.

This was a new and startling situation. It did not startle us, but it certainly 'put the wind up' among many people at home, including one or two eminent members of the British Cabinet. There was, at this very time, a real if somewhat melodramatic war, intermittent but lowering, on the eastern marches of German's next-door neighbor, the newly created State of Poland, with a real 'Red Army' threatening the Poles, a threat which came to a head some four months later. If the Western marches of unoccupied Germany, in other words the Neutral Zone, were now also threatened by an indigenous 'Red Army' on the spot, what would happen to Germany with the two Red Armies converging on her, the Russian Red Army sweeping across Poland from the East and a German home-grown Red Army, with the Neutral Zone as its base, sweeping across Central Germany from the West? And what would then happen, in due course, to our armies of occupation on the Rhine? The situation certainly looked grave. On 20 March the German Press announced in large headlines 'The Fall' of Essen and Mulheim, on the following day Duisburg and Dusseldorf 'fell.' On 21 March it was announced that the Reichswehr garrison had been compelled to evacuate the great Rhine port of Duisburg-Ruhrort. The Red Army of the Ruhr, according to the German Nationalist newspapers, was in wireless communication with Moscow, and one enterprising journal, published at Wesel, gave currency to a rumor that Lenin, who appeared to be ubiquitous, was in Dortmund—in the very heart of the Ruhr.

This sudden conflagration in the Neutral Zone was a new political phenomenon and the more surprising because, from the moment the Allied Armies of occupation had, immediately following the signature of the Armistice in November 1918, marched into the Rhineland and occupied the Rhine bridgeheads, the Zone, commanded as it was by their guns, had been comparatively free from disturbances of any kind. The transient epidemic of 'Bolshevism' which had burst out in Berlin and Munich in the early days of the Armistice had never extended to the Ruhr.[2] With the end of the Armistice and the coming into force of the Treaty on 10 January 1920, the Neutral Zone, by that time extended [3] to a boundary fifty kilometers east of the Rhine, was largely beyond the range of our guns, but the sedative effect of the Allied occupation in the immediate neighborhood across the Rhine continued to make itself felt. It was not till two months later, namely on 17 March, that the new trouble in the Ruhr began. The German Government had, it is true, always professed anxiety about the 'neutralization' of the Zone. Neutralization meant, of course, the immediate evacuation of the territory by all the armed forces of Germany and their substitution, if necessary, by reinforcements of German police. The creation of such a Zone was an obvious military precaution on the part of the authors alike of the Armistice terms and of the Treaty, for without it the territory in question, immediately contiguous as it was to the occupied territory and divided only from it by the river, might be used by our late enemy for the assembly of covering troops to mask a prospective attack on the armies of occupation. None the less, the German Government had, as early as August 1919, pressed the Allied Governments to be allowed, in the interests of 'peace and good order,' to retain troops in the fifty-kilometer zone after the Treaty came into force. This was conceded, subject to two conditions imposed on the advice of

[2] There had been an industrial disturbance in the Ruhr in February 1919 in the form of a general strike for the nationalization of the coal-mines. It soon petered out and there was very little bloodshed.

[3] By the terms of the Armistice (Article v) it was provided that 'A neutral zone shall be reserved on the right bank of the Rhine between the river and a line drawn parallel to the bridgeheads (i.e. the principal crossings of the Rhine, Mainz, Cologne, Coblenz), and to the river and 10 kilometers distant from them, between the Dutch Frontier and the Swiss Frontier.' By Articles 42 and 43 of the Treaty this 'Zone' was, in effect, extended to a distance of 50 kilometers east of the Rhine.

Marshal Foch, one limiting the effectives, the other limiting the period of their retention. The effectives were to be limited to twenty battalions of infantry, two squadrons of cavalry, and two batteries of artillery. The period of their retention was to be limited to three months after the date of the Treaty.[4] We always found, in dealing with the German Government, that, in the matter of concessions, it was invariably a case of *c'est le premier pas qui coûte*—the 'cost' always falling on us. The more we conceded, the more they asked. No sooner had the 'Advanced Guard' of our Commission arrived in Berlin than, on 9 October, barely seven weeks after this concession had been made, we were assailed with a protest from the German Government, that the forces authorized to remain in the Neutral Zone for the time being were 'very insufficient.' They did not ask for more than the twenty infantry battalions already concerned. But they pressed for no less than twenty batteries of artillery. Twenty batteries of artillery to 'deal with' the civil population of a zone in a state of profound domestic peace was a novel proposition. We rejected it. The demand was, as will duly appear, significant of much to come—how significant we did not know at the time. The Note in which it was conveyed to us also contained a hint that the limitation of the period, the three months at the end of which the German troops were to evacuate the Zone altogether, might not be easy to observe owing to a 'difficulty' in finding German police to take their place. Germany was at this very time swarming with 'police.' Whole companies of all the demobilized regiments of the Guard were being transformed, almost *en masse*, into 'centuries' (*Hundertschaften*) of the new *Sicherheitspolizei*.[5] Wherefore we were unimpressed. But this hint was, as also appeared in due course, significant. Well has it been said that the Germans think of everything while the British think of nothing, if by 'thinking' is to be understood looking ahead.

The date on which the troubles broke out in the Ruhr was 17 March. This was just twenty-four days before the German troops were due to evacuate the Ruhr district, together with the other sectors of the Neutral Zone. Within the next ten days, the Reichswehrministerium proceeded to dispatch into the Ruhr sector, without our

[4] i.e. the date of its ratification, namely 10 January 1920.
[5] i.e. the 'Security Police.'

foreknowledge or consent, no less than twenty-eight batteries of artillery, together with fourteen more infantry battalions, in addition to the authorized twenty battalions which were already concentrated on the spot. Armored car units, 'minenwerfer' companies, companies of sappers, motor-transport columns, followed hard on their heels: all of these being formations unauthorized by Marshal Foch's Note. And, oddly enough, twenty 'centuries' of the Security Police were suddenly found to be available and posted to the Ruhr at the same time as the German Army reinforcements surged into it. Then, on 9 April, exactly twenty-four hours before the German troops were due, under the terms of the concession made by the Supreme Council of the Peace Conference in the preceding August, to evacuate the Neutral Zone altogether, the Reichswehrministerium demanded that the evacuation be postponed for another three months, at the same time requesting our *ex post facto* approval of the presence of the heavy reinforcements they had dispatched there. Unfortunately for this belated request, we received within the next forty-eight hours the report of Commandant Graff and Captain Wauchope, who returned to Berlin on 11 April. That report was devastating. A copy of it was sent by courier the same night to the 'Conference of Ambassadors' in Paris, which had taken the place of the now defunct Supreme Council of the Peace Conference, and its effect was instantaneous.

Graff's report was a brilliant piece of 'Intelligence' work. He was an Alsatian by birth, a Breton by domicile, tall and dark, with an air of distinction, a lover of the *beaux arts*, and a discriminating collector, with a numismatist's passion for coins, images, and superscriptions. Like many another French officer serving on our Commission, he had an excellent literary taste and was deeply read in his country's great treasury of *belles lettres*. To him, indeed, I owe—and the debt is a great one—my introduction to Renan, which commenced on the day when he walked into my room, which was next to his at the Bellevue, and asked me to accept, with a graceful inscription ('*un souvenir du travail en commun*'), a copy of *Ma Soeur Henriette*. Not that any of these artistic accomplishments intruded into his report, which was a soldierly effort, precise, closely reasoned, 'documented,' and totally devoid of rhetoric. He had been everywhere in the Ruhr, interviewing the Bürgermeisters of Essen, Duisburg, Dusseldorf,

Dortmund, and all the rest of its thickly congregated factory towns which are hung together like pearls, if very black pearls, on a string. He had been in constant personal touch with the German staff officers on the spot who were only too anxious to see him and to impress him. As Gladstone said of Wellington, Graff had 'a wonderful gift of listening.' It was to prove very useful just now. The German officers talked—and he listened. And the more he listened, the more freely, and indeed indiscreetly, they talked. Germans, I have often observed, always assume that silence means acquiescence. They are accustomed to interrupt violently every one with whom they do not agree, which probably accounts for their assumption. Wherefore, if you listen long enough, and are careful never to interrupt, they often give themselves away in the most handsome manner. But unlike the German officers, Graff had also established close 'contacts' with the leaders of the 'Red Army,' in other words, the local Communists, and equally with the Socialist and Trade Union leaders all over the Ruhr.

And this was his Report. When the news of the revolt of the Reichswehr against the Republic reached the Ruhr, the Trade Unions there, who were Socialists almost to a man,[6] responded, as everywhere else in Germany, to the appeal of the Republican Government by declaring a General Strike. In the Ruhr district there were a number of units of most unpleasant 'toughs' known as 'Free Corps,' whose acquaintance we have made in an earlier chapter,[7] and they had no business to be there. The workmen with such arms in their hands as they had—many of the demobilized men had kept possession of their rifles—chased these unwelcome visitors out of the neighborhood. The regular Reichswehr troops were content to look on, their officers waiting, apparently, to see which way the cat would jump in Berlin. When, a few days later, the news arrived, on 19 March, of the collapse of the Reichswehr revolt in Berlin, the vast majority of the workmen laid down their arms and went home. Up to this time, hardly a shot had been fired. The General Strike was called off as a matter of course, and the men went back to work. On the following day, however, posters appeared on the walls of Essen, and other towns in the Ruhr, in the name of the three 'Socialist' parties, the

[6] The Communist element in the Trade Unions was always extremely small. How small it was, the reader may discover later in these pages.

[7] See above, Chapter IV, 'The Revolt of the Reichswehr.'

'Majority' Socialists, the Independent Socialists, and the Communists, inviting the workers to 'down tools' again. The local leaders of the first two of these parties, Otto Brass, a Landtag Deputy, and Joseph Ernst, informed Commandant Graff that their respective parties knew nothing of this poster, and disavowed it. It was, indeed, a remarkable fact that, during the whole of the troubles that followed, every mine, forge, factory, and workshop in the Ruhr continued to work full time. Still more remarkable was the fact that in the great towns, Essen, Mulheim, Dusseldorf, and Duisburg, whose 'fall' before the assaults of the 'Red Army' had been reported all over Germany, and, in consequence, everywhere abroad, 'the most perfect order' prevailed from first to last.[8] None the less, on the day the fictitious posters appeared, the two companies of the Reichswehr quartered in Essen evacuated the town. Not a shot had been fired and the troops retired in perfect order. A few hours later the same scene was witnessed—by one of Graff's junior officer-interpreters, M. Breistroffer —at Mulheim, which was evacuated by two other companies of the same regiment. Within the next twenty-four hours, Dusseldorf and Duisburg were evacuated—also without a shot being fired. Such was 'the fall' of these great citadels of industry. Flitting from one to the other of them, Breistroffer and the other junior officers serving under Graff had been looking for the 'Red Army.' It was like looking for a needle in a haystack. They found no traces of it. The troops, thus ostentatiously withdrawn, were concentrated at Wesel under General von Kabisch who announced, by the agency of his 'Press Bureau,' which was as active all the time as his Army was inactive, that he was awaiting 'reinforcements' from the center of Germany. For five days he sat tight at Wesel while bands of armed Communist workmen, mostly youths, roamed at large over the Ruhr, doing a little looting, a little shooting, and a great deal of drinking. At Duisburg, the local Communists did indeed set up a 'Soviet' under the magic name of *Vollzugsrat*, announced the sequestration of all banking accounts, and put the Bürgermeister under 'arrest.' It was, however, very 'open' arrest, as they begged him to continue to carry on with his municipal duties and gave him a free hand with the telephone. He took it, and

---

[8] 'Le fait est que dans les villes (Essen, Mulheim, Dusseldorf, Duisburg) l'ordre le plus parfait régnait et que le travail avait été repris partout'—Graff's Report.

was 'on' to General von Kabisch's headquarters during the whole
time that the 'Soviet' lorded it over Duisburg. Their style was, indeed,
badly cramped at the outset by a plain intimation from the local railwaymen, postmen, and transport workers that if they did not mind
their own business they would throw them out. Thenceforth they
had to behave themselves like a constitutional monarch, reigning
without governing. Later they mysteriously disappeared. Graff, on
the evidence of local trade unionists, came to the conclusion that
these 'Communists' were in the pay of General von Kabisch. They
were, in fact, *agents provocateurs*.

During these five days of complete inertia at von Kabisch's headquarters, the German Press was flooded with reports of terrible
'atrocities' committed by the 'Red Army,' reports of 'Russian agents'
being busy in the Ruhr, and reports of a threat by the miners of the
Ruhr to flood the pits if the coal deliveries to the Allied Governments, under the terms of the Treaty, were not suspended. The
source of these reports was obvious, for Kabisch and his staff officers
had attempted to put the wind up with the imperturbable Graff by
telling him these very things a few hours before they appeared in the
Press. They were particularly eager to convince him that the Allied
Governments [9] were vitally interested in authorizing reinforcements,
as otherwise they would get no coal. Also, the 'Russian' agents 'would
provoke an attack on the Armies of Occupation.' 'When I asked
them for their proofs,' wrote Graff, 'they always shied'—*ils se sont
toujours dérobés quand je leur ai demandé des précisions*.[10] To a blunt
question from Graff, 'Why don't you *move?*' General von Kabisch
naïvely replied, 'I have *instructions* to wait for reinforcements.' At
the end of these five days, on 25 March, reinforcements arrived, and
two days later the Reichswehr troops began to take the offensive.
The 'Red Army' immediately began to 'go to pieces' (*se désagréger*)
as Graff put it. The older men, who knew what they were in for if
they remained, dropped out, leaving an 'army' of immature youths
who knew nothing of the realities of war, having been too young to

[9] I use this term, for the sake of brevity, to describe the Governments of
Great Britain, France, Belgium, and Italy.
[10] One of the Trade Union leaders, Herr Max, subsequently informed Commandant Graff that Kabisch's statement, that the Ruhr miners were opposed to
the coal deliveries to the Allied Governments, was wholly untrue.

be called up to the colors during the years 1914-18. Just as the offensive was getting under way, the Prussian Minister of the Interior, Herr Severing, a Socialist, arrived on 31 March at von Kabisch's headquarters and, horrified, no doubt, at the prospect of the butchery which he foresaw, tried to arrange an 'armistice,' backed by a telegram from the Reich Government in Berlin ordering the suspension of operations. Kabisch and his staff officers became 'very excited,' telling Graff that the Allied Governments had 'authorized' their reinforcements—which was quite untrue—and that they would send 'an ultimatum' to Berlin if they were not allowed to continue the offensive. They continued it. What exactly took place at the interview between von Kabisch and Severing no one ever knew, but it was clear from the apology he made to Brass, Ernst, and the other local leaders of the Social Democratic party who repeated his remarks to Graff, that the unhappy Minister lost his nerve. Like Noske on another occasion in the presence of another general, General Maercker, Severing 'came sharply to attention.' 'I could do nothing with the General so long as he had so many troops at his disposal,' pleaded the unhappy Minister. 'We don't care a damn for this fellow Severing,' declared one of Kabisch's staff officers to Graff.

Within less than a week, it was all over. It was, in fact, a butchery. The 'Red Army' was no match for the Reichswehr. Their raw levies had no higher organization, so far as they were organized at all, than companies of infantry, they had no staff, little transport, no cavalry, no signaling detachments, and only eight old guns very ill-provided with rounds of ammunition. By this time, there were thirty-four batteries of Reichswehr artillery and thirty battalions of infantry, all up to full strength, in the field against them. Graff, who was present at one of the 'battles' just north of Duisburg, reported that the Reichswehr casualties were negligible, but the losses of the 'Red Army' were very heavy, particularly as the Reichswehr 'took no prisoners.' Every man who surrendered was shot, usually by an officer with a revolver. Of this, the Reichswehr officers made no secret. 'You see,' said one of them, Major von Guishandt,[11] to Graff,

---

[11] 'Le Major von Guishandt me disait que les troupes *ouvrières* étaient composées de jeunes gens auxquels avait manqué pendant cinq années l'éducation paternelle et que, comme il était trop tard pour les dresser, le mieux était de les anéantir.'

'*most of these fellows are young men who during the five years of the war have had no paternal discipline, and, as it is too late to train them, the best thing is to wipe them out.*'

Graff's conclusions as to all this were irresistible. At the very commencement of the troubles, on 19 March, his officer-interpreter, M. Breistroffer, an Alsatian, had encountered on the outskirts of Essen the two companies of infantry whose evacuation of the town was so blithely reported in the German Press the next day as 'The Fall of Essen.' He asked one of the officers, a second lieutenant, what it all meant, remarking that he had just left the town in a state of profound peace. 'Can you no longer count on the Reichswehr?' he exclaimed. 'Oh, yes,' replied the German subaltern, 'we are only retiring according to plan, it is just *to prove to the Entente* that our forces in the Neutral Zone are not sufficient to maintain order.' This, indeed, was the explanation of the spectacular withdrawal of all the garrisons from the great towns of the Ruhr, and the ostentatious flight of three Reichswehr battalions, without a single casualty among them, across the river into Cologne—no doubt in the hope of exciting despondency and alarm in our army of occupation with tales of a 'Red terror' in the Ruhr. 'I am convinced,' wrote Graff, 'that the object of it all was to impose the conviction (*imposer la conviction*) on the Entente that a vast Bolshevik movement was on foot, directed by the Russians and likely to extend to the whole of Germany and even to the left bank of the Rhine.' The Reichswehrministerium were, in fact, as we shall see later,[12] playing for much higher stakes than the reinforcement of the authorized garrisons in the Neutral Zone and their retention. Two momentous 'Notes,' one addressed to us in Berlin on 24 April, the other to the Allied Governments in Paris on 20 April, just after the Ruhr troubles were all over, made that clear enough. Meanwhile, their attempt to secure the consent of our Governments to the indefinite retention of the reinforcements in the Ruhr met with a very disconcerting reply, for which Graff's report was no doubt responsible. That reply was: When you have withdrawn these reinforcements from the Ruhr, the French troops will evacuate Frankfurt.

This was a decidedly neat rejoinder. For the Germans were ex-

---

[12] In a second volume to be published later.

tremely sore at the presence of French troops in Frankfurt who had crossed the Rhine and occupied that historic city the moment the Reichswehrministerium began to move reinforcements into the Ruhr. The whole German Press was mobilized to denounce what they called this 'outrage.' Loud and vociferous was the Nationalist Press, in particular, at this act of 'aggression,' as they termed it. And yet it was their own action which had invited it, provoked it, and indeed justified it. For the Treaty of Versailles laid it down in clear and unmistakable terms that if Germany maintained, or assembled, any armed forces, or carried out any 'military maneuvers,' in the Neutral Zone without the consent of the Allied Governments, she should be 'regarded as committing a hostile act against the Powers signatory of the present Treaty and as calculated to disturb the peace of the world.[13] By her dispatch of the unauthorized reinforcements into the Ruhr, to say nothing of their 'maneuvers,' she had committed just such an act within the definition of the Treaty. The reaction of the French by the occupation of Frankfurt was therefore entirely justified, both legally and morally. The Germans, however, seized on this occupation as an opportunity, by the industrious use of *agents provocateurs*, of compromising the French in the eyes of the world, particularly of America and our own country. They were determined to provoke the French troops, particularly their Moroccan troops, beyond endurance. That a few Germans might get shot in the process, they, no doubt, confidently hoped and expected. Human life is cheap in Germany. In this they were, as will presently appear, disappointed by the extraordinary self-restraint of the French troops. These colored troops were, however, an admirable target for German propaganda, and it was now that the great imposture of 'The Black Shame' (*die schwarze Schande*) made its first appearance. Stories, all of them false,[14] of the excesses of the colored troops, and more par-

[13] Article 44.

[14] See Chapter XI, 'Germany in Defeat,' Section III, for an account of certain investigations by the writer into this matter, also Section IX, for some remarkable admissions by a German writer as to the shameless pursuit of the colored troops by German women. I am indebted to my friend Sir Malcolm Robertson, who was Rhineland High Commissioner in 1921, and who has read the above paragraph in proof, for the following observations: 'There was only a handful on the Rhine of really "black" troops, namely Soudanese. There was a Moroc-

ticularly of 'outrages' by them on German women, began to circulate
abroad and found a credulous ear in the Liberal Press of our own
country.

I got a vivid glimpse at first hand of the methods of the German
agents provocateurs against the French troops of occupation as early
as April 1920, methods which reached their climax during the French
occupation of the Ruhr three years later, by which time English
credulity left nothing to be desired by the German propagandists.
The occasion was a visit of inspection of mine to Frankfurt, where
we had one of our District Control Committees stationed. Immediately on my arrival I called on the officer in command of the French
troops of occupation, General Demesse. He was a tall, weather-beaten
soldier with a flowing mustache, and a quiet, gentle manner, who
reminded me in some subtle way of Colonel Newcome. Certainly a
man 'sans peur et sans reproche.' I noticed that he was wearing the
Morocco medal and the French war medal with no less than six
palms. I asked him about the behavior of the 'colored' troops under
his command. They were, in fact, not 'black' troops at all, but Moorish with a well-deserved reputation for both courage and discipline.

'I will tell you,' he said quietly. 'I had a company of them stationed
in the street in case there was any trouble. They had strict orders to
avoid any contact with the civil population and at all costs to avoid
any "incident." I don't know whether my orders got known among
the populace. It is possible—the German police are not exactly help-
ful and on this occasion they were quite invisible. At any rate, a
crowd of roughs hustled my men. They seemed determined to provoke them beyond endurance. They even tried to seize their rifles
and some students attempted to carry off a machine-gun. Fortunately
my Algerians are pretty stout fellows and they managed to knock out
some of the rioters with their fists, whereupon the rest ran away. A
few days later a group of German students called at my headquarters.'

'To apologize?' I asked.

'Well, not exactly,' replied Demesse with a faint smile. 'It was to
tell us to "clear out." They told one of my staff officers that "Lloyd

can Division that had won the *fouragère* and were *some of the best behaved
troops on the Rhine.* Hitler's friend, General Franco, does not hesitate to use
Moorish troops in his own country.'

George" and "*die Amerikaner*" would have nothing more to do with us.'

The impudence of the Frankfurt students was not the mere irresponsibility of adolescence. They knew what they were talking about. Theirs was, in fact, the first manifestation of the German Government's policy of driving, by subsidized agitation, studied mendacity, foreign propaganda, and all the black arts of *Scharfmacherei* peculiar to the German official mind, a wedge between the British nation and the French. They were 'banking' on the temperamental instability of our own Prime Minister who had been a most reluctant convert at the Peace Conference to any military occupation of the Rhineland at all, being apparently under the comfortable delusion that the Treaty of Versailles would execute itself. Moreover, he had already addressed a sharp Note, of which Germany knew at once, for no secret was made of it, to the French Government, admonishing them for their impropriety in taking unilateral action by marching into Frankfurt, on 6 April, without first consulting him and acting, if need be, in concert. But if the French had waited to debate the question of action with Mr. Lloyd George—and the debate would probably have been interminable—there would have been just such a 'rough house' in Frankfurt as the German Nationalists were determined to provoke in order to have an excuse for pouring troops into the city on the pretext of 'restoring order' in the same way and on the same scale as they were doing at this very moment in the Ruhr. Before the French troops marched in, the hotel in Frankfurt in which our Control officers were billeted had already been besieged by a belligerent crowd of 'toughs' who threatened them with violence if they did not 'clear out.' But they met their match in one of our French officers, Captain de Pomeraze, a resolute and resourceful man who, anticipating some little trouble of the kind, had thoughtfully laid in a stock of Very lights. And on the night of the assault he promptly sent up a dazzling 'S O S' display of fireworks from the roof of the hotel. The nearest French troops, with whom he had already been in communication by courier (we never trusted the German telephone), saw it. They saw it and promptly marched in.

On the evening of my interview with General Demesse, I dined with Gosling, the British Consul-General stationed at Frankfurt, who, of course, had a much better perspective of the local situation than

Lloyd George. What he told me was significant. 'The bourgeoisie here in Frankfurt,' he observed, 'are *glad* the French have come *and hope they will stay*, because for the first time for weeks the local rabble are feeling the hand of a master, General Demesse, and decent folk can sleep soundly at night. You see,' he added significantly, 'the German police here either cannot *or will not* keep order.' Three weeks after his reproof to the French, Mr. Lloyd George suddenly, like Saul on the road to Damascus, 'saw a great light.' The light was Commandant Graff's report. And on 26 April he joined with the French Government in the neat rejoinder, as I have called it, that the French would evacuate Frankfurt as soon as the German forces evacuated the Ruhr, and not before.

In due course, indeed only two months later, on 17 May, the French, who had not the slightest desire to exasperate German feeling by prolonging their occupation, evacuated Frankfurt. They had never fired a shot. Their conduct had been admirable. Indeed, in face of the provocation to which they were exposed and, it is sad to have to say it, the gross misrepresentations to which they had been subjected by certain newspapers in England always curiously susceptible to German propaganda, their conduct was nothing less than chivalrous. I never saw General Demesse again. But the impression which his demeanor—patient, forbearing, slow to anger and of great kindness—made upon me abides. Like Gouraud, Nollet, Foch, and many another of the paladins of the French Army whom I have had the good fortune to call my friends, he was everything that a German officer is not. He was humane. He might have walked straight out of the pages of De Vigny's little classic, *Servitude et Grandeur Militaires*. That afternoon I paid a pilgrimage to the charming old house in the Grosser Hirschgraben in which Goethe was born. My mind was still dominated by the impression Demesse had made upon me. Where and when, I had been asking myself, have I met the General before? And as I ascended the oak-stairs of the home of Goethe's childhood, I suddenly remembered. It was in the pages of *Dichtung und Wahrheit*, that enchanting autobiography in which Goethe has left us such an unforgettable portrait of the French officer, Count Thorane, who was billeted on Goethe's petulant father in the far-off days of the eighteenth century:

He behaved himself in a most exemplary manner. He would not even have his maps nailed on the walls for fear of spoiling our new wallpaper. He practised the severest disinterestedness; he even declined gifts to which his position entitled him; he refused the most trivial present which might have looked like a bribe. He took the greatest pride in absolute justice, integrity, and honorable behavior, determined to conduct himself in an exemplary manner towards those upon whom he was quartered, and, in fact, he never deviated from this code of conduct in all the changing circumstances of the years he stayed with us.

That passage in Goethe had often recurred to me when, serving in France during the first winter of the war, I heard from the lips of British officers, including no less a person than the C.I.G.S., General Sir Archibald Murray, what they had seen of the heartless desecration and unspeakable defilement by German staff officers of the homes in France in which they had billeted themselves before our Armies advanced, after the battle of the Marne, and drove them out.[15]

Three years later, the German *agents provocateurs* succeeded in doing in the Ruhr what they quite failed to do, in April 1920, in Frankfurt, namely, in provoking the French beyond endurance. I will not discuss here the justification, or otherwise, for the occupation of the Ruhr by the French, although, in my opinion, its justification was ample. In our own country, it was, of course, severely criticized. But English sympathy for the Germans was, in any case, a little misplaced, for, paradoxical as it may sound, all the reactionary elements in Germany *welcomed* the French occupation. 'Thank God,' said the Minister-President of Bavaria, von Kahr, to me a few weeks after the French had marched in, 'the French have occupied the Ruhr.' It was a dark saying and at the time of its utterance it puzzled me greatly. But there is nothing hid that shall not, in the fullness of time, be revealed. A few weeks later, 'the Bavarian Nationalists,' to quote the words of an English historian whom no one could accuse of any want of tenderness for German susceptibilities, 'poured their murder gangs into the Ruhr and most of their undesirables.'[16] These 'toughs' had been living, like a lady of doubtful virtue, under

---

[15] As to this, see below, Chapter XI, 'Germany in Defeat,' Section IV. German officers behaved in exactly the same way in the Franco-Prussian War of 1870-71, as readers of Mrs. Belloc-Lowndes's famous book, *I too have lived in Arcadia*, may discover for themselves.

[16] R. T. Clark, *The Fall of the German Republic*, p. 91.

'the protection' of von Kahr, who had stubbornly opposed all our demands for the dissolution of the semi-military formations in which they were incorporated. With their incursion into the Ruhr and their sabotage of French transport, the French were forced at last to shoot. And some of these intruders got shot, though nothing like as many as the Führer shot, just eleven years later, on that fateful night of 30 June 1934, when the rest of them began to get out of hand. The blood of these 'martyrs' of the Ruhr became the seed of the new Nazi church. The whole of Germany was convulsed with a carefully exploited campaign of hatred [17] against the French who were accused of the shedding of innocent blood. The dead 'toughs' took their place in the national martyrology. There were some who even placed them on the same pedestal as Arminius. Then I understood the reason for von Kahr's gratitude to God.

I do not say, because I do not know, that von Kahr himself instigated the sabotage in the Ruhr, although he unquestionably welcomed the rage which the French reprisals excited in Bavaria and elsewhere. He was at heart a kindly man and one whom I liked. I think he never realized with what two-edged tools he was playing in giving official protection to these unlicensed corps of 'irregulars.' A terrible fate was to overtake him at their hands. Eleven years later on, on that dark day of 30 June 1934, he, by that time a frail old man of seventy-three, living quietly at home in honorable retirement, a man who had 'done the State some service,' was roused from his sleep in the dead of night by Storm-troopers whose attachment to the Führer was beyond dispute, and hustled into a waiting car outside. They drove him some miles out of the city to a lonely spot. The next day his body was found upon the moors. The face was almost unrecognizable. It had been crushed out of shape by the iron-heeled boots of his assassins.

II

I have always thought it a great misfortune for the peace of Europe that Commandant Graff's report was never published. If it had been, it would, I think, have nipped in the bud the great German 'drive' against the Treaty of Versailles which found its full efflor-

---

[17] As to the manifestations of this hatred, see below, Chapter XI, 'Germany in Defeat,' Section VI.

escence in the notion that if the Treaty were executed in all its rigor, which it never was, particularly in the matter of disarmament, if, indeed, Germany were not, as a certain British statesman suggested, 'set upon her feet,' then Germany would 'go Red.' The notion came to stay. Long after it had done its worst in seducing English Liberals, it was once again exploited by Hitler to 'dope' English Conservatives who, for quite a long time, accepted at its face value his assurances that he had saved Germany from 'Bolshevism' by his exertions and would yet save Europe by his example. Carefully nursed as early as 1920 by a vast foreign propaganda organization, the *Fichte Verein* of Hamburg, which was heavily subsidized by the German Government, the notion got a real strangle-hold upon Liberal opinion in England, and not upon Liberals alone. How real I only realized when von Seeckt made his first move against disarmament with certain momentous 'Notes' to the Allied Governments demanding the revision of the Treaty, and the Liberal Press, in particular the *Westminster Gazette*, urged their acceptance upon the British Government with the argument that our enforcement of the Disarmament Articles, as they stood, would expose Germany to the dangers of 'Bolshevism.' It was the beginning of a campaign in England in favor of tempering the wind to the shorn wolf which was destined to cripple the work of the Control Commission for years to come, indeed to the very end. As it was, it was 'touch and go' at this very time, i.e. in the summer of 1920, with von Seeckt's first move, which amounted to nothing less than a carefully camouflaged plan for the retention of the old Army in *cadre* and the preservation 'in cold storage' of conscription. That move very nearly captured our own Government, but at the eleventh hour I managed to get my reports on the implications of von Seeckt's plan brought to the direct notice of Mr. Lloyd George through the agency of my friend Philip Kerr who, after reading those reports, advised the Prime Minister to reject von Seeckt's proposals. Rejected they were at the Conference of Spa in July 1920, as we shall see, but von Seeckt refused to accept defeat and fell back on a second move. A little later, a certain British statesman, in all sincerity, published a lurid article in a London newspaper warning the British public of the 'danger' of a Bolshevist invasion of Germany and depicting the Russian Army sweeping across Central Europe in overwhelming hordes 'like a plague of locusts.' Yet a little while and Lord D'Abernon, who ought to have known better, was coquetting with the delusion that 'a good bargain' might be made with the German military leaders in 'co-operating against the Soviet.' [18] If the imaginative statesman in question or Lord D'Abernon himself had ever seen the Bolshevist Russian Army *of those days* at close quarters, as I was destined, under somewhat dramatic circumstances, to see it, and as they were not, they would never have entertained these spectral fears. As we shall see in due course, the danger of a Bolshevist invasion of Germany was quite as imaginary as the danger of a 'Bolshevist' insurrection in Germany itself, and the Reichswehrministerium was equally busy in conjuring up apprehensions of both in order to arrest the work of our Control Commission and, indeed, to secure its withdrawal altogether. Their official Notes to our Commission returned to this theme again and again. Unfortunately, the German Government with the as-sistance of General von Kabisch's Press Bureau in the Ruhr, had got a long start and had completely duped even the British Military Attaché, Major-General Temperley, at The Hague. How completely, I only realized when I read his published reminiscences many years afterwards. Therein I read that the Communist 'rising' in the Ruhr had 'nearly succeeded.' [19] On the publication of that astounding state-ment—it was in 1938—I wrote to Temperley giving him a *précis* of Commandant Graff's report, which he had never seen, and accom-panying it with a copy of an article in the *Quarterly Review* in which, with official permission, I had first disclosed some of the facts. Temperley replied with a very good grace, saying that he had been misinformed—German propaganda in Holland had seen to that—and adding 'What an arraignment it [i.e. Graff's Report] is of German cunning and duplicity!' But Dutch opinion, at that time very 'sym-pathetic,' as Temperley puts it, to Germany, was as completely se-duced by the German fairy-tales of a 'Red Army' in the Ruhr as Temperley himself. Under these circumstances, it is not surprising that English opinion should have been no better informed.

[18] In a letter written to Sir Maurice, now Lord Hankey, on 11 August 1920, see *The Eighteenth Decisive Battle of the World* (London, 1931), by Lord D'Abernon, at p. 72.

[19] *The Whispering Gallery of Europe* (London, 1938), by Major-General A. C. Temperley, at p. 12.

This obstinate credulity of the English mind where Germany was concerned, and the consequent instability of our own Government in the matter of German disarmament, were destined to be the cause of infinite distress, and no less surprise, to the French officers on our Commission. The only explanation I could give them was that the right of private judgment, the privilege of dissent, the 'liberty of prophesying,' are so innate in the English people that whatever be the policy of our Government there will always be a very powerful minority who differ from it, and that an opportunist Prime Minister, which Mr. Lloyd George most certainly was, is subject to the temptation to put his foreign policy 'in reverse' if at any time he thinks that the minority opposed to it may suddenly become a majority. It is the only explanation of the disconcerting half-heartedness which he exhibited at intervals in the matter of German disarmament, although, as we shall see, he had one heroic moment. But long after Mr. Lloyd George's Coalition Government had fallen, unwept, unhonored, and unsung, his successors exhibited the same lukewarmness in 'backing up' the Control Commission except for one emphatic moment, namely in January 1925, by which time, having resigned my appointment on the Commission, I had come home and got into direct personal contact with two new members of the Government, Lord Birkenhead, who was an old friend of mine, and Sir Austen Chamberlain, and with the new D.M.I. at the War Office, General Burnett Stuart. General Burnett Stuart and the new head of M.I.3, Colonel Finlayson, were, unlike their immediate predecessors, fully alive to the reality of the German danger. The trouble was that until that date the Control Commission's case was never presented to the British public,[20] for none of our reports was ever published, while the

[20] As I have already explained in my 'Introduction,' in October 1924, I published with the permission of General Burnett Stuart and of Colonel, now General, Finlayson, at that time head of M.I.3 War Office, the substance of some of my reports to the War Office in an article, 'The Disarmament of Germany and After,' in the *Quarterly Review*. A few months later, in January 1925, the Allied Governments intimated to Germany that in view of her 'numerous defaults' in the matter of disarmament, they were not prepared to evacuate the Cologne bridgehead. On 25 June 1925, just three years after the House of Commons had been told by the then Secretary of State for War in Mr. Lloyd George's Administration, that Germany had been 'completely and effectively disarmed,' the British Government, in an Allied 'Note' informed the German Government that these numerous defaults constituted 'a serious menace to the peace of Europe' (White Paper Cmd. 2429, p. 3).

Reichswehrministerium's 'case' was publicized for all it was worth, which was not much, and more than all by German propagandist activity, and the British public were completely taken in by it. To the French we seemed at once forgetful and uncertain of ourselves, and they could not understand how a nation which had been so resolute in the prosecution of the war should be so infirm in the enforcement of the Peace. 'It is all very well for your people,' said a French officer to me one day, more in sorrow than in anger, 'the threat to you, the German Navy, is now at the bottom of the sea, but the threat to us, the German Army, is still there, it has been twice on our soil within living memory, *and it may be again*.' Which was true enough, but it was not the whole truth.

The truth lay deeper. It was to be found in our national character, in other words in a certain anxious conscientiousness, at times an almost morbid introspection, the presence of which in the English character, and its absence in the Germans, disarmed us, as it may disarm us yet again, the moment we had defeated them. As we profess standards which the Germans do not, we feel a compulsion to observe them from which they are wholly emancipated. We were therefore pressed by them, and will be again, to behave with a consideration which, given the chance, they would never extend to us. To a casuist their reasoning would seem flawless, but to a moralist it suggests nothing so much as a case of 'Heads I win, tails you lose.' More than that, we always make allowances for our enemies, we nurture doubts about our own honesty of purpose, we interrogate our consciences, and have no sooner won a victory than we begin to ask ourselves whether we have any right to keep the fruits of it. The extraordinary growth, during the years immediately preceding the second war, of English sentiment in favor of restoring to Germany the colonies we had redeemed from her ferocious tyranny by force of arms was a case in point. Many Englishmen were seriously disturbed by Goering's shameless accusation that in 'taking' the German colonies we had played the part of a receiver of 'stolen goods'—a shameless accusation because Bethmann-Hollweg, when interrogated in Berlin by the British Ambassador, in the fateful days of July 1914 at the moment Germany was about to make 'her tiger-spring at the throat of Europe,' [21] as to what would happen to the French colonies if we

[21] I owe this vivid expression to the late Lord Birkenhead.

accepted the German invitation to 'stay out' while she invaded France, replied in language which made it painfully clear that Germany would 'take' the French colonies without more ado.[22] But the English people whose consciences were so seriously disturbed, as he meant them to be, by Goering's exhortation to repentance and atonement—had forgotten all about Bethmann-Hollweg, as we forget everything. Germans have always shown an almost uncanny insight into our weakness, and known how to play upon it, even as they have shown, fortunately for us, a curious blindness to our strength. Our weakness lies in our doubts as to our honesty of purpose, our strength in their lack of foundation.

Such self-catechism, such searchings of heart, are entirely foreign to the German character. Nothing impressed me more during the whole time I served in Germany than the total absence of anything in the nature of a public conscience. Modern Germany produced on my mind the same impression as the national sculpture in which her artists have embodied their ideas—some soulless force, resistless, ruthless, and elemental. Krupp's seemed to me symbolical in that respect. The huge hydraulic presses in that stupendous 'shop of war' gave me the impression of vast forces all directed towards destruction with a blind inhumanity of purpose as though the soul of the German people, like a Samson Agonistes, was imprisoned in the heart of them. A kind of idolatry of force is the very spirit of Krupp's. Its sunless shops are a twilight of the gods in which every steam-hammer is fondly idolized by the workmen with its legendary name—'Hercules,' 'Thor,' 'Fritz'—and endowed with a kind of mythological personality. Looking at them, I saw where the architects of those colossal monuments in granite which crown every hill-top in Germany had caught the secret of their inspiration. Not beauty of line, not grace of form, but an almost oppressive strength is the dominant impression of all the national sculpture, finding as it does its most complete expression in the overwhelming ugliness of the 'Völkerschlachtdenkmal' at Leipzig, in the twilit interior of whose Pantheon the eponymous figures are endowed with such enormous sinews, such gigantic hands, such disproportionate feet, that they have lost almost all human semblance,

[22] See the Report in the White Paper issued by the Foreign Office (Cmd. 7860 of 1915) and Sir Edward Grey's scathing comment on Germany's attempt at 'this disgraceful bargain' at p. 77.

and the dwarfed head on the colossal body suggests the debilitating conquest of matter over mind, the expulsion of almost all human expression from the human face. They are the impersonation of brute force. And I sometimes think that in them you have the real Germany.

In any case, this English solicitude for the domestic peace of Germany was wholly misplaced. The idea that she would ever 'go Red' could never have been entertained by so many people in England if they had followed at close quarters the course of the revolutionary movement which ended in the establishment of the Weimar Republic. Its course in the winter of 1918-19 was, indeed, obscured from all foreign observers because the drama was played out behind the curtain of the Allied blockade which was not lifted till several months later. In those early days of the Armistice, Germany was as completely isolated from all foreign contacts as if she had been shut off by a barbed-wire fence, as indeed she was, literally and not metaphorically, in the west. The Allied Governments did not allow any of their subjects to enter Germany nor were diplomatic relations resumed until the Armistice had run its full course,[23] and, except for a small 'Military Mission,' we British officers of the 'Advanced Guard' of the Commission were the first Englishmen to enter Germany since the outbreak of war five years earlier. And by the time of our arrival, in September 1919, the Revolution had run its full course. The disturbances which heralded it had, in fact, come to an end six months earlier in the month of March. They were neither as catastrophic nor as bloody as, for reasons which will appear later,[24] the German Government subsequently found it convenient to represent them. In fact, the Revolution in Germany had never, except for a very brief moment in the winter of 1918-19, borne the slightest resemblance to the Russian Revolution, either in theory or in practice. Such resemblances as there were, or rather appeared to be, were as local as they were transient, being confined to isolated political experiments in the establishment of 'Soviets' at Kiel and Berlin, Halle and Munich,

[23] The Armistice lasted no less than 14 months, i.e. from the date on which it was signed, namely, 11 November 1918, till the date on which the Treaty of Versailles was ratified, namely 10 January 1920. It was, of course, as an Armistice always is, merely a suspension of hostilities.
[24] In a second volume to be published later.

and a few other towns, none of them flowering for more than a few weeks and most of them wilting in a few days. 'Soldiers' and Workers' Councils' did, indeed, spring up like mushrooms on the morrow of the signature of the Armistice all over Germany and within the Army Commands themselves, but wherever and whenever their leaders found themselves masters of the situation they completely lost their nerve. What happened in Berlin in November and December decided the issue once and for all. A 'Soviet' of a kind was set up in the capital under the imposing name of 'The Executive Council of Workers' and Soldiers' Councils of Greater Berlin,' *Der Vollzugsrat der Arbeiter und Soldaten-Räte von Gross Berlin.* Like the Paris Commune of 1871, it aspired to rule the whole country as a 'Dictatorship of the Proletariat.' It was equally short-lived. It consisted entirely of untutored demagogues, not one of whom had ever sat in the Reichstag, and it was cleverly out-maneuvered, not without considerable secret assistance from the German General Staff, by the 'old Parliamentary hands' of the Social Democrat Party, led by Ebert, Scheidemann, and Landsberg, a triumvirate who, like their followers, were no more revolutionary in temper than the rest of the German people.

The contrast between what happened in Berlin in the winter months of 1918-19 and what had happened in Moscow is instructive. In Germany the Revolution began where the Russian Revolution had ended—in the triumph of the extremists; it ended where the Russian Revolution had begun—in the triumph of the moderates. The Social Democrat deputies, who assumed office in Berlin immediately on the flight of the Kaiser and proclaimed a Republic, were astute enough to bow their heads to the revolutionary storm, knowing that it would soon pass. They agreed to an ultimatum from the Berlin *Vollzugsrat,* or 'Soviet,' demanding that, until such time as a national Congress of delegates should meet and elect a national *Vollzugsrat,* in other words a national Soviet, they should subscribe to the formula that they derived their authority from the Soldiers' and Workers' Council of Berlin. They were then, not without a grimace, forcibly baptized, like Charlemagne's converts, with the Muscovite name of 'Commissars of the People' (*Volksbeauftragte*), only to repudiate it when, in a few weeks' time, they had shaken off the yoke of the Berlin Communists. This they soon succeeded in doing by pressing for the immediate convocation of the national Congress, sustained by the cheerful conviction that the Socialist party throughout the country would be more than a match for the Communist faction. And so it proved. When the Congress met, the Socialist delegates were found to be in an overwhelming majority. As a result, it was not only the first 'Soviet' Congress to meet in Germany but the last. Within three days of its meeting on 16 December it repudiated, in effect, all affiliation to its Russian prototype by voting, after heated protests by the Communists, for its own extinction. The Socialists proposed and carried a resolution for the immediate election of a national Constituent Assembly to draft a constitution, an election in which all classes of the community, whether *bourgeoisie* or proletariat, were to participate on equal terms. This amounted, as a German constitutional lawyer duly pointed out, to the decisive rejection (*Verwerfung*) of a Soviet system on the Russian model and to the diversion (*Uberleitung*) of the revolutionary movement into Parliamentary channels.[25] In vain did the Communist spokesman, Richard Muller, plaintively protest that the adoption of the resolution would be 'a sentence of death' (*Todesurteil*) for him and his like. It was meant to be. The elections for the Constituent Assembly a month later confirmed his gloomy premonition.[26]

The Russian ideology was, in fact, never accepted by the German workers, nor was it ever likely to be. The mystical internationalism of Moscow did not appeal to them. All they were concerned about was to secure by the new Weimar Constitution, and the emergency legislation preceding it, a 'Workman's Charter,' in other words the removal of the existing restrictions on collective bargaining and the establishment of an Eight Hour Day. This they got, with the result that the membership of the trade unions, which under the old régime

[25] Thus Hatschek in his commentary on the Weimar Constitution, *Deutsches und Preussisches Staatsrecht*, Vol. I, pp. 129, etc.

[26] At these elections, the Majority Socialists secured 165 out of 469 seats. The Independent Socialists, who had originally 'fathered' the Communist movement, secured only 22, while the Communists, having 'split off' from the Independents, secured none at all. At the Reichstag Election of June 1920 the Communists secured 2 seats. By 1922 their membership had increased to 26, but they multiplied only to divide and the greater fraction of them was careful to protest its national character, thereby earning for itself the derisory name of 'The National Bolshevists.'

had existed only on sufferance, jumped from less than two millions to nearly ten. All 'Marxist' ideas of the abolition of capital were side-tracked. Indeed, capitalism became more strongly entrenched after the advent of the Weimar Republic than before it.[27] Within a few months of the establishment of the Republic, Noske, the Socialist-Minister of Defense, blithely declared 'The Revolution is ended.' And so it was. Most of the revolutionary changes foreshadowed by the Weimar Constitution, which was admittedly a 'programmatical'[28] (*programmatisch*) document, were tacitly dropped and the legislation necessary to 'implement' its pompous abstractions was never introduced. It remained a *lex imperfecta*. This was conspicuously the case with its singularly modest proposals for 'socialization' (*Sozializierung*). Qualified, indeed in the eyes of a Communist adulterated, though those proposals were the most respectful provision for 'compensation' (*Entschädigung*) in the case of expropriation of the individual, they never materialized. Herr Stresemann, discussing them with me at a dinner-party in Berlin in February 1922, said, 'We Germans will have nothing to do with *Sozializierung;* the Socialist leaders themselves don't believe in it, but they have to pretend they do.'

The fate which overtook in Germany the most fundamental institution of the Russian Revolution, the conception of a 'Soviet,' is a striking illustration of the eternal truth that in every nation which catches the contagion of a 'world revolution' the domestic revolt, after its first lyrical outburst, always reverts to type. The nearest equivalent the Germans could find in their own language for the spell-binding term 'Soviet' was *Rat*, or 'Council,' and the November Revolution began as a *Räterepublik*. The body politic suddenly became honeycombed, amid the apparent dissolution of the old order, with thousands of *Räte*, in other words, Workers' and Soldiers' Councils, all over Germany. But this exotic institution disappeared almost as suddenly as it had arisen. Something, however, had to be done by the Socialists to keep up appearances. No doubt they felt that the Revolutionary slogan of the *Räte* might yet cause trouble again if it was allowed to be at large. They therefore put it under restraint by domesticating it in the Weimar Constitution itself. This

[27] See Chapter XI, 'Germany in Defeat,' Section VII.
[28] Thus Meissner in *Das neue Staatsrecht des Reiches* (Berlin, 1921), at p. 281.

rogue and vagabond of a word became a respectable member of bourgeois society by being sublimated into 'industrial' and 'economic' *Räte* (*Betriebsräte* and *Wirtschaftsräte*) which, by the terms of the Constitution in which they were interned, were, as a German commentator observed, 'deprived of all real political significance.' [29] Every factory and every industry was to have a *Rat* in which employers and workmen were to reason together. Every industry, every factory, and every workshop was to be 'self-governing.' They never were. The *Betriebsräte* became nothing but debating societies and every German industrialist whom I interrogated on the subject made no secret of his contempt for them. Thus ended the 'Workers' Councils' of the November Revolution.

As for the Soldiers' Councils, they, too, were quietly asphyxiated with a legal catchword. The law for the establishment of the Reichswehr substituted, for Soldiers' Councils, Soldiers' Delegates to be known as *Vertrauensleute*, who were to reason with the officers on behalf of the men, and, like an orderly officer, to deal with 'complaints.' The word *Vertrauen* literally means 'confidence,' and was not inappropriate, for the new institution turned out to be no better than a 'confidence trick,' designed to assure recruits that they were joining a 'republican' army. Some of them may even have thought that in the *Vertrauensleute* of their battalion they were going to find 'People's Commissars,' keeping a watchful eye on their C.O. If so, they were soon undeceived. The *Vertrauensleute*, who had not even the disciplinary powers of an N.C.O., never came to anything. Reichswehr officers, discussing them with me, always spoke of them as though they were a joke, as indeed they were, continuing to be funny long after they had ceased to be 'vulgar.' 'We know how to deal with them,' said a German sapper, Captain Luise, who accompanied me on an inspection of the forts of Königsberg. How the officers 'dealt with' them, if they made any trouble in the orderly-room, will duly appear.[30]

The November Revolution was, in fact, neither as catastrophic nor as bloody as it appeared to be to untutored observers in our own

[29] Hatschek, *op. cit.*, at p. 135.
[30] See above, Chapter VI, 'The German Officers' Corps,' at p. 122, and below, Chapter XI, 'Germany in Defeat.'

country and everywhere else. The fearful hemorrhage which characterized the Russian Revolution was conspicuously absent in Germany and such bloodshed as there was was almost entirely due either to troops who had got out of hand, like the *Volksmarine* of Kiel, or to the troops who were used to suppress them. The really catastrophic event of the Revolution, namely the expulsion, or rather the abdication, of the reigning dynasties, was so bloodless that one might say of this phase of it that the revolution was 'made with rose-water.' Not a single Ruling Prince ever had violent hands laid upon him, either before his abdication or after it. When the Revolution came on the morrow of the Armistice like a thunderclap, *Fort mit den Fürsten* ('Away with the Princes') was its battle-cry. Within the space of little more than twenty-four hours 'twenty-two thrones and scepters,' as the *Vorwärts* proudly trumpeted a year later in celebrating the anniversary, 'tumbled into the dust.' Kings, Grand Dukes, Dukes, Serene Highnesses bolted for cover like rabbits, stole down the backstairs of palaces and vanished across the German frontier. Never was a 'republican' revolution more complete, but never was a dynastic capitulation more abject, or even, it may be, more premature. In Baden, the 'revolution' was made by twenty drunken marines from Kiel in a motor-lorry, and the Grand Duke fled without striking a blow. In Württemberg the appearance of a handful of Prussian workmen from Berlin provoked the instant abdication of the King. Yet none of these *rois fainéants* were ever in the slightest danger of personal violence and those of them who remained at home after their abdication, such as the Grand Duke of Hesse and the King of Württemberg, were quite unmolested. The contrast with what happened in Russia, in this respect, is too obvious to need emphasis.

Even the dual abdication of the Kaiser as German Emperor and King of Prussia, which, when it came, was made in the most equivocal terms, need not have involved the abolition of the monarchy at all if he had been prepared to nominate a 'Regent.' That is quite clear from the subsequent revelations of the last Chancellor of the old Reich, Prince Max of Baden.[31] The Socialists were, up to the eleventh hour, by no means anxious for the abolition of the mon-

---

[31] See his *Memoirs* (English translation), vol. ii, at pp. 302, 313, 318, 357.

archy.[32] The Kaiser himself, was, it is true, unpopular with the people, or at least with the people of Berlin. A German friend of mine told me that, as early as 1915, he saw, one summer morning in Berlin, a top-hat stuck on the railings of the royal palace in the Unter den Linden. To the hat was attached a slip of paper on which was scrawled in a rude hand a single word. The word was 'Wilhelm.' A prophetic pleasantry, for when an officer is retired in Germany he is said to be 'given the top-hat,' even as we speak of giving a man the boot. When the saddler of Heidelberg, Herr Ebert, called to be President of the new German Republic, slept for one night in the Kaiser's bed at the old 'Schloss' in Berlin, the whole of Berlin applauded uproariously, regarding it not only as a good jest but as a democratic gesture. But it was the last gesture of the kind the Socialists ever made and it was easy to exaggerate its significance. How easy I learned when in July 1922 I paid my first visit to the Reichstag. I had a seat in the *Diplomaten-Loge*, the Diplomatists' 'Box,' and I noticed that my chair still bore the Kaiser's initial 'W,' with a crown above it, stamped imperiously upon its red leather back. More remarkable still, the very chair in which the 'Speaker,' the President as he was called, of the Reichstag sat, presiding over its republican deliberations, still bore the insignia of the Crown and the Black Eagle, and so indeed did all the chairs for members of the Cabinet on the Rostrum. All this was symbolic and more than symbolic. The professed Republicans, in other words the Socialists, after their reluctant adoption of Republicanism, were, even when in office, never in power. This momentous fact was never realized in England.

Even in the Constituent Assembly, when it met at Weimar, the Socialists had not an absolute majority and the old Nationalist parties, thinly disguised under new names, were there as in the old Reichstag and as nationalist, as monarchist, and indeed as belligerent as ever. A study of the Weimar debates is extremely illuminating on that point. The very instruments with which the Socialists, so long as they were in office, had to govern, the courts, the bureaucracy,

[32] *Ibid.* See also the remarkable evidence of General Groener in the 'Dolchstoss Prozess' (the Stab in the Back Trial) in the published shorthand report of the proceedings (Munich, 1925), at page 217, where Groener testifies on oath that the Majority Socialists strove to save the Monarchy during November 1918, in order to 'stop' (*verhindern*) the Revolutionary movement.

the police, the army, were all equally nationalist and monarchist in training and in sentiment.[33] The Constituent Assembly at Weimar, which met under the protection of seven thousand bayonets and a German general, General Maercker, began its deliberations with a draft of the new constitution providing that members of the princely families, including, of course, the Hohenzollerns, should be disqualified from election to the office of President of the new Republic. Some one must have dropped a hint. It was probably General Maercker. Or it may have been General Groener and his intermediary, Major Schleicher, who had been in constant liaison with Herr Ebert ever since 11 November 1919, and indeed earlier. At any rate, the disqualification was quietly dropped.

The truth is that, if there had been no revolution in Berlin in November 1919, the German General Staff would have found it necessary to invent one. A revolution, or at least the appearance of one, was necessary to them, for the time being, to preserve their prestige by posing, in due course, as having been forced to give the order for retreat across the Rhine not by defeat in the field but by defection at home. The only hope of that was to find a 'revolutionary' Government in Berlin, who would take the odious responsibility of negotiating and signing the Armistice and whose action both they and the Supreme War Lord, the Kaiser, could subsequently repudiate when the Allied Governments had demobilized. This, unquestionably, was why Hindenburg counselled the Kaiser to retire 'temporarily' into Holland. The Kaiser's obstinacy defeated this part of their plan. But in one direction they were supremely successful. Eager though they had been for an Armistice on their own terms early in October when the situation in the field was desperate, they were not less eager to avoid being implicated in the responsibility for an Armistice on the Allies' terms when, a month later, they realized that no other kind of Armistice was possible. The astute General Groener who succeeded Ludendorff, on his dismissal, at the German G.H.Q. on 26 October, and who played so large a

[33] By Article 176 of the Weimar Constitution all Civil Servants and Army Officers were to take an oath of loyalty to the Republic. When a Civil Servant in Hamburg refused to take it, the 'Disciplinary Court' decided that the requirement of the oath could not be enforced—The *Vorwärts*, 6 August 1921.

part, behind the scenes, in the handling [34] of the Revolution in Berlin, was determined that, whatever happened, no member of the German General Staff should either negotiate or sign the Armistice.[35] In this he was successful. The Armistice delegation was carefully 'made up' of obliging civilians.[36] In other words the German General Staff 'left the baby,' of which it was unquestionably the father, on the incipient Republic's doorstep. In due course it repudiated paternity and started the myth of an undefeated Army 'stabbed in the back' by revolutionary pacifists at home. The German Officers' Corps, which soon re-established itself as the only element of any potency in the body politic, saw to it that the myth of *Der Dolch in Rücken* ('the stab in the back'), should grow into a legend, and the legend into a creed. From them Hitler borrowed this myth, so comforting to national pride, and exploited it as an explanation of the moral degeneration of post-war Germany, a degeneration which he made no attempt to deny. He refused to admit that the mortifying fact of her having lost the war had anything to do with the moral catastrophe that followed it. To admit as much would, indeed, have been too prejudicial to the current and recurrent German doctrine that war is a cleansing agent of human progress, a kind of purification of the nation's soul. It is sheer nonsense (*Unsinn*), argues the Führer in *Mein Kampf*, to contend that the war, and the loss of it, was responsible for the decadence of Germany which he paints in those pages in such lurid colors. The loss of the war, he contends,

[34] General Groener, at the Munich Trial, the *'Dolchstoss* case,' already cited, gave evidence that on 8 December 1918, he, with Hindenburg's approval, 'concluded' (*geschlossen*) an 'alliance' (*Bündnis*) with the Majority Socialists, of which the terms were that troops should be placed at their disposal in order to establish their party's control of the 'Revolutionary' Government. From that moment the Army G.H.Q. and the Socialist Chancellor, Ebert, afterwards President were in constant communication by a 'secret telephone line' (*Geheimdraht*)—pp. 224, *op. cit.*

[35] The Chancellor, Prince Max of Baden, was of the same opinion, and naïvely exposes the whole maneuver in his *Memoirs*. See Vol. II, page 305 of the English translation where he speaks of 'our relief that at least *the Army* would not have to wait on Foch.'

[36] There was one Army officer upon it, but he was neither a member of the General Staff nor was he authorized to represent it. He was, in fact, a 'dug-out,' a former German Military attaché at Paris, General von Winterfeld, and he hastily retired from the subsequent negotiations for the renewal of the Armistice.

was not the cause of her decadence but the result of it. She had already been 'poisoned' (*vergiftet*) by the Jews.[37] They, he insists, were the assassins.

If Hitler's contention were indeed the real explanation, it would leave the historian of modern Germany with another problem as inexplicable as that which Hitler's explanation purports to resolve, namely, how a great nation of sixty-six million people could be so lacking in moral stamina as to be immediately responsive to the 'toxic' influence of a race, namely the German Jews, so infinitesimal in proportion that it numbered less than one per cent of the German population. His contention was not less fantastic than mean. Once upon a time I wrote that 'every nation gets the Jews it deserves.' I have since been told that my aphorism was not original and that others had said or written the same thing before me. No doubt. But so far as Germany was concerned, I was wrong. Germany, or modern Germany at least, never deserved the Jews she had got. They were much too good for her. No one with any claims to an intimate knowledge of Germany could, with any honesty, deny that in law, in medicine, in bacteriology, in chemistry, in physics, in archaeology, in economics, and in nearly every other department of human thought and science, the contribution of German Jews to German intellectual achievement has been so great, and indeed so out of proportion to their percentage of the population, as to suggest that they were nothing less than a *corps d'élite*. So far from being responsible for Germany's losing the war, the Jews were responsible for her not having lost it long before she did. It was the discovery by a German Jewish chemist, Professor Haber, of synthetic ammonia that enabled Germany to weather the blockade so long when the supply of Chile nitrates for high explosives was cut off. So much indeed was admitted by a German general in an official history of the German war effort[38] but, characteristically, he was careful not to admit that it was to a Jew to whom the General Staff was indebted for their salvation.

If our English statesmen had graduated in a 'school' of modern history, they would never have taken fright at the specter of a 'world

[37] *Mein Kampf* (135th German edition), at p. 253.
[38] General Wurtzbacher in *Der Grosse Krieg*, vol. i, p. 82.

revolution,' threatening, or rather appearing to threaten, from its storm-center at Moscow the foundations of society in England and Germany alike. They would then never have lent such a credulous ear to German propaganda about the dangers of 'Bolshevism.' For the Russian Revolution followed, in the long run, the same paradoxical course abroad, and even in its own home, as another great European movement, the French Revolution of 1789, and for the same reasons. The French Revolution, like the Russian, in its first flush captured the imagination of all the 'intellectuals' in Europe and of not a few in England including the sober Wordsworth who became quite lyrical on the subject. Equally, it frightened all the conservative elements for whom, in Burke's wistful words, 'the age of chivalry' was now 'gone.' Both the lyrics and the elegiacs proved to be equally out of place. For the theories of the Jacobins only commanded such a wide acceptance because they were couched in such abstract, not to say universal, terms that each country could put its own interpretation upon them. 'Every one agreed with them,' a great French historian has remarked not without irony, 'until they tried to explain them.' [39] The moment each nation attempted to put them into practice, it put an entirely different construction on them to that which they bore in the country of their origin—*en réalisant la doctrine, on en faussa le sens.*[40] And, in so doing, it extracted nearly all their sting. This, indeed, as we have seen, is exactly what happened in Germany in 1919 with the gospel of Moscow. The secret of its diffusion abroad was to be found in its abstraction. Like the 'Liberty, Equality, and Fraternity' tocsin of the French Revolution, the Russian trumpet-call, 'Workers of the World, unite!' might mean anything or nothing. It appeared on every Russian ruble note and, like the ruble, the more it circulated abroad the more it depreciated in exchange value.

In our own country, the Labour Party, to the dismay, indeed the fright, of the two older political parties, welcomed, at the outset, the Bolshevist movement with effusion, only to be told eventually by the sardonic Trotsky that they did not understand it, and were no better than the *bourgeoisie,* which, from the Russian point of view,

---

[39] Sorel, *L'Europe et la Révolution Française,* vol. i, p. 182. De Tocqueville in his *Ancien Régime* has made the same observation.
[40] *Ibid.,* at p. 185.

was true enough. The great French historian, Albert Sorel, writing with large discourse and 'looking before and after,' observed that in the case of France itself the changes in the structure of its political society made by the French Revolution which endured most were those which innovated least. Revolutionary France, within four years of 1789, became as absolutist, as centralized, as intolerant, as the Bourbon régime it had displaced and, in due course, exchanged the role of liberator of Europe for that of a conqueror as aggressive as Louis XIV himself. All political revolutions have a way of conforming to Machiavelli's law of history that the world is for ever moving in cycles; they return, after some eccentricities, to the point from which they started. The German Revolution of 1919, like the French Revolution of 1789, began by 'decreeing liberty *en masse*' and ended by 'taking it back in detail.' [41] Long before the accession to power of Hitler, for whose dictatorship the Weimar Republic itself, from October 1923 onwards, had obligingly provided any number of precedents with its periodical proclamations of *Aufnahmezustand* or Martial Law, the Republic was rapidly becoming as despotic as anything which had preceded it. In that respect the Weimar Republic like the Jacobin Republic, 'reverted to type'—to the traditional autocracy of Prussia.[42] In Russia itself the Revolution, beginning with the exotic liberalism of Kerensky, 'found itself' in a form of government as autocratic as that of the Tsars and, to that extent, as habitual to her. Indeed, having begun by being almost mystically 'international,' Soviet Russia has now become even more 'nationalist' than under the Romanoffs, but in a far more patriotic and, indeed, nobler sense.

As Sorel has profoundly observed, it is the habits, the customs, the traditions, and the temperament of the nation which invariably

[41] *Ibid.*, at p. 233.

[42] By Article 48 of the Weimar Constitution itself, the President of the Reich was endowed with power to declare 'Martial Law,' an almost despotic power originating in the law of Prussia and extended to the Kaiser by the Reich Constitution of 1871, as to which see above, Chapter VI, 'The German Officers' Corps,' at p. 128. The organ of the legal profession in Germany expressed the opinion that Article 48 invested the republican President with 'extraordinary powers far exceeding those of the ex-Kaiser' (*ausserordentliche Machtfülle die weit über die Befugnisse des früheren Kaisers hinausgeht*)—thus the *Juristiche Wochenblatt* as early as May 1923. This opinion proved to be only too well-founded.

determine the course that a national revolution will ultimately take. For that very reason, it is idle for Englishmen to expect that the German people will oblige them with a revolution, either now or later on, which will embody the English idea of self-government and thereby bring lasting peace to Europe. Idle and, indeed, a little egotistical, for it assumes that the Germans are men 'like as we are.' The outstanding characteristic of Englishmen is, as Newman observed, their insistence on 'the right of private judgment' and their capacity for it. It is the secret of their success in governing themselves. But it is a right of which a German has no conception. The innate individualism of every Englishman is something entirely foreign to the German character. This fact accounts for the German's passion for something which, except when he is on duty, only makes an Englishman feel acutely self-conscious: a uniform. The German idolatry of uniform is the outward and visible expression of their 'herd-instinct.' A German, unlike the strong man of Ibsen's play, seems incapable of 'standing alone.' By a kind of law of molecular attraction, he feels irresistibly compelled to unite with somebody else before he can trust his own judgment and even so, having formed one of those 'unions' (*Vereine*) which in Germany are, or were till Hitler forcibly amalgamated them, as countless as the sands of the sea, he must have an official superior at the head of it to decide for him. 'Ein Deutscher,' said a philosophical Nazi Storm-trooper to me in 1936 who had been placed at my disposal when I was the guest of the Gauleiter of Hesse, 'nichts! Zwei Deutschen ein Verein! Drei Deutschen ein Partei!' [43] Heine had said the same thing nearly a century ago but in ruder language.[44] A German writer in 1921, in the most searching study of his fellow countrymen I have ever read, put it in sorrowful language as follows:

It is sad to have to write (*es ist traurig schreiben zu mussen*) that the average German would a thousand times rather be a slave, shrinking from all responsibility, and a blind, if conscientious, executive machine than a

[43] 'One German, nothing! Two Germans a union! Three Germans, a Party!'
[44] 'The German is like a slave who obeys his master without chain, or whip— a word or a look is enough. Servility (*Knechtschaft*) is in his very soul.' Ernest Toller, in his *Letters from Prison*, has written the same thing in noble language.

free man bearing the burden of responsibility and depending on his own judgment.[45]

In that tragic confession is to be found the explanation of why the essay in self-government of the Weimar Constitution failed so ignominiously. Is there any reason to suppose that another such essay will be any more successful?

[45] *Die Tragödie Deutschlands, von einem Deutschen* (Germany's Tragedy, by a German), Stuttgart, 1921, at p. 63. As to this remarkable book, see below, Chapter XI, 'Germany in Defeat,' Section IX.

PART FOUR

PART FOUR

X. 'GOETHE IN WEIMAR SLEEPS'

And he was happy, if to know
Causes of things, and far below
His feet to see the lurid flow
Of terror, and insane distress,
And headlong fate be happiness.

I HAD LEFT BERLIN to seek in the enchanted land of Thuringia, haunted by all the legends of the Nibelungen, and in Weimar, the home of Goethe and Schiller, some respite from the vulgarity, the meretriciousness, and the brutality of Berlin. Goethe, as was the case with Beethoven, did not like Berlin and called it names. What, I wondered, would he have called it today? Sodom? Gomorrah? Babylon? To seek Weimar was like seeking sanctuary.

I had another reason. From the day I learned his lyrics at my mother's knee, for she knew many of them by heart, I had cherished a kind of passion for Goethe. This very day of my quest, a passage in *Die Leiden des jungen Werthers*, the 'Sorrows of Werther,' of which I had brought with me a pocket edition as the book for a pensive mood, had suddenly brought back with peculiar poignancy a wistful memory of my early childhood. It was the passage in which Goethe, coming to fetch Lotte in her home, describes how he found her engaged in one of her loving ministries, presenting 'the most charming spectacle I have ever seen.' In my mother's room there had always hung an old German engraving—a picture of a beautiful girl in flowing robes cutting bread and butter for a group of children who clung importunately with their little hands at her dress. In the background stood the youthful Goethe awaiting her. The picture bore the superscription 'Lotte.' The artist's Lotte was the very image of my mother.

I had visited Goethe's house, austere and stately, in Weimar. The experience would have been a moving one but for the guide, who talked too much. One of two plaster medallions of Napoleon in Goethe's study, which had been so hung by the poet as to face him when he wrote at his desk, had a damaged look. I noticed it, and the guide immediately sought to improve the occasion by explaining that it had fallen from the wall on the day of the battle of Leipzig. No doubt he had told the story so often that he had come to believe it. Perhaps it went down well with German patriots who found it hard to forgive Goethe for his superb tribute to the genius of Napoleon. And harder still perhaps, in these days of virulent propaganda against the French, to forgive him for having loved France. Children were being taught, so a German told me, in the *Volkschulen*, as early as 1923, to lisp 'Frankreich ist unser Feind'— 'France is our enemy.' To the Germans, patriotism means aggression and something even worse. For them, to love your country you must hate its neighbor. Goethe refused to admit the necessity.

The prolegomenous guide, who dogged my footsteps in Goethe's house, had been too much for me. After one quiet moment alone in the little room by the side of the humble truckle-bed where Goethe breathed his last, I had fled to a place where I knew I should be unmolested. It was Ilmenau. There is a tradition that it was on this lonely hill that Goethe had written the greatest of all his lyrics— *Über allen Gipfeln*. Rain was falling heavily as I left my car at the foot of the hill. But I minded it not, for it secured me the solitude I sought. The steep slopes of the hill were thickly wooded with beech and birch and larch. An impenetrable mist obscured the view, wrapping the wood and the valley below in a ghostly mantle like cotton-wool. Even the nearest trees, silhouetted against the mist like shadows on a screen, were unsubstantial as a forest of dreams. Not a sound was to be heard but the soft patter of moisture dripping from the leaves. Gradually the rain ceased, the sky cleared, the curtain of mist became diaphanous. A slight breeze sprang up and drove wisps of mist before it like thistledown. It stirred the trees in the valley below to a whisper. *Kaum einen Hauch!*—'scarcely a breath'—I repeated to myself as I listened to that faint sigh of the birches transmuted into those wistful lines by him who had sat here and invested just such a moment of time as this with immortality:

> Über allen Gipfeln
> Ist Ruh:
> In allen Wipfeln
> Spürest du

Kaum einen Hauch;
Die Vögelein schweigen im Walde,
Warte nur, balde
Ruhest du auch. [1]

The breeze died away, the mist thickened, and the rain descended again. I sat there for many hours, oblivious of the flight of time, unconscious of the rain. I fell to thinking of another poem of Goethe's, wondering whether it had any lesson for the distracted Germany of these days. I had never heard, nor was I ever to hear, Goethe's name mentioned outside Weimar during all the years I served in Germany. But a Lutheran pastor, in a sermon I had heard in the Nikolai Church in Berlin a few weeks earlier, had begged his congregation, not, so it seemed to me, without some timidity, to 'learn to suffer without complaining.' Listening to him, I had suddenly been reminded, even as I was now on that lonely hill in Thuringia, of Goethe's lines:

Wer nie sein Brot mit Thränen ass,
Wer nicht die kummervollen Nächte
Auf seinem Bette weinend sass
Der kennt euch nicht, ihr himmlischen Mächte.[2]

But the pastor's was only 'a still small voice.' The Germans could not learn to suffer without complaining and, suffering, learn the divine secret of contrition. They were filling the world with their complaints. A vast propagandist organization, the *Fichte Verein*, heavily subsidized from public funds, was flooding the world with shrill outcries in fly-sheets. In all these ululations there was not one expression of regret for the cruel things they had done upon the

[1] Over every hill-top
'Tis still,
In every tree-top
List you will
Scarcely a breath;
Soft you, soon enough
Cometh still Death.

[2] Who never ate his bread in sorrow,
Who never spent the darksome hours
Weeping and watching for the morrow
He knows you not, ye heavenly powers.

earth and in the depths of the sea. Germany was learning nothing
from defeat except how to exploit it.

'It is here, Herr General,' said my chauffeur. And he bared his
head although we were still outside the 'Court of Peace.' [3] I liked
the gesture, even as I liked the man, for it was characteristic. He
was not a Prussian but a Saxon, which may have accounted for it.
We had left Ilmenau, where he had waited for me at the foot of the
hill, and had come to the place which was to be the end, even as it
had been the goal, of my pilgrimage. For I had come to Weimar to
pay my small tribute of respect at Goethe's last resting-place. I
passed through the gates, found the caretaker, an old man, and entered the chapel. In the crypt below was the Grand-ducal vault. We
descended the steps. I observed a notice requesting visitors to remain
silent. It seemed to me unnecessary, but in Germany one is told to
do, or not to do, everything. I missed, however, the familiar 'Nicht
zu spucken!' [4] In Weimar, perhaps, they do not spit. I found what I
had sought—two plain wooden coffins by the side of the stately
sarcophagus of the Grand Duke in all the undeniable equality of
Death. In one of those two coffins lay the mortal remains of Schiller,
in the other those of Goethe. As I stood in silence, the caretaker by
my side, I caught sight, in the dim crepuscular light, of two glazed
wooden frames, lined with velvet, at the head of each coffin. They
were just such reliquaries as people fashion to enshrine the medals
and decorations of some one they have loved and lost. But they were
empty. As I stood gazing at them in some perplexity, the caretaker
touched me lightly on the elbow and, without uttering a word,
pointed to a kind of vent-hole in the roof of the vault above us.
It was small in diameter and barred with iron, admitting a faint light
into the darkness of the vault. I turned to him interrogatively. He
made no reply but beckoned towards the stone steps by which we
had come. Clearly he had something to tell me but felt that the
vault was no place for speech. Possibly he felt that what he had to
tell me was almost unspeakable.

When we had mounted the steps and left the vault, he explained.
'Those two frames contained two wreaths, *mein Herr*. One of gold,

[3] *Friedhof*, the German name for a cemetery.
[4] 'Don't spit.'

pure gold, the other of silver. One for Goethe, one for Schiller. They were greatly honored, you see. Those wreaths had been placed there when they died. A year ago they were stolen. When I arrived one morning, they were no longer here.'

'Stolen?' I inquired in astonishment. 'Stolen! But how? By whom?'

'By two men, sir. Did you not see the vent-hole? They filed through the iron bars and let down a rope-ladder. I found it hanging there after they had gone.'

'But here in Weimar?' I exclaimed. 'This sort of thing?'

'Alas, sir,' said the caretaker with a troubled look, 'since the war the Germans are up to everything. A good man is no longer respected.' [5]

[5] 'Leider, mein Herr, nach dem Krieg die Deutschen machen alles. Ein guter Mensch ist nicht mehr geachtet.'

XI. GERMANY IN DEFEAT

Questa selva selvaggia aspra e forte
Che nel pensier rinnuova la paura.[1]

I

The 'jungle' beyond the Rhine—The Contrast with the Rhineland—German propaganda and its five trump cards—Another 'scrap of paper'—Persistence of the War psychosis—The spoils of war—The loot of France and Belgium.

II

The 'Hunger Blockade' fiction and the reality—General Lewin's testimony—The German food racket—*Homo homini lupus*—Callousness of the German character—An Englishwoman's sentimentalism—Brockdorff-Rantzau and Clemenceau at the Peace Conference—Bismarck on a short way with the French.

III

The real malady of post-war Germany: a corruption of the soul—The abdication of the Churches—'Rotten and worse than rotten'—Hitler's telltale diagnosis—The 'night life' of the German cities—'Harem Nights' and the legend of the 'Black Shame'—The 'unmentionable vice' in Germany—Von Bülow's admissions.

IV

Filthy-mindedness—The German idea of humor—Behavior of German officers in France and Belgium—General Gouraud's testimony—Treatment of British prisoners of war—The character of German officers and men—The German officers' code of honor—The morals of the Army—The abiding influence of Frederick the Great and his character.

V

Cruelty—The Murder Clubs and their origin—The cult of the assassin—Influence of the Prussian military tradition—Brutality in the Army—Sir Malcolm Robertson's testimony.

[1] 'That savage forest, fierce and intractable, the very thought of which renews the horror of it.'—Dante's *Inferno*.

VI

German rage in defeat—The 'Teutonic fury' in German history—The cult of Hate and its manifestations against the French, the British, and the Belgians—Bethmann-Hollweg's admission, 'We must stop at nothing'—Goethe's repudiation—A pathological explanation of the cult of Hate.

VII

The epidemic of crime among ex-service men—The demoralization of the civil population and its causes—The German financial gamble on 'a short war' and crushing reparations—Inflation during the war and its effects—War profiteering—Ludendorff's admissions: a 'catastrophic' epidemic of greed and cheating—The infection of wholesale fraud—How the big industrialists 'got away with it' after the war—'Am I my brother's keeper?'

VIII

Reaping the whirlwind—Paralysis of public opinion in Germany—Absence of a public conscience—The German Press—'We have the worst Press in the world'—The German Universities during the war and after it—The Professors as camp-followers of the German Army, and their servility—The fiction of German 'culture'—Goethe and Kant—Kant's cowardice—A visit to the shrine of Kant.

IX

A German's testimony as to 'the fearful demoralization' of Germany and its cause: her cult of war—The origins of Hitlerism: its 'pathological impulse'—Hitler's affectations of moral reform and social reconstruction —His obligations to Ludendorff and the General Staff—Hitler as the instrument of the German High Command—Military preparations camouflaged as 'social reforms'—Continuity of Hitler's aims and policy with those of his predecessors—The 'annihilation' of France and the 'extermination' of the Poles—The German passion for destruction—The idolatry of war—War as 'the highest goal of human achievement'—The teaching of Clausewitz and his disciples: Moltke, Ludendorff, Seeckt, von der Goltz, Beseler, and the German General Staff—German outrages and their inspiration: the Gestapo as the camp-followers of the Army—Seeckt on the ideal Führer—The fundamental mistake of the Disarmament articles of the Treaty—The solution of the problem: the only hope for Germany.

To PASS FROM Cologne to Berlin was like exchanging light for darkness. And so indeed with the rest of trans-Rhenan Germany. The Englishman at home who thought about the Germans in those days, if he ever thought about them at all, saw them through the rose-colored spectacles of his fellow countrymen who, quartered in the

Rhineland or flocking there on the heels of the Army of Occupation like so many camp-followers, returned to England without ever having so much as crossed the Rhine. The hinterland of unoccupied Germany beyond the great river these itinerant Englishmen saw not at all or saw only as through a glass darkly. They saw the clearance on the Rhine but they never saw the jungle beyond it, dark and sinister and swarming with predatory life, from which the Allied troops of Occupation had reclaimed it. They saw the orderly, docile, not to say plausible, demeanor of the Rhinelanders and thought this Prussian province typical of Prussia which it had never been and was never less so than now. In the Rhineland, or rather in the British zone of occupation the Germans were on their best behavior. That behavior may, indeed, have been, and probably was, inspired and instructed by the Government in Berlin whose agents in the local administration of the province we, wisely or unwisely, left undisturbed. The German Government, as Lord Birkenhead remarked on a memorable occasion, 'think of everything,' and the authorities in Berlin unquestionably saw immense possibilities in the Rhineland of 'doping' English opinion by appeals to that humanitarian sentiment of ours which they always both exploit and despise. A great German, the only German who dared to raise his voice against the outrages in Belgium and who was driven into exile in consequence, Professor Foerster, relates that a fellow countryman of his was reproached with those outrages early in 1918 by a Swiss who asked him, 'What will Germany do, what can she expect, after such iniquities if she loses the war?' Quick as light came the reply, 'Oh, then we shall organize sympathy.' [2]

In the occupation of the Rhineland the Germans saw their chance. The Wilhelmstrasse had five trump cards in their hand and played them all in due course with consummate skill. One was to take the captivity captive by representing the occupation itself as an intolerable 'servitude' upon their sovereignty. The facts that the Germans had themselves occupied the fairest provinces of France for three years after the Franco-Prussian War until France paid the uttermost farthing of 'reparations' did not, of course, deter them. They had no intention of ever paying reparations and, as all the world now

[2] Oh, dann organisieren wir die Sympathie'—*Europa und die deutsche Frage,* by F. W. Foerster, at p. 349.

knows, they eventually secured the evacuation of the Rhineland by tendering a promissory note, known and now notorious as the Pact of Locarno, and then dishonored their note by repudiating reparations altogether. All that was to come. At the moment of our arrival in Berlin they were playing three other cards. One was the 'misery' of the German people, induced, it was insinuated, by the 'Hunger Blockade,' and in the Rhineland this 'stunt' was worked for all it was worth. A second was the 'Black Shame' of quartering colored troops on the Rhine. A third was the specter of Communism, but here the venue was shifted to the Ruhr. As will be seen in the pages that follow, each and every one of these appeals was spurious.

The contrast between the rest of Germany and the Rhineland was startling enough. But the contrast with our own country was even more startling. In England people, as is the English way, were already forgetting the war and all its asperities. In Germany beyond the Rhine the Germans were remembering it and remembering nothing else. As early as February 1920 the most topical song in German cabarets, outside the Rhineland, was a song with the refrain *Nur Papier*—'Only Paper.' I first encountered it on a visit to Königsberg. One evening I sat in mufti in a local cabaret with my staff officer, Major Ewald, over a bottle of bad wine. One variety 'turn' had succeeded another, each characterized by the usual lecherous humor and topical satire, and had left the audience languid and unmoved over their beer-mugs. But when *Nur Papier* was announced the audience visibly brightened as at a star turn. *Nur Papier* more than justified expectation. It was a comic song of misadventure attuned to the ears of an audience whom the exigencies of the war had made disagreeably familiar with paper substitutes for everything from string to underclothing, and the comedian, with much dramatic expression, told a forlorn tale of how he had been left a legacy in marks. When he sought to collect it, he had found it was 'only paper.' He had bought an 'ersatz' suit-case, and when it caught in the carriage door it had ripped in two, for it was 'only paper.' He had purchased an umbrella, and when exposed to the rain it had drooped and wilted, for it was 'only paper.' He had bought a pair of ready-made trousers, and—but Prussian humor is not delicate. The audience followed the tale of comic disillusion with increasing merriment, but it was the last verse, unfolding the parable, which

brought the house down. One morning, sang this political trouba-
dour with a communicative wink, the Entente would wake up to
find itself faced by a strong and united Germany, and to discover
the Treaty of Versailles to be 'only paper.' In a tumult of guttural
applause, the singer subsided.

Everywhere and at every turn one seemed to encounter the War
psychosis in all its melancholy rancor. In the shops of numismatists
and booksellers unpleasant reminders stared one in the face such as
one never saw in Cologne where, indeed, in view of the presence
of the Allied troops, they had been spirited away. There was a
good deal of 'window-dressing' in Cologne in more senses than one.
One day I paused outside a numismatist's shop in Berlin, in the Friedrichstrasse, the windows of which were filled with war medals com-
memorative of German victories. My eye caught sight of a real
trouvaille among the display. It was the famous—or infamous—
Lusitania medal, struck by the German Government in 1916, when
flushed with that dreadful triumph. I bought it. I bought it just in
time, for the German Government furtively withdrew it from circulation when the tide of tourist traffic began to flow into Germany
again. It was a ghoulish thing. On one side, most artistically executed, was the figure of a grinning skeleton gloating over the heads
of the drowning victims in a troubled sea. On the reverse was the
mocking inscription, 'To him who disregarded our warning.' [3] Just
fifteen years after this exhibition in the Friedrichstrasse, a German
newspaper decorously saluted the new Anglo-German Naval Agreement, withdrawing the ban imposed by the Treaty of Versailles on
the construction of submarines, an Agreement into which we were
decoyed by Germany's undertaking to observe the Rules of Submarine Warfare for all time to come. The salute took the form of a
touching narrative by the commander, Captain Karl Scherb, of the
submarine which had sunk the *Lusitania*. He wrote of the deep
regret 'as a man' with which he had sunk her. 'We all regretted,' he
proceeded, 'that so many innocent lives had been lost.' [4] I sometimes
wonder whether Captain Scherb's contrition ever moved him to
destroy his medal.

[3] 'Dem Verachter der Warnung.'
[4] The *Völkischer Beobachter*, 7 May 1935.

As in Berlin, so elsewhere. The whole country was glutted with loot. One heard a great deal during the war of the deliberate destruction by the orders of the German General Staff [5] of the industries of Belgium. The object of it all was to reduce Belgium and the occupied districts of Northern France to a state of economic servitude, in other words commercial exploitation by the German export trade, for all time to come and thereby to ruin France and Belgium beyond hope of recovery. There had been nothing like it in any European campaign since the devastation of the Palatinate two centuries earlier. My friend General Barthélemy told me that at Lille the Germans carefully removed all the vital parts of the machines in the textile factories and crushed them under a hammer. At Denain-Anzin they had done the same with the metallurgical industries. The sugar-refineries they destroyed everywhere. According to German writers themselves this wholesale 'liquidation,' as they called it, of Belgium and France was part of a deliberate policy on the part of the German General Staff acting in collusion with the big industrialists, in particular that evil genius Hugo Stinnes.[5] The deliberate destruction of the coal-mines at Lens and the factories at Lille I had seen with my own eyes, and many a British officer was struck by the melancholy sight, immediately after the declaration of the Armistice, of the factories, in particular the glass factories, wrecked not by shell fire but by the sabotage of German sappers all along the line of the Meuse between Liège and Namur. Now, on the arrival of the Control Commission in Germany, we were forcibly reminded of these things, things which we should have been only too glad to forget. Like the spoils of the looted homes of France in the antique shops of Berlin, the loot of the gutted factories stared one in the face. Colonel Beasley, of our Armaments Sub-Commission, told me that on his arrival at Dresden he found huge barges, still unloaded, crammed with costly machinery which had been 'lifted' from the factories of France and Belgium. At this very time I read, with extremely mixed feelings, reports in the English newspapers of a move-

[5] General Wurtzbacher's plea of confession and avoidance, in the German official publication, *Der grosse Krieg*, I, p. 76, makes interesting reading. His chief defense seems to be the thoroughness with which the thing was done. See also Dr. Hermann Brinckmeyer in his *Hugo Stinnes*, at p. 33, also Arnold Rechberg, 'Innere Einflusse im Weltkrieg,' in *Das Tagebuch* for 31 March 1923, at pp. 437, etc.

ment in Downing Street and among the City of London Bankers to 'set Germany on her feet.' Meanwhile, as we shall see, the big industrialists in Germany were having the time of their lives. Profiting by the German Government's policy of inflation, largely inspired by themselves, they were paying off the whole of their debentures, dodging the burden of income-tax *en masse*, and renewing their plant with such success that by 1922 our Armaments District Committee in the Ruhr reported to us that they were even better equipped to resume war manufacture than in 1914.

II

The sight of these things considerably tempered the commiseration which we otherwise might have felt for the civil population of Germany and the short commons to which some, but by no means all, of them had been reduced. The Allied blockade may have inflicted some hardship and it may have been as well that the British Government took the initiative, largely on the representations of General Plumer who was then in command of the British Army of Occupation on the Rhine, in raising it at the earliest possible moment. But, as we shall see, there was nothing like starvation in Germany; it was Austria, her ally, which was left to starve by the Germans themselves who, in Ludendorff's brutal phrase, regarded her as a decomposing 'corpse' (*eine Leiche*). General Plumer was deeply moved by certain reports of 'famine' in the Rhineland or rather in Cologne. Whether he would have been equally moved if he had seen what one saw in Berlin and what one never saw in Cologne, namely the sight of well-fed *Schieber* (profiteers) eating gluttonously in fashionable hotels, I do not know. There was, indeed, another side to the picture presented to the eye of the casual observer in Cologne and one had only to travel a few miles outside the city to see it in all its invidiousness. A British officer, Brigadier-General Harry Lewin, serving with the Army of Occupation in a rural district in the immediate neighborhood of Bonn, was approached, almost immediately on his arrival, by a German official, the local 'Landrat,' with an appeal for his assistance as a commanding officer in compelling the rural inhabitants to observe the German Food Control regulations. While the British troops were living on bully beef, tinned milk, and salt butter, the

Rhineland farmers and smallholders were, despite the continuance of the blockade, 'doing themselves well,' according to the Landrat, on an abundance of fat geese, succulent hams, fresh milk and butter, and newly laid eggs. General Lewin was at first incredulous, as any Englishman accustomed to the rigid enforcement of the Food Control regulations in our own country would have been. Moreover, German propaganda, already in full cry against the iniquities of the 'Hunger Blockade,' had led him to believe that the stores of food in Germany were completely exhausted. But an accidental discovery aroused his suspicions.[6] He soon found himself on a hot scent. Subsequent investigations confirmed all that the Landrat had said. One day, the General happened to enter a large barn which we had requisitioned as a storeroom for a British battery. Glancing upwards, he was astonished to see the cross-beams festooned with large Westphalian hams, a delicacy very dear to the German palate. 'What's the meaning of this?' he asked the N.C.O. in charge, 'are you running a ham and beef shop?' The N.C.O. explained. 'A lot of Jerrys' had come to him by night, each bearing a ham hidden under his coat, and had asked him to 'take care of it.' In a mood of misguided charity, the N.C.O., who knew nothing of the German Food Control regulations, had agreed. 'I've got 'em all here down in my book, sir,' he added as he produced for General Lewin's inspection his 'Squad-book' in which he had noted down the names of each individual ham owner. 'When a Jerry comes to draw his ham,' the N.C.O. continued, 'I make him sign for it in my book.' On examining the hams, the General discovered that each bore a different German name, rudely incised with a jack-knife upon the rind. It was the name of the hoarder, designed to serve the purpose of a 'cloak-room ticket' when he came to the barn to recover it. In the meantime, the barn was as good as a 'strong-room' for the

[6] General Lewin, to whom I owe the story, writes to me as follows: 'Lord Plumer's appeal (as G.O.C. the British Army of Occupation asking for the termination of the blockade) gave enormous support to the German yarn. I had the deepest respect and admiration for him, but in this particular matter he was most partially and carelessly advised.' General Lewin adds that, at the request of the Landrat, he reported to our G.H.Q. at Cologne the names of forty German landowners in his district who had refused during the war, and were continuing to refuse, to hand over, for the relief of German people in the towns, the quota fixed by German law.

custody of this illicit treasure, for no German Food Control officer would dream of attempting to search a place requisitioned by the British Army authorities.

Was this ugly incident typical? Yes. Englishmen were much more distressed by the signs of hungry German townsmen in Cologne than their rural neighbors ever were. If the common people in Germany 'starved,' it was largely, though not entirely, owing to the selfishness of their 'betters' and, in the case of the rural population, their equals. German 'Food Control' utterly failed to equalize the burden between one man and another owing to the impunity with which people, more fortunately placed than others, were allowed to disobey the Food Control regulations. In England, as we all know, such regulations were honorably observed during the last war by all classes of the population. In Germany they were not. It was a case of *homo homini lupus*. This is not mere speculation. There is abundant German testimony to the dismal truth of it. Town and country in Germany treated each other, during the war, 'like enemies,' the rural population refusing point-blank to provision the towns.[7] In a German encyclopedia of high authority, published immediately after the war, and dealing with the German 'War Economy' (*Kriegswirthschaft*) the writers declare that the Food Control legislation was so 'riddled' (*durchlöchert*) with loopholes and the public 'conscience' (*Gewissen*) so lax that 'usury and profiteering flourished' like a fungus—'Wucher und Schiebertum blühte.'[8] A neutral observer in the service of the German Government during the war as their chief aircraft designer, the famous Anthony Fokker, subsequently put on record, in scathing language, his disgust at the universal selfishness in this matter which he encountered everywhere in Germany. Supplies were always available, he tells us, 'legally or illegally,' if you knew where to look for them. 'Bootlegging of foods became a widespread industry.' From the very start, each man did that which was right in his own eyes and food distribution cards served, paradoxically enough, not to distribute food but to monop-

---

[7] See, for example, Schucking's book, *Die innere Demokratisierung Preussen*, p. 17, where the writer says in so many words that the country people 'refused' (*versagte*) to supply the towns as though they and the townspeople were 'mutual enemies.'

[8] *Handbuch der Politik* (Berlin, 1921), iv, p. 134.

olize it, the cards being bought up in order to accumulate food in the hands of the purchaser and thereby becoming a kind of 'base currency' in more senses than one:

Bread was the first article to be distributed, each family being limited to so many ounces in proportion to its size. Butter was next. Graft began to show at once, with families obtaining tickets for absent members. People who could buy through illegitimate channels would not use up their food cards, but would sell them to less fortunate neighbors, the old law of supply and demand dictating the prices. Fairness and even common decency were forgotten in the struggle to get all the food one could lay one's hands on.[9]

According to Mr. Fokker, 'the army delegations' in the Home Commands behaved as badly as everybody else.

Why was it that Englishmen fulfilled the law of Christ and bore one another's burdens while Germans did not? Was it the spectacle of those in authority being favored, as they were, by the Food Control regulations in Germany that led the common folk to break them? 'The English,' observed a shrewd Frenchman, 'respect law and despise authority.' The Germans respect authority and despise law. That is one explanation. Another is the habit of self-government in England and its absence in Germany. Self-government induces self-control. It seems to be a law of life, for nations in great emergencies, not that they must be bond that they may be free but that they must be free in order that they may be bond. Otherwise there are no conscious ties of mutual obligation to bind them. With a nation habituated to self-government, the service of its citizens, in the crisis of its fate, is that service which is 'perfect freedom.' But it may well be that the true explanation goes deeper than any difference in the forms of political institutions in the two countries and that it is to be found in racial character. One cannot live long in Germany without being driven to the inexorable conclusion that the mutual consideration, the kind-heartedness, which so honorably distinguishes the English people above all others in the world, is entirely alien to the German character. Indeed, the most popular of

---

[9] *Flying Dutchman*, by Anthony Fokker (English translation), p. 181. Exactly the same scuffle among the German people took place in the years 1914-18, to escape the burden of war taxation, and the big industrialists 'got away with it.' See below, Section VII, etc.

German historians has boasted as much. The secret of German
'greatness,' he tells us, lies 'in their total lack of kind-heartedness.' [10]
No doubt Hitler gave his audience what they wanted when he
boasted in one of his war speeches that he was 'the hardest man in
German history.'

I came across a painful example of this sort of thing when I tried
to enlist the assistance of one of the great German industrialists,
Herr Arnold Rechberg, with whom I was on friendly terms, in aid
of one of the most distinguished musicians in Germany, the Director
of a famous Berlin Orchestra, and his family. The latter had been
reduced to something very like starvation by the collapse of the
mark, and I was no longer able to continue to relieve, as I had been
doing, his necessities sufficiently out of my own comparatively modest resources. 'Starving!' replied Rechberg, 'I dare say they are. So
are lots of others. Let them starve! *The fact is there are too many
people in Germany!*' I replied with a tart reminder that he was always complaining to me of the burden of 'reparations' upon the
German people, whereupon he changed his tone with the words,
'Well, I'll see what I can do.' I learned afterwards from my friend the
musician that Rechberg eventually sent him the equivalent, in English
currency, of half a crown. Rechberg was one of the wealthiest men
in Germany. This indifference of the Germans to each other's priva-
tions may, or may not, account for the Führer's institution of his vast
system of *Hilfsdienst* and 'Winter Relief.' The sight of a large and
formidable Storm-trooper with a collecting-box acted like a charm
and was irresistible. The trouble was that the *Hilfsdienst* accounts
were never audited and German refugees tell us that the Storm-
troopers pocketed the proceeds.

The truth about the spurious appeal of German propaganda to
British humanitarianism in 1919 is important because an appeal in
much the same terms was made by Germans during the Second
World War to the humanitarianism of all the belligerents against
our naval blockade. The appeal affected a solicitude, which no German ever felt, for the hungry non-Germans in the territories overrun and occupied by German troops. In due course, when the

[10] Thus Treitschke in *Das deutsche Ordensland Preussen*, at p. 6, where he
says of the Prussians: 'Much of their greatness lay in their total lack of that kind-
heartedness (*Gutmütigkeit*) which is so wrongly exalted as a German virtue.'

Germans themselves were on the run, the appeal was switched on, as in 1919, to humanitarian opinion in England with importunities to relax our blockade in favor of 'hungry' Germany. Indeed one of our irrepressible bishops took the field quite early in the war with the naïve suggestion that we should temper our blockade of Germany itself by making 'arrangements' with the Nazi Government to allow food cargoes to go through under a kind of 'gentleman's agreement' that the food should be 'reserved' for the civil population of Germany. Apparently the bishop thought the Nazis perfect gentlemen. As late as November 1939, a sentimental Member of Parliament, Miss Jenny Lee, gave to the world an autobiography in which there re-appears without qualification the old fairy-tale about the hungry Rhinelanders in 1919. Some twenty years ago she made one of those fugitive intrusions into the Rhineland to which itinerant politicians in those sentimental days were so addicted and was greatly moved, she tells us, at the spectacle of 'a quarter million British soldiers' who were 'the despair of their commanding officer' because they were, according to her, suffering from 'malnutrition' owing to their 'lavish bestowal' of their rations among the 'hungry' Germans. 'A precious memory,' she tearfully adds, and 'the basis of all my hopes' for the future. If only Europe had been governed by the spirit of this mythical quarter of a million soldiers during the last twenty years, Europe would, she suggested, have escaped the present catastrophe.[11]

There are other aspects of the 'Hunger Blockade' about which German propaganda was discreetly silent and which our humanitarians completely overlooked. There was the responsibility of Germany herself for the starvation of the civil population of Belgium and the occupied districts of France. General Lewin reminded me of it recently when discussing the subject of Plumer's intercession. 'I also,' he told me, 'served, like "Plum" himself, in the British Army of Occupation. Some people in the Rhineland, I dare say, went hungry,

---

[11] General Lewin's pungent comment on this lady's fatuous illusions is of peculiar value at the present moment. After describing her statements as wildly imaginative, he adds: 'It is all rot for any one to say that our men suffered from malnutrition. I hope, even at this late hour, I may see the quietus given to this spurious piece of Boche propaganda which is always seized on by our pacifists and highbrows and believed by many reasonable people. When we have beaten the Boche for the second time in our lifetime, I have no doubt the story will be worked up again with many trimmings.'

but it was nothing to the hunger I saw among the Belgian people when we marched through Belgium and France immediately after its evacuation by the German troops. *The Belgians were yellow with hunger.*' As for the French, 'I shall never forget,' continued General Lewin, 'the look of misery on the faces of the women and children as we passed through Avesnes; the women were gaunt specters and the children listless little skeletons with skins like parchment. The moment we crossed the frontier into Germany, near Malmedy, I noticed that every one we met looked well fed and well clad, the children looking particularly rosy and well nourished.' The plea that the German troops in Belgium may have been hard put to it to feed themselves during the last two years of the war, when the Allied blockade had been tightened up would, even if it were true, avail nothing to acquit the German authorities of this inhumanity. Long before the blockade, indeed from the very commencement of the war, the German General Staff, by its ruthless policy of 'requisitioning,' set itself to starve out the people of Belgium. Had it not been for the vast organized charity of the United States, at that time neutral, and the Hoover Commission, the Belgian civil population would have been exterminated by hunger.[12]

When present, as a member of the British Military Delegation, at the historic ceremony of the signature of the Treaty of Peace in the Salle des Glaces at Versailles, I listened to the famous outburst of the German plenipotentiary, Herr Brockdorff-Rantzau, against the 'inhumanity' of the blockade. Now so far as its enforcement during the period of war is concerned, it was a measure which every great maritime power is entitled to enforce when fighting for its own existence and there can be no question that, had Germany succeeded in securing the command of the seas, she would have enforced it not less,

[12] The observation of the American Ambassador, Walter Page, on this aspect of the matter are very much to the point. Writing in 1916 he said: 'In the country over which the German Army has passed, a crow would die of starvation and no human being has ten cents of real money. Our Belgian Commission is spending more than 100 million dollars a year to keep the Belgians alive—only because they are robbed every day. They have a rich country and could support themselves but for these robbers.'—*The Life and Letters of Walter Page*, vol. ii, pp. 153-4. When, in due course, America entered the war all this relief work inevitably came to an end and the Belgians were left to starve—as their German conquerors never starved.

indeed perhaps more, rigorously than ourselves. Long after Brock-dorff-Rantzau's outburst, I encountered in a bookseller's shop in Königsberg a German war pamphlet with the expressive title of 'The Starving out of England' (*Die Aushungerung Englands*), in which the writer gloated over the prospect of our being reduced to famine by the German policy of submarine warfare. As for the continuance of the blockade after the war, in other words during the early months of the Armistice, there was a precedent which many of those present at Brockdorff-Rantzau's allocution, M. Clemenceau among them, had painful cause to remember. That precedent was the siege of Paris by the German armies in 1871. A siege is a blockade, no less and, indeed, a good deal more. During the negotiations between Thiers and Bis-marck for an armistice, the former attempted to secure permission for the revictualling of Paris, whose people were dying of hunger. He was met with a blunt refusal. This is a matter of history. Very different was the attitude of the Allied Governments in 1919. The ink was hardly dry on the terms of the Armistice when they con-certed plans for the dispatch of food to Germany. But the Germans, in pursuance of their ruthless campaign against shipping, had sent so many of our own ships to the bottom that we were constrained to stipulate that the German Government should supply ships for the purpose. With singular indifference to the 'hunger' of their own people with which they had so loudly reproached us, the German Government, no doubt with an eye on the renewal of hostilities, held up the ships for nearly three months.[13]

Watching Clemenceau as he listened patiently, with his gloved hands clasped in front of him, to Brockdorff-Rantzau's carefully cal-culated tirade against the 'Hunger Blockade,' I found myself wonder-ing what were the old man's thoughts. Under his beetling brows, his magnetic eyes sunk in a face yellow with age like an old parchment, he appeared to be watching intently, with a faintly ironical expres-sion, every flicker of the German's eyelids, every tell-tale muscle of his face. Perhaps Clemenceau was living over again the days of

[13] 'After having side-stepped the issue for over two months, Germany finally accepted the inevitable and began the delivery of her ships.'—*American Food in the World War*, at p. 194. See also Temperley's *History of the Peace Confer-ence*, vol. i, at pp. 318, etc., for the story of Germany's disingenuous behavior in this matter.

France's agony and famine in 1870-71. Perhaps he was recalling, for he was an omnivorous reader, the *ipsissima verba* of Bismarck in those days as he gloated over the starvation of the people of Paris hemmed in as by a ring of steel with the German troops investing the city and refusing to allow a single wagon of food-supplies from humanitarian neutral countries to go through. The story is worth telling and never more so than now. Here it is.

One December day in the year 1870 when the German armies were investing the city of Paris, Bismarck sat at meat in a château at Versailles meditating on how to bring the war with France to a speedy conclusion. Moritz Busch, predestined to go down to history as the Boswell of the Iron Chancellor, sat with him, taking careful mental notes of the conversation. A strange creature this Busch— obscure, obsequious, and always burrowing underground in news- paper offices. He was Bismarck's 'Press Officer.' In other words he was, in some sense, but a relatively decent sense, a predecessor of Goebbels, describing himself and his job, as he does in his Remi- niscences, as 'all ears' except that his description was purely meta- phorical, his head being, in fact, quite a presentable head and not in the least like the unlovely, rabbit-like head of Goebbels with its protruding pair of ears. Also Bismarck who, after all, was an aristo- crat with a sense of proportion, never dreamed of elevating Busch to ministerial rank. He kept him as a kind of literary scullion to do the dirty work of his politics. No one in Germany dreamed in those days of being ruled, as Germany was later ruled, by the scum of the scullery and the refuse of the basement. France was at that moment fighting a rear-guard action, hoping for a peace by agreement. Thiers was negotiating with Bismarck for an armistice. Paris was starving, and the countryside had been stripped by the German troops as though by a plague of locusts. They called it 'requisitioning.' There was a growing movement in two neutral countries, England and Belgium, for the collection and dispatch of food to the starving Parisians. At the same time, Thiers was pleading with the Germans that the proposed armistice should permit of the passage of food supplies to the civil population.

Bismarck was extremely indignant. He had dined well, Busch tells us, discussing the excellent quality of the Swiss cheeses they were eating and of the wines with which the Germans always 'wash down' their food with noisy sounds suggestive of the emptying of a drain-pipe. And the more he ate and drank—he was famous, and much admired, in Germany for his gigantic and indiscriminate appetite —the more eloquently did he declaim to Busch against 'these thoroughly foolish proposals,' as he called them, for relieving the hunger of the French. 'These projected supplies,' he indignantly de-clared, 'are to prevent the Parisians starving *after* they shall have capitulated.' Nay, worse, the free passage of such supplies, under an armistice would, he protested, delay the capitulation itself.

'The French,' he proceeded, 'should not merely be allowed to capitulate, they should be *forced to* an immediate capitulation,' amounting to an unconditional surrender. '*They should be forced to it by starvation.* And then we are told to spare people who are searching for potatoes!—on the outskirts of Paris. They should be shot too, if we want to reduce the city by starvation.' [14]

Thus Bismarck and his *ipsissima verba.* The diplomatic historian of the Franco-Prussian War, Albert Sorel, subsequently told the world, with chapter and verse, the full story of the failure of the French negotiations for an armistice. Germany, he revealed, finally refused to allow any *revitaillement* of the besieged towns, 'hoping to reduce them by famine.' She succeeded.[15]

III

The real malady from which Germany was suffering in 1919 was not starvation of the body but corruption of the soul. It was the malady of 'a mind diseased' to which none could have ministered but the patient herself. Only a great spiritual revival could have cured her, but of such there was no sign. One day I attended divine service, as I have remarked in an earlier chapter, in the Nikolai Church in Berlin. The service of the Lutheran Church is a thing of singular beauty and when the preacher gave out his text the whole congre-gation, as is the custom, rose to their feet and stood in silence. One sentence of the sermon has stamped itself upon my memory. It was

[14] *Bismarck, Some Secret Pages of his History* (English translation), by Mo-ritz Busch, vol. i, at pp. 357, 362.
[15] *Histoire diplomatique de la guerre franco-allemande,* by Albert Sorel, vol. ii, pp. 79, etc.

'Meine Gemeinde, lernet leiden ohne zu klagen'—'My people, learn to suffer without complaining.' It was, however, a singularly sterile sermon. While there was much exhortation to national endurance, there was not a word about national repentance. Contrition found no place in it. Of atonement there was not a word. I doubt indeed whether any German pastor's life would have been safe if he had dared to condemn the barbarous conduct by Germany of the war which had just ended. Neither Niemoller, who, indeed, had peculiar reasons for silence,[16] nor any other ever did so, and the only man who did, Professor Foerster, was driven into exile by the murder gangs of Munich. Even so, the preacher's voice in the Nikolai-Kirche was as that of one crying in the wilderness. Germany never learned to suffer without complaining. She was too busy 'organizing sympathy' by filling the world with complaints of the *Gewaltfrieden*, the 'Peace of Violence' as it was common form to stigmatize the Treaty of Versailles, and utterly forgetting the violent 'peace' she imposed, when flushed with victories in the field, only a few months earlier upon Rumania and upon Russia as they lay prostrate at her feet. Equally forgotten were not only the plans of her General Staff to reduce Belgium to eternal servitude but the appalling massacres of Aerschot, Louvain, Tamines, Tintigny, Andenne, and that field of blood, Dinant. Just as, in 1914, not a single voice was lifted up, even among the clergy, in Germany to condemn these appalling cruelties,[17] so now no one was heard to regret them, much less to exorcise the evil spirit which had inspired them. The soul of an erring nation, like the soul of the individual, may be saved by contrition, even as the dying knight in the *Purgatorio* was saved by *una lagrimetta*—'one little tear.' The history of the English people is full of such great expiations— the abolition of the slave trade, the enfranchisement of conquered peoples, the restoration of independence to the Irish and to the South African Dutch—but such acts of magnanimity have been as fugitive

[16] Niemoller had not merely been one of the practitioners of ruthless submarine warfare as a U-boat commander but, in April 1920, took a hand along with the Free Corps 'toughs' and the Reichswehr in the bloody massacres in the Ruhr where he so distinguished himself as to be offered by von Seeckt a commission in the Reichswehr.

[17] 'Must not we Germans feel ashamed that not a single voice (*nicht eine einzige Stimme*) amongst us, neither in the Reichstag nor among the dignitaries of our Christian Church, was lifted up to protest against these things.'— Foerster, *Europe und die deutsche Frage*, p. 357.

as they have been rare in German history, which is one long story of concessions made only to be withdrawn—of caresses always followed by blows, as a sardonic German has said of Prussian administration in Poland.[18] Germany did, indeed, weep in 1919 and copiously, as Germans often do, for there is no people more lachrymose, but they were, as always, tears of rage, not of sorrow.

In the evening of his days Treitschke, the lifelong apologist of German ruthlessness, was filled with misgiving, when it was too late for misgiving, at the 'moral deterioration' of the German people.[19] He traced the cancerous growth to a decay of spiritual life in Germany and to nothing else. In this he was right. He would have been still more right if he had probed a little deeper, to find the cause of this decay in the cult of that brutal militarism which he had done so much to exalt. And now, just twenty-four years after his valedictory lament, his misgivings had come home to roost. The state of Germany, as Goebbels freely admits in his naïve autobiography, was 'rotten and worse than rotten,' [20] not only, he adds, in 1919 but in 1914—a curious admission from one whose political stock-in-trade it was to place all of the blame on the Weimar Republic. The autobiographies of the other members of the Nazi triumvirate vie with Goebbels in fouling their own nest. Germany, they tell us, was 'decadent,' [21] 'corrupt, immoral, and indecent in every walk of life' [22] not only in those days immediately after the war but even before it. Of that 'rottenness' we, on our arrival and long after it, were to see enough and more than enough, as will presently appear. But of the healing agencies of contrition there was never a sign. In one fugitive sentence, lighting up the dark background of implacable hate which disfigures so many of its pages, the author of Mein Kampf has speculated on the possibility of the German people having accepted defeat 'in quite another spirit' than that in which they had, in fact, accepted

[18] 'One should not treat the Poles, as we have done, to sweetmeats one day and thrashings the next (heute Zuckerbrot und morgen die Peitsche)'—von Treschkow, Von Fürsten und anderen Sterblichen (Berlin, 1922), p. 189.

[19] Thus Treitschke in his valedictory lecture, 'Zum Gedächtnis des grossen Krieges,' on 19 July 1895.

[20] 'Faul und oberfaul'—Goebbels in his Vom Kaiserhof zum Reichskanzlei, p. 17.

[21] Hitler in Mein Kampf (135th German edition), at pp. 252, etc.

[22] Goering in Aufbau einer Nation, p. 22.

it. If, he suggests, they had really been beaten in the field, a fact which it does not suit his purpose to admit, they might have been 'overwhelmed by sorrow'—*von Schmerz uberwältigt*. But he entertains the disturbing idea only to dismiss it. Even had Germany been defeated by the Allies and not, as he will have it, by the 'poisonous' elements at home, 'rage and fury,' he tells us, would have filled the hearts of the Germans 'against the enemy to whom *destiny* had given the victory.' In that case, he speculates, as he surveys the Bacchanalian orgies of post-war Germany, Germans would have 'danced' and rioted less shamefully after the war and 'hated' more robustly. It is an extraordinary diagnosis of his adopted fellow-countrymen, suggesting nothing so much as a bad loser, but it is not for an Englishman to dispute it. That the German has, and always will have, a quarrel with 'destiny' is certainly not to be disputed. The naïve Goebbels got very near the mark when, enlarging with all the intrepidity of a non-combatant on the heroic capacity of Germans in 'knowing how to die,' he admitted that they might not know how to live.[23] The same might be said of the Gadarene swine.

The 'rotten' Germany we of the 'Advanced Guard' now encountered was like a bad dream. The Cities of the Plain were not more vile. A gifted Polish writer, who lived through it all, in no way exaggerates when he observes that 'one year in Germany, especially in Berlin, revealed more of the perversions in which man's lower nature can indulge than a lifetime spent anywhere else.' [24] The social life of the country, if one can speak of a savage horde as a society, was flagrant beyond belief, savage with all the lusts of that dark forest of the great Florentine poet's somber imagination:

> Questa selva selvaggia aspra e forte
> Che nel pensier rinnuova la paura.

The Germans themselves made no secret of these things and the German Press recurred to the subject again and again as though at once fascinated and repelled.[25] I often discussed it with the chiefs of

[23] 'Zu leben verstehen wir Deutschen vielleicht nicht; aber sterben, das konnen wir fabelhaft. Wie mancher S.A. Mann hat dieses Wort wahrmachen mussen!'—p. 258 of *Vom Kaiserhof zum Reichskanzlei*.

[24] Rom Landau in his book, *Seven, an Essay in Confession*, p. 76.

[25] For example, a Berlin newspaper, the *Berliner Tageblatt* of 23 January 1921, in which the writer, a police official, lamented the powerlessness of the police to cope with these evils.

the German Police in Berlin, with whom my military duties brought me into frequent contact, and they professed themselves powerless to deal with the malady just because of its universality. As night fell, the torpid city seemed to wake like a beast of prey. Vice walked the streets, lurked in underground cabarets, and was rampant in the theaters. It was not merely that women were to be seen everywhere naked on the stage. The same thing might have been seen, and was, in nearly every city upon the Continent. 'Nudism,' or something very like it, was not unknown, for a time, behind the footlights in London. The whole of Europe seemed possessed by a mania for ridding itself of its clothes, vicariously, if not otherwise. It is, as alienists well know, a familiar symptom of insanity, and who shall say that, after all the horrors of the great catastrophe, Europe was wholly sane? But in Berlin I saw things which I never saw in London and Paris or even in Vienna or Budapest. If it be true that, in the famous phrase of Burke, 'vice lost half its evil by losing all its grossness,' then the 'night life' of Berlin had nothing indeed to redeem it. One evening, some of us went to a theater in the Kurfurstendamm which had become one of the sights of Berlin. There we saw four women, naked as Eve, executing a *danse de ventre*, with weary faces and bodies glistening with sweat in the limelight. One of them was a mere child. The performance was as crude as it was disgusting. There was no suggestion of art, no diaphanous veils to grace the contour of the limbs, no woodland scenery to suggest the frank simplicity of nature, no pipe of Pan, no song of Spring, such as charmed the eye and ear upon the stage of Paris. The scene was too gross for art and too artificial for nature. The sight of those tired women and their writhing bodies, hired for a song to divert the crowd who sat noisily eating and drinking at little tables in the auditorium below, suggested nothing so much as the horrors of a White Slave Traffic.

Another theater, the Apollo Theatre, drew all Berlin to a review known as 'Harem Nights' (*Harem Nächte*), presenting the spectacle of a seraglio of naked women raided by black men, almost as nude, who, rushing on to the stage from the wings, seized the women in their arms and bore them off amid storms of applause as the curtain fell. The enterprising management saw to it that the public craving for realism should not be disappointed and proudly advertised that the ravishers were 'real blacks from Africa' (*echte Schwarze aus*

Afrika). By a curious irony, at the very time that all Berlin was flocking to 'Harem Nights' the whole German Press was launching the vast campaign of propaganda, directed principally to the ears of Americans, against the 'infamy' of 'black troops on the Rhine.' Doubtless they hoped that the world had forgotten to what use the German forces in East Africa had, according to the reports of General Smuts, put their black subjects as guards over Englishmen and Englishwomen interned as prisoners of war. The propaganda did its work, and not in America alone. When home on leave and dining with Lord Haldane, who knew as little about Germany after the war as he did before it, I was gravely told by my host that his German friends had informed him that there had been 'sixty rapes' of German women by 'black' troops on the Rhine. On my return from leave, I paid a call on General Degoutte in the Rhineland and asked him about it.

'The trouble is,' Degoutte said grimly, 'that all the prostitutes in the Rhineland solicit them. Naturally we don't encourage that sort of thing. After all, we are a great Colonial Power and we don't want our "colored" troops to return, on demobilization, boasting of their conquests over white women. "Rape" did you say? There have been only two cases of rape, or rather attempted rape, by our colored troops. Both men were sentenced by a *conseil de guerre* to be shot. I saw to it that the sentence was duly carried out, and in view of the propaganda beyond the Rhine, I ordered the local Bürgermeister to be present at the execution.'

Years later—it was in 1926—I spent a convivial evening at Geneva in company with a German lawyer from Bonn at a *Bierabend* organized by the German colony in the Swiss town. He was a genial man, *gemütlich* as only a Rhinelander or a Saxon among Germans can be.

"How have the French soldiers behaved during the Occupation?' I asked.

'Very well, on the whole,' was his answer, 'but I preferred the black troops to the white.'

This was a new point of view to me and I said so. 'I always heard in Berlin,' I replied, 'that the "black" troops insulted your women.'

'Gott im Himmel, Nein, das war nur Propaganda,' [26] he replied,

[26] 'Good Lord! No! That was only propaganda.'

looking at me sideways with a twinkling eye. 'You don't think the French officers would be so foolish as to tolerate that sort of thing? As a matter of fact, my wife told me that whenever one of those dark-skinned fellows—they're not really "black" you know, they're Moors—passed her on the pavement, he would pull in the skirts of his wide trousers so that even his clothes should not brush against her. They seemed frightened of our women somehow. Oh, yes, the French know how to keep these fellows in order. I don't like the French, but they're not fools, you know.'

'Harem Nights' was not, to be sure, a very edifying spectacle nor were those gyrations of naked women, to be seen on almost every stage and in every cabaret in Berlin, exactly a pretty thing. But, at least, their 'sex-appeal,' such as it was, was natural. What repelled British officers in Berlin and elsewhere with an almost physical nausea was the open and blatant evidence, which confronted us wherever we went, of the unnatural. That 'dark' offense, as the great Blackstone called it, 'which is not so much as to be mentioned among Christians,' flourished like a horrible fungus in the moral decay around us. It seemed to be accepted as a matter of course. 'Soliciting' by men was practiced with the most shameless impudence in the streets, the Tiergarten, the foyers of fashionable hotels, as though they were licensed by the police. Even in polite society one German would say of another, and his tastes, 'Er ist homo-sexual,' as one might speak of a man being fond of cricket or of golf. A friend of mine in 'A.G.3' at the War Office, Major Macmahon, wrote to me one day saying that he had heard there was a 'Society' of homo-sexualists in Germany, that they published a journal of their own, and would I get him a copy of it? I thought at first that Macmahon was pulling my leg, until a German friend assured me that there was indeed such a 'Society' (a Verein) and that there was just such a journal, published under the name of Freundschaft. So it proved. I bought a copy for my correspondent at a newspaper kiosk in the Unter den Linden, where I found it openly displayed. One glance at its contents was enough.[27] Some months later, when our Commission got to work, a

[27] The character of this horrible periodical is sufficiently indicated by the fact that it flourished a leading article claiming Jesus Christ's affection for the beloved disciple as a proof that the founder of Christianity approved and practised sexual perversion. The periodical was not new. In the autobiography of a Commissioner of Police in Berlin, the author tells us that it 'appeared regularly'

British officer serving under me asked one of the heads of the German C.I.D. in Berlin, with whom we were on good terms in spite of our duty to 'control' the police or perhaps because of it, if he would show him the 'night life' of Berlin. The German detective agreed and they visited, in mufti, one haunt after another until they arrived at a kind of night-club in which pale youths, with painted faces and dressed in women's clothes, were dancing with middle-aged men. It was obvious what the place was. 'But isn't this sort of thing an offense under German law?' inquired the British officer. 'Well, yes,' replied the policeman tranquilly, 'but we can't go against public opinion.'

It is a curious trait of the German character to impute to others, with every affectation of horror, the vices to which they themselves are most addicted. Of that there was any amount of evidence in the Second World War. When, in 1870, the German armies had conquered France and were investing Paris, one of their chaplains preached an improving discourse at Versailles in which he called the world to witness that the German victories were the judgment of God upon 'Sodom.' The Sodom of his sermon was Paris. He exhorted the German soldiers to smite her people and spare not. A great French historian, stung to passionate indignation, emerged from the twilight of the scriptorium and, putting aside his texts and manuscripts, replied with a mordant pamphlet [28] in the form of an 'open letter' addressed to the German Army chaplains, in which he protested against the attempt of the victors to defame the country and people they had ruined. He threw back the insult. 'You gentlemen talk of the "abominations" of Parisian life,' he retorted, 'do not worry! I can tell you that more than one-third of the sort of people you have in mind come to us from Germany.' [29] And now, fifty years later, by a strange irony, it was Berlin, and not Paris, Germany, and not France, which had become a by-word among Germans themselves as the home of the unmentionable vice. The sardonic von Bülow, in a book published

(regelmässig), even in the days before the war. It was never suppressed—see *Von Fürsten und anderen Sterblichen* (Berlin, 1922), by Hans von Treschkow, p. 110.

[28] *A Messieurs les ministres du culte evangélique de L'armée du roi de Prusse*, by Fustel de Coulanges (Paris, 18 October 1870).

[29] 'Mais quittez ce souci; je vous dirai que plus du tiers de ces personnes-là nous viennent de l'Allemagne.' Fustel de Coulanges added that 'not ten per cent' of those who sought to satisfy their depraved tastes in Paris were Parisians. They were mostly German visitors.

as recently as 1931, freely admitted it. 'It is doubtful in my opinion,' he writes in his Reminiscences, 'whether Berlin is not more reminiscent of the city of Nebuchadnezzar than Paris.' Paris, at least, he pointedly observes, 'redeems with wit and grace the worse aspects of sin.' In the modern Babylon on the river Spree he could find no such signs of redemption.[30]

IV

There were other vices. Bestiality met one at every turn, on the stage, in the Press, in the shop-windows, and was the current coin of political controversy. One of my officers stationed in Dresden, Captain Hennessy, told me that Herr Lipinski, the Minister-President of Saxony and a Socialist, wound up a debate in the Landtag, in the course of which he had been violently attacked by the Nationalist Opposition, with the sardonic observation that he did not mind their defamation of his character but he did wish that they would abstain from sending him parcels of human excreta through the post. I was incredulous until Hennessy produced the Parliamentary report in the *Leipziger Neueste Nachrichten*, which was conclusive. My incredulity was, indeed, misplaced. Misplaced because evidence of an almost insane obsession with the lowest functions of the body assailed one everywhere in Germany. In this respect there was nothing whatever to choose between Prussia and Bavaria, Saxony and Württemberg. In a numismatist's window in a fashionable shopping quarter in Berlin, the Friedrichstrasse, one could see, day after day, a grimacing statue of a human figure in a stooping posture engaged in the act of excretion. On the stage, as Lord Birkenhead remarked with characteristic incisiveness after a flying visit to Germany, German humor 'reeked of the lavatory.' Comedians and comic journalists vied with one another in pleasantries that affected an Englishman with the same sense of nausea as a bad smell. Any one who takes the trouble to look through the files of the great comic journal *Simplicissimus*, published in Munich, the home of the arts, will discover scores of

[30] The observations of a gifted Polish writer, Mr. Rom Landau, on this subject are both illuminating and suggestive. In his book, *Seven*, quoted above, he observes: 'Whenever Germany suffers from an inner crisis, all her latent sex distortions break out. The post-war years, as well as 30 June 1934, were merely part of the convulsions without which Germany seems unable to fulfil herself.'

cartoons, many of them directed against our Control Commission, of quite indescribable filthiness. They were not the less remarkable for being the work of finished artists, witnesses to the eternal truth that the Germans are educated without being refined. These draftsmen's passion for introducing a latrine, and things even more repellent, suggests nothing so much as the pathological impulses of a patient defacing, as patients so often do, the walls of a lunatic asylum with his obscenities.

This filthy-mindedness was not, however, the aberration of a people whose minds had been estranged and disordered by defeat. It was, in fact, nothing new. It is always repeating itself in German life and character, even in public life. As it was in the Saxon Landtag in the year of disgrace and defeat in 1922, so it was in the year of grace and triumph in 1938 in the 'Party' rally at Nuremberg. On the eve of 'Munich,' Goering, in the course of a savage attack on the people of Czechoslovakia, delivered himself of a sentence which the discreet correspondents of *The Times* and the *Daily Telegraph*, present at the meeting, decently veiled by describing it as 'a Rabelaisian jest very much to the taste of his audience.' It was, in fact, quite unprintable in an English newspaper, and cannot be reprinted here. It threatened the Czechs with the same nasty pleasantries as those of which Herr Lipinski complained. They are common form among 'the best people' in Nazi circles, and the stock-in-trade of all their political troubadours.[31] The English reader may think it strange that a Field-Marshal of the Reich and the Minister-President of Prussia should make a ministerial utterance to a listening world in a European crisis the occasion for a filthy jest and a not less filthy threat. But there was nothing strange about it. Goering was merely running 'true to form.' He was a Prussian officer, educated at Gross Lichterfelde, the Sandhurst of the German Army, and the obscene behavior of the fine flower of that academy, the German staff officers, has always stunk, in the most literal sense of the word, in the nostrils of every British officer who ever found himself billeted during the last war in a château evacuated by the German staff. When I joined the A.G.'s

[31] For a case in point, see the Nazi Youth song quoted in *The Dear Monster*, by G. R. Halkett, an exiled Prussian officer of Scottish descent, p. 380. The keyword to this disgusting threat is '*scheissen*,' for the nasty meaning of which I must refer the reader to Muret-Sanders' German dictionary.

staff at G.H.Q. at the end of 1914, one British officer after another told me the same tale. An experience related to me by the C.I.G.S. himself, General Sir Archibald Murray, is typical of all the rest. After the battle of the Marne he and his staff took possession of a beautiful country house hurriedly evacuated by German staff officers. They found it almost uninhabitable. The German officers had systematically defiled every bed in the house. My friend Brigadier-General Miller, on entering another château, found the German officers who had been occupying it had defiled a Sèvres service of dinner-plates in the same way. They did the same thing in the Royal Palace at Brussels and in the palace of the Prince de Croy.[32] They behaved in exactly the same way in the Franco-Prussian War of 1870-71, as readers of Mrs. Belloc-Lowndes' *chef d'œuvre* [33] may discover for themselves.

'Faugh!' the reader may well exclaim, 'fetch me an ounce of civet.' But these nasty things have, unfortunately, a deep, a pathological significance for any one who really seeks to understand the German character. The tragedy will be ours if we do not. For where there is bestiality, as the great Florentine poet discovered, in the dark places of the human soul, you will almost invariably find malice. The German officer was and is always both bestial and malicious, and the flowering of the Nazi is the efflorescence of his decay. It is a complete delusion to suppose that the German Officers' Corps is, or ever was, a corps of 'perfect, gentle knights' who view with distaste the atrocities practiced by the Gestapo. Professional jealousy, not moral distaste is, as we shall see, the true explanation of any antipathy, if such, indeed, there be. The obscenities practiced by the German officers in the last war were almost invariably as malicious as they were bestial. Pepys Cockerell, our A.P.M. at Hazebrouck in 1914, when looking for a billet one day at Doue, entered a house and asked the occupant, an old lady, if she could give him a billet. 'I will do what I can,' she said with tears running down her face as she threw

[32] The testimony of British officers with personal experience of this sort of thing, is overwhelming. See an article in the *Journal of the Royal United Service Institution* for February 1923, at p. 143, where the writer speaks of 'the bestialities perpetrated by the staff of von Kluck in the French châteaux that they occupied.'

[33] *I too have lived in Arcadia,* at pp. 179, etc.

open the door of her little *salon*, 'but German officers have been here. Look!' In the middle of the room was a pile of sheets of fine linen, foul and disordered. The German officers had taken them out of the press, where they were kept in lavender, and had urinated over them, after smashing her old china and piercing the prints on the walls with their swords. Years later, I received a letter from my friend General Gouraud who had been reading an article of mine in the *English Review* about these things. He wrote as follows:

Of the cruelty or more exactly the malicious joy, 'Schadenfreude' as they call it, which the Germans feel in hurting other people, I can give you an instance out of my own experience. I was in Morocco when the war broke out and I was only able to return to France after the battle of the Marne, when I received the command of the xth Division in the Forest of Hess to the West of Verdun. I slept one evening in a little village, called Aubreville, in the cottage of a peasant. In the morning the woman of the house kindly brought me a cup of coffee. Having noticed some words in German scrawled on the door, I said to her,

'So you have had some Germans here before the battle of the Marne, madam?'

'Yes,' she said to me, 'but they were very unkind.'

'What have they done? Have they molested you?'

'Oh, no,' she replied, 'I am too old. But in the room where you have been sleeping, there was a German officer who left in the morning after you had won the great battle. He came out of the room holding a little framed photograph. It was a picture of my poor husband in uniform. The German said to me, "Is that your husband?" I said, "Yes, sir." And then with an evil laugh (*un mauvais rire*) he shouted, "Ah, well! you'll never see him again." And he threw the little photograph on the ground and crushed it with the heel of his boot.'

'I do not believe,' added Gouraud, 'that any Frenchman or any Englishman would ever treat a defenseless woman like that'—*Je ne crois pas qu'aucun Français, qu'un Anglais se conduirait pareillement vis à vis d'une femme sans défense.* And of that there can, indeed, be no doubt.

Of such bestial cruelty at the hands of German officers and men— there was not much to choose between them [34]—there were innumer-

---

[34] As to German officers, quite apart from what may be called official cruelty in the execution of the German doctrine of 'breaking the spirit' of the civil population of enemy countries by deliberate massacre, as to which see the last section of this chapter, there is only too much evidence of the sadistic delight of

able examples in the last war. There are on record thousands of depositions, never published, most of which passed through my hands as Vice-Chairman of the Government Committee appointed in 1918 to inquire into the Breaches of the Laws of War. They are the depositions of British soldiers taken prisoner by the German troops and subsequently repatriated. They tell an almost uniform tale of illtreatment, a tale the truth of which is emphasized by an occasional remark, plaintive in its sincerity, such as 'one of the guards was decent to us,' 'one of the doctors was not too bad.' Our men were starved, assaulted with the butt-end of a rifle, forced to work under fire at the Front, but that was not the worst of it. 'The Sub-Committee feel,' it was reported to us by those who took down the depositions, 'that the only explanation of this unjustifiable treatment is the remark made in broken English by a German officer to Corporal Joseph Page on 22 March 1918, at Marchiennes: "We will break your brave English hearts tomorrow!"' The process of 'breaking' usually consisted in depriving the prisoners of sanitary conveniences of any kind, and humiliating them by forcing them to relieve themselves in public in the sight of German soldiers and, later on, in the prison camps in the interior in the sight of German civilians, men and women, who assembled in crowds to enjoy the spectacle. Almost invariably on the long journey, sometimes lasting many days, on the *via dolorosa* from the Front to the Internment Camp, our men were locked up in cattletrucks, sometimes ankle-deep in manure, to be let out eventually in a state of indescribable filth and then marched through jeering crowds to the camp. Any one who has read the reports in our newspapers of Polish men, women, and children herded into cattle-trucks and locked up therein with the same circumstance of bodily discomfort and physical humiliation, will see now the source of Nazi inspiration. The Nazi leaders, nearly all of whom served in the ranks in the First World War, learned their methods in the school of the German Army, the greatest school of brutality in the world. The British Government White Paper containing the reports of the treatment of

individual German officers, both in this war and the last, in acts of cruelty. See, for example, the report in *The Times* of 9 June 1940, entitled 'German Tactics at Sea,' a report of the sinking of a British merchantman in which the U-boat commander directed his crew to push off into the water, with boat-hooks, the British sailors as they tried to clamber on to the submarine while he took photographs of them in their death agonies.

German Jews in the Nazi concentration camps reads almost like an unconscious 'reconstruction' of what took place in the Prisoners of War Camps in Germany during 1914-18. Every book by a German refugee [35] who has survived the horrors of a concentration camp tells the same tale of studied attempts to humiliate the interned by making them an object of obscene amusement to their tormentors. I sometimes think that the most appropriate emblem of the Nazi creed should be not a swastia but a latrine.

It may be that every nation gets the army it deserves. If that be so, the German nation is past praying for. If not, the only way to save it is to destroy the German Army altogether. For the Army, as idolized as it was privileged, invested every vice it patronized with a kind of meretricious prestige. The whole nation took its cue from the Army. And vicious that Army certainly was. Its sense of honor and its morals were equally perverse. German testimony itself—much of it unconscious testimony—on that point is, as we shall see, pretty conclusive, quite independently of the appalling record of the Army's behavior in France and Belgium. Of the German officer's code of 'honor' I shall have much to say in due course. It is enough to say at this stage that it 'rooted in dishonor stood.' We British officers serving on the Commission almost invariably found that when a German officer gave us his 'word of honor,' his *Ehrenwort*, that a certain thing was true, it was untrue. Nor was he in the least dismayed when he was caught out. An experience of ours with General von Stempel, of which I will tell in its proper place, was most illuminating in that respect. An Englishman who is surprised in a lie has at least the grace to be ashamed, a German never. The English are indeed the most truthful people in the world, even as the Germans are the most mendacious. In England it is a rule of etiquette, to say nothing of ethics, that men do not lie to one another in social intercourse. In Germany there is no such rule—certainly not in the case of officers. I have sat at meat with a German general, von Kluck, whom we have

[35] The testimony of such books on this point is too uniform, and thus too corroborative, to be lightly dismissed. It is confirmed in a remarkable book by Miss Dodd, the daughter of the late American Ambassador in Berlin in the following words, 'Most of the men and women (in the concentration camps) were given the jobs of cleaning out the *Toilets* (i.e. the latrines) with their bare hands and told, if they wanted their hands clean before eating or retiring, they could lick them.'—*My Years in Germany*, at p. 259.

already encountered in this book,[36] and have been told by him a story which, at the very time he told it, I knew to be a falsehood. I had a similar experience with Ludendorff. The only 'honor,' either in word or in deed, which a German officer feels constrained to observe is towards his fellow-officers. Towards a German civilian, to say nothing of foreigners whether civilians or not, he feels no such obligation. A German officer has put it on record that the caste to which he once belonged, and which he has now repudiated for all time, never hesitate to cheat a civilian, whether at cards or anything else, seeking to justify themselves, so far as they trouble about justification at all, with the excuse that the civilian will cheat them first if he gets the chance.[37] The excuse may be true of German civilians—no doubt the devil knoweth his own. Be that as it may, the German cadet was from the very beginning taught, as one of them has told us, that all civilians were 'swine' and were to be treated accordingly.[38]

One cannot say of the vicious behavior of German officers, what Burke said of the laxity of morals in the French nobility of the *ancien régime*, that their polished manners were such that, in them, 'vice lost half its evil by losing all its grossness.' The lechery of German officers was too ostentatious and too flagrant for that. In a remarkably courageous book, a German writer tells us that during the war 'the majority of German officers' set an example of unbridled licentiousness. '*Officers' brothels* swarmed behind the lines (*Die Bordelle für Offiziere überschwemmten die Etappen*) like fashionable hotels.'[39] This was flagrant enough but, however shameless, it was not abnormal. There was something far more sinister in the morals of the German Army. They were the morals of Sodom. One day, in 1922, I picked up a newly published book in Berlin which lit up the dark and sinister character of the German Army with almost blinding

[36] See above, Chapter v, '*Ausser Dienst.*'
[37] See the extremely illuminating analysis of the German military caste by G. R. Halkett, a former German officer, in *The Dear Monster*, at p. 68. See also above, Chapter vi, 'The German Officers' Corps.'
[38] *Das alte Heer* (1920), at p. 3, where the writer observes that the cadets had it 'hammered into' them (*eingehammert*) that there were only two classes of human beings, 'soldiers and swine' (*Es gibt nur Soldaten und Schweinehunde*).
..[39] *Die Traögdie Deutschlands* 'by a German' (*von einem Deutschen*). The author of this devastating study of the German Army published his book anonymously. He would certainly have been 'beaten up' if he had revealed his identity. As to this remarkable book, see further below, Section ix.

illumination. It was by a Commissioner of the C.I.D., a 'Kriminal-kommissar' of the Berlin Police, Hans von Treschkow. Much of it was devoted to his experiences of sexual perversion and of the symptomatic vices which, according to him, almost invariably accompany it, namely 'Blackmail' (*Erpressung*), 'Hypocrisy' (*Heuchelei*) and 'Lying' (*Lüge*). These three are vices which every Englishman knows to be as indelibly the stigmata of Nazi politicians and diplomatists as the swastika itself, and, as we shall see, there is good reason to believe that here too the pathological explanation is the same. Von Treschkow records with the utmost nonchalance his conviction that the paragraph of the German Penal Code, the *Strafgesetzbuch*, making the practice of sexual perversion punishable, is both 'purposeless and obsolete.' This 'ever-growing vice,' he urges, claiming at least 'one hundred thousand' addicts in Berlin alone known to the police, to say nothing of the unknown, must be recognized as too popular to be put down. After all, he urges, it is undeniably fashionable in the Army, as if that settled the question. The Postdam garrison, he points out, was 'absolutely infected' (*verseucht*) with it, the German Officers' Corps, 'particularly the Guards,' was rife with it and the men of the Guards regiments, soliciting in the Tiergarten when off duty, were, being soldiers, the most popular of 'prostitutes.'[40] At Gross Lichterfelde, the Sandhurst of the German Army, as also in the Prussian preparatory cadet schools, sexual perversion was openly pursued and officially tolerated.[41] All this was in the Prussian military tradition. As an accomplished American historian has pointed out, Frederick the Great encouraged the practice both by precept and example, and encouraged it all the more because he forbade his Guardsmen to marry.[42]

[40] Von Treschkow's *Von Fürsten und anderen Sterblichen* (Berlin, 1922), pp. 110, 118, 123, 185.

[41] There is first-hand testimony as to this, quite independently of Herr von Treschkow's disclosures, e.g. G. R. Halkett who in his reminiscences of Gross Lichterfelde, where he was a cadet, writes: 'The majority of the cadets indulged in homo-sexualism and *there were no illusions among the commanding officers as to what was going on.*' (Halkett, *The Dear Monster*, at p. 59.) In a book by another German officer, the writer says of the Preparatory Cadet Schools: 'Every kind of sexual perversion flourished (*blühten*) and was openly pursued' —*Das alte Heer, von einem Stabsoffizier*, at p. 3. No one, he adds, felt any shame about it.

[42] *Frederick the Great*, by Victor Thaddeus, pp. 300, etc.

Filthy in mind and body, brutal, perverted, cruel, treacherous, the true character of Frederick the Great and his corrupting influence on the German people has been wholly obscured from Englishmen by the panegyrics of Carlyle who prostrates himself, and prostitutes his intellect, before the image of the debased soldier with that idolatry so peculiarly characteristic of men of letters bewitched by men of action. It is a kind of vicarious violence, a form of frustration felt by the men of words in the presence of the men of deeds. Carlyle is at times as violent as another non-combatant, Dr. Josef Goebbels, and it is no matter for surprise to find that the ruthless Treitschke claims him as 'the only Englishman who absolutely understood the Germans,' by which he means the only Englishman who has flattered them without restraint. Carlyle sank to his lowest level of sycophancy when he had to deal with a filthy poem of his hero, on the morrow of Rossbach, in which the Prussian King 'with a wild outburst of spiritual enthusiasm' becomes lyrical on the subject of sodomy. 'Smutty enough,' Carlyle is constrained to admit, but with the abject plea '*though in theory only.*' [43]

To the Englishman who wishes to understand the German people, and the German Army in which the national, or, to be more precise, the Prussian character is reflected as in a mirror, the character of Frederick the Great is much more than a matter of mere historical interest. For he is a ghost who walks. He is one of those war-gods of his race who, in Heine's vivid metaphor, periodically rise from their graves and, rubbing the dust of centuries from their eyes, let loose upon mankind 'the senseless fury of the brutal German joy of battle.' Even in the days of the Weimar Republic his uneasy spirit was abroad. One day I went to see a famous Ufa film, *Fredericus Rex*, which was the talk of Berlin and was enjoying a record run. Its realism was very much to the taste of the packed audience among whom I sat and who seemed to take a peculiar pleasure in contemplating the vindictive execution of Lieutenant Katte high on the gallows in the fortress of Custrin. But it was the all too faithful impersonations of Frederick, with his vulpine face, and of his cohort of generals, 'those strange, sadistic, military types,' [44] as Mr. Sitwell has called them, 'with their essentially beastly countenances,' which moved that au-

[43] *A History of Frederick II of Prussia*, vol. x, Chapter VIII.
[44] *German Baroque Art*, by Sacheverell Sitwell, at p. 24.

dience to tears as he and they were shown upon the screen unctuously chanting 'Nun danken alle Gott' on the stricken field of Rossbach. The film was not more belligerent than the audience, which greeted one battle-scene after another with frantic applause. At the time, one of my old tutors at Oxford, a distinguished historian, no less a historian than Herbert Fisher, was on a short visit to Berlin and, after seeing the film, he came to tea with me one afternoon at the Adlon. 'A most significant spectacle and disturbing,' was his comment. And so it was. But it required a historian to divine its significance in those delusive days.

The true character of Frederick the Great is to be found in the pages not of Carlyle, who writes like a lackey, but of another English man of letters with none of his servility. And, on a considered and careful judgment, he finds him totally devoid of 'purity, sensibility, generosity, honor and respect for human nature.' [45] A 'most execrable cynic,' as Morley rightly describes him, 'indecent,' 'infamous,' 'always spiteful and sneering and cruel,' a man 'who never found so much pleasure in a friendly act as when he could make it a means of hurting the recipient,' [46] he is the supreme example in German history of that ugly national characteristic known as *Schadenfreude*, a characteristic so foreign to the English people that, unlike the German language, our own has not even a word for it. *Schadenfreude* can only be translated into English by a circumlocution. It means a malicious delight in the sufferings of another. The ingenuity of this hero of the German people in inventing occasions of pain to others, in order to enjoy the spectacle of their suffering, was inexhaustible, as any reader of his biographers can discover for himself. What, however, is more to the point is that the doctrine of 'terrorism' (*Terrorismus*) inculcated by the German General Staff in its notorious *War Book* and the inhuman methods of the Gestapo reproduce down to the last detail the precepts and the practice of the Prussian King.[47] His published instructions for the use of his generals read

---

[45] Morley's *Voltaire*, p. 166.

[46] *Ibid.*, at pp. 168, 203, 207.

[47] See, for example, his precepts as to how to compel a man to turn informer. He advised that one should 'choose a man who has a wife and children' and threaten him that if he refused to inform, 'his wife and children shall be hanged,' adding with characteristic complacency, that he himself had had recourse to this practice and that 'it succeeded.'—Quoted in Morley's *Miscellanies*, vol. iv, p. 329.

like a compendium of the conduct of the Second World War by the German rulers in all its ruthlessness, even as his foreign policy anticipates their diplomacy in all its duplicity. The description by a contemporary of his treatment of Poland after he had torn the unhappy country asunder might be written today, word for word, of Hitler's spoliation and oppression. He 'reduced the inhabitants to a state of despair' by requisitioning all their cattle and goods, affecting to pay for them with a spurious currency, and by abducting seven thousand of their young daughters.[48] He followed all this up with a jest at the expense of the victims so horrible that it touched the lowest depths of blasphemy.[49] The passage of his armies over the countries he conquered and devastated was such as to move another contemporary to write that there had been nothing like it since the Huns and Goths of the Dark Ages.[50] Such was the god of the German Army's idolatry. He at last came into his own. He was saluted by Baldur von Shirach, in the name of the German Youth Movement, as 'A revelation to our people of religious doing, an example of a faith such as is honored and admired by German Youth.'

v

Nor was it only the bestiality of post-war Germany which could be traced to the Army. There was the love of cruelty, which one encountered everywhere. In the Nazi concentration camps a favorite form of torture was running the gauntlet. It was a punishment devised by the sadistic imagination of Frederick the Great, not merely for deserters but even for minor offenses. In the Army of Kaiser Wilhelm that form of punishment was, indeed, no longer practiced but the spirit which inspired it was still there. When at last, after repeated obstruction by the Reichswehrministerium, I succeeded in securing the demobilization, in part, of the N.C.O.s of the old Army, who

[48] Sorel, La Question d'Orient au xviiie siècle, p. 206.

[49] Writing to Prince Henry a triumphant letter, after the partition of Poland between the three Powers whose established religions were Catholic, Greek, and Protestant, he compared 'the body' of the martyred country to the body of Christ with the jest, 'We three have now joined in a rare performance of holy communion: we have partaken of one and the same eucharistic body (le même corps eucharistique), namely Poland.'—See Sorel, La Question d'Orient, p. 207.

[50] Sorel, L'Europe et la Révolution française, vol. i, p. 85.

mustered something like a hundred thousand of its 'peace strength,'
I let loose upon the community the most brutal 'toughs' who had
ever disgraced a uniform.[51] Many of them joined a notorious 'Murder
Club' known as the Organization 'Consul' in Munich, and innumerable other associations of a similar character, and there formed the
nucleus of the future Storm-troopers. Their demobilization was a
case of 'Othello's occupation's gone,' but they found an outlet for
their lethal instincts in that form of political assassination which,
according to a careful estimate by a German writer,[52] claimed at
least three hundred and seventy-six victims in the first three years of
the Weimar Republic. Rarely were these outrages followed by a trial
and conviction, the reason being, according to the same authority,[53]
that the juries at the Assizes (the *Schwurgerichte*) were 'packed' by
the bureaucracy, responsible for empanelling them, who were reactionaries almost to a man. Behind the republican façade, the old order of the bureaucracy were strongly entrenched and so far as the
Republic was not, as indeed it was, in the custody of the Reichswehr
and the big industrialists, it was enmeshed in their toils. Without their
co-operation the police, in spite of 'Police Presidents' of republican
complexion, could do little or nothing. The police could prosecute
the assassins, but they were powerless to secure a conviction. It is,
indeed, significant that only five per cent of these political murders
were committed by 'Communists.' They were almost invariably the
work of the reactionary parties, in other words of the elements most
closely associated with the Army and the old order for which the
Army stood. The fact in no way deterred those parties and, as we
shall see, the Reichswehrministerium itself from blandly protesting,
alike by official representations to us and by world-wide propaganda,

[51] About 60,000 of the regular N.C.O.s of the old Army were actually discharged or rather passed into the 'Security Police,' the remainder, in defiance of
all our efforts to enforce their demobilization, being kept with the colors in
pursuance of General von Seeckt's design to preserve in cadre the nucleus of the
old Army, a design in which, as is disclosed later in this book, he was only too
successful. In addition to the 100,000 N.C.O.s on the peace-strength of the old
Army, there were, of course, a vast and unascertainable number of temporary
N.C.O.s, promoted from the ranks during the war, and such men, unlike the
regular N.C.O.s, who had a legal claim under the German military laws to employment in the civil service, were now without a job and game for anything.
[52] Gumbel, *Vier Jahre Polilitischer Mord* (Berlin, 1922), pp. 6 and 80.
[53] Gumbel, *Verschwörer* (Vienna, 1924), p. 63.

against the disarmament of Germany on the ground that the result would be to expose Germany to a 'Red Terror' which, in fact, did not exist.

For every man who was actually done to death by these illicit associations, or *Vereine* as they were generically known, a dozen men were 'beaten up' during the years we were stationed in Germany. It is difficult for an Englishman at home to understand the German habit of knocking a defenseless man about with clubs and whips, even as it is difficult to understand Hitler's lust for blood, but he would have no difficulty in understanding it, or rather the state of mind which sees no shame in it, if he knew a little more of the Prussian military tradition. In the British Army it is fatal to the career of a N.C.O., still more to that of an officer, to knock the men about. I have known of a particular case—I had to deal with it—in which a choleric brigadier-General was court-martialed for merely flicking a man on parade with his cane. But in the German Army the kicking and beating of the men was not merely tolerated, it was encouraged. It was encouraged on principle. The principle was that if you want, as the German General Staff has always wanted, your men to be brutal in war you must brutalize them in time of peace. 'Service' journals in Germany during the war made no secret either of the principle or of its objective,[54] although an earlier generation of German soldiers were a little more reticent.[55] German officers whom I interrogated on the subject were, as might be expected, usually evasive. But one of them, Major Wolff of the 25th Dragoons, when accompanying me on a long drive as liaison officer on one of my inspections of regimental units in Württemberg, completely gave the show away. Except in Saxony the N.C.O.s were, he admitted, 'often very brutal.' Of course, the officers, he hastily added, did not approve of that sort of thing. It required a good deal of credulity, I reflected, to believe that German N.C.O.s would venture to indulge in practices of which their officers did not approve, but I preserved a tactful silence. The same evening, when Wolff and I dined together

[54] Thus, for example, the *Deutsche Wehr* for 9 August 1936, in an article on 'The Conduct of the Next War' in which the writer emphasizes 'the necessity' of training the German Army in 'the highest degree of brutality.'

[55] See, for example, Field-Marshal Hohenlohe's Reminiscences, *Aus meinem Leben*, vol. ii, p. 237, and vol. iii, p. 191, where he admits the practice but makes light of it.

at Ulm and he was off his guard, having drunk a good deal, he completely forgot all he had said earlier in the day about the disapproval
of the officers as he became expansive in his cups on the 'paternal'
behavior, as he engagingly called it, of a German C.O. in the orderly-
room when dealing with delinquents. 'He always gave a man his
choice,' explained Wolff. 'He would say to the man, "Will you take
a box on the ear (*eine Ohrfeige*) from me or three days C.B.?"' 'A
box on the ear from the heavy fist of a Prussian officer is a knock-out
blow, calculated to break the ear-drum of the object of it. Remembering Major Wolff's touching revelation of the magnanimity of
German commanding officers, I once asked an ex-private, Herr Kape,
whom we had met before,[56] what happened on such occasions to the
soldier who told his C.O. that he would prefer the three days' confinement to barracks to the paternal box on the ear. 'That's no good
(*Das geht nicht*),' was the prompt reply, 'the silly fellow got both.'

Is all this brutality in the Army the cause or the effect of the German love of cruelty? It is a hard saying and who shall answer it? For
myself, I think the answer is contained in the words of a distinguished
Englishman, Sir Malcolm Robertson. Writing to me on this subject
after reading this particular page in manuscript, he observed as long
ago as 1938:

As regards the sheer brutality of the German military, I could give you
example after example extending over the twenty years before the last
war. In 1903-4, when I was at our Embassy in Berlin, there was a fearful
scandal in the Third Regiment of Foot Guards resulting from the suicide
of several of the men who had been so badly ill-treated by their N.C.O.s
and officers that they preferred to put an end to their own lives! An inquiry was held and disciplinary action taken against various officers and
N.C.O.s. On the whole, however, I know that it is true to state that the
German does not object to ill-treatment as such. He cannot understand
any kind of gentle treatment. 'Blut, Eisen, Gewalt,'[57] are what he wor-
ships and what he understands. People in this country seem to have forgotten German brutality during the last war or prefer to believe that it
was greatly exaggerated by propaganda. Little do they realize that 'frightfulness' is part and parcel of German military methods and in the next
war we may expect further ghastly examples of it.

Sir Malcolm Robertson's expectations have been more than fulfilled.

---

[56] See above, Chapter III.
[57] 'Blood, Iron, Violence,' a favorite 'slogan' among Germans.

VI

The internecine fury with which the Germans turned on one another during these years of defeat was not, as some of their apologists would have us believe, the transient mood of a people driven desperate by the harsh terms of a 'dictated' Peace. No terms of Peace, whether dictated or not, would have placated German temper, short of an admission by the victors that they were not victorious. What enraged the German people was not so much the Peace itself as the defeat which had made it possible. Hence the fury with which the Nationalists sought a scapegoat for their outraged pride in the Social Democrats to whose 'defection' at home they preferred to attribute the demoralization of the troops at the Front. They studiously ignored the fact that the defection, if defection it was, followed on the demoralization which, indeed, was the cause of it. It was, however, inevitable that defeat should produce in the German mind a feeling of savage exasperation which, failing a return to Christianity or at least a repudiation of the German gospel of force, must find an outlet either in vice or in violence. One man may be cruel without being vicious and another vicious without being cruel, but both are victims of a malady of the soul and its name is frustration. A common prison, as in the seventh circle of the *Inferno*, confines them both in a dark abyss of anger and despair. Having grown great by three wars of aggression within living memory, Germany had learned to idolize war as, in Clausewitz's famous phrase, an 'instrument of policy' and indeed something more—an article of belief. Three successful campaigns had convinced her that history was on her side—'Die Weltgeschichte ist das Weltgericht' [58] and now 'history' had decided against her. The God of Battles, for the first time for a century, had turned a deaf ear and the priesthood of Baal was confounded and 'cried aloud and cut themselves with knives.' Hitler's strange words, insane though they seem, about a quarrel with 'destiny' are profoundly significant of this mood. The rage with which Germans now turned on one another and shed each other's blood with a kind of

---

[58] 'The world's history is the world's judgment,' a favorite catchword of German historians when in search of a justification for the success of German wars of aggression.

delirious satisfaction was like a discharge of nervous energy on the part of men whom the mere fact of defeat had made not less insane than incredulous. The day after the assassination of Rathenau, I read in the *Berliner Tageblatt* that his 'Nationalist' enemies were repeatedly ringing up his bereaved mother to tell her that her son was a Jewish 'traitor' who had only got what he deserved. Hitler was equally vindictive. The sight of blood streaming down the faces of interrupters at one of his meetings in Munich in 1922, after his Stormtroopers had set about them, gave him, he tells us, a 'thrill of joy.' [59] Hitler was in this respect a kind of 'common denominator' of the popular mind. The secret of his success as an orator was, as a German writer acutely observed, not that he had any ideas of his own but that he had none at all. He kept on repeating what every one else was saying at every beer-table,[60] voicing what every one else was thinking, or rather feeling, for his appeal was always to the emotions, never to the reason. That feeling was Hate. Hitler's expression of it in those days was discreetly directed against the German Socialists and the Jews who had 'corrupted' the Socialists. The French Army of Occupation was too near to make it either convenient or safe to switch the corrosive rays on to the foreigner. All that was to come later.

'He that hateth his brother is in darkness.' Such is the hatred which has always lurked in the subconscious self of the German people like some beast of prey in the 'dark forest' of the lusts of the flesh. It is a permanent, psychological fact, to the sinister presence of which innumerable German thinkers and statesmen, as various in their outlook as Treitschke and Goethe, Bismarck and Bülow, Heine and Foerster, have borne witness, deploring it or exploiting it according to their mood and vocation. In an illuminating sentence the cynical Bülow says of that faked dispatch of Bismarck's, known and notorious in history as the Ems telegram, which precipitated the Franco-Prussian War at the moment most opportune for the Prussian General Staff: 'By means of this masterly dispatch Bismarck released the *furor Teutonicus* at home and created a unified German fighting front.' [61] He

---

[59] *Mein Kampf* (135th German edition, Munich, 1935), p. 567.
[60] *Hitler ist ein ausgemachter Demagoge: ein Mensch, unfähig einen eigenen Gedanken zu haben, aber gerade darin liegt seine Stärke. Denn er sagt was an jedem Stammtisch jeden Tag wiedergekäut werden kann.—Verschwörer,* by E. J. Gumbel (1923), p. 178.
[61] Bülow's *Memoirs*, vol. iv, p. 163.

writes of the 'release' as though he had in mind the letting loose of a beast of prey, and no metaphor could be more apt. The turbulent history of the German peoples right down to the year 1870 is the bloodiest in Europe, a volcanic history of dark, subterranean fires now quiescent, now flagrant, but never quenched. The most popular of all German historians, Treitschke, treats this 'Teutonic fury' as something self-evident, insisting, not without pride, that 'the Germans are the most passionate people in Europe.' Wherefore, he explains, 'they cannot live happily without hating their neighbors.' Hence, he tells us, 'the boundless hatred' of the Saxons and Rhinelanders for the Prussians, of the Prussians for the Bavarians, of the Germans of the North for the Germans of the South.[62] To the Prussians, in particular, 'the art of live and let live was utterly unknown.' [63] Bismarck made no secret of it. It was the instinctive 'inclination' (*Neigung*) of the Germans to cut each other's throats 'with even more zeal' (*Eifer*) than the throats of their neighbors which determined him, he coolly explains, to abstain from the annexation of Bohemia after the defeat of Austria in 1866.[64] The presence of the wedge of a non-German people in Bohemia would, he calculated, keep the Germans and the Austro-Germans from flying at each other's throats, and serve as a counterirritant to the mutual hatred of the two great German stocks. In a common animosity against the Czechs they might find a kind of lightning-conductor for their hatred of one another.

During the first three years of our time in Germany the German people, like a spirit in prison, vented this wrathful temper upon themselves. It was only in 1923, with the French occupation of the Ruhr, that it found an outlet against the foreigner. In that occupation, which the behavior of the German Government had done everything to provoke, German 'patriots' saw their chance. Ludendorff and von Kahr, and, at a later date, Otto von Bismarck spoke to me of its advent in curiously identical words: 'Thank God the French have occupied the Ruhr!' The occupation, explained Ludendorff with his usual naïve bluntness, had united the Germans as nothing else could.

---

[62] Treitschke's *Deutsche Geschichte im 19ten. Jahrhundert* (Leipzig, 1895). The passages quoted will be found in the English translation, *History of Germany in the 19th Century*, vol. ii, p. 545; vol. iv, pp. 301, 308, 556.
[63] *Ibid.*, vol. ii, p. 557.
[64] *Gedanken und Erinnerungen* (Volks-Ausgabe, 1905), vol. ii, p. 273.

It had revived all the secular hatred of the French, with the decline of which the infuriated Nationalists had so often reproached the 'internationalist' Jews and Socialists at home, and there can be no question that, as is related elsewhere,[65] the Nationalists did everything in their power to provoke the French troops of occupation beyond endurance. The one thing the French G.O.C., General Degoutte desired was, as he put it to me, to make his occupation as 'invisible' and as unobtrusive as possible. He was not 'out for trouble.' But the Nationalist 'toughs' who swarmed into the Ruhr with sticks of dynamite were out for nothing else. Some of them were promptly, and very properly, shot, and from that moment, as if at a given signal, the 'Teutonic fury' was let loose.

The outburst was so perfectly orchestrated, its manifestations so remarkably synchronized, that there can be little doubt that a signal was given. In the State elementary schools the teachers suddenly began teaching their pupils to lisp in unison, 'France is our enemy,' *Frankreich ist unser Feind.* In public places notices appeared overnight, in identical terms, offering a reward of 2,000 marks to the first German who should spit in the face of a Frenchman. In restaurants the incitement was slightly varied by an invitation to spit in a Frenchman's plate. It all left the French officers on our Commission, whom it was designed to intimidate, quite unmoved. 'Spitting is a German's way of expressing himself,' remarked the imperturbable General Nollet to me, *c'est un mode d'exteriorisation.* This is true enough. Bülow, in his *Memoirs,* informs us that honorable members of the Bavarian Parliament, the Landtag, spat at one another when words failed them to express their political differences. To a race denied, according to Bülow, the gift of debate, expectoration is perhaps the easiest form of repartee. Others now relieved their political feelings against the French in very much the same manner as the Nationalist opponents of the Socialist Minister-President of Saxony. My friend the Comte St. Quentin, Counsellor of the French Embassy in Berlin, told me that the ambassador was the recipient, among other nasty things, of a large parcel by registered post which, when opened in the Chancellery, was found to contain the carcass of a dog in an advanced stage of decomposition. The label bore the super-

[65] See above, Chapter IX, at p. 197, and below.

scription, 'The first and last payment of Reparations!' 'What did you do with it? Bury it?' I asked. 'Mais non,' replied the imperturbable St. Quentin, 'we sent it to the German Foreign Office with a note drawing their attention to an infraction of the *police vétérinaire* which the sender, we suggested, had apparently overlooked.'

In 1914 German nurses in Red Cross uniform 'tempted British prisoners of war, who were in the last extremity of hunger and thirst, by holding coffee and soup out to them and then at the last moment spitting in the glass or cup.' [66] With the occupation of the Ruhr, German women once again competed with their menfolk in malevolence. A young married girl, waiting on one of my officers, Major Bennett, in a restaurant, said to him, 'If I had children, I would inoculate (*einimpfen*) them with my mother's milk (*mit meiner Mutter-Milch*) with hatred of the French.' Greater hate hath no woman than this. Feminine fury was carefully stimulated by disgusting cartoons in *Simplicissimus* representing 'black' French soldiers in the act of ravishing German girls, cartoons which were as false as they were outrageous, but which the German Government did nothing to discountenance or suppress. As the popular fury waxed, the zeal of the German authorities in protecting the officers of our Commission waned. It was quite useless for a French officer, traveling alone and unarmed, to appeal to German policemen when hustled and assaulted, as began to happen with increasing frequency, by Nationalist 'toughs.' The policemen merely looked the other way. This was our reward for agreeing to relax the terms of the Treaty by conceding to the German police a strength in effectives far beyond that to which those terms entitled them. The 'Security' Police, who were armed with revolvers and very quick to use them, could easily and effectively have dealt with such incidents if they had been, as they were not, so minded. The reason why soon became apparent. One day a young French officer serving on our Commission, Captain Morange, who was traveling from Cologne to Berlin, was set upon by a group of young 'Reserve' officers who spat in his face and,

---

[66] *The Times* of 23 February 1918, a report of the evidence of British prisoners of war interned in Switzerland. My friend, Colonel Maxwell Earle of the Grenadier Guards, who was wounded and taken prisoner at the First Battle of Ypres, has told me of similar treatment of our men. In many cases German nurses threw a basin of scalding hot soup in the face of British soldiers with the words, 'That's good enough for an Englishman.'

after a struggle in which they were six to one, ejected him from the train. This was the culmination of a series of similar attacks on Control officers at Passau, Ingolstadt, and elsewhere, and the Control Commission addressed a Note to the German Government demanding the punishment of the police authorities who had failed to protect French and, more rarely, British officers from these assaults. The result of these representations was not the punishment of the authorities but an intimation that, in view of 'the public feeling' about the occupation of the Ruhr, the German Government could not accept any responsibility for the protection of Control officers, particularly if we continued to carry on our work of disarmament by inspections of munition factories and of barracks. Now it was a curious and notable fact that demonstrations against Control officers had very rarely taken place in any factory, though in barracks they were frequent enough. The workmen were by no means friendly to our operations, but the only demonstration which ever took place during our inspections of factories, except in the case of the Rockstroh affair, was against a German liaison officer, at the sight of whose gray uniform the men downed tools and shouted 'Out with him! Out with him!'—*Heraus! Heraus!* [67] But the German Government's representations found, unfortunately, a credulous and sympathetic British ear in Lord D'Abernon. We, of the British Delegation, were suddenly ordered to suspend our Control operations. They were never resumed.[68] Such an order was fatal, for without British co-operation the French Delegation could do nothing. For the remaining four years of our time in Germany the Commission could do little more than mark time. The whole episode was typical of the German Government's habit of releasing the *furor Teutonicus* to serve its own purposes.

This careful exploitation of the worst passions of the German people by their governors occurs and recurs throughout German history. In this respect there is nothing to choose, and never was, between the military authorities and the civil. They have always been equally cynical, and equally successful, in directing the congenital hate of the populace, turning it on and off, directing it this

[67] See above, Chapter III, page 64.

[68] A 'trial' inspection was made late in 1924 after a lapse of nearly two years, but it was so frustrated as to be largely illusory.

way and that, like a 'flame-thrower.' One might even say equally impartial. Early in the last war it was directed against the British and the Belgians, later against the French, in 1938 against the Czechs, in 1939 against the Poles, in 1941 against the Russians, and then against any one who would not bow his head to the German yoke. The manifestations of it against the French which we encountered in Germany in 1922-3 were quite curiously similar in form and character to its exhibitions in 1914-15 against the British. A gifted Polish writer, resident in Germany during those earlier years, has put on record his observations of it in Munich in 1914 in the following terms:

I had never believed that such hatred was possible as that against the British. Few ideas in English minds are based on falser premises than that the English people were popular in Germany in pre-war days. Of course, the English tourists and students were flattered, for no foreigners were more generous or better customers. But in 1914 and 1915 stamps with 'Gott strafe England' were used on letters as well as ordinary stamps, there were posters, leaflets, postcards bearing the ominous words. You saw them on the windows of shops and private apartments, on benches in the parks, on the doors of trains, on your parcels, on sausages, on butter and in the drawing-rooms of your acquaintances.[69]

This mobilization of the passions of the people unquestionably accounts for the peculiar malevolence with which British prisoners of war were treated in the earlier stages of the war of 1914-18. The troops were put through a regular catechism of hate against the British, and there was nothing whatever to choose between the conduct of the Prussians and the Bavarians in this respect. When serving on the A.G.'s staff with the B.E.F. in 1914-15 I was shown a copy of an Army Order by Prince Rupprecht, found on a Bavarian officer whom we had taken prisoner, instructing the troops to treat the British with particular ferocity. This they accordingly did. No distinction was made between officers and men. One of the British officers serving under me in Berlin in 1921, Captain Evelyn Smith, who was taken prisoner at the First Battle of Ypres, told me he was repeatedly struck by German N.C.O.s who believed, or affected to believe, that our troops gouged out the eyes of German prisoners of war. No doubt they had been so instructed by a higher authority, for

[69] *Seven,* by Rom Landau (London, 1936), p. 37.

an exactly similar charge against the Belgians, and an equally false one, duly appeared in the notorious German White Book with which the German Government attempted to justify before an outraged world of neutrals the massacres of men, women, and children by German troops at Dinant and elsewhere.

When conducting a kind of 'C.I.D.' investigation of these things for our own Government at G.H.Q. in 1914-15, I encountered a peculiarly horrible, not to say bestial, example of the sinister tactics of the German General Staff in alternately checking and encouraging the worst passions of the troops as a matter of policy. At Bailleul scores of French women were outraged by German officers and men with every circumstance of brutality. After studying the depositions of these outrages, handed to me by Major-General Swinton and taken down by the Commissaire of Police immediately on the evacuation of the town by the German troops, I motored out to Choques to make further inquiries of Colonel, now Field-Marshal, Lord Gort at the H.Q. of our First Army. He told me that there was nothing further of the kind to report in the vicinity, and that the German troops had left the women quite unmolested in villages at a distance of only two miles from Bailleul. 'You see,' Gort explained, 'they thought Bailleul was on the Belgian side of the frontier and *they know no mercy against the Belgians.*' His explanation is more than confirmed by a distinguished German writer, Professor Foerster. A peculiar animosity against the Belgians, Foerster tells us, manifested itself in Germany among all classes of the population, whether because Germans find it impossible to forgive those whom they have injured, or more probably, because they had been deliberately inoculated by their rulers with a malicious hatred of the victims. He records, on the authority of a German officer of his acquaintance who was a witness of the scene, a terrible spectacle at Charleroi when Belgian men, women, and children, whose ages varied from 15 to 65 were being driven into cattle-trucks after being rounded up for forced labor in Germany:

The people were only half clothed and without coats, carrying in their hands little parcels with a few of their belongings hastily snatched up. On passing through the station they protested against the brutality with which they were being treated, whereupon the German stationmaster turned a fire-hose on them and the wretched people, drenched to the skin, were thrust into the trucks in freezing weather 16 degrees below zero.

Professor Foerster's German friend apparently thought it necessary to offer some excuse for his non-intervention. 'It was impossible for me to interfere,' he added, 'for even the uniform of a German officer would not have saved me from lynching by the soldiers if I had attempted to stop this sort of thing.' The excuse is quite incredible and in the very next sentence he adds, 'Soldiers *and officers* alike burst into shouts of laughter and applauded with all their might the stationmaster's practical joke at the expense of these poor people.' [70] The soldiers were, in fact, officially inoculated by their superiors with hate against the Belgians like a serum. The German Government issued an official 'White Book' purporting to record that little Belgian girls of 'eight to ten years old' were observed 'busying themselves' in gouging out the eyes of wounded German soldiers with the contents of their mothers' workboxes in the presence of a whole column of German troops on the march.[71] In support of this fantastic story they published 'depositions,' quite obviously faked, to that effect, in a vain attempt to allay the outbursts of execration excited in America and other neutral countries by the organized massacres of Belgian civilians at Dinant and elsewhere. But while this calculated defamation of the civil population of Belgium entirely failed to convince neutral opinion, it was only too successful in its incitement of the *furor Teutonicus* against that unhappy people.

Just five years later, the Weimar Republic empaneled a Reichstag Committee to inquire into the conduct of the war. It was sitting at the time of our arrival in Berlin. A pertinacious Reichstag deputy pressed Bethmann-Hollweg as to why, when Chancellor, he had tolerated these iniquities in Belgium. 'Are you aware,' asked the deputy, 'that thousands of Belgians,' as the result of the brutalities practiced upon them, 'died?' The Imperial Chancellor, driven into a corner, let the cat out of the bag. The German High Command, he pleaded, had silenced all his protests with the curt reply, '*In war*

[70] *Europa und die deutsche Frage,* by F. W. Foerster, p. 350.
[71] The German White Book, Appendix 56. The 'depositions' are to be found in *German Atrocities, an Official Investigation* (London, Fisher Unwin, 1916).

we must stop at nothing.' [72] It was the voice of tradition. But, having elicited this damning admission, the Reichstag Committee apparently got frightened. It was characteristic of the weakness of the Republic in face of the military caste that when Hindenburg and Ludendorff refused to answer questions about these things the Committee threw up the sponge. No doubt its members feared the knife of the assassin. The Committee hurriedly 'shut down,' and whole volumes of the evidence were suppressed. It was, indeed, too late to disinfect the wells of truth in Germany poisoned for years by the lying propaganda of the German Higher Command. It would have required then, as it would require now, generations of ethical teaching to induce a change of heart in the people, and the teachers were not to be found.

Such was the German cult of hate in all its ugly manifestations. As it was in 1914, so it was in 1919. So it was in the Second World War. In one of his belligerent utterances to the German people Hitler, exhausting the whole vocabulary of lethal fury, used the word 'Hate' no less than fourteen times in successive sentences in a single speech.[73] The inflammatory passages of *Mein Kampf* in which he declares that Germany would never rest until she had achieved 'the annihilation' (*die Vernichtung*) of France are neither as new nor as transient as some amongst us fondly believed in the years of 'appeasement.' They were, and were intended to be, the Austrian convert's pledge to the German people of his unimpeachable orthodoxy. More than a century ago, it became the cherished creed of German patriotism that to love your country you must hate your neighbor. Alone among Germans, Goethe in Weimar refused to admit the necessity. When asked by Eckermann—'a little incautiously' (*etwas unvorsichtig*) as that worthy scribe admits—why he had not made a single contribution to the hymnology of hate composed by German patriots against the French, he repudiated the whole creed in unforgettable words:

How could I have written songs of hate (*Lieder des Hasses*) when I felt none? I never hated the French, however much I may have thanked

[72] See the shorthand report of Bethmann-Hollweg's evidence published in *Official Documents relating to the World War* (Carnegie Endowment, 1923), pp. 412, etc.

[73] See *The Times* and *Daily Telegraph* reports of 9 November 1939.

God that we are quit of them. How could I, to whom civilization and barbarism are the only things that matter, hate a nation which belongs to the most cultivated in the world and which I have to thank for the greatest part of my own culture? [74]

National hatred, Goethe proceeded, will always be found at its strongest and in its most violent form 'on the lowest plane of culture.' On such a plane do the Germans, with all their lip-service to 'culture,' live. That, no doubt, is why Rathenau had the courage to proclaim that he would like to see the catchword 'culture' banished from the German vocabulary. Goethe declared, in a sorrowful moment, that it would be 'a few centuries' (*ein Paar Jahrhunderte*) before the Germans would cease to be 'barbarians.' [75] To those of us who lived and moved in the Germany of 1919-23 those 'few' centuries sometimes appeared to be an under-estimate.

This *furor Teutonicus* with its facile changes of mood, savage one moment, ingratiating the next, has often suggested to my mind something feline in the German character. Or is it something pathological? There is a form of epilepsy—what the French call *petit mal* —in which the patient, after periods of normal behavior as a law-abiding citizen, will suddenly, as in a trance, commit the most atrocious crimes and, when the fit of 'automatism' has passed, will remember nothing of them. This pathological explanation might hold good of the German rank and file and of the populace, but it fails when applied to their leaders for they, as we have seen, are only too conscious of the malady and leash and unleash its savagery with studied calculation. There is an amazing passage in the German White Book in which a German staff officer, Major Bauer, records that, after the German troops had butchered nearly seven hundred civilians in cold blood at Dinant, they 'manifested a most notable kindness' to the survivors—'All received coffee from the field-kitchens,' deposes the Major, and a girl 'of about five years of age,' who was discovered by a German staff-surgeon 'quite unhurt' among a heap of forty corpses of 'women and young lads,' was given chocolate and 'was quite happy.' The 'kindness' thus shown to the bereaved was so 'notable' that the Major suggested it was 'worthy

---

[74] Goethe's *Gespräche mit Eckermann* (Insel Verlag), p. 534.
[75] *Ibid.*, p. 319.

of recognition.' He evidently thought it a case for the Iron Cross. The people, however, remained provokingly insensible to the consideration thus shown them, with the result that the Major could hardly contain his indignation.[76] And so today. After thirty thousand civilians had been slaughtered at Rotterdam by German bombers in 1940 and the Germans settled down to occupy the country, the German soldiers, we are told, had been most ingratiating in their attempts to make themselves agreeable to the Dutch population and were really hurt to find they were not loved. They behaved like the most mild-mannered men who ever cut a throat. They had been ordered to be kind, even as they had been ordered to be cruel, and it is 'theirs not to reason why.' Their astonishment that their victims were unable to see it in the same light may have been genuine. German Army discipline in all its ruthlessness has made them the automata they are. But the problem of their strange mentality remains. And its diagnosis is a European problem, a problem which will have to be faced. It may well be that 'the most passionate people in Europe' are a hysterical race. For susceptibility to 'suggestion' is, quite notoriously, one of the recognized symptoms of hysteria. The records of Charcot's famous clinic are full of examples of the responsiveness of hysterical patients to hypnotism, under the influence of which they will commit any deed, good or bad, benevolent or malevolent, according as they are directed by the master-mind of the hypnotist.

One torrid day in India, when a guest of the Maharaja Gaekwar of Baroda, I went hunting buck in the jungle with a cheetah. The cheetah sat between me and its keeper on the seat of our car, as we lurched along the rough uneven tracks under a blazing sun in whose hard, brilliant light the leaves of the banyan trees glittered like so many patterns cut out of burnished metal. The strange beast, more feline than canine, with its abnormally long forelegs, its curious head, flat as a cobra's, its wide, whiskered mouth, sat quietly between us, its eyes hooded like a falcon's, while the *shikari* held it in leash. It was as friendly as a domestic cat and, when I stroked it, purred luxuriously. The car slowed down as we sighted a herd of black buck browsing peacefully in the distance, lovely and graceful to look

[76] The German White Book, Documents C. 44 and 51.

upon. Doves cooed softly in the banyan trees and it seemed impossible to believe that savage and predatory life lurked in the long, spear-like grass of the undergrowth. The car stopped, the *shikari* unhooded the cheetah and let slip the leash. The animal shot from the car like a streak of light and with long, loping strides made for the herd, hustled a buck off its feet and got it by the throat. As we arrived on the scene, the buck was lying prostrate, looking up at us with inexpressible anguish in its glazing eyes as it lay with its throat gripped as in a vice by the cheetah which crouched over it intent and motionless except for the strangely measured beats of its long tail. The *shikari* took out his hunting knife and waited, until the last agonized convulsion of the victim, for the cheetah to relax its hold. Then he gave it its coveted reward, the bloody testicles of the buck. When it had satiated its appetite, it allowed itself to be hooded and leashed with the utmost docility and resumed its place in the car. As we drove slowly away, the jungle suddenly came to life. Crows appeared as from nowhere and settled on the still writhing entrails of the disemboweled buck, kites swooped down and scattered the crows, and, after a pause, vultures lumbered heavily down and scattered the kites. As we left the obscene feast far behind us, the sinister beast in the car, having licked its bloody chops, settled down quietly on the seat with ingratiating friendliness as I shrank away from it. When I think of the German people, I am reminded of that cheetah.

VII

Each and every one of these moral disorders which ravaged the social life of Germany in Defeat was directly attributable to her idolatry of war and of the instrument with which, in all its brutality, she waged it. The dual German doctrine that war itself is, in von Seeckt's tell-tale phrase, 'the highest goal of human endeavor,' and that every means, however foul, is legitimate to prosecute it to a successful conclusion, ends in a hopeless moral cul-de-sac. The moment the disciples of such a doctrine are defeated, they are left without any law of life, human or divine, to govern their conduct. The very license with which they waged the war poisons all their attempts to accommodate themselves to a state of peace. License of conduct inevitably ends in licentiousness of mind. For four years

millions of German men had been licensed by their officers to indulge
in the vices of cruelty, bestiality, lust, cupidity, hate, and rapine at
the expense of the vanquished, and on their return to civil life they
behaved like men who had lost their moral sense. They were as
men 'of sense forlorn.' In this morbid atmosphere, crime flourished
like a poisonous weed in a manure heap. A German Socialist newspaper, the *Vorwärts*, in an article on 'The Housing Question' (*die
Wohnungsfrage*) made the sardonic observation that the question
was most acute in Germany's prisons, presenting, as they did, a
housing problem of their own. It seemed at times as if the judges of
the civil courts had themselves lost all sense of right and wrong, so
trivial were the sentences they imposed, particularly if the offender
were an ex-service man, for the most atrocious crimes. One day, at
Leipzig, I read in a local newspaper [77] the report of a case in which
the accused was convicted of the rape of a little girl of six years of
age under the most revolting circumstances. The court imposed a
nominal sentence of four months' imprisonment. A man had only
to plead that he had been a 'Front-Soldat' and the judges seemed
to be hypnotized by the plea. They could not have been more indul-
gent if they had served at the Front themselves and there committed
the same offenses. Perhaps they had.

The civilian population was, in one respect, even more demoral-
ized by the conduct of the war than the soldiers. This sounds like
a paradox but is none the less true and is attested, as we shall see,
by the evidence of German writers of the most authoritative kind.
The fiscal policy of the German Government in financing the war
can only be described as not less rapacious than short-sighted. Under
the inspiration of the General Staff and its confederates, the great
Federations of German Manufacturers generically known as *die
Grossindustriellen* or 'Big Industrialists,' the German Treasury decided in 1914 to impose no taxes for the prosecution of the war.
To that decision it adhered for nearly two years. It viewed the war
and its conduct as a vast predatory enterprise which should, and
would, pay for itself. It was to pay for itself by the exploitation of
the economic resources of the occupied countries, by gigantic 'fines'
imposed on their inhabitants and by the exaction, at an early date,

[77] The *Leipziger Abend Post* for 14 July 1921.

of enormous 'reparations' from all the enemy belligerents.[78] Reckoning on a 'short war,' a crushing victory, an equally crushing peace, and the payment of the entire cost of the war by the ruin and exploitation of the vanquished, the Treasury deliberately spared the German taxpayer the imposition of any war taxes right down to March 1916.[79] The war was financed by the flotation of War Loans, which were all the more blithely taken up by the German public owing to their sure and certain hope that the interest thereon would be paid and the capital redeemed not by the German taxpayer but by the vanquished people of England and France. When, in the middle of 1916, this golden mirage began to recede, the Reich Government was compelled to resort to taxation to meet the debt-charges but, having deluded the public so long with the promise of a crushing victory and equally crushing 'reparations,' it had not the courage either to tell the German people the truth or to demand of them taxes adequate to meet its own necessities. It therefore resorted to 'a fatal policy of depreciation' of the currency by ever-increasing inflation.[80] 'The seed' of all the financial troubles which overtook Germany after the war, German authorities tell us, was 'sown' by the German Treasury in the middle of it.[81] Every sort of financial trick was invoked to disguise the growing inflation, but 'inflation it was.'[82] German writers find themselves forced to admit that no such sacrifices as were demanded of the taxpayers of France and England for the prosecution of the war were ever asked of the German people and more than hint that the lust of gain, 'the most wanton cupidity,' which characterized the war fever in Germany, made it hopeless to expect them.[83] The Government had encouraged this mood of cupidity by its promises that the war would pay for itself

[78] That this was the basis of the fiscal policy of the Reich is freely admitted by German writers on German war finance, in particular by Arthur Dix in his *Wirtschaftskrieg und Kriegswirtschaft* (Berlin, 1921), at pp. 228-9. See also the authorities quoted below.

[79] Professor W. Piron, *Die Finanzen des Reichs* in *Handbuch der Politik*, vol. iv, p. 2. The same authority says 'the deciding factor' in this policy was the expectation of 'a speedy victory.' See also Reichsminister Dr. Schiffer in Dix, at p. 235.

[80] Dix, p. 243; *Handbuch der Politik*, vol. iv, at p. 2.

[81] *Ibid.*, iv, at p. 5 (Professor Piron) and p. 40 (Professor Diehl).

[82] 'Die Inflation war da'—*Handbuch der Politik*, vol. iv, p. 2.

[83] See the scathing criticism of this aspect of the war fever in Germany by Reichminister Dr. Schiffer in Dix, at p. 235.

and they were now powerless to exorcise the evil spirit they had fostered. The 'moral evils' resulting from this evasion of responsibility by the Government and the governed were described by Dr. Schiffer as 'enormous' (*ungeheuer*),[84] and the writers already quoted depict the demoralization of society during the last two years of the war, in consequence of the Government's fiscal policy, in terms which remind one of nothing so much as the demoralization which characterized Germany during the years of peace that followed. But by that time a scapegoat had been discovered in the Reparations clauses of the Treaty of Versailles. That vast propagandist organization, the *Fichte Verein* at Hamburg, subsidized by the German Government, flooded the world with pamphlets inviting it to contemplate the ruin wrought in German finances and German morale by the monstrous shadow of the Treaty. The sinners summoned their late enemies, whom they had hoped to despoil, to repentance, and many an unshriven Englishman, deeply moved, did public penance for the terms of the Treaty. Germans have no use for atonement themselves, but they have no objection to vicarious atonement.

Even more disastrous than the indoctrination of the German people by the German Government with the belief that the war would pay for itself was its encouragement of the idea that war would enrich them. Profits, not sacrifices, were, a German writer tells us, the bait held out to the armaments industries by the Government to stimulate them to increased production,[85] it being regarded as a matter of supreme importance 'to keep the big industrialists in a good temper'[86] with the result that their profits attained 'fantastic' dimensions.[87] Ludendorff himself, although as responsible as any one for the indulgence granted to the armament firms in their financial exploitation of the war, admits the disastrous 'moral consequences' of this 'conscienceless' (*gewissenlos*) scramble to make huge profits.[88]

---

[84] *Ibid.*
[85] Heymann, *Die Rechtsformen der militärischer Kriegswirtschaft* (Marburg, 1921), p. 181.
[86] '*Man, wahlte den bequemsten Weg die Grossindustriellen bei guter Laune zu erhalten,*' Dix, *op. cit.*, at p. 321.
[87] '*Phantastische' Gewinne,* Dix, at p. 321.
[88] Ludendorff, *Kriegführung und Kriegpolitik*, p. 123, etc. In his *Kriegserinnerungen* (p. 269) he expresses 'deep regret' that he had not taken measures to stamp out all this profiteering.

War profiteering, another writer tells us, flourished 'like a noxious weed.'[89] Everybody was out to get rich quickly. The Civil Service itself caught 'the infection' (*die Verseuchung*) of the riotous luxury (*Luxusleben*) around it and became hopelessly corrupt.[90] It is a surprising picture of the 'home front' in Germany, during the war, with which these German writers present us. There is not a word about a distressful Germany languishing under the pressure of the 'Hunger Blockade.' All that was an afterthought of post-war propagandists. Indeed, a German writer bluntly admits as much. The 'Hunger Blockade' was, he writes, 'not in the least the cause' of the decline in public morale which overtook Germany towards the end of the war.[91] The real cause of the decline, he proceeds, was the big profits and the high wages exacted by employers and workmen alike in the armaments and munitions industries. Hence the total failure of the attempt of the German General Staff to secure conscription of labor in any real sense of the word. The workmen and their representatives in the Reichstag, the Social Democrat Party, refused to consent to it unless the employers would agree to a limitation of their profits, and the employers refused. Every one tried to 'shirk' their duty to the common weal and 'the rift,' between the men at the Front 'risking their lives for a few pfennig a day' and the men wallowing in luxury at home, grew ever wider.[92] Greed and cheating of the most 'repulsive' kind grew to 'catastrophic' dimensions.[93] It is not a pretty picture of German devotion to the Fatherland with which these German writers present us. If, as Ludendorff and his disciple Hitler would have us believe, the German armies were not defeated in the field but 'stabbed in the back' by dark forces at home, those forces were not the hidden hand of Bolshevism but the itching palms of German citizens. One of these writers, a writer whom Ludendorff himself quotes as worthy of respect whenever it suits his purpose, sums it all up in some damning observations on the national character of his fellow countrymen as compared with our own. The longer the war lasted, he observes, the more faint-hearted did the

[89] Dix, *op. cit.*, p. 321; also Professor von Eheberg in *Handbuch der Politik*, vol. iv, p. 64.

[90] Dix, *op. cit.*, p. 212.

[91] Heymann, *op. cit.*, p. 181.

[92] Dix, *op. cit.*, p. 321.

[93] Ludendorff, *Kriegserinnerungen*, at p. 277.

German people become. The civil population were wholly wanting in 'public spirit' and the Army alone possessed any will of its own. The English people, he adds, were inspired by 'the will to conquer,' the German, from the moment things began to go wrong, were not. The longer the war lasted and 'the more they were defeated,' the more resolute did the English become.[94]

It was an extraordinary delusion on the part of the Allied statesmen at Paris, when drafting 'the Reparations' Clauses of the Treaty, to believe that a country which had thus deliberately shirked the burden of taxation to pay its own costs of the war, would now dutifully impose it to pay the costs of the victors. Germany never had the slightest intention of paying any reparations, whether large or small, excessive or not excessive, 'liquidated' or unliquidated, if she could possibly avoid payment. The only way to secure payment would have been to establish an Inter-allied Reparations Commission in Berlin instead of at Paris, to put in a Receiver-General of German revenues and to increase progressively the strength of the Armies of Occupation on the Rhine, instead of steadily diminishing it, until the German Government imposed adequate taxation and, what is more, enforced the payment of it. As it was, the propaganda against 'reparations' directed by the *Fichte Verein* abroad had its repercussion at home in the form of wholesale fraud by the German taxpayer. Many a factory-owner said to me and to other British Control officers, 'Of course I keep two sets of books—one for the *Finanzamt* (the Inspector of Taxes), the other for myself. Why should I pay taxes for the French if the more I earn the more I shall have to pay?' The excuse was not more honest than the practice which it pretended to justify. The fraudulent state of mind which it revealed was, as we have seen, an 'infection' already active in the body politic of Germany during the war. The German Government, reaping where it had sown, was now confronted with the problem of a whole community of taxpayers making, whenever they could, false returns. Shirking—*Drückbergerei* as it is called in German—became the accepted policy of every industrialist and, indeed, almost every capitalist, in dealing with the Income Tax authorities. One day, in May 1922, I questioned the *Chef de Cabinet* of the Reichs President,

[94] Dix, *Wirtschaftskrieg und Kriegswirtschaft*, at p. 3.

Dr. Paul Meissner, on the subject, when he came to lunch with me at the Adlon. He told me that the Reich taxes were two years in arrears and that it was almost impossible, in the case of the big industrialists, to assess them. 'As soon as the Revenue Department has trained officials to audit the books of the big firms,' Meissner explained, 'the Directors offer the auditors six or seven times their official salary to join their firms and instruct them how to dodge the audit.' If only twelve 'Big Business' men were 'sentenced to imprisonment' (*Zuchthaus*), added Meissner, 'all the rest would pay up.' But they never were. The Government of the Weimar Republic would no more have dared to lay its hands on a big industrialist than on the Lord's Anointed.

Whatever one may think of its morality, the strategy of the big industrialists, during these years immediately after the war, was brilliantly successful. They were themselves largely responsible for the inflation policy of the Treasury and the discount policy of the Reichsbank which was itself governed by representatives of the great banking corporations who were only the big industrialists under another name. In 1923-4 inflation was carried to lengths it had never been carried before, ostensibly to finance 'passive resistance' to the French in their occupation of the Ruhr. But there was more in it than that. To the industrialists inflation meant a golden harvest in the way of cheap labor, an expanding export trade, and the redemption of all their debentures for a song. At the height of the inflation Krupp's took advantage of it to pay off the whole of their debentures on merely nominal terms, and by this astute operation made a profit of some ten million pounds sterling, equivalent to nearly 100 per cent on their pre-war capital. The fact that the debenture-holders were ruined in consequence did not trouble the directors at all. Those of the *rentier* middle class who had invested in War Loans were ruined in any case by the resulting repudiation by the State of its indebtedness to the subscribers. The small trader was also overwhelmed. Obtaining money, as banking corporations, at 18 to 30 per cent, the industrialists, through the banks which they controlled, fleeced the small trader by re-discounting his bills at 500 per cent. At the same time the industrialists scored heavily in the distribution of the burden of taxation. While the workmen paid income-tax weekly on their wages, which were known, the industrialists paid only on their yearly profits which, as we have seen, were almost unascertainable. The assessment on the workmen's wages was in current values; the assessment, such as it was, on the industrialists' profits was in values so obsolete, owing to the continuous fall of the mark, that by the time the assessment was made and the demand-note presented the amount payable to the tax-collector was almost nominal. The victims of this fraudulent fiscal policy, the ruined middle classes and the impoverished working classes whose 'real' wages were continually diminishing, were ceaselessly told by the Press, which had been largely bought up by the industrialists and by the two great news agencies of which they were in complete control, that all their afflictions were due to the Treaty of Versailles, and more and more of them came to believe it. The Treaty was a very present help to the industrialists in this respect, acting, as it did, as a kind of lightning-conductor to divert from the real culprits the stroke of popular indignation. In this fertile soil was the seed of Hitlerism sown.[95] It was no mere accident that Hitler, beginning as the foundling of the Reichswehr, was launched on his political career as the hireling of the industrialists.

The callousness of the industrialists, the real rulers of Germany in those days, was as shameless as it was ruthless. One day in January 1923 Arnold Rechberg, himself a big industrialist and one of the heads of the great Potash Syndicate, called on me at the Adlon. He was surprisingly cheerful about the French occupation of the Ruhr. 'Nothing is here for tears,' was his attitude, which was almost bois-terously complacent.

'But what about the fall of the mark?' I asked.

'Oh, that's very good for us,' was the reply. 'We shall get big ex-port orders.'

'But what about the increased cost of German imports?'

'Our big profits on the export trade will meet that all right,' re-plied the imperturbable plutocrat.

'And what about the middle classes?' I retorted.

'Oh! they are ruined, of course.'

---

[95] One or two German writers attempted to expose the imposture, e.g. E. J. Gumbel in his book *Verschwörer*, at p. 214, where he wrote: 'It is, in fact, simply not true (*in Wirklichkeit ist es einfach nicht wahr*) that the Versailles Treaty is the cause of Germany's financial misery.'

'But isn't that a tragedy?'

Rechberg was not at all discomposed. 'Of course it's a tragedy,' he replied with a cheerfulness more appropriate to a comedy, 'but when a man's dead, he's dead, isn't he?'

This attitude of 'Am I my brother's keeper?' was characteristically German. It is strange that the idealists of Geneva and Locarno should have cherished the idea that a people who are so ill acquainted with fraternity at home would ever become converts to the doctrine of the brotherhood of man abroad.

VIII

Thus did Germany, having in war sown the wind, in peace reap the whirlwind. Nemesis overtook her and would not be denied. Was there no one in Germany to remind her that God is not mocked? That the cruelty, the lust, the bestiality, the mutual hatred, the cupidity and the callousness which now ravaged her were the measure of what she had meted unto others during the war when she had practiced just these vices upon the unhappy peoples of Belgium, France, and Russian Poland, ground down under the heel of her occupation? There was no one. The Churches in Germany, by their ignominious silence throughout the war, had abdicated. There remained only the Press and the Universities, as organs of public opinion and of the education of opinion. What were they doing to cure these fearful maladies in the now disordered nation to which they ministered? The answer is nothing. There was indeed, there never has been, such a thing in Germany as public opinion, as Englishmen understand it and give expression to it, still less a public conscience. In a remarkable passage in his Reminiscences, a passage almost blinding in its fierce illumination of German mentality, Bismarck speaks contemptuously of the alien ideas represented by 'such words as Humanity and Civilization *imported into Germany from England*,' [96] and boasts of his success in extirpating such exotic ideas before they could take root. Germany had no more use for these 'imports' in 1919 than in the days of Bismarck, except to re-export

[96] 'Die Redensarten von Humanität und Civilisation die aus England bei uns importiert werden'—Bismarck's *Gedanken und Erinnerungen* (Volks-Ausgabe), vol. ii, at p. 132.

them for foreign consumption by plaintive appeals, against the terms
of the Treaty, to the humanity and civilization of the non-German
world.

Let us take a brief look at the German Press and the German
Universities in order to discover why and how they failed the German people in these disordered days. When serving in Berlin, I not
only read every German newspaper I could lay my hands on, but
consorted, as opportunity offered, with many German journalists.
The first thing that struck me about the German Press was the total
absence of a feature as conspicuous as it is characteristic in the Press
of our own country, namely a 'Correspondence Column.' Every
English newspaper is a kind of open forum for the discussion of
public affairs. Therein you find a forensic display of every shade
of opinion, opinion, as often as not, criticizing the editorial outlook of
the newspaper itself. But during the whole of the time I served
in Germany I never once encountered a single 'Letter to the Editor'
in a newspaper. One day I questioned Herr Victor Hahn, the editor
of a Berlin newspaper with a large circulation, the *Acht Uhr Abendblatt*, on this point.

'Do you *never* publish letters from your readers?' I asked.   .

'No, of course not,' was the surprising reply.

'Do you never receive any?' I asked, and was told that he did.

'Then what do you do with them?' I persisted. 'Do you shoot
them into an *oubliette?*'

'Oh,' replied Hahn, 'we answer them *privately*, if they are important.'

The effects of this policy on public opinion were profound and
far-reaching. No German newspaper-readers ever became acquainted
with the two sides of any public question. What the newspaper editor, or rather its proprietor, wanted him to believe he was told and,
being told it, he believed it.

The passive receptivity of the reading public in this respect was
almost childish. One day a great German banker, Herr Geheimrat
Widding, President of the National Bank and former Oberbürger-
meister of Posen, was brought to see me at the Adlon by Arnold
Rechberg. I asked him what he thought of the German Press. He
told me.

'Our Press is the worst in the world,' he exclaimed. 'It passes by all the great events in the world outside Germany. What is worse, Germans believe everything it says. Our public believes everything that is underlined (*unterstrichen*). Hauptmann is not a great poet, Rathenau is not a great political thinker, but our Press has been saying they are, twice a day for years, and so everybody thinks so. The French public is much more critical. If they read in the papers that Madame So-and-so is a great actress, they say, "Either the writer has been bribed or he is in love with her." German journalists,' he added, 'are not like yours, distinguished men. They are little people (*kleine Leute*) and will do anything for you if you ask them to dinner.' He hinted, not obscurely, that they were always open to bribes.

Of German newspaper proprietors Herr Widding had an equally poor opinion. 'We have no Northcliffes, no Beaverbrooks, as you have,' he proceeded, 'those men are statesmen, they have a policy, they *believe* in things.'

'But what about Stinnes?' I asked in astonishment, 'surely he's a man who has a policy, a man who "believes in things"?'

'Not at all,' was the reply, 'Stinnes is a child (*ein Kind*) in politics, like all the big industrialists, and isn't really interested in them at all. He has only bought newspapers to find a market for his cellulose.'

All this explains why the German public never sees any side in any great international controversy or crisis except their own. During all the years I served in Germany I very rarely saw a single article, much less a letter from a reader, in any newspaper which so much as hinted that Germany might have been in the wrong either in the initiation of the war or in the conduct of it.[97] Still less did I ever encounter any admission that the Treaty of Versailles, or even a single article of it, had any justification whatsoever or that Germany herself had provided the Allies with precedents for it, far exceeding it in harshness, in the inexorable treaties she had imposed on Russia and Rumania. Germany was invariably presented to the public by the German Press as the innocent victim of the cupidity

[97] To this there was one exception, the sort of exception that proves the rule, *Die Menschheit*. But *Die Menschheit*, which was an organ for the promotion of international peace and good-will, was, in October 1923, proscribed by the German Government and its editor had to take refuge in the occupied territory at Wiesbaden where it was thereafter published.

of the Allies, never as the prisoner of her own. Meanwhile, day after day our pacifists at home were being given the run of the correspondence columns of the English Press to declaim against the 'harshness' of the Treaty of Versailles, often finding excuses for German policy which the Germans had never found for themselves. All this was meat and drink to the German Press which seized upon it as an excuse for the moral disorders of post-war Germany with the specious pretext that those disorders were due to the 'despair' induced in the German people by the terms of the Treaty. As a matter of fact, the German Press had itself done its best to deprave the mind of the German public instead of elevating it. What could one expect, in the education of the public conscience, of a Press one of whose leading journals published with approval, early in the war, the letter of a German officer describing the 'brilliant idea' (*ein guter Gedanke*), as he called it, which inspired him, during the invasion of France, to place French civilians on chairs in the middle of the street of a town, in which the German troops were in action, and use them as a screen for his men against the French troops in spite of their 'prayers of anguish.' [98]

The Universities were as impotent for good, in the midst of all this social evil, as the Churches—and for the same reason. Like the Churches, they too had abdicated in the most critical hour of Germany's spiritual life. Just as the Churches had been silent throughout the war in the face of all the crimes committed in Belgium, so the Universities had been silent, indeed worse than silent, in the face of the greatest crime of all—the violation of Belgian neutrality. That outrage was the most flagrant offense against the Law of Nations, the public law of Europe, since the Partition of Poland and not less cynical. It was, in fact, the one outrage which the German delegation at the Peace Conference made no attempt either to palliate or to deny. The Delegation, in so many words, pleaded guilty.[99] The sanctity of the Treaty of London guaranteeing the neutrality of

[98] The *Münchener Neueste Nachrichten*, 7 October 1914.

[99] 'Germany accepts the obligation to pay for all damage sustained by the civil population in the occupied parts of Belgium and France, *inasmuch as she brought upon them the terrors of war* by a breach of international law through the violation of Belgian neutrality.'—Reply of the German Delegation to the draft Treaty of Versailles.

Belgium, the sacred obligations of its guarantors, of whom Germany
was one, the catastrophic effects upon international morality of any
repudiation of it, had been laid down again and again in every text-
book of International Law and, in earlier days, in none more forcibly
or more eloquently than those which emanated from the Law Faculties of the German Universities.[100] When, on that fateful day in
August 1914, the German Chancellor suddenly declared the Treaty
to be nothing more than 'a scrap of paper' and the German troops
swept into Belgium, laying waste this sanctuary of International Law
with fire and sword, not a single voice among the Professors of International Law in the German Universities was raised in protest.
This was bad enough. But what followed was worse. Just ten days
after the outrage, a Manifesto was issued to the world attempting
to justify it. It was issued from the German Universities and bore
the signatures of forty professors, the accredited spokesmen, and the
most eminent, of their tribe. In this encyclical the Agnostic and the
Christian, Haeckel and Harnack, joined hands. The sciences and the
arts united in a common apostasy. From that moment, the German
Universities were doomed to ignominious acquiescence, throughout
the war, in each successive violation of all the rules of international
law by the German Government, as they followed hard on one
another. They became the camp-followers of the German Army,
prostituting their intellects in its service by justifying each violation,
as it occurred, with one sophistry after another. Frederick the
Great's contemptuous estimate of German learning came home to
roost: 'I snatch what I want at the start; I can always find German
pedants to prove my right to it after I have taken it.' The leaders
of German thought and culture became more and more enmeshed in
the web of their own weaving. Harnack, the fine flower of the
theological faculties, 'surpassed,' as Bülow tells us, 'in chauvinism all
the other German *savants* during the war.' [101] This professed cham-

---

[100] One quotation, typical of all the rest, will suffice: 'The Treaty is a landmark of progress in the formation of a European policy and no Power has ever
dared to violate a guarantee of this kind. He who injures a right does injury
to the cause of right itself and in these guarantees lies the express obligation to
prevent such things. Nothing could make the situation of Europe more insecure
than an egotistical repudiation by the great States of these duties of international
fellowship.'—Holtzendorff, *Handbuch des Völkerrechts*, vol. iv, pp. 93, etc.

[101] Bülow, vol. iv., p. 272 (French edition).

pion of German Christianity, according to the same unimpeachable
authority, touched bottom by declaring that the only soldiers, among
all the belligerents, who were in such a state of grace as to be 'ready
to die' were the Germans.[102] This was too much even for Bülow,
who makes no secret of his contempt for Harnack and all his colleagues. Perhaps it was Harnack who inspired the invidious inscription [103] which the German War Graves authorities thought good
enough for British soldiers, fast bound in misery and iron and dying
like flies in the internment camps, when death put an end to their
sufferings.

When Nemesis overtook this repudiation of all law, both human
and divine, and Germany reaped in demoralization what she had
sown in aggression, not one of the forty professors had the courage
to abjure that fatal Manifesto. Harnack knew well enough into what
an abyss of moral declension he and his confederates had led the
people whom they were supposed to guide and control. He admitted
it, but was careful to confine his admission to a private letter. 'Arro-
gance, godlessness, Mammon-worship, *lack of ideals*,' wrote in 1919
this disillusioned realist of 1914, were devouring the German people
like a Black Plague. But the Manifesto of Harnack and his thirty-
nine colleagues was not an aberration. In that Manifesto the professors merely ran true to form. The German Universities had always
been the academic garrison of German militarism. In Prussia, in
particular, for nearly a century every member of the Faculties of
History of any eminence in the Universities had been a professional
apologist of Prussian militarism,[104] with the single exception of Ranke
who was the only approach among them to 'a good European.' Even
when, like Sybel and Treitschke, they flirted with Liberalism in
the days of their youth, they had always ended by coming to heel

[102] *Ibid.*, p. 273.
[103] In a letter to the *Daily Telegraph* of 28 January 1941, Brigadier-General
E. G. Wace records that in 1920 he visited a cemetery in Germany near Saar-
brucken where German and British soldiers had been buried during the war.
The graves of the German soldiers bore the inscription 'Hier ruht in Gott'
('Here rests in God') on a cross, those of the British the words 'Hier ruht'
('Here rests') only, the words 'in God' being deliberately omitted.
[104] The consistent teaching of the German Universities in this respect has been
set out, with chapter and verse, in *L'Allemagne et ses historiens*, by Antoine
Guilland.

behind the jack-boot of Prussia. Mommsen himself, intractable Radical though he remained in domestic politics to the end of his days, joined the academic camp-followers in the Franco-Prussian War and demanded the forcible annexation of Alsace-Lorraine in the authentic accents of German 'Nationalism,' anticipating with sophistical arguments the creed of Hitler in all its aggressiveness.[105] His attitude, like that of all his colleagues, on that fateful issue was the same as Treitschke's: 'We Germans know better what is good for Alsace than the unhappy people themselves. We will give them back their own identity *against their will*.' [106] In this, as in every other direction, Hitlerite Germany merely reverted to type.

It is not surprising that under these circumstances the German Universities were hot-beds of reaction as early as 1920 and that the current of opinion was running more strongly within them than in any other centers of thought in Germany in the direction of aggressive nationalism at the very moment when, by her entry into the League of Nations, Germany appeared to be converted to the ideals of internationalism. Yet in such spiritual homes of German culture one would have expected to find, if anywhere, a sympathetic response to such ideals, or rather one would have expected it if one did not know a little more about them and their peculiar constitution. I read in 1941 a glowing passage in a great English newspaper [107] in which a gifted writer put his hopes, for the future, of some kind of regeneration, after the present war, in the Universities of Germany. 'Think of them,' he wrote, 'with their marvelous century's work,' before Hitler debased them, '*the fruit of free thought, free speech, free inquiry*.' It left me wondering whether the writer was aware that throughout the whole of that 'century' every holder of a chair in a German University held it at the pleasure of the State, by whom

[105] Mommsen joined with Treitschke in denying the right of the people of Alsace-Lorraine, the whole of whose Parliamentary representatives without a single dissentient protested against annexation to Germany, to choose their own destiny on the ground that, although they had been part of France for two centuries, they were of German 'race.' He would not hear of a plebiscite. In a devastating reply, Fustel de Coulanges prophetically pointed out the disintegrating effects on the whole of the European States of such racial claims by German historians.—*L'Alsace, est-elle allemande ou française? Réponse à M. Mommsen* (1870).

[106] Treitschke's pamphlet, *Was fordern wir von Frankreich?*

[107] The *Sunday Times*, 9 February 1941.

he was appointed and by whom at any moment he might be dismissed. Even the academic head, the 'Rector Magnificus,' of every German University, and, as such, its *primus inter pares*, only enjoyed his primacy for a year, as the Rector of Munster University himself mournfully explained to me when I met him. Rectors came and went, professors rose and fell, but, added his Magnificence, the 'Kurator,' lording it over all the Faculties, remained. The Kurator is a Government official, the representative of the State with power to bind and loose, always keeping a watchful eye on the professors to see that they mind their step. Every German University, and all the spiritual life within it, has for a century, and much more than a century, been thus completely subject to the secular arm of the State. Hitler was not by any means the first ruler of Germany to sack professors who showed symptoms of 'free thought' and 'free speech.' The fact explains why the German Professors, from Kant [108] to Harnack, have always come to heel.[109]

English writers, with characteristic generosity, are always imputing to German scholars a humanitarianism which they rarely possess and still more rarely practice, although they sometimes profess it. Such writers seem to confuse intellectual distinction with moral elevation. The striking thing, the disturbing thing, about the German intellect is the presence of the one without the other. There is, indeed, no necessary connection whatsoever between the two. The writer in the *Sunday Times*, quoted above, reminded his readers of 'the debt' the world owes to 'Goethe and Kant and Helmholtz.' Goethe and Kant may, for the moment, abide our question. Helmholtz was a great physicist and no one will dispute his eminence. But what has the eminence of German scientists got to do with any hopes for the 'regeneration' of Germany? What have the natural sciences to do with the moral law? I am reminded of a disconcerting experience which befell my friend Lord Haldane who

[108] As to Kant, see the scathing description of his intellectual 'surrender' to Prussian authority in Wallace's *Kant*, p. 74, where the biographer bluntly says he behaved 'like a coward before his king.'

[109] The moral cowardice of 'Germans of intellectual eminence' was the subject of scathing comment by the last Chancellor of the First Reich, Prince Max of Baden, in his *Memoirs*, where he speaks of their dread of assuming 'personal responsibility' in public affairs—*op. cit.*, I, pp. 80, etc.

was always exhorting English audiences, in season and out of season, to remember 'the debt' which civilization owed to German science. One day in 1923, after a lecture of mine on 'The Present State of Germany' before a University audience at which he did me the honor to preside, Haldane—not very seasonably, for memories of the war of 1914-18 were still both fresh and raw—launched out into his favorite theme of our indebtedness to German science. 'Even during the war,' he blithely proceeded, 'German men of science made great discoveries of which we in England had no conception.' Quick as light came the rude interruption of an undergraduate in the gallery: 'Poison gas!' The roar of laughter which followed was too much for Haldane. It badly cramped his style for the rest of his discourse. Yet undoubtedly the German professor, Dr. Haber, who was responsible for poison gas and incidentally for that synthetic ammonia which revolutionized Germany's production of high explosives, was a most distinguished man of science. He was none the less lethal on that account.

Goethe and Kant call for rather close attention. For we were hearing a good deal of them till now in the intermittent newspaper controversies which were going on, a little prematurely, as to what is to be done with Germany when we have defeated her. Our leading literary journal has gently chided Lord Vansittart, on the occasion of his trenchant 'broadcast' analysis of the German character, for forgetting 'the Germany of Kant and Goethe.' [110] I doubt if he had forgotten anything. His answer would probably be that after a long and peculiarly intimate acquaintance with Germany, he, like myself, has never been able to discover that other Germany, which, the more you seek it on the spot, the more it eludes you like some 'fairy land forlorn.' There is, in fact, little or nothing characteristically German in Goethe's teaching but very much to the contrary. Goethe repudiated German 'nationalism' altogether, which is why he has had no influence whatsoever on German thought and action in the sphere of conduct. He thought the German people hopelessly 'barbarian' and said so repeatedly, as the reader of Eckermann's *Conversations* may discover for himself. Germans lisp his lyrics, when they are a little drunk and not a little sentimental, and once a year you

110 *The Times Literary Supplement*, January 1941.

may see, as I have seen, *Faust* admirably acted, without 'cuts,' at Weimar, but you will see it acted nowhere else. Germany has only produced one Goethe in two hundred years. If she had produced ten, then, like the Cities of the Plain which she so intimately resembles, there might be some reason for sparing her. But, as security for her good behavior, one seems a little inadequate.

As for Kant, there are, to be sure, few things nobler, certainly none more edifying, in the literature of Ethics than his speculations on the problem of conduct, and nothing more aspiring than that essay of his, *Zum ewigen Frieden* ('To the Everlasting Peace'), envisaging a Universal World State in which wars shall be no more. But was that essay, was it intended to be, anything more than an academic exercise? Would he have been prepared to fight for such a peace? Or even to bless those who were? I doubt it. For his attitude towards the principles of political obligation was as Prussian as the King of Prussia himself, before whom he trembled 'like a coward,' could have desired. Certainly no German professor has ever written in more abject terms of the indefeasible duty of rendering unquestionable obedience to the powers that be, however despotic their character. The subject of a State, he has told us, ought never to raise any questions as to the source, the exercise, or the limits of the sovereign power. It is something mystical, 'inscrutable,' 'holy and inviolable, so that *even to question it is a crime.*' [111] This is pure 'Nazi' doctrine. And so too when he comes to discuss the crucial issue of 'Freedom.' No man has ever written more eloquently or more nobly about the freedom of the will, 'that transcendent will whose voice is the moral law.' But, as one of his most accomplished English interpreters dryly remarks,[112] when we descend from these high altitudes of metaphysics and attempt to apply his metaphysic to human conduct, we get from Kant the most 'unsatisfactory replies.' He shirks the issue. And for a good reason. He knew, by a bitter experience of his own, that while a German professor was, and is, as free as he pleases to speculate at large in the icy altitudes of the philosopher's 'Absolute' and on the cold peaks of 'Transcendentalism,' the moment he descends into the habitable valleys of so-

[111] See the passages from Kant's writings on this subject collected in Caird's *Critical Philosophy of Immanuel Kant,* vol. ii, pp. 332, etc.
[112] Professor William Wallace in his *Kant,* at p. 211.

cial life and begins to discuss the duty of man to man, and citizen to citizen, he is in danger of the Kurator and the long arm of the Prussian police. Which is perhaps why even the famous tract on 'Everlasting Peace' has had no successors in Germany, even as its teaching has found no disciples.

One day in the summer of the year 1920, when inspecting the forts of Königsberg, I decided to pay a visit to the shrine of Kant in the cathedral church of that city. It took some finding. The cathedral itself was visible enough. In the choir of the vast brick building, pugnacious in its very ugliness, I found myself confronted with the carved oak stalls of the Teutonic Knights, their helms and steel gauntlets impaled upon the walls, their faded banners drooping from the vaulted roof. That choir was like a temple of the Mailed Fist. In its sacerdotal commemoration of the rough 'exterminating' host of warriors, as Treitschke proudly called them, one seemed to discover the dark secret of that lust for blood which lurks deep in the German character under the thin veneer of German Protestantism and which nowhere finds more appalling expression than in the writings of Luther himself.[113] Below the choir, in a crypt like a cavern, was the pewter sarcophagus of the last Grand Master of the Knightly Order. But the shrine of Kant was nowhere to be seen, and I had to ask the verger where to find it. Perhaps the rude burghers of Königsberg felt some little difficulty in finding a place in that Temple of Mars for the lonely pacifist philosopher whose project of Perpetual Peace was followed by twenty years of almost perpetual war. Perhaps they felt his Peace was a peace which passeth all understanding in Prussia. Their solution was not without a certain grim significance. In an obscure corner on the north side of the choir wall,

---

[113] In his tract against the Peasants' Revolt, Luther incited the ruling Princes to massacre them with the words: 'A Prince can now obtain merit better by shedding blood than other men in prayer.' German historians have estimated the victims of the resulting massacre at 100,000. The full story, in all its horror, is to be found in Zimmermann's *Allgemeine Geschichte des grossen Bauern-Krieges*, at pp. 711, etc. Luther's lethal fury against the oppressed German peasants found expression in language which sounds like the authentic voice of Hitler himself. For example: *Man soll sie zerschmeissen, würgen und stechen, heimlich und öffentlich, wer da kann,* which literally translated, is: 'One must dash them in pieces, slaughter them, stick them like pigs, both in private and in public, wherever one gets the chance.'—Luther's tract, quoted in Zimmermann, *op. cit.*, at p. 712.

placed like an excommunicant outside the cathedral, is a small Gothic chapel. It seems like a Chapel of Dissent. It is the tomb of Kant.

On this pious pilgrimage I had with me my staff officer, Major Ewald, a hard-bitten infantry officer of the old school. He had followed me in silence as I entered the little chapel, somewhat mystified, apparently, by this vagrant excursion of mine and, as we came away, he said, 'Say, General, who was this bloke who called himself "Immanuel Kant"? Sounds a bit Jewish to me.'

'Not at all,' I replied, 'he was a German of Scottish descent.'

'Oh,' said Ewald, thinking, when he heard of his British extraction, rather better of Kant than he did of most foreigners. 'But what did he *do?*'

'He was a famous German metaphysician,' I replied. 'Wrote the *Kritik of Pure Reason.* The founder of Transcendentalism—*and all that,*' I added hastily and vulgarly as I caught a look of suspicion on Ewald's face at my 'highbrow' expressions. I felt I was rapidly losing caste in the British Army.

My explanation left Ewald unimpressed. 'Yes, but what did he *do?*' he persisted.

'What *did* he do?' I reflected. 'Well,' I said desperately, 'he taught. Taught philosophy in the University here.'

'What! To all these toughs we're up against in East Prussia?'

'Not quite so recently. He may have taught their great-grand-fathers.'

'Well,' said Ewald meditatively, 'I reckon that the chap who invented my safety-razor has done more for the world than this fellow Kant.'

I felt that Ewald had had the best of this dialectic. As regards Germany at any rate. Nine out of ten Germans use a safety-razor. But not one out of ten has ever heard of Kant.

IX

The reader will now, I think, not be disposed to quarrel with my description of Germany, the Germany with which we officers of the Control Commission were so familiar in the years we served there, as a 'savage forest,' a human jungle swarming with predatory life, a society ravaged with such passions that it resembled a ferocious horde rather than a civilized community. If the reader thinks the picture overdrawn, he had better get hold, if he can, of a book written by a thoughtful and humane German in 1921.[114] It was published, significantly enough, anonymously, no doubt because its author would have been promptly 'taken for a ride' if he had dared to disclose his identity. The book passed almost unnoticed in Germany. Like the seed in the parable, it fell among thorns, the thorns of the savage forest, and they sprang up and choked it. In this book the writer says in so many words that Germany reaped in defeat what she had sown in conquest, and that the 'fearful demoralization' of the post-war years was the Nemesis of her idolatry of militarism (*Militärismus*). She, and she alone, he wrote, was responsible for her own debasement. The picture he draws of that debasement is quite as somber, and as repulsive, as anything I have written above. A single extract will suffice:

The war had been conducted by us without the slightest chivalry, without the slightest nobility and with the most appalling hatred. That is why the moral brutalization (*die ethische Verwilderung*) which the war produced among us now knows no limits (*ist so grenzenlos*). The instincts of an unlicensed soldiery dominate today the whole of our public life. The hand-grenade is the chosen method of expressing a difference of opinion, the revolver and the rubber truncheon take the place of argument, murder has become a recognized instrument of politics, calumny of the vilest kind is the order of the day in our political Press. Nay, more, in certain of our newspapers one reads open incitements to the murder of political opponents.

It would be a complete mistake to stigmatize the Revolution as the cause of this brutalization of our people. That is clear enough from the fact that its symptoms are most apparent in just those classes who from the beginning have been the opponents of the Revolution. But those very classes were *the friends of War* (*Sie waren aber Freunde des Krieges*). That the craft of war brutalizes there can be no doubt whatsoever. And it brutalizes the young among us far more than the old, because a young man is far more susceptible to impressions, he succumbs far more easily to bad examples, than the man of mature age who has already got a firm hold on life and vocation. *It simply brutalized the very soul of the German people.*

Nowhere was this brutalization more apparent than in matters of sex. During the war hundreds of thousands of children were born infected with syphilis. The officers set the example (*Die Offiziere gaben ein Bei-*

114 *Die Tragödie Deutschlands, von einem Deutschen* (Germany's Tragedy, by a German), published at Stuttgart in 1921.

spiel besonderer Zügellosig-keit) in all this unbridled licentiousness. Special brothels reserved for officers flooded (*überschwemmten*) every place occupied by the Army. This brothel system was simply nauseating (*ekelerregend*). The utter licentiousness of the Army debauched the whole civil population at home and hundreds of thousands of German girls were corrupted. In this respect the Revolution could do nothing to corrupt the people, for they were already corrupted. It was merely that, once the war was over, the shamelessness of it all became yet more evident. Degenerate German women, in the hundreds, pestered the black soldiers who were taken prisoner during the war and equally the black troops of the French Army of Occupation after it. These women were responsible for a 'white shame' (*eine weisse Schmach*) for which they ought to have been whipped. All self-control and sense of discipline in Germany disappeared. The German people, steeped in war, became dirty to the very depths of their souls (*schmutzig bis in das tiefste Herz*).

During the war German literature and art were utterly debased. The nation was flooded with pictures of war in all its most lethal brutality, with pictures of cruelty and of almost insane horror. The Press systematically, and under official direction, indoctrinated the whole people with a cult of hate, of brutality, of blood-lust and of cruelty. Most of the newspapers would have seen their circulation disappear altogether if they had not co-operated in these orgies of Hate (*die Orgien des Hasses*). But there is an old saying that he who sows hate reaps it. All this fearful cult of hate came home to roost after the war.[115]

Out of this primeval chaos, as of night, the Nazi world was created. Adolf Hitler, as we know, claimed that he and his like saved this chaotic Germany from herself, and from the alien yoke of that 'Peace of Violence,' that Treaty of Versailles, which he would have us believe was the sole cause of her degeneration.[116] This new Messiah claimed to have purged her of her moral maladies, restored her stricken industries, liberated her from a paralyzing tribute, cured her of unemployment, and founded a new form of political society which, in the language of Burke, was destined to be 'a partnership in every virtue and in all perfection.' Many people in our own country believed this for quite a long time, even as they believed his claim that he had rescued Germany, and Europe with her, from the menace of 'Bolshevism.' All these claims were spurious, and none

[115] *Die Tragödie Deutschlands*, at pp. 281-3.

[116] I refer here to his speeches after he came into power and 'showed his hand.' In his earlier speeches, and in the pages of *Mein Kampf*, he put it all on the Jews.

more spurious than the last. Germany was never, as I have shown elsewhere in this book, at any time in danger of going 'Bolshevist' at or after the November Revolution of 1918. It was the Weimar Republicans, most notably the first President of the Republic, Hans Ebert, who disposed of the Bolshevist menace, if menace it was, once and for all in November 1918, and there never was a meaner travesty of history than Hitler's claim that, in destroying the Republic, he destroyed an outpost of Bolshevism. The Communists were never, at any Reichstag election during the fourteen years of the Republic, within measurable distance of assuming office. As for the moral maladies of Germany, the lust, the cruelty, the bestiality, the homicidal fury, which disfigured society in the years we served in Germany, it is a simple fact that those whose practice of these vices was most notorious were the very men who formed the spearhead of the Nazi conspiracy against the State. Almost without exception, the Nazi leaders were known and notorious as practitioners of these repulsive vices. As early as 1924, a German writer, in a carefully documented study of the innumerable 'para-military' societies of conspirators which ultimately coalesced into the Nazi Party, remarked, only too truly and with uncanny insight, that there was 'a strong pathological impulse' (*ein starkes sozial pathologisches Moment*) inherent in these subterranean forces in the body politic.[117] A homo-sexual taint, to say nothing of the other vices, he observed, seemed characteristic of them all. This is an unpleasant subject, but having already said so much of the infection of the Army, of which Hitler was at once the foundling and the chosen instrument, with this horrible vice, I think it as well to emphasize the truth of the writer's observations. For it may well be that in it is to be found one clue to the other pathological aspects of the Nazi movement, in particular the sadistic fury which, confined at first within the domestic circle of the concentration camps in Germany, have been wreaked upon Russia, Serbia, Poland, and other countries under the twin yoke of the German armies and the Gestapo. A British consular officer, of whom I saw a good deal when I was serving in

[117] *Verschwörer* (Conspirators), *a contribution to the history and sociology of the German National Socialist secret organizations*, by E. J. Gumbel (Vienna, 1924), at p. 216. The fact that this work had to be published outside Germany, i.e. in Austria, is significant.

Germany, Mr. Smallbones, in a report on the treatment of German nationals in German concentration camps has remarked, with considerable acuteness, that 'the explanation of this sadistic cruelty may be that sexual perversion and, in particular, homo-sexuality, are very prevalent in Germany.' [118] As I have observed elsewhere in this chapter, this 'mass sexual perversion,' as Mr. Smallbones rightly calls it, of the German people was, in the opinion of one of the heads of the C.I.D. in Berlin, Herr von Treschkow, such a deeply rooted national characteristic that it was futile to entertain any hope of eradicating it or the 'hypocrisy, lying, and blackmail' which, he tells us, are almost invariably associated with it and which, therefore, he presumably regards as equally characteristic of his fellow countrymen. The reputation of the organizer of the Nazi movement, Captain Roehm, was notorious in this respect in Germany even during the early years of the movement when I was serving there. It was only when Hitler found Roehm's political rivalry inconvenient, and decided to murder him, that he affected to discover in this boon companion and political bed-fellow, as in all the other victims of the massacre of June 1934, vicious habits which had long been known to every one else. With edifying unction the Führer suddenly claimed the murder of his rivals as a sacrifice offered up on the altar of social purity. After that bloody episode, Hitler appeared to lose all interest in such lustrations except when he wanted to discredit the Catholic Church by staging mass-trials of Catholic priests and accusing them of a vice which is, as a matter of fact, as shocking to a Catholic as it is venial to a Nazi. It is not less shocking to the Jews,[119] whom Hitler affected to treat as the source of all the moral pollution of Germany. But as an instrument for the blackmail of their opponents the Nazis found in the imputation of this vice, to which they themselves were so addicted, an invaluable political instrument. To the innocent the preferment by the Public Prosecutor of such a charge was, of course, always intimidating. And so it was, although to an infinitely less extent and in a different way,

[118] 'Paper concerning the Treatment of German Nationals in Germany,' issued by the British Government as a 'command' paper in 1939 (Cmd. 6120), at p. 20.

[119] Herr Gumbel in his book, already cited, points out that any question of the practice of this vice by the Jews in Germany may be 'ruled out' (ausgeschlossen), Verschwörer, at p. 217.

LIEUTENANT-GENERAL SIR G. M. W. MACDONOGH

BRIGADIER-GENERAL J. H. MORGAN

to the guilty. For it is a curious paradox, running through the whole of Police Commissioner von Treschkow's book that, according to him, this nasty vice was and is in Germany at one and the same time the secret of political success, if practiced discreetly, and the ruin of the practitioner if, in practicing it, he is indiscreet. 'In an earlier age,' he tells us, 'a man who wished to advance his career had to be a freemason or the gallant courtier of influential ladies, but to-day it is more practical (*praktisch*) in Germany to have homo-sexual tastes, or to affect to have them.' [120] At the same time, he suggests, such practices have their dangers as they lend themselves so easily to blackmail, publicity being attended not, indeed, so much by shame as by ridicule.

So much for Hitler's claim to have cleansed Germany from vice. The reader can judge for himself, from the evidence of authoritative German writers on finance and fiscal policy whom I have cited so abundantly in this chapter, whether his claim to have delivered Germany from the economic distress induced, as he would have it, by the burden of 'reparations' is any better founded. As I have pointed out, the financial disorganization of Germany after the war and, with it, the dishonesty, fraud, distress, and corruption accompanying it, had their roots in the fiscal policy of the German Government itself during the years 1914-18. Paradoxically enough, it was not the reparations imposed on Germany by the Treaty of Versailles but the reparations the German Government and the High Command so confidently hoped and expected to extort from their enemies which started Germany on its 'rake's progress' of inflation. Nor was the unemployment which Hitler affected to have cured, together with its resulting distress, any more attributable to the Treaty of Versailles. As for the 'cure' itself, it was nothing more, and nothing better, than a rest-cure for the restoration of the German Army. For quite a long time, indeed right down to September 1939, many people in our own country were quite bewitched by what they regarded as the marvelous achievements of the Nazi régime in solving a problem we ourselves had failed to solve, namely, the problem of unemployment. Even as late as December 1941,[121] Hitler affected to regard the war he had planned from the moment he came into power as a rude and

---

[120] Treschkow, *Von Fürsten und anderen Sterblichen* (Berlin, 1922), at p. 191.
[121] See his New Year speech in *The Times* of 1 January 1942.

unwelcome interruption of a cherished dream of his to give social and industrial stability to Germany in the arts of peace. As a matter of fact, the whole of his social and industrial program during the years 1933-9 was nothing but a closely integrated preparation for war, camouflaged as a holy crusade of 'social reconstruction.' *Wiederaufbau* as it was enticingly called. A writer, Major von Collenberg, in the official organ of the German Ministry of War, let the cat out of the bag as early as the year 1936 when he pointed out that it was *the rearmament of Germany* which had 'solved the unemployment question.' [122] Unfortunately for us, few people in this country were in the habit of reading the *Militärwissenschaftliche Rundschau* or we should never have had so many admirers among us of Hitler's work of 'reconstruction,' or so many apostles of 'appeasement.' As early as 1935, as I discovered for myself on a visit to Germany in September of that year, the great armament factories were working night and day in triple shifts, but, on my return to England, I could find no one who would believe me.[123] The whole of Hitler's work of 'reconstruction' was, in fact, borrowed from the archives of the German General Staff. It was an appropriation, and an extension, of a program of Ludendorff's during the last war, which he had failed to put into execution owing to the opposition of the Reichstag, a program for harnessing to the mills of war every man, woman, and child from the age of 15 to 60 by a Bill for the conscription of labor under the name of the Auxiliary Service Law, or *Vaterlandhilfsdienstgesetz*.[124]

And so with much else besides. From Ludendorff, his patron, Hitler, unquestionably, learned that his first moves, on his accession to power, must be the destruction of the party system represented by the Reichstag and the dissolution of the Trade Unions, the two

[122] In an article *Die Erneuerung der allgemeinen Wehrpflicht* ('The Restoration of Universal Military Service') in the *Militärwissenschaftliche Rundschau* (1936), vol. i, at p. 145.

[123] I disclosed these facts at the time to an audience at Chatham House at the suggestion of my friend the late Lord Lloyd, who had asked me to attend and 'support' him at an address he was to deliver on 'The Need for the Rearmament of Great Britain.' The curious reader, if such there be, will find the report of my speech in *International Affairs*, published by the Royal Institute of International Affairs (1936), vol. xv, No. 1, at pp. 74-7.

[124] As to Ludendorff's plans, see his *Kriegführung und Politik*, at pp. 121, etc., and his *Kriegserinnerungen*, at pp. 259, etc.

institutions to which Ludendorff always ascribed, alike in speech and in writing,[125] the frustration of the ideas of the German High Command and the loss of the war. Having achieved this at the outset in 1933, Hitler proceeded to put into operation *in time of peace* all the military plans for industrial conscription and economic mobilization which the German High Command had failed to carry through in time of war. Some of these plans, most notably the plans for an *Allgemeine Wirtschaftspflicht*, or universal economic service, had already, in part, been unobtrusively put into operation by the so-called Republican Government as early as 1923 at the instance of the Reichswehr High Command, to whom that Government could refuse nothing, and put into operation under the very nose of our Control Commission. Not that we did not know all about them or failed to report them.[126] Others, such as the reintroduction of conscription under the mask of 'Compulsory Physical Training' for all youths of 'military' age, had been taken out of their pigeon-holes in the Reichswehrministerium and actually submitted to the Reichstag in the form of draft bills as early as 1922, but had been hurriedly withdrawn when our Control Commission had insisted on their withdrawal. And so with the plan of a *Reichs-polizei*, the germ of the future Gestapo, which we also knocked on the head. But by the time of Hitler's accession to power, there was no longer an 'Inter-allied' Control Commission in Berlin to report upon the true character and significance of German legislation. The Commission had been hustled off the scene, its work still undone, in January 1927, as the price exacted by Stresemann for the ill-fated 'Pact' of Locarno. Its withdrawal was one of the unwritten conditions of that stupendous confidence-trick. With the withdrawal of the Commission one of the two securities invaluable, if only as a *poste d'observation*, to the peace of Europe was, as Foch remarked to me at the time, surrendered. The other security was, of course, the 'demilitarization' of the Rhineland. With the premature withdrawal of our troops of

---

[125] In conversation with myself Ludendorff returned again and again to this theme as though it were an obsession of his. Parliamentary Government, he insisted, was a thing for which Germans had no use. As to his writings see the works mentioned in the preceding footnote.

[126] A summary of them was published as early as October 1924, in the article by the present writer in the *Quarterly Review* under the title of 'The Disarmament of Germany and After.'

occupation, that also was foredoomed. Thenceforth the moribund
Republic, as it came more and more under the influence of such
Ministers as Schleicher and Papen, was free to put into operation,
more or less furtively at first, all the plans in the pigeon-holes of the
Reichswehrministerium for the restoration and renewal of Germany's
military might. Indeed Stresemann himself had already lent a hand in
that direction when the ink was barely dry on the Pact of Locarno.[127]
With Hitler's accession to power, there was thus no real break in the
continuity of German policy. New and upstart men, *novi homines*,
appeared on the scene, but their ultimate aims were not intrinsically
different from those of the men whom they replaced, except that
they were in a greater hurry to realize them. New words for old
plans were coined in order to give Hitler's policy an appearance of
originality, but the imprint of these words meant no more, if no less,
than the impression of a new monarch's image on a coinage already
in circulation. It was merely a new issue of an old currency. *Gleichschaltung* became a word to conjure with in the Nazi vocabulary,
but the 'co-ordination' which it represented was already in process
of achievement. There was indeed another and more sinister reason
for the new political vocabulary of the Nazi régime than the investi-
ture of Hitler with the spurious prestige of the creator of a New
Order. It was to mask the true character and objective of the plans
he borrowed from his predecessors while he speeded them up. Speed
them up he certainly did and in that sense, if in no other, his advent
to power was indeed a revolution, that sort of revolution in which,
in the classical diagnosis of Thucydides, 'frantic energy becomes the
true quality of a man.' *Gleichschaltung* was, in fact, an essay in the
art of camouflage, the exploitation of a political term to conceal a
military objective. Hitler's 'co-ordinated State' was merely the mobilized State of Ludendorff's dreams and the Reichswehrministerium's plans under a new and disarming name. To those of us who
had served on the Disarmament Commission it was simply amazing
how, from the year 1933 right down to 1936, and indeed later, Hitler
disarmed nearly all criticisms, quieted all fears, and put to sleep all
suspicions in England by masking one military measure after an-

---

[127] In the financial year following the signature of the Pact, the German Army
Estimates went up by leaps and bounds—see the analysis by the present writer
in *The Times* of 15 November 1928.

other with the drapery of social reform. Under the specious names of the 'Youth Movement,' 'Community of Labor,' 'Reclamation,' 'Co-ordination,' and the like, he put into operation, in time of peace, a program of 'social reconstruction' whose sole aim was the destruction of society all over Europe.

As with measures, so with men. The difference between Hitler and his predecessors is not so great as it appears. General Schleicher, Herr Stresemann, and even Ebert, the Socialist and first President of the Weimar Republic, were not so far removed from him in their ideas as English observers have imagined. Schleicher never made any secret of the fact that his objective was the restoration of the old Army. Stresemann, before he took office, had inscribed on the program of the Deutsche Volkspartei the 'abolition,' *die Aufhebung,* of the Treaty of Versailles and his substitution on his accession to power of the catchword 'fulfillment,' *Erfüllung,* was merely a disguise for those sapping and mining operations against the Treaty which he initiated with the demand for the withdrawal of the Control Commission and the evacuation of the Rhineland. Ebert himself prepared the way for the legend of an 'undefeated' Germany, tricked into capitulation by the Fourteen Points of President Wilson, by greeting the returning regiments of the Guard on 11 December 1918, at the portals of the Brandenburger Thor with the words, 'I salute you on your return *undefeated* from the field of battle.' It was Ebert and that catspaw of the Reichswehr Herr Gessler, the 'Republican' Minister of Defense, who aided and abetted all the devices of General von Seeckt to defeat our work of disarmament. After all, had not Ebert and his party, the Social Democrats, been *particeps criminis* in the great crime of 1914 when, with only two dissentient votes, that party, over a hundred strong in the Reichstag, declared themselves by the mouth of their chairman, Haase, in favor of the war, to be greeted by the rest of the Reichstag, as a German chronicler tells us, 'with tempestuous applause.' [128] The identity of outlook of these

---

[128] Thus Dr. Jakob Reindl in his history of the German Trade Union movement, *Die deutsche Gewerkschaftsbewegung* (1922), at p. 249. The writer adds that 'the whole of the Socialist Press' (*die gesammte sozialdemokratische Parteipresse*) associated itself with this declaration. See also the article, 'Sozialdemokratie' in the *Politisches Handwörterbuch* (1923), vol. ii, at p. 625, where it is recorded that the Socialist Party in the Reichstag voted 'solidly' (*geschlossen*)

three men, Ebert, Stresemann, and Schleicher and, indeed, of *all* their colleagues in their determination to recover, either by guile or by force, everything Germany had lost in 1919 was obscured from foreign eyes by the violence of their domestic differences and the fury of their party feuds, but the identity was there. The homogeneity so suddenly imparted to Germany by Hitler on his accession to power seemed to untutored minds in our own country as miraculous as Newton's synthesis of the colors of the spectrum but was, in fact, capable of the same explanation. Like the primary colors, the complexion of each political party in Germany blended into the complexion of its neighbor. A respect for force and a belief in guile were common to them all and Hitler gave them both. Hitler was, in fact, a Messiah who, so far as Germany herself was concerned, came not to destroy but to fulfill. The Weimar Revolution, such as it was, had spent its force long before he appeared on the scene, and of the counter-Revolution he was the creature, not the creator. The secret of his hold over the German people was not that his mind was, or ever had been, original, but that it was the opposite. Any one deeply versed in German history would have no difficulty in showing, by way of an exegetical commentary, that every page of *Mein Kampf* is second-hand. Its author is the greatest plagiarist who ever presumed to be ambitious. All his ideas were already current coin in Germany. He did, it is true, debase the currency but, in so doing, he did but increase its circulation among the vulgar. Again and again he speaks the language of Treitschke and Mommsen, of Bismarck and Bülow and Kaiser Wilhelm the Second, in their most aggressive moments except that he speaks it with a plebeian accent. The notorious passage in *Mein Kampf* about the necessity of 'a final reckoning' (*eine endgultige Auseinandersetzung*) with France, ending in her 'annihilation' (*Vernichtung*), which one of Hitler's many apologists in this country obligingly explained away, in the columns of *The Times* on Hitler's accession to power, as a kind of eccentricity of his political adolescence, merely blurted out what had been whispered by Kaiser Wilhelm to Bismarck in the Chancellery of Berlin some

for the war. Not till mid-January 1917, when hopes of victory began to fade, did a small fraction, less than one-fourth, of the Party dissociate itself from this belligerent policy.

thirty-six years earlier [129] and had been common talk for years among the German General Staff. So with his speeches. When in October 1939 he proclaimed 'the extermination' of the Poles, he was merely lisping the authentic language of that first German Chancellor of the First Reich who declared, 'Let us strike the Poles until they lose the courage to live.' [130]

It is true enough that neither Bismarck, nor Bülow who shared his sentiments, ever attempted, brutal and oppressive though their administration of the Polish Provinces was, actually to exterminate the Poles as Hitler attempted, with too much success, to do during the Second World War. So long as Polish territory was incorporated in Prussia, it was neither practicable nor profitable to exterminate millions of frugal and industrious German subjects of Polish blood, subjects who, moreover, provided Germany with two Army Corps of admittedly excellent soldiers. But the Prussian lust to exterminate was there and the moment Germany was compelled, by the Treaty of Versailles, to cede her Polish Provinces to the restored State of Poland, the fate of the Polish people was sealed. As we shall see later,[131] it was painfully obvious as early as 1920 to those of us who served in East Prussia that, if Germany was not effectively disarmed, the days of the Polish people were numbered. So much I wrote to Mr. Wickham Steed at the time. The secular hatred of the Prussians for the Poles, a sentiment I encountered everywhere east of the Elbe in the most malignant form, was inflamed, by the cession, to fever heat. Thenceforth, it was as certain as anything could be that when the German attack upon Poland came, as come it did, like a thief in the night, little less than the extermination of the Polish people would satisfy the military hierarchy. There were 'too many'

[129] See the remarkable letter, dated 10 May 1888, of the Kaiser to Bismarck, first made public in 1919 in Bismarck's posthumous volume of reminiscences, in which he expresses his regret that Germany failed in 1871 to 'really annihilate' (*wirklich zu vernichten*) France altogether as a Great Power—*Erinnerung und Gedanke* (Stuttgart, 1919), at p. 137.

[130] Thus Bismarck in a letter written to his sister Malvina in 1861. His words were *Haut doch die Polen dass sie am Leben verzagen,* of which the words in the text above are a literal translation. The text of the letter is to be found quoted in *Bismarck und die Osten* (Leipzig, 1934), by Hans Rothfels, at p. 45: 'I have every sympathy for them,' added Bismarck sardonically, 'but we cannot do other than exterminate (*ausrotten*) them.'

[131] In a second volume to be published later.

Poles in any case Ludendorff hinted some twenty-two years ago in a sinister sentence.[132] The lethal ferocity of the Prussian Officers' Corps towards the Poles was traditional, and here again Hitler owed their support of him to his having identified himself with their unchanging sentiments. As it was in 1848, so it was under Hitler. In that year the 'Prussian' Poles, having joined hands with the Liberal elements in Berlin in a transient movement for constitutional reform, secured a promise from the King of Prussia, temporarily frightened, to grant them a form of 'Home Rule.' But they had reckoned without the Prussian Officers' Corps and the General Officer, von Colomb, in command of the local garrisons. Von Colomb, 'with the willing support of the German burghers and soldiers, found it easy,' in the words of an eminent English historian, Professor Alison Phillips, 'to create pretexts for using force,' in order to make short work of the promised autonomy. What followed reads like an exact and faithful description of the German campaign in Poland in 1939 and the horrors which have followed it:

'Reports of horrible cruelties perpetrated by the Poles,' says a contemporary English eyewitness, 'were industriously circulated by the German newspapers.' Imaginary outrages led to very real retaliation and the war—if it can be called so—that followed assumed the ferocious character with which the world is now (in 1915) all too familiar. 'All the rules and usages of civilized warfare were totally disregarded by the Prussians. Prisoners were slaughtered; the wounded in the hospitals were killed, and in one instance burned to death, the hospital having been set on fire by the victorious party. Other prisoners were marked with vitriol on hands and ears.' [133]

There were some Germans, but not many, in those days, adds the historian, who, horrified by these outrages, anxiously asked themselves 'whether this ferocious desire for murder, which delights in exterminating and tormenting even a conquered enemy, is inherent in the nature of the German.' [134] Adolf Hitler has supplied the answer. It was the secret of his ascendancy.

So too with Hitler animosity against the Jews. The only difference between him and his more reputable predecessors is not in

[132] See his *Kriegführung und Politik*, at pp. 286-7.
[133] *Poland* (London, 1915), by Professor Alison Phillips, at p. 188.
[134] *Ibid.*, at p. 188.

his sentiments, much less in his arguments, but in the violence and vulgarity with which he expressed them. His argument that the Jews are a disintegrating influence, destructive of German national sentiment, is as old as Treitschke, who set the fashion of making the Jews a kind of 'whipping-boy' for all the congenital weaknesses of the German character. That accomplished cynic, Prince von Bülow, is almost the only German 'Nationalist' of eminence, with the exception of Bismarck, to admit frankly that 'the national sentiment of the German is weak' [135] in any case, if, indeed, it ever existed at all except in the most negative form, namely a consuming hatred of all neighboring peoples in whom the sentiment is as strong as in the Germans it is feeble. What Treitschke said a succeeding generation repeated, accusing the Jews of seducing German democracy with 'international' sentiments and of inducing in the strangely responsive German mind an enervating feeling of inferiority to other nations.[136] Hence, according to General von der Goltz, the unfortunate national habit, which, he tells us, the German eagle has, of fouling its own nest (Selbstbeschmutzung), a habit of which the pages of Mein Kampf present so many examples as to suggest the singular paradox that, of all Germans, the most susceptible to the Jewish 'poison' was Hitler himself. Ludendorff went a step farther than von der Goltz, and in one summary sentence provided Hitler with every count in his indictment against the Jews.[137] Even Hitler's defamation of the Jews as the cause of Germany's defeat in the last war was not original. It was advanced by Ludendorff [138] before Hitler was ever heard of. In all this racial intemperance the ex-corporal was a docile, not to say servile, pupil of his military superiors, the German Officers' Corps, of which one of its most distinguished members boasts, in a glowing tribute to the Corps as the nursery of German national sentiment, that it was its peculiar privilege to have 'defended' (gewehrt) the German Army against the 'penetration' of Jewish blood.[139] This it

[135] Memoirs (English translation), vol. i, p. 556.

[136] Thus General von der Goltz in Meine Sendung in Finnland (Leipzig, 1920), at pp. 16, 17, and 39.

[137] 'Judah led to the complete destruction of the physical, economic, and spiritual strength of the (German) people'—Ludendorff in Der totale Krieg, at p. 13.

[138] In his Kriegführung und Politik, at p. 190, etc.

[139] General von Rabenau in Hans von Seeckt, at p. 62

succeeded in doing by a boycott so effective that, as we have seen in
an earlier chapter, no Jew could ever hope to obtain a commission in
the standing Army or even, except in time of war, in the Reserve.[140]

To the German mind the greatest of all 'blood-sports' is war or,
failing war, that violence which found its outlet in the old Army in
'beating up' conscripts and, with our demobilization of that Army,
in the beating-up of one's fellow citizens. Hitler was like a huntsman
who gratified this apparently ineradicable instinct by showing the
populace sport. His first step was to organize the rival packs. He did
not create the 'Storm-troopers.' He merely took them over from the
innumerable 'toughs,' Ehrhardt, Rossbach, Aulock, and their confederates, with whose illicit 'para-military' formations our Commission had failed to deal effectively owing to the supineness, in fact the
cowardice, of the Republican Government. In other words he disciplined the terrorism (*Terrorismus*) inherent in the German people
and made it an instrument for his own ends, first 'blooding' it by
letting it loose upon the defenseless Jews at home before unleashing
it in all its carnal horror abroad upon the peoples of Poland, Czechoslovakia, Serbia, and Russia. The reader who recalls the historical
review, which I have attempted earlier in this chapter, of the
periodical convulsions of the *Furor Teutonicus* throughout German
history will now, I think, understand my observation that Hitler
came, so far as Germany herself was concerned, not to destroy but
to fulfill. He fulfilled her abiding passion for destruction.

Of this passion for destruction the German Army has always been
the instrument, even as it has been the unabashed teacher and ex-

---

[140] Paradoxically enough, some German Jews, in spite of this invidious treatment by the German Gentiles, were quite as 'pan-German' and anti-English,
both during the war and after it, as the Prussian *Herren-volk*, if one may believe Lord D'Abernon. Thus at p. 236 of Volume I of his *Reminiscences* he
quotes a statement made to him in 1921 by Dr. Weizmann that 'Jewish intellectuals were the most overbearing and aggressive Prussians of the whole
crowd.' And in September 1923 Lord D'Abernon had come to the conclusion
that 'the leading Jews' in Germany under the Weimar Republic were 'definitely
and temperamentally anti-British,' and that he found little or no evidence of
any 'gratitude' among them 'for the relatively generous attitude of England
towards their race as shown in the absence of anti-Semitism in England'—*op. cit.*
Vol. II, at pp. 251, etc. If this be true, it may account for what Lord Vansittart,
in a remarkable letter in the *Manchester Guardian* of 6 June 1944, has described
as a certain agitation in our own country during the war by some of the German
refugees amongst us in favor of 'a peace acceptable to Germany.'

ponent. The English reader will do well to realize, what indeed very few Englishmen appear ever to have understood, for the very idea is repugnant to our national character, that the German military hierarchy, which begat Hitler, idolizes war as a kind of religious cult with all the hieratic fervor of a privileged caste. The more destructive war becomes, the more do they idolize it. Writing in the *Hamburger Nachrichten* in 1914, shortly after the destruction of Louvain by the fury of the German troops, Major General von Disfurth glorified the act, and other acts like it, in the following terms:

We have nothing to explain, even as we have nothing to excuse. If all the monuments and all the pictures in the world be destroyed, the fact is of no importance so long as their destruction facilitates a German victory. War is war and should be conducted with the utmost harshness. The rudest stone that marks the tomb of a German grenadier is more glorious and more to be worshipped than all the cathedrals of Europe. We are called barbarians. I hope that in this war we have done our best to earn the epithet.[141]

This idolatry of war does not stop short of exalting it as an end in itself. It is, indeed, a remarkable fact that later generations of the accredited spokesmen of the German General Staff have gone far beyond Clausewitz's famous saying that 'War is an instrument of policy.' They have indoctrinated the nation with the creed that war should be not merely a means but an end. From Moltke onwards there has been a progressive accentuation, by each generation of German military writers, of this doctrine of destruction, as it may be called. Writing barely three years before the latest catastrophe burst upon the civilized world, and no doubt coldly envisaging it even as he had coldly prepared for it, the creator of the Reichswehr, General von Seeckt, delivered himself as follows: 'War is the highest summit of human achievement; it is the natural, *the final stage* in the historical development of humanity.' [142] In other words the goal of civilization is the destruction of civilization. Ludendorff, the advocate of war in its most destructive form, and, as such, once again the source of Hitler's inspiration, even as he was also the originator of 'unrestricted'

141 Reprinted in *La Menace allemande* (1934), by André Chevrillon, at p. 256.
142 'Der Krieg ist die hochste Steigerung der menschlicher Leistung; es ist die natürliche letzte Entwickelungstufe in der Geschichte der Menschheit.'–von Seeckt in the *Militärwissenschaftliche Rundschau*, vol. i (1936), p. 2.

submarine warfare in all its cruelty, and of the notorious Belgian deportations in all their misery, did not hesitate, after all the horrors of the last war, to proclaim his impenitent adherence to the pagan belief of Moltke in the 'divinity' (*Gottesweltordnung*) of war.[143] And what Moltke wrote, in so many words, was that 'Want and misery, disease, suffering and war'—the conjunction of words speaks for itself—'are all permanent elements in man's destiny and nature,' to be welcomed as indispensable to his 'development' (*Entwickelung*).[144] Development in what direction? one may ask. The only answer to be elicited from Moltke's writings and those of all his tribe is a periodical return to nature red in tooth and claw. In language which is common form among all German military writers he declares that the more inhuman a soldier, the more humane he is.[145] To the English reader such thinking, if thought it can be called, must seem to be the symptom of a mind diseased, but every German military writer on war and its conduct uses exactly the same language, as indeed does nearly every German jurist of the last two generations. These doctrines have, in fact, worked such a corruption in the soul of Germany as to prostitute the German conception of law itself to the lust of conquest. Nothing is more remarkable, or more sinister, in the history of German thought than the ferocious casuistry with which the modern school of German lawyers, 'barrack-room' lawyers as they have been aptly called, set themselves during the last forty years to sap and mine the very foundations of international law by their invention of the doctrine of 'necessity' and its application to the laws of war—the necessity which knows no law. The teaching of the German schools of history ever since the year 1871 has been exactly the same. It is, indeed, a curious fact, and suggestive of much, that the deterioration

---

[143] Ludendorff in *Kriegführung und Politik* (1922), at p. 333.

[144] 'Noth und Elend, Krankheit, Leiden und Krieg sind nur einmal gegebene Elemente in Gottes Weltordnung.'—Moltke's letter to Lueder published by the latter in Holtzendorff's *Handbuch des Völkerrechts*, vol. iv, p. 210.

[145] 'Man mag es beklagen aber es bleibt richtig dass die Humanität im Kriege dem Kriege nachstehen muss and dass die energische Kriegführung zugleich die humanste ist.'—*Ibid*. It is clear from the context that 'energetic' (*energisch*) as used by Moltke is a euphemism for ruthless. This sinister paradox is to be found in German military text-books as early as Clausewitz and as late as the manual issued by the German General Staff, *Kriegsbrauch im Land-Kriege* (1913), which instructs the German officer that in ruthlessness, in time of war, lies 'the only true humanity.' See above, Chapter VII.

in German thought and culture is directly traceable to the years 1866-71 when, as the result of two great wars of aggression, 'Germany' ceased to be a geographical expression for a group of virtually independent States and became a political one. Germany, as a nation, was conceived in war and brought forth in aggression. German nationalism thus became identified with war and has never got rid of this congenital taint. A kind of obsession that, having achieved union by war, Germany could only preserve it and 'keep fit' politically by a periodical return to war took possession of the German mind. Writing in 1889, von der Goltz, surveying the military triumphs of 1866 and 1871, expressed himself satisfied that Germany was now strong, united, and with every guarantee of a long existence. There was, indeed, at the time he wrote not a cloud upon Germany's political horizon. But, he concludes, there has *got* to be another war. There remains 'a final struggle' which is 'unavoidable.' [146] Why, or where, or for what cause, he does not pretend to know. But here is the authentic source of Hitler's obsession of 'a final reckoning.' A generation later, another German general, Beseler, gives expression to the same baneful creed in language quite curiously anticipatory of the Nazi slogan of *Lebensraum*. Writing in 1913, he glorified the German Army as the indispensable instrument of German policy to secure for the nation more and yet more 'space, light and air' (*Raum, Luft und Licht*).[147] It is the language of claustrophobia, and who shall say it is wholly sane?

This excursion of mine into Hitler's intellectual antecedents, both political and military, has seemed to me the more necessary, as no one in our own country appears ever to have undertaken it. Hence the delusion, still dangerously persistent among us, that the Hitler movement was a kind of aberration in German history, that somewhere or other, in some yet undiscovered 'No Man's Land,' there is another Germany distinct and distinguishable from 'Hitlerite Germany,' and that the German people are not fellow principals in Hitler's crimes against civilization, that they are not even accessories either before the fact or after the fact. This strange delusion, which could never have been entertained by any one deeply versed in the political and

[146] *Germany in Arms* (1889), English translation, at pp. 390, etc.
[147] Beseler in *Die allgemeine Wehrpflicht* (1913), p. 40.

military history of Germany, still less by any one who had lived and served in Germany during the years following upon the last war, found its supreme expression in a leading article in a great English newspaper in September 1939, on the day of the declaration of war. It found expression in the strange caption, 'One Man's War.' The war, the article suggested, was a little private affair of Hitler's, a kind of game of 'patience' played by the Führer, with the German people looking on at once intimidated and dissentient if not aghast. Such a comfortable delusion can only be compared with the naïve observation of that unfortunate English ambassador in Berlin who expressed his profound conviction that there would have been no war if Marshal von Blomberg had not married his typist.

As in his preparations for war, so in his conduct of it, Hitler was the docile pupil of the German Army, or, to be more precise, of that German Officers' Corps whose enduring authority and unique prerogatives have been described in an earlier chapter of this book. The appalling outrages committed by the German armies, and their camp-followers the Gestapo, nearly all of whose leaders were time-expired N.C.O.s of the Army itself, in Poland, in Czechoslovakia, in Russia, in Serbia and elsewhere, owe nothing whatsoever to Hitler in originality or even in inspiration. They were almost identical in character with those committed in the last war except that they were still more atrocious, even as their sphere of operation was more extensive. Between the holocaust of tens of thousands of inoffensive civilians at Tournai and Rotterdam, Warsaw and Belgrade by bombing during the past war and the massacres of thousands of men, women, and children by shooting at Dinant, Aerschot, Louvain, and Andenne during the First World War there is nothing to choose either in the barbarity of the act or the cold brutality of the motive. At both times the German High Command was merely applying the policy taught in the Kriegsakademie in Berlin by Clausewitz a century ago and indoctrinated by each generation of his successors, namely the 'necessity' of 'terrorism' (*Terrorismus*) in war in order to break 'the spirit' (*der Geist*) of the civilian population. At both times, as each country was invaded in turn, the prospective victim was subjected to a campaign of calumny in order that the zest of the troops in the field and the applause of those at home for the butcheries would be stimulated to fever-heat. Goebbels was no more original than Hitler in this respect—he was merely putting into operation the counsel of the Emperor Wilhelm that it is no good Germany going to war unless the Government can first be sure of mobilizing the latent ferocity of her people.[148] And so with the enslavement of prisoners of war for military purposes, the wholesale deportations for purposes of forced labor in Germany of the inhabitants of occupied countries, and much besides. Here too the difference is merely one of degree. In the First World War, according to German testimony itself, 'thousands' of the victims of these flagrant violations of international law 'died;'[149] in the second war the number who perished of such barbarities is beyond computation. Ludendorff slew, in cold blood, his thousands, Hitler his tens of thousands. That is the only difference. The policy itself is the same.[150]

In an article in a German military periodical, in the year 1936, General von Seeckt, in describing the ideal 'Führer,' laid it down that he must learn above all 'to be hard' (*hart zu sein*) and ruthless.[151] His article apparently gave Hitler his cue, for Hitler boasted, in one of his most violent utterances during the war, that he was 'the hardest man in German history.' That speech was, no doubt, intended to assure, or reassure, the German Army as to his credentials for the assumption of the Supreme Command. For of such stuff is the German officer made, a kind of intellectual savage, educated without being refined, in whose vocabulary one will look in vain for the word Pity, for he knows it not and has no use for it. It is related of Wellington, a humane man as British officers invariably are, that he once said there was only one spectacle almost as sad as that of a battle lost. It was that of a battle won. But of Clausewitz,[152] the idol of the German

[148] See the remarkable letter of the Emperor to Bismarck published in the latter's posthumous volume, *Erinnerung und Gedanke* (1919), at p. 139, in which he points out that before undertaking yet another war, he and the Chancellor must be quite sure that the conditions are such that 'the indispensable German ferocity' (*der so nothwendige furor Teutonicus*) can be aroused.

[149] Thus Dr. Sinzheimer in the Report of the Reichstag Committee of Inquiry, translated in *German Official Documents Relating to the World War* (Carnegie Endowment), vol. ii, p. 415.

[150] *Ibid.*, p. 412, where Bethmann-Hollweg admitted, under cross-examination, that the deportations were the deliberate policy of Ludendorff and the German High Command 'for the purpose of carrying out the Hindenburg program.'

[151] The *Militärwissenschaftliche Rundschau* (1936), vol. i, pp. 2 and 285.

[152] In his brilliant and suggestive little book, *Ordeal by Battle*, the most distinguished military writer of his generation, Captain Cyril Falls, says of Clause-

General Staff, we are proudly told by one of his disciples that the sight of the bloodiest battlefield left him not only quite unmoved but exultant. The bloodier a battle, 'the more,' held Clausewitz, should one 'esteem war' (*die Kriege mehr wurdigen*).[153] When Wellington was asked whether the news of the death of Napoleon in exile moved him to compassion, he replied, after a moment of reflection, 'No! *For he loved war.*' The German officer loves war. Wherefore it is not enough to make an end of the Nazi régime. We should, now the day of reckoning has come, end the German Army altogether. For between the Nazi régime, with all its abominations, and the German Army, there is nothing to choose. The former is the off-spring of the latter, and what the German Army begat once it may beget again. The fundamental mistake of the 'Disarmament' articles of the Treaty of Versailles was that they left Germany with any Army at all. The attempt of those Articles to enforce the transformation of the old Army into something different neglected to take account of the fact that a new Army entirely officered, as it was and was bound to be, by the German Officers' Corps of the Army which it was intended to displace would merely preserve the traditions of its predecessor in all their aggressive brutality and thereby only serve to 'mark time' for a military revival. If, as has been observed earlier in this chapter, every nation gets the Army it deserves, Germany as a nation is past praying for and the only way to secure the peace of Europe is to 'break up' the nation which, *ex hypothesi,* is responsible for such a scourge of humanity. If, on the other hand, the German nation does not deserve the Army, which, indeed, has chastised her with whips in preparing to chastise her neighbors with scorpions, if the German people have, in fact, been not the corruptors of the Army but corrupted by it, then the only hope for the regeneration of Germany as a nation is to deliver her from this yoke of iron. There is no escape from this dilemma. We must either abolish the German nation or abolish the German Army. It is, indeed, more than possible

witz, whom he justly acclaims as 'the great philosopher of war,' that subsequent generations of German military thinkers have been 'permeated and soaked in the thought of Clausewitz.' Captain Falls is, of course, speaking of his teaching of strategy and tactics. But the observation is applicable also in another and a sinister sense. For Clausewitz, a typical Prussian, indoctrinated the same German military thinkers with the 'philosophy' of brutality.

[153] General von Kuhl in *Der deutsche Generalstab* (Berlin, 1920), at p. 229.

that by the abolition of the German Army the political problem presented by the difficulty of breaking up any nation, if, indeed, Germany *is* a nation with any claim to be regarded as such, would solve itself. The German 'nation' is the artificial creation of the Prussian Army—how artificial a student of Bismarck's policy can discover for himself. It was conceived in war and brought forth in aggression, as I have previously remarked, and all within the short space of five years, barely two generations ago. The strong 'particularist' tendencies, always latent in the different German peoples of the north and south, the east and west, and only kept in check by the Army, would, with the total disappearance of that Army, most certainly reassert themselves and 'Germany' would, in all probability, 'break up' of its own accord.

APPENDIX I

A letter from Lieut.-General Sir George Macdonogh [1] to the Author.

LENSBURY CLUB,

TEDDINGTON

18 *May* 1942

MY DEAR MORGAN,

I was very pleased to get your letter of the 12th instant, and would have replied to it earlier, had I not been away on a short holiday.

I am very glad to hear that you are about to publish your book, for it would be a thousand pities if all your knowledge and experience were not available when peace comes.

I don't suppose any one knows as much as you do of the subterfuges employed by the Germans to evade the terms of the Versailles Treaty, and it is essential that those who will have to deal with the disarmament of Germany after this war should start their work with all your experience behind them instead of having to learn it for themselves.

I would be delighted to write a Foreword to your book if you wish me to do so, but as I have not much experience of that sort of thing I shall be glad if you will let me know the sort of thing you want me to say and the length. Unfortunately all my papers, with all my other goods and chattels, have been destroyed by enemy action, so I am no longer able to look up the reports you used to send me when I was A.G., and which I have treasured ever since.

Hoping all goes well with you,

Yours sincerely,

G. M. W. MACDONOGH

[1] A poignant interest attaches to this letter and to the Preface to *Assize of Arms* which was the sequel to it. A few days later, General Macdonogh died suddenly.

317

APPENDIX II a

PRÉFACE BY GENERAL WEYGAND

Au début d'une conférence sur 'Le Problème de la Sécurité,' que le Brigadier-Général Morgan faisait le 4 mai 1925 au Centre Européen de la Dotation Carnegie, il disait: 'Après six ans de discussion, nous ne sommes pas plus avancés à cet égard que nous ne l'étions en 1919. Nous sommes censés être en état de paix, je suis plutôt enclin à dire que nous vivons sous un régime d'armistice. . . Tout le monde parle de désarmement, personne ne le met en pratique.'

En dehors de la sûreté de jugement dont ces paroles apportaient le témoignage, il est important d'en retenir que le désarmement ne constitue que l'une des parties d'un ensemble, le problème de la Sécurité. C'est dans ce cadre qu'il faut le considérer pour en bien juger.

Trouver la sécurité dans la victoire, tel était le plus fervent désir des nations qui avaient été contraintes à la guerre, et, en particulier, de la France, quatre fois envahie en un siècle. Comment le Traité de Versailles assura-t-il cette sécurité? La promesse d'une convention particulière qui devait garantir à l'Europe Occidentale, dans l'éventualité d'une nouvelle aggression, le concours des Etats-Unis et de l'Angleterre avait amené la France à renoncer aux garanties substantielles réclamées par le Maréchal Foch. Par là cette convention devenait pour la sécurité la pièce maîtresse du système. On sait que le recul des Etats-Unis n'en permit point la ratification. Dès lors, sans parler du pacte de la Société des Nations, dont l'influence ne pouvait se faire sentir que beaucoup plus tard dans le règlement des problèmes de sécurité, il ne restait plus en face de l'Allemagne, debout dans son unité renforcée au milieu des ruines, que l'occupation des Pays Rhénans et le désarmement, sur lequel, fatalement, on reporta des espoirs accrus en raison des déceptions subies d'autre part.

C'était peu raisonnable. Au cours de la Conférence de la Paix, le Maréchal Foch avait fortement exprimé l'opinion qu'il était vain de prétendre désarmer véritablement un pays comme l'Allemagne, grand non seulement par le chiffre de sa population et la puissance de son industrie, mais plus encore par la ferveur de son sentiment national et par sa volonté de relèvement. Il avait rappelé l'exemple de Napoléon qui y avait échoué après une victoire cependant bien complète puisqu'elle l'avait conduit à Berlin et avait porté ses soldats jusqu'aux rives de la mer Baltique.

Le Commandant des Armées Alliées ne fut pas écouté. Il ne le fut pas davantage lorsqu'il affirma dangereux d'imposer à un pays, aussi essentiellement militaire dans ses préférences et ses méthodes, une armée de 100,000 gradés servant douze ans, plutôt qu'une armée d'effectifs doubles ne demeurant qu'un an sous les drapeaux.

Une fois les clauses militaires arrêtées dans cet esprit, le Maréchal Foch, placé par les Gouvernements à la tête d'un Comité Militaire Allié, fut chargé de veiller à leur exécution. Il se donna tout entier à cette mission. Son premier acte fut l'organisation de la Commission Militaire Interalliée de Contrôle, qui devait exiger de l'Allemagne l'observation de ces clauses militaires, tâche difficile entre toutes. Le Brigadier-Général Morgan comptait au nombre des Membres de la Délégation Britannique dans cette Commission. Il y occupait le poste de Deputy Adjutant-General. Bien qu'il ne fut pas un 'soldat de carrière,' il avait si rapidement acquis une telle compétence dans les questions militaires, qu'il fut choisi, de préférence à tout autre, comme Vice-President de l'importante Commission des Effectifs. Il eut de ce chef à s'occuper de toutes les questions concernant l'organisation de l'Armée Allemande. A une grande finesse, il joignait une connaissance parfaite de la langue, du tempérament et des coutumes des Allemands. Il put ainsi dévoiler la véritable portée de certains documents règlementaires ou législatifs allemands, et les faire redresser, conformément aux stipulations du Traité. L'inspection des Commandements de Wehrkreis, lui donna l'occasion de visiter à l'improviste un grand nombre d'unités de la Reichswehr dans leurs casernes. Sa perspicacité était bien connue. J'ai entendu raconter—je ne sais si le fait est exact, mais, selon un vieux proverbe français: 'On ne prête qu'aux riches'—que, mis en éveil par l'inégalité d'un plafond, il y avait fait découvrir un lot important d'armes. Son expérience lui avait permis d'établir un 'plan de contrôle' si bien conçu qu'il fut adopté comme guide des Officiers Britanniques et Français appelés à servir dans la Commission.

Comme le plus ancien des Officiers Britanniques, il était chargé de tenir directement le War Office au courant de la réorganisation de la Reichswehr. Dans ses rapports il fit preuve à la fois d'une clairvoyance aiguë, car il avait pénétré jusqu'au fond les intentions allemandes, et aussi d'une grande indépendance d'esprit et de caractère, car il eut le courage d'exposer et de défendre ses opinions même s'il savait ne rencontrer que peu de personnes pour les partager.

La Commission Militaire Interalliée de Contrôle a rempli, aussi bien qu'il était possible de le faire, une tâche ingrate et d'une difficulté considérable. Il est permis de penser que l'activité du Brigadier-Général Morgan a été pour une grande part dans cet heureux résultat, et qu'il a rendu à son pays et aux Alliés un très grand service, en leur faisant connaître la vérité. C'était bien l'avis du Maréchal Foch, qui avait de son travail en Allemagne une si haute opinion qu'en 1927, peu de temps après la cessation des fonctions de la Commission de Contrôle, il écrivit au Ministre des Affaires Etrangères, M. Aristide Briand, une lettre personelle pour lui demander la nomination du Général Morgan au grade de Commandeur de la Légion d'Honneur. [1] Le Maréchal avait vivement re-

---

[1] A copy of Marshal Foch's letter to M. Briand was attached to General Weygand's 'Préface,' and is therefore reproduced below, as an integral part of it.

gretté que la règle fixée par le Gouvernement Britannique de ne pas accepter de décorations étrangères pour les membres des commissions interalliées n'ait pas permis de faire aboutir cette proposition.

Ce livre n'est pas sa première publication sur l'important sujet du désarmement. Un article paru en 1924 dans la *Quarterly Review* a soulevé un très vif intérêt en Grande Bretagne et sur le continent. L'ouvrage qu'il publie aujourd'hui est l'histoire complète du désarmement de l'Allemagne. L'auteur expose dans le détail la lutte pied à pied qui eut lieu pendant des années entre des défenseurs du Traité et les représentants du Gouvernement allemand. D'un côté, une activité, une vigilance, une patience jamais lassées, pour tâcher de n'être pas dupes; de l'autre, un mélange de volonté, de rudesse, d'ingénuosité et de souplesse pour sauver tout ce qui pouvait l'être de l'organisation et des traditions militaires du passé, et, en tout cas, rendre aussi prompte que possible, dès que le masque pourrait tomber, la résurrection de l'armée allemande.

Ce temps est arrivé. L'armée allemande est redevenue la plus forte armée du monde. Tous les efforts de la Commission de Contrôle décrite par le Brigadier-Général Morgan auraient donc été inutiles? Oui, sans aucun doute, si l'on se refusait à tirer des faits accomplis depuis l'armistice les conclusions qui s'imposent. Mais, si l'on veut reconnaître les erreurs commises à la base, c'est-à-dire dans le Traité de Paix et dans la façon dont il fut appliqué, et comprendre que la limitation des armements ne pouvait donner qu'une sécurité illusoire, il est encore temps de les réparer.

WEYGAND

62 RUE DE COURCELLES,
PARIS
1938

APPENDIX II *b*

COMITÉ MILITAIRE ALLIÉ DE VERSAILLES

LE MARÉCHAL FOCH,
PRÉSIDENT DU COMITÉ MILITAIRE ALLIÉ DE VERSAILLES,
À M. LE MINISTRE DES AFFAIRES ÉTRANGÈRES,
À PARIS

23 *novembre* 1927

MONSIEUR LE MINISTRE,

Pendant que la Commission Militaire Interalliée de Contrôle en Allemagne était en fonction, vous avez bien voulu, à diverses reprises, accorder des distinctions dans l'Ordre de la Légion d'Honneur à des officiers alliés appartenant à la dite Commission.

Parmi ceux-ci ne figurait aucun officier anglais, par suite de la décision prise par le Gouvernement Britannique de ne plus donner son assentiment à l'attribution de décorations étrangères proposées pour ses ressortissants.

La Délégation anglaise à la C.M.I.C. comptait, alors, parmi ses membres un officier, le Général Morgan, qui au sein de la Commission, nous a rendu les plus grands services.

Ses conclusions ne négligent aucun des intérêts des Alliés.

Croyant savoir que le Gouvernement Britannique ne s'oppose plus formellement à ce que ses nationaux reçoivent des ordres étrangers, j'ai l'honneur de vous demander de bien vouloir proposer le Général Morgan pour le grade de Commandeur de la Légion d'Honneur.

(Signé) FOCH

APPENDIX II c

Letter from General Weygand to the Author.

62, RUE DE COURCELLES,
PARIS

Paris, le 13 Janvier 1938.

MON CHER GÉNÉRAL,

Je vous envoie ci-joint le texte que j'ai préparé pour la préface que vous m'avez fait l'honneur et l'amitié de me demander.

Je n'ai pas craint de m'élever du particulier au général, et je pense que cela n'est pas pour vous déplaire. Naturellement si vous jugiez nécessaire de me demander quelques modifications ou complément, je vous prie de la faire tout simplement, puisque je tiens, avant tout, à vous être agréable.

Veuillez, mon cher Général, agréer l'expression de mes sentiments de très distinguée considération.

Bien sincèrement votre,

(Sgd.) WEYGAND

APPENDIX II d

GENERAL WEYGAND'S PREFACE

(ENGLISH TRANSLATION)

IN A LECTURE [1] on 'The Problem of Security' which Brigadier-General Morgan delivered on 4 May 1925, to the 'European Centre' of the Carnegie Endowment (in Paris), he began by saying: 'After six years of discussion of this problem, we are no nearer a solution than we were in 1918. We are supposed to be living in a state of peace but I should be more inclined to call it an armistice. . . . Every one is talking of disarmament, no one is practicing it.'

Quite apart from the sureness of judgment to which these words bear witness, it is important to bear in mind their implication that disarmament

[1] The text of the lecture in question was subsequently published in the *Revue des deux Mondes* for June 1925.

constitutes only one part of a larger whole: the problem of Security. It is
within this setting that one must look at it in order to judge it.

To find security in victory—this was the most fervent desire of the
nations who had found themselves compelled to go to war, particularly
France which had been four times invaded within a single century. How
did the Treaty of Versailles assure this security? The promise of a special
convention to guarantee to Western Europe, in the event of a new attack,
the co-operation of the United States and of England had led to the
renunciation by France of the substantial guarantees demanded by Marshal Foch. As a result, this convention became the keystone of the arch of
the system of security. As we all know, the United States recoiled from
this proposal, and its ratification became in consequence of that recoil,
impossible. From that moment, apart from the Covenant of the League of
Nations, the influence of which in the regulation of problems of security
could only make itself felt much later, there was left to face Germany,
now on her feet again and her unity strengthened after her catastrophe,
nothing but the Occupation of the Rhineland and the Disarmament of
Germany herself—a disarmament on which we fell back all the more
hopefully but all too fatally in consequence of our disillusionment as to
the guarantee which had failed us.

The hope was ill-founded. During the Peace Conference Marshal Foch
had forcibly expressed the opinion that it was a vain aspiration to attempt
to disarm effectively a country such a Germany, great as she was not only
owing to the size of her population, and the potentialities of her industry
but even more so in virtue of the fervor of her national sentiment and her
determination to rise again. He had recalled the example of Napoleon
who failed in that direction after a victory lacking nothing in complete-
ness seeing that it had ended in his occupying Berlin and in carrying his
soldiers to the shores of the Baltic.

The Commander-in-Chief of the Armies of the Allies was not listened
to. Nor did he receive any more favorable hearing when he insisted that
it was dangerous to impose upon a country, so essentially military in its
predilections and its methods, an army of 100,000 with the men serving
for twelve years instead of an army of double that number of effectives
and serving only a year with the colors.

The military clauses of the Treaty having been thus decided, Marshal
Foch was appointed by the Allied Governments to be head of an Inter-
Allied Military Committee for the purpose and entrusted with the execution of them. He devoted all his energies to this task. His first act was to
organize the Inter-Allied Military Commission of Control which was to
exact from Germany the observance of these military clauses, a task of
supreme difficulty. Brigadier-General Morgan was one of the members
of the British Delegation of this Commission. He held the appointment of
Deputy Adjutant-General. Although he was not a professional soldier, he
had become so competent an authority on military questions that he was

chosen, in preference to every one else, to be Vice-President of the important Sub-Commission for Effectives. He had, in the exercise of this responsibility, to occupy himself with every question concerning the organization of the German Army. In addition to great acuteness, he was endowed with a perfect knowledge of the language, the temperament and the customs of the German people. As a result, he was able to unveil the true significance of certain legislative and administrative documents emanating from the German Government and to secure their amendment in conformity with the stipulations of the Treaty. His inspections of the Army Territorial Commands, the *Wehrkreise*, gave him the chance to pay surprise visits to a large number of units of the Reichswehr in barracks. His perspicacity was famous. I have heard tell—I do not know if the story is true but, to quote an old French proverb: 'One lends only to the rich'—that, put on his guard by the unevenness of a ceiling in a barracks, he discovered an important cache of arms on the spot. His experiences enabled him to draft a 'Plan of Control' so well-conceived that it was adopted as a Manual for the use of the British and French officers serving on the Commission.

As the most senior of the British officers, he was charged with the duty of reporting direct to the War Office on the reorganization of the Reichswehr. In his reports he gave proof of an acute clear-sightedness, for he had penetrated to the very heart of the intentions of the German High Command. So also he gave proof of a great independence of mind and character, for he had the courage to expound and to defend his opinions even when he knew he could find few people prepared to share them.

The Inter-Allied Military Commission of Control fulfilled, as far as it was possible to fulfill it, a none too pleasant task and one of very great difficulty. One may well believe that Brigadier-General Morgan's activities played a great part in this fortunate result, and that he rendered a very great service to his own country and to the Allies in acquainting them with the truth. This was very much the view of Marshal Foch who held such a high opinion of his work in Germany that in 1927, shortly after the functions of the Commission had come to an end, the Marshal wrote to the Minister of Foreign Affairs, M. Aristide Briand, a personal letter asking him to nominate General Morgan to the rank of Commander of the Legion of Honor.[2] The Marshal learned with keen regret that a rule

[2] The Marshal wrote as follows:

THE ALLIED MILITARY COMMITTEE OF VERSAILLES
23 *November* 1927

MARSHAL FOCH, PRESIDENT OF THE ALLIED MILITARY COMMITTEE TO THE MINISTER FOR FOREIGN AFFAIRS.

SIR,
At the time when the Inter-Allied Military Commission of Control was still functioning in Germany, you have been desirous, on several occasions, to grant

formulated by the British Government forbidding the acceptance of foreign decorations by members of the Inter-Allied Commissions made it impossible to give effect to his recommendation.

The present book is not the first publication of the author's on the important subject of Disarmament. An article by General Morgan which appeared in 1924 in the *Quarterly Review*—'The Disarmament of Germany and After'—excited a very lively interest at the time in Great Britain and on the continent.[3] The work which he now gives to the public is the complete history of the disarmament of Germany. Its author discloses in detail the struggle, step by step, which took place for years between the defenders of the Treaty and the representatives of the German Government. On the one side an activity, a vigilance, an unwearied patience in the endeavor to avoid being duped—on the other a combination of determination, rough behavior, ingenuity and suppleness to conserve everything that could possibly be saved of the organization and the military traditions of the past and, in any case, to prepare the way at the earliest possible moment for the resurrection of the German Army as soon as the time came to throw off the mask.

That time has now arrived. The German Army has become once again the strongest army in the world. Must one then say that all the efforts of the Commission of Control described by Brigadier-General Morgan have been utterly futile? Yes, unquestionably, if one refuses to draw from all that has happened since the Armistice conclusions from which there is no escape. But if one is willing to recognize the mistakes made at the outset, in other words in the drafting of the Treaty of Peace and in the methods adopted in applying it, and to understand that the mere limitation of armaments can only give an illusory kind of security, there is yet time to repair these mistakes.

WEYGAND

PARIS
January 1938.

---

distinctions in the Order of the Legion of Honor to Allied Officers belonging to the aforesaid Commission.

Among these no English Officer found a place because of the decision of the British Government to withhold its assent in future, to the conferment of foreign decorations put forward in the case of persons coming within its jurisdiction.

The British Delegation of the Control Commission included at that time, among its members an officer, General Morgan, who in the very heart of the Commission has rendered us the greatest services. The conclusions at which he arrived were in the interests of all the Allies.

Being under the impression that the British Government is no longer formally opposed to the acceptance by its subjects of foreign decorations, I have the honor to ask you to be good enough to propose the name of General Morgan for appointment to the rank of Commander of the Legion of Honor.

FOCH

[3] See Appendix v, below.

APPENDIX III

A letter from the Chief of the Imperial General Staff, General (later Field Marshal) the late Sir John Dill, K.C.B., to the Author.

WAR OFFICE,

WHITEHALL,

LONDON, S.W.1

23 October 1941

MY DEAR MORGAN,

Thank you so much for your letter and the typescript of your character-study of a German General in the chapter 'Ausser Dienst,' which I find of absorbing interest.

I regard it as important that the Public should be educated *now* so as to prevent, as far as possible, a repetition of the mistakes we made after the last war.

Sir Malcolm Robertson's remarks in his letter [1] to you on German Military Methods are only too true. In conversation with von Brauchitsch, shortly before this war, he told me that the only thing that mattered in war was that one should employ *any and every means* at one's disposal in order to bring it to a successful conclusion as quickly as possible.

Yours very sincerely,

(*Signed*) J. G. DILL

BRIGADIER-GENERAL J. H. MORGAN, K.C., D.L.,

    PRIORY COTTAGE,

        WOOTTON BASSETT,

           WILTS

[1] For the letter in question, see p. 262, above, in this book.

APPENDIX IV

[Extracts from the evidence taken by a British Committee appointed in 1918 to inquire into the treatment of British Prisoners of War by the Armed Forces of Germany] [1]

I

WORKING CAMPS ON THE EASTERN FRONT

THE 2,000 PRISONERS, divided into four parties of 500 each, known as E.K.1, E.K.2, E.K.3, and E.K.4, were collected from different camps in Germany and sent to Angersee, Mitau, Wainoden, and Libau respectively, the whole being under the command of Landwehr Captain Förster. From these central camps the men were sent to a number of working camps, where, generally speaking, the accommodation was of the roughest description, the water supply bad or non-existent, the sanitary arrangements very inferior, and various forms of cruel and brutal punishment were inflicted.

Five hundred British prisoners of war were placed under the most terrible conditions within range of the Russian guns. The horrors of the march to the camp are established beyond doubt, and the conditions of life, during the rigour of a Russian winter, constituted torture of the most deliberate kind; the accommodation and treatment were bad, the men were not allowed to receive any parcels and were deliberately starved; there was no water supply; suffering from frostbites was general, and many of the men died as the result of the treatment. That this was a deliberate act on the part of the Higher Command is shown both by the threat of reprisals, which the German Government made, and by the fact that the 500 British prisoners were paraded at the camp and a notice was read out to them stating that they were to be subjected to reprisals, that they would have to work in the firing-line, get bad treatment, bad food, bad accommodation, and that thirty-six of them had to die. At the end of April 1917, there were only 77 men left in the camp out of 500 driven there in February (23 having died and 400 having been sent to hospital) and of these 47 were certified by the doctor to be unfit to leave their beds.

One hundred of the R.N.D. were sent to Libau, where a further 400 were sent, and they were 'officially informed' that they would be sent to the trenches between Riga and Mitau, and remain within the artillery zone by way of reprisal. On 25 February these 500 men were forced to march 35 kilometres up the frozen River Aa, often through snowdrifts

---

[1] These extracts are here made public for the first time.

326

knee-deep. Sledges followed to pick up the men who broke down from exhaustion, while the escort of Uhlans drove the stragglers on with lances and whips. Those who fell were robbed of their kit and property. Two sergeants, Gibbs and West (specially mentioned by Captain Draudt as good men), remonstrated, and were singled out for special ill-treatment on the march. 'They were brought in by transport later, but through their lying in the snow they were frost-bitten in the hands and feet.'

The horrors of this march are established beyond doubt by numerous witnesses.

Arrived at their destination, the men were kept waiting outside a 'cavalry tent built on the ice of a marsh by the river. It had wire beds on three racks, the bottom one being about one foot from the ground, so that the weight of a man's body weighed it down till he was lying on the snow or the ice.'

There was no water supply, such water as there was was obtained by melting ice from the river or by digging down into the marsh, where filthy polluted water was obtained. Most of the men had no wash during the whole time they were there.

The treatment was bad. Were it not established beyond the possibility of doubt, the story would be unbelievable. Men were driven out to work —breaking ice on the rivers, felling trees, making and repairing trenches under fire—when they could hardly stand and had to be supported by their comrades to and from their work. One man died while being carried home; another, who had fallen exhausted on his way back to camp, was shot at point-blank range by the sentry; while a third man, who did not turn out quick enough one morning, was first abused and then attacked with a bayonet by the *sanitater* (medical orderly)—further investigation disclosed the fact that his sleep was the sleep of death—he had been dead some hours, frozen in his bunk. The only punishment was tying to the post outside the tent for two hours, after the men returned from work, under conditions hardly differing from crucifixion. Sergt.-Major Gibb, of the Gordon Highlanders, relates how, having been urged by the Interpreter to write home how they were being treated, he eventually did so: 'Next day,' he proceeds, 'I got the letter back marked "Five days strong arrest." After being hard at work from 6 a.m. to 6 p.m., I was tied to the pole from 7 p.m. during 36 degrees of frost.' This is corroborated by several witnesses.

That this treatment was deliberate and inspired by higher authority is evident from the fact that Sergt.-Major Gibb says they obtained a copy of the orders from the guard, which stated 'that no mercy was to be shown to us; *we were men who had, every one of us, assisted in stopping the Kaiser's army from going to Paris;* and they were to think of their comrades who were being brutally treated in France. Any soldier failing to carry out these orders was to be severely punished.'

The result of this inhuman treatment was what might have been expected. At the end of April 1917, there were 77 men left in the camp out of the 500 driven there in February.

II

WORKING CAMPS ON THE WESTERN FRONT

The complaints in the evidence may roughly be divided into the following heads:

(1) Very bad accommodation; (2) Very bad sanitation; (3) Underfeeding; (4) Overwork; (5) Brutality; (6) Compulsory work on war material; (7) Exposure to shell-fire.

There is a mass of evidence in support of these complaints. The most flagrant instance of the first two, and to some extent of the third, is, on the present evidence, Fort Macdonald. In the spring, 1917, there were a number of British prisoners confined at this place. A witness (1833) states that when he was there, for ten days, there were from 101 to 135 men in an underground cell which was only ventilated by one window; the only sanitary provision was a tub in the cell itself. During his stay there he was allowed to wash twice. The prisoners were not allowed out of the cell before the seventh day. The diet consisted of one-sixth of a loaf for each man, a drink of 'coffee' substitute at 7 a.m., thin soup of mangelwurzel and a little barley at midday and again at 6 p.m. The men by the seventh day were so weak from confinement and want of food that they staggered as they walked, and three collapsed and were removed in an ambulance. Another (2282) who was at the Fort somewhat earlier for ten days, states that 180 of them were in a cell of 25 feet by 15 feet, which had one window 6 feet by 4 feet; nobody was allowed to wash; for latrines there was a barrel in the cell, which was cleaned out once every four days; the cell was full of vermin; each prisoner had one slice of bread, soup once a day and coffee once a day. Another witness (2330), who was at the Fort for three days towards the end of April 1917, says that there were from 120 to 130 prisoners in a cell 40 feet by 15 feet on the first floor; there was no water and no means of washing; the sanitary arrangements consisted of large tubs, which were used for defecating and urinating. They were never emptied or removed while he was there, and overflowed on to the floors of the cell. He comments on the offensiveness of the stench. Rations consisted of a 3-lb. black loaf for every ten men; at midday some thin vegetable soup and at 6 p.m. acorn tea. The men were so enfeebled that at the next place to which they went 26 out of a working party broke down.

Sergeant Humphries who was at the Fort from 25th April to the end of June 1917, states that there were 350 men in a room 18 feet by 40 feet, which was filthy and full of lice. He also refers to the tub for sanitary purposes, which in his time appears to have been emptied twice a day, but it overflowed at night on to the floor, where the men had to sleep. The place was so hot that the men could not wear their clothes. He described the men as gasping for water and giving anything they had for a mouthful, while the guards, he says, laughed and jeered at the men for crying for water. They were only allowed a quarter of a loaf, what he describes as poisonous coffee, and a drop of barley-water or 'saurcraw.' The men, he states, were beaten and kicked for not moving quickly when they emerged from this prison. Witness (2361) is shorter, but to a similar effect.

Making all allowances, it appears to me [2] that Fort Macdonald is a case of shocking barbarity, and that all persons responsible for the inhuman system which prevailed there ought to be punished.

There is much evidence of the rough and brutal treatment of the prisoners by their guards, and sometimes by officers, for example, Vendhuile, where the prisoners were beaten with rifle-butts as an inducement to work (2033); Le Porer, where the prisoners are said to have been knocked down by the guards on the slightest pretext (1840); Cantin, where the guards are said to have kicked the prisoners and beaten them with sticks and rifle-butts (2033-4); Sailly, where the same things happened (2002-5); Villers, where a Prussian Guard (56th Regt.) was guilty of similar conduct (2175); Ecoust, where the sentries and an officer or under-officer in command of the camp and a sergeant-major under him, both of the 56th Regt. VII, are accused of the brutal use of rifle-butts and sticks (2175); Rethel, where men who lagged or fell down from exhaustion or illness were kicked or beaten (2206); Maretz, where a man was shot dead by a guard because he stooped down to pick up a packet of cigarettes, and where two men who attempted to escape had to stand to attention for about twelve hours a day for a fortnight and were so beaten by the Commandant and Feldwebel that they had to go into hospital (2283 and 2290); Ramecourt, where the men who were lying on the ground from exhaustion were kicked and beaten to make them resume work (2298-2300), and the guards beat the men with sticks (2351), and men who fell from exhaustion on the march were prodded with rifle-butts and kicked (2530); Amifontaine, where the guards often kicked and beat the prisoners (2298-2300); Peronne, where the same kind of thing happened, and one man was knocked senseless and died three days after; complaint was made unavailingly to the officers.

In many cases the accommodation for the prisoners was decidedly bad; and in some cases the sanitation was execrable; for instance, at Le Porer (June to August 1917) 150 prisoners were placed in a machine shop, 50 feet by 30 feet, with a sunk tub in the room for all sanitary purposes. During the first month it does not seem to have been emptied more than once, and as the windows were all boarded up, and the tub overflowed on

[2] Wherever the first person singular is used in this document it represents the Chairman of the Committee who was a distinguished Judge of the High Court. —J.H.M.

to the floor, the place 'stank horribly.' After the first month, two large bowls were substituted, but as these were not regularly emptied, 'the stench was horrible.' Taking this in conjunction with the insufficient food, it is not surprising to hear that many of the men suffered from boils and dysentery (1840). At Vendhuile the men were lodged in temporary wooden buildings, with no blankets, and the men in the top tier of beds were covered with hoar frost in the winter of 1916-17. A complaint is made of the smell from a hole in the ground, which was the latrine. Here, too, most of the men suffered from dysentery; the men were full of vermin, and about 18 died. In this, as in other cases, the prisoners' boots were taken away (2191 and 2033). At Villers (March 1918), there were 1,000 prisoners, and one hut which held 100, the rest sleeping in holes in the ground; the place was swarming with vermin; there were no sanitary arrangements and no means of washing (2175).

The evidence contains constant references to the misery which the prisoners suffered from the combined effects of starvation and exhaustion; for instance, they were glad to pick up nettles, potato peelings, and dandelions (Amifontaines, July 1918 (2298-2300); at Cantin and Sailly, April and May 1918), 'They were like wild animals with hunger and scrambled for any piece of food which might be lying about' (2002-4). They were punished for accepting gifts of food from civilians,[3] and civilians were prevented from supplying food to them, and were punished, and even fired at, if they tried to supplement the prisoners' ration. (See, for instance, Meurchin [1833], Denain [2521 and Private Beaton]; see also instances given in Cd. 8988). There are constant complaints that the men were forced to work when, in their condition of weakness, it was sheer cruelty to expect it. No parcels reached these men who were working behind the lines on the Western Front, and it was therefore impossible for them to supplement their insufficient rations in this way.

[3] The civilians in question were the French inhabitants of the occupied territories.—J.H.M.

APPENDIX V

THE STATE OF GERMAN 'DISARMAMENT' IN JANUARY 1925[1]

INTRODUCTORY NOTE

THE OBJECT of this letter to Professor Foerster and the circumstances under which it was written will be sufficiently apparent from the text of the letter itself. But it may be as well to disclose here something of the extraordinary 'reign of terror,' as the Berlin correspondent of the *Daily Mail* truly described it,[2] prevailing in 'republican' Germany at the time the letter was written. Professor Foerster attempted, in the first instance, to get it published in Berlin in the well-known 'Radical' newspaper, the *Vossische Zeitung*. After having accepted it, the Editor of this famous newspaper suddenly took fright and informed Professor Foerster he could not publish it. The Editor of another great 'republican' newspaper, the *Frankfurter Zeitung*, on being then approached by Professor Foerster, also fought shy of it. The fears of these newspapers were well-founded. A German workman in Rhenish Westphalia who, at a public meeting, read extracts from the letter, on its appearance in *Die Menschheit*, was immediately arrested on a charge of 'high treason' for so doing and sentenced to a long term of penal servitude.[3] At this time Stresemann and his colleagues were governing Germany with an iron hand, exercising dictatorial powers which, as the *Vorwärts* observed, involved the 'total suspension of freedom of opinion' (*Meinungsfreiheit*). At the same time Stresemann was declaring in the Reichstag and to audiences of foreign journalists that the disarmament of Germany was 'complete,' protesting to the Allied Governments against any further exercise of control, repeatedly demanding the withdrawal of the Control Commission, and even declaring that there had never been any obstruction to the

[1] *Die Menschheit* was a weekly German journal of Liberal views in the best sense of the word, edited by Professor Foerster, the sale of which in unoccupied Germany was in consequence proscribed by the Republican Government with the result that it had to seek refuge in the occupied territory at Wiesbaden.

[2] The *Daily Mail*, 27 February 1925, whose correspondent also observed that 'no great newspaper in Germany dared to publish' this correspondence with Professor Foerster 'for fear of proceedings for treason,' adding, 'There are 1,200 trials for treason pending, but they are held up because they will throw light on the military preparations that are going on.'

[3] The *Daily Mail*, 3 March 1925.

work of the Control Commission.[4] The publication of the letter to Professor Foerster had, however, one curious result. In consequence, perhaps, of the catechism attempted by the writer, in the form of 'a few plain questions' addressed to the German Government, the violent attacks of the Nationalist Press on the writer and his article in the *Quarterly Review* ceased as suddenly as they had begun.

(*An appeal to the German people, written at the request of the Editor of* Die Menschheit *and published in its issue of 20 February 1925, at* Wiesbaden.)

DEAR PROFESSOR FOERSTER,

Your telegraphic message of 11 January, which arrived when I was absent in Paris, was duly forwarded to me by Mr. Wickham Steed in accordance with your request. Your letter of 19 January, addressed directly to me, together with your article in *Die Menschheit*, has also duly reached its destination. In his covering letter to me, Mr. Steed has laid emphasis upon the high repute which your name carries with it as that of a German scholar of distinction and a Prussian Liberal whose conscientiousness is only equalled by his courage. Such assurances, though welcome, were unnecessary. The tone of your letter, the temper of your article, are alike such as would convince the most sceptical that they are the authentic utterances of one who is deeply concerned at the danger not only to Europe but to Germany herself, and all that is best in her, of the revival of German militarism—the utterances, indeed, of one who is a true lover of his country, who, neither loving his country at the expense of her neighbours, nor loving her neighbours at the expense of herself, avoids the two extremes of an aggressive Militarism and of a defenceless 'Pacifism,' confederates as only extremes can be.

Amid the emotional disorders induced in all the belligerent peoples by the war, it is rare, indeed, to find a patriotism so pure; yet the only hope of peace is to be found in its diffusion. It is by the reciprocity of such sentiments between us, and by that alone, that a lasting peace is to be sought and assured, and a bridge thrown across that chasm, deep beyond all sounding, of dreadful memories, of devastating asperities and of unforgettable regrets which separates your people and mine, and which estranges the German nation from our Allies.

I should be, indeed, dull and insensible if I did not respond, to the best of my ability, to an appeal so moving in its sincerity, so urgent in its apprehension. And if my response should in some things fall short of

[4] See Stresemann's papers published after his death under the title of *Stresemann: Vermachtnis*, Vol. III, at pp. 302, 315, 446, 619, 622, and 624. As will be shown in the second volume of *Assize of Arms*, to be published later, the whole of his statements on the subject of Disarmament were untrue.

what you ask, I would pray you to remember that the task you set me is a delicate one. In your telegram you invite me to reply to the attacks upon myself in the Nationalist Press; in your letter you ask me to bring 'the facts' as to the disarmament of Germany before the German people, urging on me, at the same time, the imperative necessity of their publication by the Allied Governments or on their behalf. Of these two (or three) tasks, the first is both the easiest and the least important. I reserve it for the end of this letter. Only let me say in this place that I have read the Press extracts which you sent me. Here I will say only that I should have been more impressed by these maledictions if, instead of attacking my reputation, these journals had attempted to refute my article.[5] This they have neither done nor sought to do. Yet the refutation of my statements of fact, if materials existed for their refutation, should surely have been easy, for the relations between the Reichswehrministerium (the German War Office) and the Nationalist Press have always been friendly and sometimes intimate; I have often observed in the latter a prophetic anticipation of the arguments addressed to us on the Commission by the former.

As to the publication of the reports of the Commission, I think it unlikely that they will be published; and there are reasons against publication which seem to me to be sound. Many of these reports, especially those which deal with the transformation of munition factories, would be unintelligible to the general public, for the question of what is and what is not 'special plant' in Krupp's gun-shops; the question whether the manufacture of celluloid at Reinsdorf without solvent, under conditions perilously similar to the manufacture of nitro-glycerin powder, is a 'commercial proposition'; the question whether the proportion of machines to men in the 'Deutsche Werke' [6] is or is not inconsistent with the arguments put forward by the German Government for the retention of these great arsenals in the interests of the unemployed—these questions, and others like them, are too technical for a plebiscite of uneducated opinion. Other reports, indeed, even the simplest of them, would be misleading without the publication of the earlier reports for the years 1920-22, for they are but the continuation of a serial story interrupted by the occupation of the Ruhr. Even the reports as to 'effectives' and police would be unintelligible without an exposé of army organization, and many of them would merely serve to disclose our methods of investigation and proof, with the inevitable result of stimulating the Reichswehrministerium to fresh efforts in the art of camouflage. 'Disarmament' is, believe me, not a simple subject.

[5] i.e. the article, 'The Disarmament of Germany and After,' published in the preceding October issue of the *Quarterly Review*.

[6] The *Deutsche Werke* were the State armament factories, corresponding to our own Woolwich Arsenal, as distinct from the privately owned armament factories such as Krupp's. See below at p. 337.

334 APPENDIX

You will, therefore, understand that it is my duty to be both reticent and discreet, and that what I now say by no means exhausts all that there is to say. Let me try at the outset to put the Allied case in the form of a few plain questions. And first, why does the Reichswehrministerium persistently refuse to disclose its recruiting returns,[7] the *Mannschafts-untersuchungslisten* and *Annahmebücher*. These alone can establish how many men are being called up for training by the Reichsheer (Regular Army), and for five years they have been constantly refused. Why? The reason given is that they are a matter of 'inner service' which does not concern us. But is it no concern of ours to know how many men are being trained to the use of arms? And if there is nothing to conceal, why conceal it?

In the second place, why do the Reichswehrministerium refuse to show us those registers of armament production [8] which were snatched away from under our very noses at Spandau? They alone can serve to establish what your gun establishment was in 1919 and what it is now.

Thirdly, why does the Reichswehrministerium insist on retaining control of the vast network of military establishments, artillery depots, munition depots, supply depots, remount depots, which supplied the needs of the old army and are altogether superfluous for the needs, the legitimate needs, of the new? Your Government does not expropriate these, it does not alienate them, it does not sell them, it does not convert them— it either leaves them idle or lets them to a tenant at will. They are available for the mobilization of a vast army at almost any moment. A trifling sum of 200,000 gold marks is all that appears in the *Reichshaushaltsplan* (the Budget) for 1924 as the proceeds of a sale of some two or three of them. What is being done with all the rest?

Fourthly, why is the Reichswehrministerium paying no less than twenty-two officers in the Ministry alone, without taking account of the generals in the Wehrkreis commands, as lieutenant-generals and major-generals? Why are all the captains in the Reichsheer with over two years' service drawing the pay of majors, and the oberleutnants drawing the pay of captains? Why is your Government maintaining an establishment of *Feldwebels* and *Unteroffiziers* [9] sufficient for an army thrice, and more than thrice, the Treaty strength? To a soldier there is only one explana-

---

[7] The returns in question were Army registers showing (1) the number of men presenting themselves for medical examination with a view to enlistment in the Reichswehr; (2) the number of men who, after such examination, were actually attested. The German authorities, from first to last, always refused to disclose them to the Commission.

[8] These were the records kept by the Prussian Ministry of War Supply Department from 1914-19 showing the number of guns, etc., manufactured by the armament factories. The Commission was never allowed to see them.

[9] A *Feldwebel* was a sergeant-major and an *Unteroffizier* an ordinary N.C.O., i.e. a sergeant or corporal.

tion of these things and that is that this army is, and is destined to be, a cadre for expansion.

What of your 'Security Police'? The question whether they should live in barracks or out of barracks, whether they should be organized in *Hundertschaften* (centuries) or not so organized, whether every twenty men should be armed with more than one machine-gun—all these are minor questions compared with the profoundly significant fact that they are, by one statute after another, made interchangeable with the Reichsheer in pay, promotion, pensions, grades, and a dozen other things, so that the two forces match one another even as the wards of a lock match the key which fits it. Behind every Reichsheer soldier there stands, like a silhouette, a 'police official.'

As to your army expenditure—and I have studied your Budget—I will only say this: if your army is really as small as your Government says it is, then your Government is the most extravagant Government in the world; and if your Government is not extravagant, then your army is far larger than it ought to be. Your Reichsheer, in theory small in stature, projects in reality a gigantic shadow across the map of Germany, and the shadow is the greater reality of the two. That shadow is the old army. Everything that an ingenious brain could devise and a subtle intellect invent, down even to giving the companies of infantry of the new army the numbers and badges of the regiments of the old, has been done to ensure that, at a touch of a button, the new army shall expand to the full stature of its predecessor. The proofs in my possession are overwhelming.

Your Government tells us repeatedly that our work is done and that there is nothing left to find out. They tell us that the Treaty of Versailles has been loyally executed. How then do they explain the astounding paradox that every time a store of hidden arms in a factory is revealed to the Commission by a pacifist workman, the workman, if discovered, is immediately arrested and sentenced to a long term of penal servitude? There have been scores of such cases, and I am told that the unhappy German workman, who only the other day disclosed to us the great stores of arms in Berlin,[10] is the latest, but I fear he will not be the last, of the victims. If, as your Reichswehrministerium informed the Commission when disputing the necessity of an enactment by the Reichstag to abolish compulsory service, the military clauses of the Treaty 'are part of the law of Germany,' these unfortunate workmen were merely assisting in the execution of the law. If these concealments of arms are not approved by the German Government, why are the workmen who disclose them ruthlessly punished and the factory owners who conceal them allowed to go free?

To me, with my four years' experience of the work of the Commission, it seems that there was, and is, a deep and fundamental difference of view

---

[10] The stores in question were 113,000 rifles discovered by Control officers in December 1924, in the Wittenau factory.

between the Reichswehrministerium and the Control Commission. The former regarded the military clauses of the Treaty as merely an armistice, and suspensory; the latter regarded them as a Treaty, and definitive. The former thought it was our duty to make the resumption of war manufacture cheap and easy; we, on the other hand, conceived it our duty to make such resumption expensive and difficult. If the astonishing Note addressed to us by your Government on 24 April 1920 were ever published, as I hope it will be, all this would be clear beyond refutation.

Your Nationalist Press informs the world that the Control Commission, and more particularly the British section of it, are merely 'commercial spies,' that their real object is not to disarm German industry but to cripple it. Never was a charge more undeserved; never, I venture to say, was an imputation more ungenerous. If that had been our object, the first thing we should have done would be to pack the Commission with business men disguised as officers. There was not a single man of that character on the British Delegation. Even our chemical expert was unconnected with any British firm, and for a considerable time after leaving the Commission was, I am told, without employment. None of the reports on the factories has ever gone outside our War Office; even our Board of Trade has not been allowed to see them. But the charge is not only groundless, it is, as I have said, ungenerous. How ungenerous I will show by making public for the first time certain decisions of the Control Commission. Early in 1920 an officer, with great experience of munition manufacture, submitted a report to the Commission on the machinery in your munition factories—and there were 7,000 such factories. He pointed out that there was an enormous stock of machines in those factories which had been installed during the war solely for the purpose of the war; that these machines, particularly the lathes, though capable of conversion to ordinary commercial use, could easily be reconverted to a warlike use. He showed that these machines were far in excess of the normal needs of German commerce—it was the very time when your Reichswehrministerium were urging us to allow the retention with the colours of twice the number of soldiers allowed by the Treaty, on the ground that there were so many men unemployed. He insisted that all such machines in excess of the normal requirements of your commerce should be destroyed. Yet we did not destroy them. You have been left with every lathe that ever turned a shell.

Here is another example and an even more striking one. At Krupp's factory at Essen there is a great gun-shop, known as 'Shop No. 10,' which is one of the most perfectly equipped shops for the manufacture of heavy artillery in the world, unique of its kind. It was equipped—and is still equipped—with 78 big machines: heavy lathes which plane, mill, rifle, and polish heavy guns, and during the war had done nothing else. Eleven of these machines were sufficient, and more than sufficient, to manufacture the heavy guns authorized for the new German navy, but not authorized for the new German army, which is prohibited such armament by the Treaty of Versailles. For the remaining 67 machines there was no commercial use, except a temporary contract for compressed-air cylinders for the Badische-Anilin Fabrik. The continued existence of those machines was regarded as such a potential menace to peace that the Allied Naval Commission urged us to destroy them all. We did not destroy them. With no conviction that they could ever be used to meet any lasting or genuine commercial demand, we authorized the retention of 31 of them—subject to a pledge which has never been kept. For that concession also, I—who am now denounced by the whole of the Nationalist Press as one of the commercial 'spies' and an enemy of the German people—not very wisely perhaps, voted.

Yet another example is the 'Deutsche Werke,' the new name for your State arsenals, some seventeen of them, with the historic Spandau at their head. They were the most belligerent institutions in Germany; they were built for war and expanded for war; by war they were justified, and by war they were condemned. Under the terms of the Treaty every one of them was to have been closed down altogether, closed down finally, unequivocally, ruthlessly, never to resume again. We decided, and here also I was a party to the decision, to leave them open, in deference to an appeal from your Government that they might be converted to the arts of peace, our only condition being that they should be converted to genuine commercial use, their special plant destroyed, their surplus machines dispersed. But we had no sooner made one concession than another was demanded; having made a surrender of a principle we were called upon to surrender every safeguard against its abuse. We asked for the dispersal of the surplus machines, and the trade unions of Germany were officially mobilized against us. We pressed again for the dispersal, and the whole Press of Germany denounced us as bent on 'the destruction' of German industry. Never was a more spurious agitation foisted upon a credulous public. We were accused of seeking to take the bread out of the mouths of German workmen—and not more than 3,500 workmen were involved. This, too, at a time when the Reichswehrministerium were telling us that they could not compete for 12-year recruits with the demands of German employers for labour. And what was the sequel? In December 1922 the directors kept the machines and began to dismiss the men—I have a German official Note which will prove that.

Am I not right when I say that these reproaches of an intemperate harshness to German industry and trade, these accusations of a base conspiracy against German commerce, now so freely directed against us, are unjust? Do I go too far when I say they are ungenerous? Would a German Commission have been equally tender to Allied industries if the Allies had lost the war, instead of winning it? Does the German exploitation of Belgium and the occupied districts of France suggest it? Did the German Treaty with Roumania forebode it? And if every concession we make is thus abused, if every amelioration of the Treaty terms we admit is thus misrepresented, can your people be surprised if there are those among us who say, as I heard a distinguished British diplomatist say after the Treaty of Rapallo, 'There is no helping the German Government; the more you try to help them, the more they take advantage of you.' I will not endorse that sentiment—I am anxious to avoid all asperities—but I cannot think that it is wholly without justification.

As to the results of the present inspections [11] by the Commission of Control, they are secret and I must not disclose them. This only I will say: your Nationalist Press makes much of the fact that hundreds of 'visits' by our Control officers have been freely allowed by your Government for the last five months; and it cries: 'Enough! What more do the Allied Governments want?' Yes, but what kind of visits? It requires two parties to make a visit a success—one to call, the other to receive; one to ask, and the other to reply. How have our Control officers been received? The host whose visitor is received with the words, 'Not at home,' is not more inhospitable than the commanding officer of a German unit who meets all inquiries from a Control officer as we have been met with the negative formula of 'Innerer Dienst,' in other words, 'Mind your own business!' The number of visits of inspection we have made, and have had to make, is a proof not of how much we have been told but of how little. I could say much more on this point, but at the present moment the less said the better.

You have asked me to reply to the attacks of the Nationalist Press upon myself. I have read them. They could not be more ferocious if the object of them was the President of the German Republic himself, nor do I suppose that I should be any more successful than he in obtaining redress. I regret them, but I do not fear them. I regret them because, after four years' residence in Germany, I am convinced that the greatest danger, not only to the peace of Europe but to Liberal institutions and to Parliamentary Government in your own country, is the license of the Nationalist Press and the violence with which your public men are attacked by those who differ from them, a violence which often aims not only at taking away a man's character, but at depriving him of his life. Where distinguished Germans such as Erzberger, Rathenau, Ebert and a score of others have suffered thus at the hands of the Nationalist Press, where one German University professor after another has been hunted from his chair for daring to tell the truth, it is not to be expected that a foreigner should escape. But what is the pretext for all these attacks upon me? It is an article which I wrote for an English review of high reputation for sobriety and truthfulness, the *Quarterly Review* of October last,

[11] They took place in the autumn of 1924. The results of these inspections were embodied in a confidential report by the President of the Commission, General Walch, who forwarded a copy to the writer. It has never been published.

on the subject of 'The Disarmament of Germany and After.' It was no propagandist article, and it may interest my Nationalist critics, who call me a newspaper propagandist, to know that during the whole fifteen months since I resigned my position on the Commission in October 1923, I have not written a single newspaper article on this subject of any kind whatsoever, with the exception of an article which appeared in the *Morning Post* of 29 December 1924, and which was merely an elucidation of my article in the *Quarterly Review*. I have, of course, often been solicited by newspaper editors, both in England and America, to write, and I have as often refused .The offers were lucrative and I was invited to name my own price, but they had no attractions for me. I remained silent because I wished to say nothing that might prolong the occupation of the Ruhr, an occupation which, whether justified or not, I have some-times deplored. But the discussion of the 'Protocol' at Geneva brought the whole question of security and disarmament into the arena of public debate, and I could no longer remain silent. My article may have been wise or unwise; what is certain is that every statement contained in it was true. Those statements can be proved by the publication of official documents in London and in Paris. The article was read in proof before publication, and approved by two of the most distinguished generals in the British Army, both of them men of moderate views. It has now been read by Marshal Foch, and I do not think I am guilty of an indiscretion if I say that he has expressed to me his entire agreement with it.

In circumstances such as these I do not think the attacks on me in the German Press call for any reply except on one issue. Nearly all the state-ments made about me are untrue and many of them mutually contra-dictory. One newspaper, I observe, anxious to convict me of ignorance, says I am no soldier and do not know what I am talking about; another, less charitable and determined to inculpate me in mendacity, says I am the most inexcusable of all liars because I am an 'expert' and ought to know better. One newspaper accuses me, none too politely, of having lived in Berlin a life of idle luxury; another reproaches me with having been notoriously the most energetic (*eifrig*) member of the Commission. A fifth attempts to satirize me as a poor man whom the high emoluments of his position on the Commission endowed with the income of a rich one, but he omits to explain why I, of my own volition and against the express wish of General Nollet, gave that position up. A sixth explains, at great length, that I am a person of no importance, while a seventh insists that I am the true author and only begetter of all the Notes of the Allied Governments. But what has all this to do with the question of whether Germany is or is not disarmed? Is all this cloud of abuse merely a smoke-screen to obscure from the German public my statements of fact? I can see no other explanation.

Let me confine myself to the one issue in all these attacks which really has some relevance. It is this: I am accused by the Nationalist Press of being an enemy of the German people, defaming them in war and 'hating' them in peace. I find it a little difficult to recognize myself under this invidious description. Within three months of having recovered, by my resignation, my liberty of opinion, I published a little book, *The Present State of Germany,* which you, in common with the Swiss Press and certain Democrat organs in the German Press, have been good enough to acclaim as 'chivalrous.' Therein I pleaded for the evacuation of the Ruhr, the liquidation of reparations, the mutual forgiveness, by the Allies on the one part and the Germans on the other, of all the wrongs they may have inflicted on one another. Was this the language of 'hate'? I am reproached with having, during the war, published things sullying the fair fame of the German Army. I have published nothing which was not the result of judicial inquiry, and of official scrutiny by others than myself, and the only publication for which I was in any way responsible was published by authority. Your own Foreign Office published in 1915 a German White Book [12] of which I will say nothing, although I could say much, except that it was an indictment against a whole people, the people of Belgium, whose only offence in our eyes was that it had attempted to preserve the inviolability of its soil. Does the Nationalist Press really wish all these questions to be reopened? Is their demand for acquittal from the imputation of 'guilt' in the inception of the war to be extended to a demand for acquittal from guilt in the conduct of it? When I read their apologetics I find that never, according to them, was a war more righteously begun or more chivalrously conducted. Perhaps! But the Allied Governments and peoples will never be induced to believe that. They will never believe that they sacrificed the flower of their youth and the hope of their generation for an idle cause and a foolish quest. And is it not more than a little dangerous to reopen these things? I say dangerous because there is locked up in the archives of our Government material about these things so inflammable that, if published, it might set a spark to all the belligerent elements in Europe. Does your Nationalist Press really want these things published? Towards the end of the war, in October 1918, our own Government established a Committee which Mr. Lloyd George rightly described as a committee of the most eminent jurists ever empanelled in England (a future Lord Chancellor and the present Lord Chief Justice sat upon it), and not of jurists alone but of naval officers of distinction, military officers, civil servants. It laboured for many months and collected and subjected to the most searching scrutiny an enormous mass of evidence of alleged breaches of the laws of war by the German forces on land and sea. I have seen all that evidence—I will not discuss whether it was true or untrue, I will only say that the Committee, of which I was the Vice-Chairman, was painfully and sincerely impressed by it. No punitive action has ever been

[12] See above, p. 271.

taken by the Allied Governments upon it and the Leipzig Trials were but an experiment, and a very small one, in that direction. Many people in my own country and in France have clamoured for the publication of the Committee's reports; others for stern retribution and punitive action by the Allied Governments. If any one man might reasonably have been expected to aid and abet these demands, it would have been myself. Yet in the little book, to which you have so generously referred, I pleaded, with all the power at my command, that these sorrowful things, so exasperating in their retrospect, so estranging in their prospect, should now be put behind us, that they should be wiped out as with a sponge, and that your people and mine should blot out all memories of transgressions like a cloud and of iniquities like a thick cloud. Was this the language of 'hate'?

Let me, in conclusion, lift the veil, ever so slightly, which still enshrouds many of the deliberations of the Peace Conference. It fell to my lot to suggest, devise, and pilot through the Supreme War Council at Versailles in 1919, the Convention which was to regularize the occupation of the Rhineland. If I had been animated—as well I might have been, coming straight from the deliberations of the 'War Crimes' Committee in London of which I have already spoken—by feelings of hatred and animosity towards the German people, nothing would have been easier than for me to gratify them by making that convention the instrument of a military despotism to crush the people of the Rhineland. But I strove to make that burden upon your people easy, and that yoke light; there is in our Foreign Office a report by my own hand in which I urged that everything should be done that could be done to keep the Allied forces from wanton or oppressive interference in the life of the German people and to assure to your Bürgermeisters and police the exercise of their own authority and the respect that was due to it. In the establishment of that principle I succeeded. It was not always easy. I had to encounter much opposition. The German people do not know, no one among our own people outside official circles knows, that, at one stage in the deliberations, one of the very highest authorities in Paris pressed on me the insertion of a clause in the Rhineland Convention which should authorize the Allies to occupy, if need be, not only the Rhineland, but any German territory beyond it, even to the uttermost parts of East Prussia. If I had admitted that clause, the whole of Germany, even Berlin itself, would have been liable to the 'servitude' of a military occupation by the Allies in the exercise of their own discretion. I did not insert it.

Alike in all that I have done and in all that I have refused to do, I have striven to save both your people and mine, both the German nation and the French, from the catastrophic horror of another war. It may well be that I have made some mistakes but, if that be so, those mistakes have proceeded from fallibility of judgment, never from asperity of temper. I am not conscious, despite the maledictions of my critics, of having ever sought my own interest; I have been outspoken in office when silence would have been advantageous; I have been silent in retirement when speech would have been lucrative. Whatever faults may attach to my opinions, servility is not one of them; they have never been the docile echo of another voice. I have never allowed myself to believe a thing merely because the German authorities affirmed it nor to disbelieve it simply because the French denied it. The French military authorities, it is true, gave me their trust, but it was an uncovenanted trust, honourable in its terms to them and not dishonourable to me. If they and I have reached identical conclusions about the 'disarmament' of Germany it is due to the inexorable logic of facts and to nothing else.

To your observations on the danger to Germany of the ascendancy of the Nationalists in her councils, it would, I feel, be unbecoming in me to reply. You, as a patriotic German who has suffered for his patriotism, have every right to make them; I, as an Englishman and a foreigner, am unenfranchised and have no claim to endorse them. As an Englishman I owe your Government charity, as a foreigner, respect. For a foreigner to attempt to separate a people from its rulers is a perilous thing and invidious. The surest way to unite, and indeed to exasperate, a country is for an alien hand to attempt to divide it; the most certain course to strengthen a Government in reactionary tendencies is for a foreigner to attack it. Moreover, the head of your Government, Dr. Luther, has recently given utterance to an allocution, in this vexed question of disarmament, which, if it accomplishes nothing, promises much, and is at least conciliatory. I can but await the pledges of his good faith. But when you assure me that there are just and enlightened men in Germany whose one desire is to know what cause the Allied Governments have for their anxieties and who would, if once convinced that such cause exists, do all in their power to remove it, I cannot but subscribe to that opinion and respond to the invitation which accompanies your noble expression of it.

Believe me,

Yours most sincerely,

J. H. MORGAN

LONDON, 31 *January* 1925

APPENDIX VI

Letter from the President of the Inter-Allied Military Commission of Control to the Chief of the Imperial General Staff.

'HEADQUARTERS,'

INTER-ALLIED COMMISSION OF CONTROL,

BERLIN

16 *juin* 1922

A. M. LE GÉNÉRAL LORD CAVAN,

  CHEF DE L'ETAT-MAJOR IMPERIALE,

  WAR OFFICE

MON GÉNÉRAL,

Le Brigadier-Général Morgan, Colonel-on-the-Staff, Deputy Adjutant-General, Chef par interim de la Délégation Britannique à la Commission Militaire Interalliée de Contrôle me fait savoir qu'il doit quitter la Commission le 1er juillet prochain.

J'ai demandé au Général Morgan de soumettre sans delai cette question au War Office [1] et je m'autorise de nos si bonnes relations de 1917, pour vous demander directement de vouloir bien intervenir et la régler sans retard.

Le Général Morgan remplit entre autres fonctions, celles du membre du Conseil de la Commission et d'Adjoint au Général President de la Sous-Commission des Effectifs; il y rend les services les plus distingués par son intelligence, sa haute culture et son sens des réalités. Il a actuellement en main une serie de questions qui prennent de jour en jour plus d'ampleur, et qui ne peuvent rester sans solution. Le remplacer par un autre expert qui, si distingué fût-il, devrait se mettre au courant d'une situation très compliquée, serait compromettre gravement la rapidité et la sécurité des operations de la Commission.

L'importance des intérêts en jeu me determine à vous demander de consacrer à cette question quelques uns de vos moments dont je sais le prix. Je le fais d'autant plus volontiers, que j'y trouve l'occasion de me reporter aux souvenirs communs de la forêt d'Houthulst sur laquelle nous avons marché la main dans la main.

Veuillez agréer, mon Général, l'assurance de mes plus cordiaux sentiments.

                    (Signed) NOLLET

[1] This I naturally could not bring myself to do. The issues as to disarmament raised by this letter and Marshal Foch's personal intervention in the matter are dealt with in a second volume to be published later.—The AUTHOR.

9.7.27

Mon cher Général,

Nous n'avons pu retrouver, malgré de soigneuses recherches, la lettre demandée.

Peut être n'avons nous traité que de vive voix (ou bien en transmettant et en appuyant une lettre du g.al Nollet) votre maintien jugé nécessaire à Berlin —

Je regrette beaucoup de ne pouvoir vous dire mieux.

C'est avec un grand plaisir que je recevrai votre "Problème du Rhin" — J'ai été enchanté de la réception d'Oxford.

Croyez moi bien à vous,

F. Foch

INDEX

Allied Army of Occupation, 10, 25-6.
See also British Army of Occupation
Allied blockade after war of 1914-18, 232 ff.
Allied Military Commission. *See* Inter-Allied Military Control Commission
Alsace-Lorraine, German annexation in 1870 of, 289, and *n.* 105, 106
Alte Heer, Das, 137 *n.* 1, 138 *n.* 4, 139 *n.* 6, 140 and *n.* 7, 142 *n.* 8, 156 *n.* 37, 255 *n.* 38, 256 *n.* 41
Altrock, Lieut.-Gen. von, 111 *n.* 1, 2
Ambassadors, Conference in Paris of, 61, 75
American Food in the World War, 239 *n.* 13
Ammonia, synthetic, 291
Anglo-German Naval Agreement, 230
Armaments, German, 31, 65-6, 278; *caches* discovered, 35, 335; *Deutsche Werke* (State arsenals), 333, 337
Armistice (1918-20), the, 204 *n.* 23; German General Staff and, 211-12
Austria, 232

Bart, Herr, 161-4
Barthélemy, Gen., 5-6, 46-7, 75, 173-4, 231
Bauer, Major, 80, 94; German massacre at Dinant, on, 273
Baum, Vicki, *Grand Hotel*, 48 ff.
Bazeilles, German massacre in 1871 in, 145, and *n.* 17
Beasley, Col. J. H. M., 35, 64, 159, 231
'Beating up' in Germany, 261, 308
Belgian Prince, German atrocity at sinking of, 175 *n.* 13

Belgium and the Belgians, German hatred of, 270-71
German treatment during 1914-18, 87-8, 145-6, and *n.* 18, 149, and *n.* 26, 168 *n.* 4, 242, 270-71; Bethmann-Hollweg and, 271-2
industries destroyed by Germany, 231
neutrality, German violation of, 286-7, and *n.* 99; German Universities' Manifesto about, 288
starvation of Belgian civilians by Germany, 237-8; Page, W. H., on, 238 *n.* 12
Belloc-Lowndes, Mrs., 197 *n.* 15, 251
Bennett, Major, 29, 95-6
Berlin, 16-17, 174
Adlon Hotel, 48 ff., 68-9, 82 ff., 92, 112
Bellevue Hotel, 47-8
'Harem Nights' at Apollo Theatre in, 245-6
homosexuality in, 248-9
post-war, 227-8, 232, 244 ff.
Reichswehr revolt in 1920, 81 ff., 95-7
Beseler, Gen., 311
Bethmann-Hollweg, Dr. von, 202-3, 271-2, 313 *n.* 150
Bieberstein, Baron Marschall von, 30, 147, and *n.* 21
Bingham, Gen., 75-6, 155, 172
Birkenhead, Lord, 48, 177, 201, 202 *n.* 21, 228, 249
Bismarck:
Bohemia in 1866, on, 264-5
Ems telegram (1870) of, 264
Gedanken und Erinnerungeren, 283, and *n.* 96, 305, and *n.* 129, 313 *n.* 148
Poles, the, on, 305, and *n.* 30
Siege of Paris (1870-1) and, 239-41